Zsolt Bottlik, Márton Berki,
Steven Jobbitt (eds.)

POWER AND IDENTITY IN THE POST-SOVIET REALM

Geographies of Ethnicity and Nationality after 1991

Bibliografische Information der Deutschen Nationalbibliothek

Die Deutsche Nationalbibliothek verzeichnet diese Publikation in der Deutschen Nationalbibliografie; detaillierte bibliografische Daten sind im Internet über http://dnb.d-nb.de abrufbar.

Bibliographic information published by the Deutsche Nationalbibliothek

Die Deutsche Nationalbibliothek lists this publication in the Deutsche Nationalbibliografie; detailed bibliographic data are available in the Internet at http://dnb.d-nb.de.

Proofreading by: Steven Jobbitt
Editorial assistant: Elizabeth Barden
Maps designed and drawn by: Zsolt Bottlik

The book was produced as part of the project "After the Post-Soviet Period: A Geographical Analysis of Social Processes within the Shifting Eastern European Buffer Zone" (K-124291) with the support of the National Research, Development, and Innovation Office (NRDIO), and the textbook support fund from ELTE University, Budapest.

ISBN-13: 978-3-8382-1399-6
© *ibidem*-Verlag, Stuttgart 2021
Alle Rechte vorbehalten

Das Werk einschließlich aller seiner Teile ist urheberrechtlich geschützt. Jede Verwertung außerhalb der engen Grenzen des Urheberrechtsgesetzes ist ohne Zustimmung des Verlages unzulässig und strafbar. Dies gilt insbesondere für Vervielfältigungen, Übersetzungen, Mikroverfilmungen und elektronische Speicherformen sowie die Einspeicherung und Verarbeitung in elektronischen Systemen.

All rights reserved. No part of this publication may be reproduced, stored in or introduced into a retrieval system, or transmitted, in any form, or by any means (electronic, mechanical, photocopying, recording or otherwise) without the prior written permission of the publisher. Any person who does any unauthorized act in relation to this publication may be liable to criminal prosecution and civil claims for damages.

Printed in the EU

Soviet and Post-Soviet Politics and Society (SPPS) Vol. 222
ISSN 1614-3515

General Editor: Andreas Umland,
Swedish Institute of International Affairs, umland@stanfordalumni.org

Commissioning Editor: Max Jakob Horstmann,
London, mjh@ibidem.eu

EDITORIAL COMMITTEE*

DOMESTIC & COMPARATIVE POLITICS
Prof. **Ellen Bos**, *Andrássy University of Budapest*
Dr. **Gergana Dimova**, *University of Winchester*
Dr. **Andrey Kazantsev**, *MGIMO (U) MID RF, Moscow*
Prof. **Heiko Pleines**, *University of Bremen*
Prof. **Richard Sakwa**, *University of Kent at Canterbury*
Dr. **Sarah Whitmore**, *Oxford Brookes University*
Dr. **Harald Wydra**, *University of Cambridge*

SOCIETY, CLASS & ETHNICITY
Col. **David Glantz**, *"Journal of Slavic Military Studies"*
Dr. **Marlène Laruelle**, *George Washington University*
Dr. **Stephen Shulman**, *Southern Illinois University*
Prof. **Stefan Troebst**, *University of Leipzig*

POLITICAL ECONOMY & PUBLIC POLICY
Dr. **Andreas Goldthau**, *Central European University*
Dr. **Robert Kravchuk**, *University of North Carolina*
Dr. **David Lane**, *University of Cambridge*
Dr. **Carol Leonard**, *Higher School of Economics, Moscow*
Dr. **Maria Popova**, *McGill University, Montreal*

FOREIGN POLICY & INTERNATIONAL AFFAIRS
Dr. **Peter Duncan**, *University College London*
Prof. **Andreas Heinemann-Grüder**, *University of Bonn*
Prof. **Gerhard Mangott**, *University of Innsbruck*
Dr. **Diana Schmidt-Pfister**, *University of Konstanz*
Dr. **Lisbeth Tarlow**, *Harvard University, Cambridge*
Dr. **Christian Wipperfürth**, *N-Ost Network, Berlin*
Dr. **William Zimmerman**, *University of Michigan*

HISTORY, CULTURE & THOUGHT
Dr. **Catherine Andreyev**, *University of Oxford*
Prof. **Mark Bassin**, *Södertörn University*
Prof. **Karsten Brüggemann**, *Tallinn University*
Dr. **Alexander Etkind**, *University of Cambridge*
Dr. **Gasan Gusejnov**, *Moscow State University*
Prof. **Leonid Luks**, *Catholic University of Eichstaett*
Dr. **Olga Malinova**, *Russian Academy of Sciences*
Dr. **Richard Mole**, *University College London*
Prof. **Andrei Rogatchevski**, *University of Tromso*
Dr. **Mark Tauger**, *West Virginia University*

ADVISORY BOARD*

Prof. **Dominique Arel**, *University of Ottawa*
Prof. **Jörg Baberowski**, *Humboldt University of Berlin*
Prof. **Margarita Balmaceda**, *Seton Hall University*
Dr. **John Barber**, *University of Cambridge*
Prof. **Timm Beichelt**, *European University Viadrina*
Dr. **Katrin Boeckh**, *University of Munich*
Prof. em. **Archie Brown**, *University of Oxford*
Dr. **Vyacheslav Bryukhovetsky**, *Kyiv-Mohyla Academy*
Prof. **Timothy Colton**, *Harvard University, Cambridge*
Prof. **Paul D'Anieri**, *University of Florida*
Dr. **Heike Dörrenbächer**, *Friedrich Naumann Foundation*
Dr. **John Dunlop**, *Hoover Institution, Stanford, California*
Dr. **Sabine Fischer**, *SWP, Berlin*
Dr. **Geir Flikke**, *NUPI, Oslo*
Prof. **David Galbreath**, *University of Aberdeen*
Prof. **Alexander Galkin**, *Russian Academy of Sciences*
Prof. **Frank Golczewski**, *University of Hamburg*
Dr. **Nikolas Gvosdev**, *Naval War College, Newport, RI*
Dr. **Guido Hausmann**, *University of Munich*
Prof. **Dale Herspring**, *Kansas State University*
Dr. **Stefani Hoffman**, *Hebrew University of Jerusalem*
Prof. **Mikhail Ilyin**, *MGIMO (U) MID RF, Moscow*
Prof. **Vladimir Kantor**, *Higher School of Economics*
Prof. em. **Andrzej Korbonski**, *University of California*
Dr. **Iris Kempe**, *"Caucasus Analytical Digest"*
Prof. **Herbert Küpper**, *Institut für Ostrecht Regensburg*
Dr. **Rainer Lindner**, *CEEER, Berlin*
Dr. **Vladimir Malakhov**, *Russian Academy of Sciences*
Dr. **Luke March**, *University of Edinburgh*

Prof. **Michael McFaul**, *Stanford University, Palo Alto*
Prof. **Birgit Menzel**, *University of Mainz-Germersheim*
Prof. **Valery Mikhailenko**, *The Urals State University*
Prof. **Emil Pain**, *Higher School of Economics, Moscow*
Dr. **Oleg Podvintsev**, *Russian Academy of Sciences*
Prof. **Olga Popova**, *St. Petersburg State University*
Dr. **Alex Pravda**, *University of Oxford*
Dr. **Erik van Ree**, *University of Amsterdam*
Dr. **Joachim Rogall**, *Robert Bosch Foundation Stuttgart*
Prof. **Peter Rutland**, *Wesleyan University, Middletown*
Prof. **Marat Salikov**, *The Urals State Law Academy*
Dr. **Gwendolyn Sasse**, *University of Oxford*
Prof. **Jutta Scherrer**, *EHESS, Paris*
Prof. **Robert Service**, *University of Oxford*
Mr. **James Sherr**, *RIIA Chatham House London*
Dr. **Oxana Shevel**, *Tufts University, Medford*
Prof. **Eberhard Schneider**, *University of Siegen*
Prof. **Olexander Shnyrkov**, *Shevchenko University, Kyiv*
Prof. **Hans-Henning Schröder**, *SWP, Berlin*
Prof. **Yuri Shapoval**, *Ukrainian Academy of Sciences*
Prof. **Viktor Shnirelman**, *Russian Academy of Sciences*
Dr. **Lisa Sundstrom**, *University of British Columbia*
Dr. **Philip Walters**, *"Religion, State and Society"*, *Oxford*
Prof. **Zenon Wasyliw**, *Ithaca College, New York State*
Dr. **Lucan Way**, *University of Toronto*
Dr. **Markus Wehner**, *"Frankfurter Allgemeine Zeitung"*
Dr. **Andrew Wilson**, *University College London*
Prof. **Jan Zielonka**, *University of Oxford*
Prof. **Andrei Zorin**, *University of Oxford*

---

* While the Editorial Committee and Advisory Board support the General Editor in the choice and improvement of manuscripts for publication, responsibility for remaining errors and misinterpretations in the series' volumes lies with the books' authors.

Soviet and Post-Soviet Politics and Society (SPPS)
ISSN 1614-3515

Founded in 2004 and refereed since 2007, SPPS makes available affordable English-, German-, and Russian-language studies on the history of the countries of the former Soviet bloc from the late Tsarist period to today. It publishes between 5 and 20 volumes per year and focuses on issues in transitions to and from democracy such as economic crisis, identity formation, civil society development, and constitutional reform in CEE and the NIS. SPPS also aims to highlight so far understudied themes in East European studies such as right-wing radicalism, religious life, higher education, or human rights protection. The authors and titles of all previously published volumes are listed at the end of this book. For a full description of the series and reviews of its books, see www.ibidem-verlag.de/red/spps.

Editorial correspondence & manuscripts should be sent to: Dr. Andreas Umland, Kyiv-Mohyla Academy, Department of Political Science, vul. Voloska 8/5, korp. 4, UA-04070 Kyiv, UKRAINE

Business correspondence & review copy requests should be sent to: *ibidem* Press, Leuschnerstr. 40, 30457 Hannover, Germany; tel.: +49 511 2622200; fax: +49 511 2622201; spps@ibidem.eu.

Authors, reviewers, referees, and editors for (as well as all other persons sympathetic to) SPPS are invited to join its networks at www.facebook.com/group.php?gid=52638198614
www.linkedin.com/groups?about=&gid=103012
www.xing.com/net/spps-ibidem-verlag/

Recent Volumes

220 Gergana Dimova
Political Uncertainty
A Comparative Exploration
With a foreword by Todor Yalamov and Rumena Filipova
ISBN 978-3-8382-1385-9

221 Torben Waschke
Russland in Transition
Geopolitik zwischen Raum, Identität und Machtinteressen
Mit einem Vorwort von Andreas Dittmann
ISBN 978-3-8382-1480-1

222 Steven Jobbitt, Zsolt Bottlik, Marton Berki (Eds.)
Power and Identity in the Post-Soviet Realm.
Geographies of Ethnicity and Nationality after 1991
ISBN 978-3-8382-1399-6

223 Daria Buteiko
Erinnerungsort: Ort des Gedenkens, der Erholung oder der Einkehr?
Kommunismus-Erinnerung an einem historischen Ort am Beispiel der Gedenkstätte Berliner Mauer sowie des Soloveckij-Klosters und -Museumsparks
Mit einem Vorwort von Sigrit Jacobeit
ISBN 978-3-8382-1367-5

224 Olga Bertelsen (Ed.)
Russian Active Measures
Yesterday, Today, Tomorrow
With a foreword by Jan Goldman
ISBN 978-3-8382-1529-7

225 David Mandel
"Optimizing" Higher Education in Russia
University Teachers and Their Union "Universitetskaya solidarnost'"
ISBN 978-3-8382-1519-8

226 Daria Isachenko, Mykhailo Minakov, Gwendolyn Sasse (Eds.)
Post-Soviet Secessionism
Nation-Building and State-Failure after Communism
ISBN 978-3-8382-1538-9

227 Jakob Hauter (Ed.)
Civil War? Interstate War? Hybrid War?
Dimensions and Interpretations of the Donbas Conflict in 2014–2020
With a foreword by Andrew Wilson
ISBN 978-3-8382-1383-5

228 Tima T. Moldogaziev, Gene A. Brewer, J. Edward Kellough (Eds.)
Public Policy and Politics in Georgia
Lessons from Post-Soviet Transition
ISBN 978-3-8382-1535-8

Contents

Introduction VII

Formation of National Identity 1

The Historical Roots of Regional Inequalities and Their Relationship with Present–Day Peripheries and Conflict Zones in the Post-Soviet Realm (1897–2010)
Gábor Demeter 3

The Faces of Russian Nationalism
Margit Kőszegi 41

Geopolitics and Language in the European Post-Soviet Realm
Zsolt Bottlik 59

Russian and Soviet Censuses in Ethnic-National Context
Géza Barta; Tamás Illés; Zsolt Bottlik 91

Local Identities under Russian Rule 111

The Layers of Post-Soviet Central Asian "Nations"
Margit Kőszegi; Zsolt Bottlik 113

Tatars in Russia and the Post-Soviet Realm
Margit Kőszegi 135

In the Net of Power: Small Nations and Ethnicities on the Black Sea Coast
Margit Kőszegi 149

Living on the Edge: The Origins and Evolution of the Kalmyk Ethno-Religious Enclave along the Southern Russian Frontier
Tamás Illés 169

"CONSTRUCTED" (SOVIET) ETHNICITIES 181

In the Contact Zone of In-Between Europe and the Post-Soviet Realm – *Notions of Karelian Spaces*
GÉZA BARTA 183

Rescaling Moldovan Identities
TAMÁS ILLÉS; ZSOLT BOTTLIK 207

The Post-Soviet Azerbaijani National Identity
MARGIT KŐSZEGI; ZSOLT BOTTLIK 227

Tajik Identities: Ageless Alternatives to an Unborn Nation
CSABA BAROCH 245

BIBLIOGRAPHY 261

Sources 263
References 266
List of figures 291

Introduction

On the European continent, which includes also the Russian sphere of power, the establishment and consolidation of today's political units can be connected mostly to the formation of modern nations. However, these processes unfolded along strikingly different trajectories, characterized by diverse causes and consequences. One of the latter is the marked difference in terms of the spatial patterns of ethnic groups, more or less along the Szczecin–Trieste dividing line. To the west of this imaginary line, one can find relatively sharp ethnic boundaries, usually aligned with national borders, whereas to the east of it, ethnic spatial patterns are highly heterogeneous despite a long history of war, (forced) waves of migration, and the ethnic homogenization efforts of the 20th century.

"Ethnicity" has undoubtedly been one of the cornerstones of social problems and conflicts in the eastern part of Europe throughout the 20th century, but it is also a crucial issue today. In addition to the societal transformation that has accompanied the change of political regimes over the last three decades, the societies of these countries have also had to deal with the difficulties of the transition to a market economy. After the turn of the millennium, and with the accession to the EU, some of these countries are now part of the European integration effort. For the time being, however, a part of the Balkans, as well as several countries of the post-Soviet realm, have been left out of European enlargement. At the same time, ethnic-related problems have not been fully addressed by the integration process, since it is organized mostly on an economic basis, and thus faces new challenges amidst the changing geopolitical situation and the globalizing economy of the past two decades. Owing to the inherent spatiality of these processes, it is evident that geographers should also focus on these issues.

Our research group has been dealing with the study of these areas and the ethnic background of economic transition processes for several years, and in so doing has engaged with topics that are not unknown to the international scholarly community. As we argue, this region deserves particular attention due to the inextricable entanglement of its complex social, economic, and political fault lines. In addition to internal societal contradictions, in many cases the region is also characterized by cross-border conflicts that often manifest as armed struggles. Evidence of these clashes also includes the numerous "frozen conflicts" and geopolitical deadlocks that pervade the region. Given the difficult and often uneasy task that newly-independent countries have faced in trying to reposition themselves both economically and geopolitically within post-Soviet space, the challenges they face are of strategic importance, not only to Europe, but also to the globalized world.

Introduction

In light of the above-mentioned considerations, our research focuses primarily on the issues of ethnicity that underlie social problems in the region. These issues range from the tensions between groups that have the potential to form nations, through the difficulties of economic transformation that accompany political transition and the possibilities of leveling regional disparities, to integration efforts that seek to address current global challenges. Though we do not consider the formulation of solutions to be the main goal of our research, we nevertheless feel that the exploration of the processes surrounding existing conflicts may help us in articulating possible future strategies.

The geographical focus

Due to its large territorial extent and its divergent historical trajectories, the region in question can be further divided into sub-regions, of which our volume focuses on the post-Soviet realm (Figure 0.0.1). With the disintegration of the Soviet Union and the end of the bipolar world order, non-Russian parts of these territories suddenly found themselves in a geopolitical vacuum, and then gradually formed a particular kind of geopolitical buffer zone during the 1990s. Stuck between European integration, on the one hand, and the reorganized Russian state, on the other, post-Soviet territories in Europe were reduced to two sub-regions after the accession of the Baltic States to the EU. The first sub-region includes the South Caucasian states of Azerbaijan, Georgia, and Armenia, which are considered to be European according to the European Neighborhood Policy. The second includes Belarus, Moldova, and Ukraine, countries that are historically and culturally more closely tied to "In-Between Europe", or *Zwischeneuropa*. In addition to these two sub-regions, our third geographical focus is on former "Soviet Central Asia." Constituted by Kazakhstan, Kyrgyzstan, Tajikistan, Turkmenistan, and Uzbekistan, this sub-region is comprised by countries that are also striving to find their place in the altered geopolitical landscape of the post-Soviet era.

Though the situation in all three of these post-Soviet sub-regions is of course unique to the contemporary period, the buffer-zone nature of the countries themselves is far from new. The eastward expansion of German, Polish, and Swedish states in the past, for example, as well as repeated Russian attempts to expand westward, have repeatedly redrawn the political, demographic

Figure 0.0.1 *The geopolitical situation in the post-Soviet realm;* (Sources: [2]; [3]; [4]; [5]; [9]; [10]; [15]; [19]; [21]; [22]; [30]; [31]; [32]; [33]; [34]; [35]; [36]; [38]; [40]; [41])

Introduction

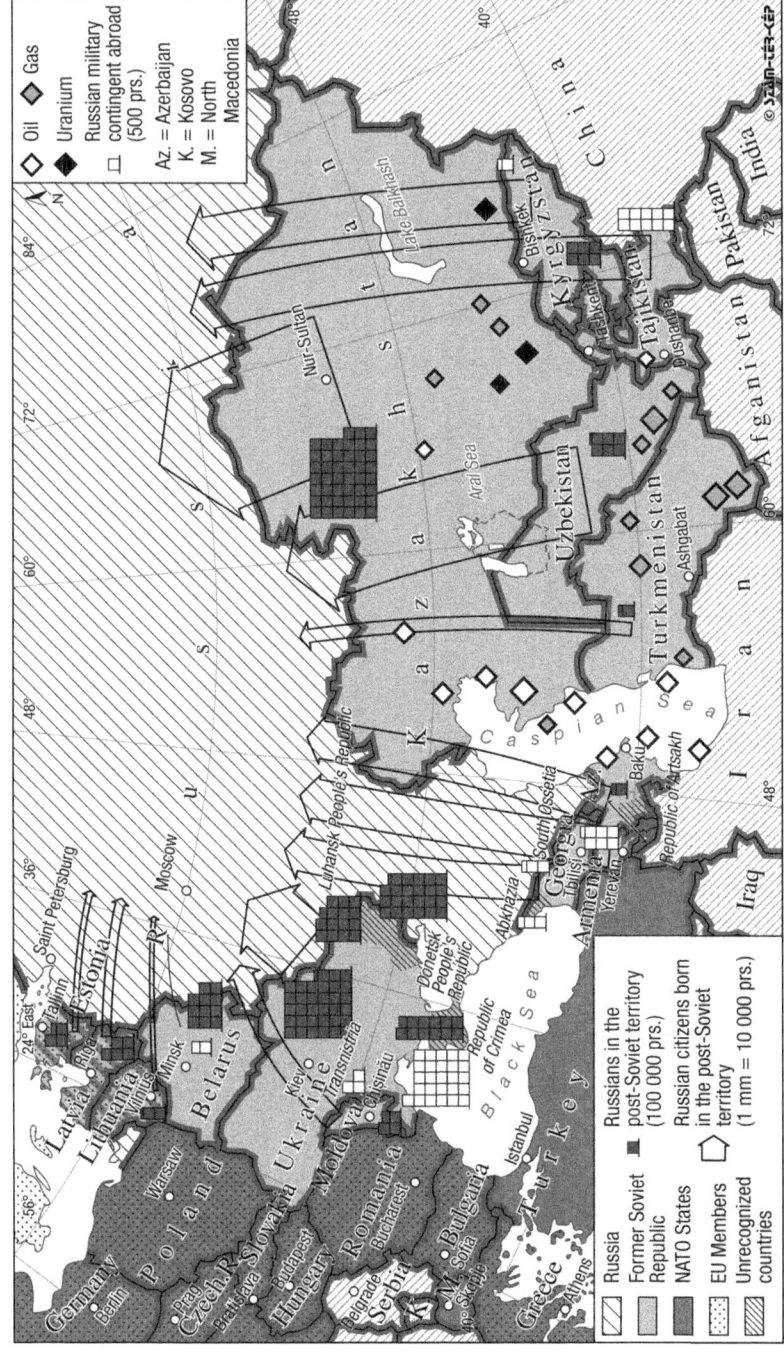

and economic map of the region that now falls within the European post-Soviet realm. Similarly, tsarist and later Soviet aspirations in the Caucasus and Central Asia during the 19th and the 20th centuries resulted in significant changes in power, and profound transformations of existing social and cultural connections.

Expansionist projects in these historic buffer zones resulted in the imposition of new structures that simultaneously erased and built upon the old ones. The borderland position of the sub-regions under examination has fundamentally determined the political culture and economic organization of local societies, with their buffer-zone nature contributing directly to their high levels of complexity. Social, political, and economic discourses pertaining to the region are, however, often based on oversimplified dichotomies such as West vs. East, developed vs. underdeveloped, and democratic vs. authoritarian. Reducing underlying dynamics to oversimplified binaries like these render local conflicts and crises difficult to interpret.

The three sub-regions that we explore in this volume consist of former Soviet republics that have experienced significant social tensions and economic problems since the political turn in 1989. Against the backdrop of a heightened geopolitical situation, the social, economic, and political instability has even led in some cases to the outbreak of armed conflicts. Our research examines some of the perspectives and also social groups that have played and continue to play a key role in the region's social and economic processes. A full appreciation of the role played by these perspectives and social groups presupposes not only studies on multiple geographical scales, but also an exploration of how geographical and social space are intertwined in the processes of the region.

Throughout this volume, we emphasize the importance of identities (and their formation) in the processes that shape the everyday life of societies. These processes and their impact on the events of recent years, however, can only be grasped in historical context. Out of the multiplicity of narratives defining the identity of certain peoples and local communities, we wanted to accentuate, compile, and geographically systematize the ones that have explicitly determined and continue to define the geopolitical situation of the region under investigation, as well as the interrelationship of local peoples and their economic attitudes.

The effort at various points in history to establish independent state structures has been a more or less characteristic feature within all three sub-regions. As much as this factor has shaped the lives of the people, an even greater role has been played by external forces whose geopolitical aims have often run counter to the aspirations of local populations. Though regional leaders and their followers have sought to create nation-states in the past, external powers have generally stood opposed to these intentions. In many ways, therefore, current state formations were already determined in earlier historical periods as a result of their buffer-zone situation.

The historical dimension of current state structures in the region cannot be underestimated. Following the collapse of Kievan Rus in the mid-13th century, for example, Eastern European powers such as the Tatars, the Polish and Hungarian Kingdoms, and later the Habsburg Empire and the Ottoman Empire, were either too weak or otherwise unable to permanently integrate the former territories of the Rus'. At the same time, however, the impact of these Eastern European state formations on local societies in the region was by no means minimal, and in fact had a pronounced influence on social, political, and economic developments. During the 18th and 19th centuries, moreover, this region became the target of Russian imperial aspirations, which also coincided with the process of modern nation-building (in the case of Belarus, this latter process continues to this day). Although the peoples of Eastern Europe were characterized by many specificities and differences, their languages, cultures, and political traditions were not markedly different from those of the Russian population (which itself was characterized by an imperial identity). During the state-socialist period, these similarities were emphasized by Soviet authorities, so that independent identities could not be developed on the peripheries of the Soviet empire.

The situation was, of course, slightly different in the Caucasus region, where, from the outset, Russian expansion often resulted in aggressive counter-responses. Similarly, in the sparsely populated Turkestani territories acquired by the tsar in the 19th century, the organization of local societies rested on different foundations than in Russia, though it is important to keep in mind that, like the societies of Central Asia, Russia was not on a fully European pathway either. These historical factors had a profound impact on local populations, and in many ways shaped the divergent attitudes of those with different cultural and linguistic traditions. Forged in the context of complex historical and geographical processes, these attitudes were difficult, and in some cases impossible, to transform, either by the Soviet integration efforts of the 1950s, or by the formation and propagation of the "*homo Sovieticus*" ideal.

Conceptual aims

The most important conceptual aim of our volume is to provide a general overview of how the factors that determine ethnicity have developed in the region, and what role(s) these factors play in the region's current social conflicts. In the eastern part of Europe (including our study area), ideas regarding national characteristics, as well as group consciousness and perceived differences with respect to neighboring peoples, have stemmed primarily from a common sense of origin, and from customs rooted in a shared sense of culture, language, and sometimes also religion. In addition, in many cases, the historical memory of states and proto-states that existed in the Middle Ages has also been important, and has often provided stronger frameworks than the dynastic empires they may have been a part of, such as tsarist Russia, which had been steadily gaining Great Power status from the 18th century onwards. On the peripheries of tsarist Russia, the most important political goal of Russian power was to integrate these regions into the structure of the empire. The main focus in this light was on economic reinvigoration and the creation of public administration. The process of integration was to be strengthened by the pursuit of cultural and linguistic homogenization as well. However, several ethnic groups that became part of the empire in the 18th and 19th centuries opposed these attempts. This opposition was fueled not only by the fact that many ethnic groups had different cultural backgrounds, traditions and languages (as was the case in the Caucasus and Turkestan), but also because some of the states that were integrated into the Russian Empire had previously enjoyed middle power status (as was the case with the Polish state).

Fundamental differences like the ones outlined above proved to be of crucial importance for the national movements that emerged in the 19th century, as well as for the creation of local factors of identity formation that have remained important in the post-Soviet realm to this day. Given this dynamic, the first section of our volume reviews the elements that have facilitated the social cohesion of the peoples living in the region. The basic tone is set by outlining the historical background of the current economic and cultural fault lines at three points in time. The first chapter employs quantitative methods to provide an historical analysis of a GIS database to support our hypothesis that previous fault lines have not been significantly reshaped by changing state borders, even over a longer time frame. Thus, in addition to the imperial frameworks that gradually developed from the 18th century onwards, the earlier state formations found in the region have also determined cultural and linguistic orientations.

The political frameworks that emerged in the region were of course key to identity formation. For some groups, these emergent frameworks provided a positive basis for national self-definition, while for others they served as unwelcome impositions against which a competing sense of community was constructed. In this light, the conditions for the development of an imperial attitude are also important in the region, as these conditions not only determined the fate of state formation for local groups since the 18th century, but also shaped Russian imperial nationalism. Amongst other consequences, these broader factors and processes resulted in the continuous evolution of the language of local groups, and gave rise to notable particularities in language use that are obvious even today.

The nuanced nature of identity formation in the region has been notoriously difficult to trace, primarily because of the data that scholars have had at their disposal. For more than a hundred years, maps showing the region's ethnic patterns and their dynamics have been based on official census data that was itself produced with frequently changing methodologies and/or in completely different political contexts. Although the figures of our volume also rely predominantly on this data, we have considered it important to present and critically analyze the contexts of these censuses.

The second and third sections of the volume present four case studies each. Some of these case studies focus on local groups that formed in alignment with Russian imperial interests. Other case studies examine how ethnic self-consciousness emerged as a direct result of Russian intervention. Intentionally separating certain groups from one another, Russian authorities shaped new identities amongst imperial populations that typically had a long history of shared cultural traits and practices.

In each of these case studies, three distinct historical periods are taken into consideration: the imperial, the Soviet, and the post-Soviet. The period of national awakening took place within a framework determined by tsarist Russia, while after World War I, identity formation was shaped by policies and structures implemented by the Soviet Union. After the collapse of the Soviet Union in 1991, nation-building processes unfolded within the successor states established according to the borders of the USSR's former member republics. Events that have taken place since the collapse of communism must be interpreted, of course, within a context that has been further complicated by globalization. At the same time, many of the elites of post-Soviet states have reinvested in national(ist) sentiments that are often imbued with the soviet frameworks of the preceding decades.

The second section of the volume begins with an examination of the former Turkestani territories of imperial Russia. The homeland of nomadic Turkic-speaking groups and agrarian Iranian peoples, this region provides an excellent example of how local identity constructions were influenced by, and interacted with, the intentions and attitudes of the Russian center. The classification of Tatars as a single, monolithic ethnic group can also be considered a Russian construct, since the relative cohesion among both smaller and larger groups scattered over this vast area was itself very much a reflection of the changing attitudes of Russian power. As with our other case studies, the case of the Tatars highlights how different groups can be characterized by highly diverse sets of relationships, not only towards each other, but also towards the Russian majority. Several smaller ethnic groups that have found themselves at the forefront of the Russian frontier, moreover, may owe their distinct identities to the imperial attitude of *"divide et impera"*. Apt examples of these are the histories of the Gagauz and the Bulgarians of the Budzhak, groups that stood in the way of Russian expansion into the Balkans. In the case of the Caucasus, the history of the Kalmyks stands as another example.

Our third section explores the distinct identities of Karelians, Moldovans, Azeris, and Tajiks, groups whose more or less compact settlement spaces were divided by the changing Russian borders in the 19th century. The border itself thus formed a significant barrier between linguistically and culturally similar communities. Trapped in different state frameworks and moving along diverging trajectories, former relations were weakened and transformed, despite the fact that, in the case of the Karelians and Moldavians at least, efforts were made to establish and maintain meaningful contact with the more stable Finnish and Romanian national communities emerging on the other side of the border. In the case of these groups, a particular communist nation-building process prevailed during the Soviet period as well. This project achieved its goal only partially, however. As a result, highly ambiguous local identity constructs have only amplified the social problems that have unfolded since the collapse of the Soviet Union.

The principal aim of our volume is to provide an overview of the ethnic background of social processes in the post-Soviet realm, pointing to both regional specificities and to temporal particularities stemming from the different historical cross-sections we investigated. These studies, we hope, will serve both as a background to, and a starting point for, further empirical research in various social scientific fields.

The research results presented in this volume can, of course, be further refined. Since the conflicts we examine are of a multidimensional nature, they can be approached from several perspectives. In addition to presenting ethnic patterns based on static census data from various points of time, the exploration and refinement of meso- and micro-level ethnic processes can also be aided by ethnographic research on the relationship within and between different ethnic groups. This may shed light on the processes connected to the use and appropriation of space by ethnic groups. The historical development and the current strength of their identities obviously also play a role in these processes. Additionally, exploring the ethnic dimension of social structures may also help us in avoiding (or at least mitigating) conflict.

Expanding our GIS database could also be a step forward, either by including additional economic datasets or by carrying out further investigations on lower (sub-national) geographical scales. Such research would be necessary in order to have a greater understanding of the local specificities influencing both the economic situation and social differences. In building on these results, and at the same time also going further, greater emphasis can and should be placed on exploring other dimensions of existing conflicts. Such investigations could include, but by no means should be limited to, explorations of underlying social-economic factors, and studies grounded in the more recent approaches of cultural geography.

Formation of National Identity

The Historical Roots of Regional Inequalities and Their Relationship with Present-Day Peripheries and Conflict Zones in the Post-Soviet Realm (1897–2010)

Gábor Demeter

The series of political conflicts that developed in the post-Soviet realm just decades after the collapse of the Soviet Union have highlighted the internal tensions within newly emergent political entities. These tensions were partly the result of economic shocks imposed on transforming economies, and partly the result of unresolved social problems. Beyond these factors, the conflicts also show a clear territorial pattern that is itself the result of the re-emergence of nationalism throughout the region (Brubaker, R. 1996, Kolstø, P. 2016, Anderson, B. 2016). Having been strengthened during the Soviet era, persistent and even revitalized forms of nationalism have re-emerged along historical fault lines and fractures. The instability of political entities, from the Republic of Moldova to the Baltic region, is partly caused by the fact that these states conform neither to the concept of the nation-state, nor to the concept of the state-nation (citizenship-nation). The instability is also partly due to the often changing political-ideological circumstances over the last hundred years. In other words, the old-new boundaries that were established after 1990 cannot fulfill — or just barely fulfill — their homogenizing and identity-forming functions, and thus have largely failed in regard to the political unification of the post-Soviet territory. Like the old imperial and Soviet boundaries before them, the borders created after 1990 have not been able to overcome historical differences in development and culture. As a consequence, historically determined structures in the European post-Soviet region still influence present political behavior (Bottlik Zs. 2008, 2016, Karácsonyi D. et al. 2014a, 2014b, Karácsonyi D. and Bottlik Zs. 2018). Problems in the region therefore become more obvious and understandable not only by tracing existing social and political fault lines, but also by examining current and historical spatial patterns through the lens of "phantom boundaries" (Hirschhausen, B. et al., 2015). Employed alongside political science, geography contributes to a better understanding of these "frozen conflicts" (Dembinska, M. and Campana, A. 2017, Tudoroiu, T. 2012, 2016).

Researchers such as Bottlik, Dembinska and Campana, Hirschhausen, Karácsonyi, and Tudoroiu have highlighted the significant parallel between political protest, economic development and the old political boundaries in East Central Europe and the post-Soviet region, and have stressed the clear spatial aspects of these social phenomena. Jańczak (2015) and Zarycki (2015) have proven that there is a significant correlation between the historical boundaries from 1795 to 1920 between Prussia, Austria, and Russia, on the one hand, and the spatial patterns of Polish parliamentary and presidential elections, on the other (Kaczynski vs Tusk, then Kaczynski vs Komorowski in 2010 and Komorowski vs Duda in 2015). Of course, one may argue that this political pattern has nothing to do with "historical roots," and instead simply reflects the present-day economic-structural differences in Poland, such as the ratio of people employed in the private sector, or the ratio of industrial employees compared to the agrarian population, or the spatial pattern of foreign investments and private entrepreneurship (Pütz, R. 1998). However, it is clear these patterns coincide not only with the historical borders, but also with the spatial pattern of railway density as well. As most of the railways were constructed before 1945, it is more likely that it was the old features that determined the development of present economic differences than to think of them developing in this pattern merely by coincidence, or as the result of differentiated regional development after 1990 (Barta G., Illés T. and Bottlik Zs. 2018). This also suggests that neither conditions in interwar Poland, which resulted in regional differences between illiteracy rates and agrarian outputs, nor the "egalitarianist" communist policies, were able to overcome regional differences that were established between 1795 and 1920. The Polish example demonstrates that historically-determined differences may persist over centuries, even in an ethnically and religiously functioning political entity.

In Belarus, the spatial pattern of the Belarusian language shows great similarity to the location of the old Polish-Russian border that existed between 1920 and 1939 (Bottlik Zs. 2016). Electoral geography exhibits the same pattern. Lukashenko's opponents are always more popular in the western fringes of the country. As can be seen in the third chapter of this volume, language use in this region can be considered as an act of political protest, as both the Belarusian language, as well as Greek Catholicism, were banned during the Soviet era. The territorial and cultural expression of this political behavior suggests that, despite the ostensible ethnic homogeneity of Belarus, latent dividing lines can still be identified. When a crisis hits, a renewal of these historical "frontlines" can be expected (Radzik, R. 2002). The Belarusian-Polish boundary represents a transitional zone between the Polish-Catholic and Russian-Orthodox ideologies. This transitional zone has manifested itself in cultural differences as well, and has resulted in an entangled, and selective, interpretation of the historical past, and the emergence of a regional identity in Belarus.

Whereas present-day Poland is a good example of the persistence of phantom borders generated by political boundaries that lasted from 1795 to 1920 where these phantom borders managed to divide or split an ethnically and religiously homogeneous state, by contrast, Belarus is an example of the persistence of differences along political borders that lasted only a short time — from 1920 to 1939 — and endured despite long-running imperial efforts at homogenization (when the country was incorporated into historical Poland or into the Soviet Union, Bottlik Zs. 2013, 2016). This also implies that differences observed in present-day Belarus can be traced back well before the establishment of the 1920 boundaries. And, unlike in Poland, the different development pattern has manifested itself in language preferences in Belarus.

Political behavior and ethnic consciousness have a strong correlation and a clear territorial pattern in Montenegro as well. Those who claim themselves to be Montenegrins, and who supported Milo Djukanović in 1997 and the secession from Serbia in 2006, live in the core area of the republic within the pre-1912 borders (Bottlik Zs. 2008, Demeter G. 2010). Those who identify themselves as Serbs live on the fringes that were occupied after 1912. The persistence of these historical structures is not only reflected in self-determination, but also was strengthened by the selection of new symbols. These symbols included a new national anthem and flag — which signaled a denial of the Yugoslavian era — as well as the codification of the new Montenegrin language, which differs only slightly from the Serbian language.

Despite the codification of the new Montenegrin language, its everyday use has been of secondary importance in ethnic identity and self-definition. Most Montenegrins speak Serbian, not Montenegrin. In Ukraine, however, the Ukrainian language is in everyday use, and does not corelate with identity, but rather has a strong correlation with political behavior. This phenomenon also has historical roots and has manifested itself in a spatial pattern, and East-West division. It also coincides with differences in physical geographical conditions, such as steppe areas versus woodland areas. These physical geographical features have influenced the history of the region, as well as its socio-economic conditions (Karácsonyi D. et al. 2014a-b, Karácsonyi D. 2006, 2008, 2009, Karácsonyi D. and Bottlik Zs. 2018). The conquest of the Crimean Tatars, and the vacuum created by the fleeing of Muslims, attracted hundreds of thousands of people who were drawn to the promise of economic prosperity, which was in turn influenced by free trade on the Black Sea from 1783, and also by western demand for grain. The colonization process supported by the state reshaped both the economic and ethnic characteristics of Crimea and Eastern Ukraine, and led to the acceleration of industrialization, urbanization, and Russification. This was further triggered by industrialization during the Soviet era when the state depended on coal and iron ore from the Donets basin. The persistence of old privileges enjoyed by the Don Cossacks also contributed to the maintenance of an east-west division. It is therefore not surprising that present-day Ukraine still exhibits these historical divisions.

Recent elections in Italy, Turkey (2018)[1], and Romania proved that this spatiality is not confined to the "transitional" regions of East Central Europe, which includes the European post-Soviet region. Instead, this spatiality seems to be a more general phenomenon. Italy's Five Star Movement is deeply rooted in the poorer, southern Mezzogiorno region, which is the former Kingdom of Naples and Sicily. Supporters of President Erdoğan in Turkey, moreover, can be defined not only on a social basis, but spatially as well. In turn, the 2014 election of Claus Johannis as president of Romania is apparently due to the votes in Transylvania and Bucovina, an electoral result that corresponds to the old borders.[2] These still-traceable internal fault lines and fractures that relied on former cultural or political boundaries, and which have been identified in Western literature as "phantom boundaries", have only come into focus through resent research (Hirschhausen, B. et al. 2015, Hirschhausen, B. 2017a, 2017b, see also the German project Phantomgrenzen in Ostmitteleuropa: www.phantomgrenzen.eu).[3]

This chapter will focus on whether present fault lines in the post-Soviet realm can be considered historically determined (that is, inherited from the past). In order to trace these fault lines, regions need to be identified with the aid of historical statistical analysis. Then, boundaries need to be studied to determine if they coincide with any previous, or present, political boundaries or conflict zones. Differences in levels of development, or other features or characteristics, between the identified historical regions also need to be identified and examined. Historical differences between urban and rural environs need to be traced and compared as well with the results of regional planning in the Soviet era. Finally, a description and illustration of regional inequalities in the post-Soviet area in 2010 needs to be compared to the pattern of inequalities in the existing conflict zones, as well as to the location of the newly identified historical regions.

1   https://www.electoralgeography.com/new/en/
2   https://azonnali.hu/cikk/20180420_a-monarchia-visszavag
3   The term "fracture, fault" is used when the spatial pattern of indicator values of neighboring entities do not show the "expected" gradual transitions (as defined by Tobler, W. R. 1970), but are very definite.

Aims and methods

The Western literature that deals with phantom borders has focused primarily on case studies (Löwis, S. 2015b, 2017, Zamfira 2015), while macroregional, historical, and statistical approaches have rarely been applied together (Löwis, S. 2015a). This chapter investigates how, and to what extent, the ethnic and regional policy first of the Russian Empire and then of the Soviet Union was both willing and able to overcome the cultural differences of the formerly incorporated areas. Simple administrative readjustments made by the state were not always enough to eliminate entrenched regional differences. With this in mind, the working hypothesis of the present chapter is threefold: 1) If regional patterns at the end of the nineteenth century coincide with old political boundaries, this implies that the Russian Empire's national and regional policy was not aimed at homogenization at all, or alternatively, that its attempt to homogenize the region had failed. 2) If the boundaries of this region at the end of the nineteenth century coincide with present-day fault lines, then this would suggest that the Soviets were also unsuccessful at eliminating existing differences. 3) If both of these assumptions are correct, then present-day fractures and conflict zones are the result of historical boundaries that are more than 200 years old.

If current tensions in the post-Soviet region are the result of ethnic and cultural divisions that have existed for two centuries, then this is interesting in two respects. First, communism in the Soviet Union lasted for more than 70 years, whereas collective memories and traditions based on oral history begin to fade after two generations, then quickly vanish (Herrschel, T. 2007). This means that collective memory and traditions based on oral history, which are contributors to the persistence of phantom boundaries, did not have an effect, because they would have faded before the end of Soviet rule. If phantom boundaries still persist, despite the lack of these collective memories, their existence is a result of political factors and other cultural determinants.

Secondly, although both tsarist Russia and the Soviet Union can be described as empires, there were significant differences between their regional and ethnic policies. The administrative uniformity of tsarist Russia was increasing by the end of the 19th century as a result of the simultaneous strengthening of nationalism and the centralizing efforts of the empire (for details see the next chapter). The creation of *guberniyas* and *uyezds* as new administrative territorial units was partly based on historical traditions; however, establishing boundaries based on ethnic differences was not the goal. Special privileges such as tax exemption for Germans settled at the Volga River, military exemption for the peasants in Bessarabia, or special development policy as in the case of the Caucasus, Crimea, or the constitution for Finland, were unique to the recently occupied frontier zones, and assisted in the colonization, pacification, and integration of these regions (Kőszegi M. 2018).

When the communists came to power in 1918, they abandoned the idea of establishing a homogeneous Russian nation. In addition to the enormous social differences across the Soviet Union, which made the nationalization of the region impossible, the communists were also aware of other regional differences and inequalities. As a result, the Soviet leadership allowed the formation of territorial (collective) autonomies based on ethnicity, as well as the use of local languages. They believed that a supranational dictatorship of the proletariat, as outlined by Karl Marx, could be achieved through the establishment of national self-government as an intermediary stage (Tolz, V. 2005).

If the homogenization efforts of both imperial Russia and the communists were unsuccessful, then the present-day fault lines, which correspond to former cultural boundaries, are a result of the limited viability of the political boundaries inherited from the Soviet era. Therefore, they suggest a failure of the administrative, regional, and national policies of the Soviet Union.

The Russian imperial census of 1897 covered most of the region that is now referred to as European Post-Soviet. This census enables us to examine the whole area by using the same indicators and there is no need for data harmonization which would be unavoidable if numerous countries are involved in such investigations. Up to now, this source has not been utilized for its regional aspects. Mironov's (2000) research relying on this source mainly focused on vertical structures (social stratification) and not on the identification of regional patterns.

The examination of regional differences after the collapse of the Soviet Union was based on the census data from the 2000s and 2010s. For the investigation a fine resolution raion-level territorial approach was used (covering 740 territorial entities), which is more sophisticated than the usually applied approach in the literature (Karácsonyi D. and Kocsis K. and Bottlik Zs. 2017, Kocsis K. and Rudenko, L. and Schweitzer F. 2008). It is also finer than the resolution of the investigation on 1897 (composed of 340 entities). The investigation of regional patterns after the turn of the millennium required the harmonization of Belarusian, Ukrainian and Russian national censuses (Karácsonyi D. 2014, Karácsonyi, D. and Bottlik Zs. 2018), and this was a limiting factor for the selection of available indicators. Thus, the indicators used in the two investigations were not the same, not only because of the above outlined problem, but also because the structure of censuses also changed in the last 100 years. Nor was the territorial coverage the same. The investigation of 1897 did not cover the Austrian part of Galicia, whereas the investigation of the situation in 2010 did not contain the Baltic states and Poland. Moreover, although the methods were the same, these limiting factors noted above should be taken into consideration during the interpretation of the results, that is the location of the fault lines in 1897 and in 2010. Despite all these constraints, it is remarkable that many fault lines in 2010 coincided with former (and in 2010 no longer existing) political boundaries and with the socio-economic fault lines identified in 1897.

Regional inequalities in 1897

The connection between historical regions, administrative systems, and present-day hot-spots

This section investigates the results of imperial homogenization efforts, the outcome of which is illustrated through the identification of historical regions, the differences in their development, and the relationship between the boundaries of historical regions and present-day hot-spots. It is important to point out that language-based national consciousness and homogenization are not the specific features of empires (Anderson, B. 2016). As in other empires, in the Russian Empire it was loyalty to the imperial state, or "Mother Russia", not to the nation, that was of prime significance (Osterhammel, J. 1997). Nevertheless, hybrid and entangled systems did exist, especially if an empire wanted to increase its level of integration, or if the elite wanted to preserve its power by utilizing nationalism as a tool. Even the Russian empire attempted to adopt nationalism to increase the level of homogenization. On the one hand, it had the option of choosing a supranational approach, which involved the creation of the "citizenship nation" (this was the path chosen in the Ottoman Empire, though pan-Osmanism ultimately failed). On the other, it could have chosen a language-based, nationalist approach, but this option was hampered by the fact that only 45% of the population spoke Russian as their mother tongue. The tools for national homogenization in an empire were the reshaping of territorial administration, education, and imperial administration.

For this investigation, several variables from the 1897 Russian imperial census were selected. The proportion of migrants was chosen, as it is generally accepted that modernization processes trigger mobility. State interventionist policies pursued by imperial Russia (such as those linked to the colonization of conquered areas) also increased migration. Therefore, the proportion of migrants can function as an indicator of the impact of modernization and/ or state interventionist policies. A rise in literacy rates, as a result of compulsory education, can also be an indicator of the effects of modernization and state intervention. The proportion of merchants, and of urban dwellers, are two different features according to this hypothesis. Although both can indicate a level of modernization, it is also assumed that a non-urban merchant population existed in Russia because of the significant Jewish population in rural areas. The correlation matrix later confirmed the assumption that the share of urban population, and the proportion of merchants, refer to different aspects. The ratio of (bureaucratic) nobility and clergy measured to merchants symbolizes the relationship between the "old" and "new" elites, which also has a territorial pattern. The assumption was that religion also has an impact on socio-cultural and economic behavior. As a result, the proportion of Pravoslavs (Orthodox people) was also used (our presumption was later confirmed by the correlation matrix). The high proportion of Orthodox people, and the prevalence of Russian as a mother-tongue, may refer to the penetration of the central power into local spheres, and the impact of centralization (Kőszegi M. and Pete M. 2018). The difference between the proportion of the Orthodox population, and the proportion of Russian speakers, indicates the level of homogenization. A map illustrating the distribution of the Russian mother-tongue in the peripheries shows the Crimean and Don-Kuban regions as target areas of Russian colonization. A map of non-Russian Orthodox people indirectly indicates Russian infiltration, or the level of Russian assimilation, in Belarus and Ukraine. The proportion of households with servants can be used as a proxy for family economic potential and social prestige. The proportion of households with more than six persons, including both family members and servants, represents a traditional behavior that is characteristic of agrarian societies in the case of values above the country average. Thus, the two indicators are not equivalent (which was confirmed by the correlation matrix). Finally, the ageing index, which indicates the proportion of the population above 60 years of age, shows the same pattern. It is not considered a sign of demographic decline when applied to the late 19th century, but is rather considered a positive feature which may indicate improvements in health care. Due to the constraints of the population census, it was impossible to include additional indicators. As a result, these data related to demographics and social behavior can only indirectly refer to development level.

    The goal of this study was to identify community characteristics other than language to delineate the regions, so the use of ethnic categories as variables was avoided. Also, the 1897 census exaggerated the proportion of Russians in the region (Bottlik Zs. 2016). After indicators were selected the relationship between the variables was analyzed. This highlighted the region's socio-economic characteristics, allowing for the elimination of variables that proved to be irrelevant for the study of development levels. The investigation was carried out at the *uyezd* level.

A strong correlation was measured between the percentage of merchants and the proportion of traditional elite, but the negative coefficient refers to territorial separation of the two social layers. The higher the proportion of the local-born population was in European Russia, the less likely they were able to read and write. In other words, the migrants of that era were educated, which indicates a higher level of capitalization (merchants, freelance professions), and also highlights the empire's efforts to colonize the area (some social layers were immobile: peasants were allowed to move only after 1861, while Jews had to live in pre-designated districts). The higher the proportion of Pravoslavs, the lower the rate of literacy. Higher education was a privilege for those who were born under the influence of western culture. Despite the colonization efforts of the state, migration was not a common behavior for Orthodox people in general. (Orthodox people were thought to be loyal, therefore one may suppose that they were overrepresented in this process. This might be true, but the large numbers of immobile rural Orthodox people decrease the possible correlation between migration and Orthodoxy). The proportion of servants was also low among Pravoslavs, and among the less-mobile autochtonous population in general. This suggests a correlation between economic potential and religion, or economic potential and education levels. The higher the proportion of servants in the population, the higher the rate of literacy as well. Large family size correlated to low literacy, and low family economic potential, and it had a relatively strong connection to Orthodoxy.

After an analysis and historical interpretation of the relationship between the selected variables, the spatial pattern of the single indicators was investigated. These individual maps are then overlain on one another. This created a complex map which indicated development levels (the values of the single variables were normalized and aggregated), and allowed for the delimitation of regions based on differences in development.

In addition to the reconstruction of development levels, cluster analysis was used in an attempt to identify regions with similar features and characteristics in order to delimit and map homogeneous regions. The territorial extent — or number — of regions delimited based on development levels, as well as regions defined by their relative similarity, do not necessarily match. The 1897 census data also provided a possibility to trace differences in the level of development between urban and rural zones within administrative units. As a result, internal inequalities could be measured and mapped.

The number of servants employed by a household, as a measure of family prestige and economic potential, was high in former

Polish and Lithuanian regions, and in the southern parts of Ukraine (Fig. 1.1.1-3). Literacy rates (Fig. 1.1.1-1) showed a similar pattern. It was high in the conquered Crimea and Southern Ukraine. This was a result of the proportion of newcomers in the area, and is confirmed by the territorial distribution of the Russian-speaking population in the region. Interestingly, the proportion of merchants, as a new social class of capitalism, was low in the Polish-Lithuanian area, but relatively high in Belarus and Crimea. This suggests that the connection between Jews and trade was somewhat weaker than originally believed. An 1804 decree had forbidden Jewish people from settling east of Kiev (Pándi L. 1997). However, a relatively high proportion of merchants was measured in the region, and was likely a result of increasing grain exports from southern Russia. At the same time, in the region of Warsaw, where the proportion of Jews was over 10% (Bottlik Zs. 2016), the proportion of merchants was low (Fig. 1.1.2-1). The ageing index was favorable in Volhynia and Crimea, but was very unfavorable in the Baltic region. The proportion of urban dwellers (Fig. 1.1.2-2) was higher in the west, but showed a gradual decrease with a broad transitional zone towards the east. The bulk of urbanized areas coincided with the boundary of Congress Poland in 1815 and the Baltic region. Finally, the map illustrating the ratio of the old and new elite — the number of priests + nobles measured to the number of merchants — shows the Polish-Lithuanian region, which up to then showed favorable tendencies, also had some retrograde features (Fig. 1.1.1-4). The old elite was overrepresented compared to the new bourgeoisie in the region of the Don River as well, because the Cossacks had managed to preserve their privileges collectively. Households larger than six, which suggested traditional structures and underdevelopment, were dominant in future Belarus and central Ukraine. At the same time, the proportion of locally-born individuals was over 90% in the areas that would become Belarus, northern Ukraine, Bessarabia, and the southern part of the Baltic region, which also suggests the maintenance of traditional structures (Fig. 1.1.1-2).

As the figures illustrate, homogeneity was not characteristic for the investigated region in 1897, despite the passing of more than a century after the partition of Poland (between 1772 and 1795) and the acquisition of the Baltic region and Crimea in 1783. As most of the single variables (cartograms) showed regional patterns and not fragmented, mosaic-like structures, we therefore attempted to identify homogeneous sub-regions with common or similar features and special characteristics (which makes them discernable from other regions) using the above analyzed indicators. For the identification of these so-called "formal regions" (regional geography usually makes a distinction between these mainly preindustrial formations and "functional regions" which are characterized by

REGIONAL INEQUALITIES, PERIPHERIES, CONFLICT ZONES

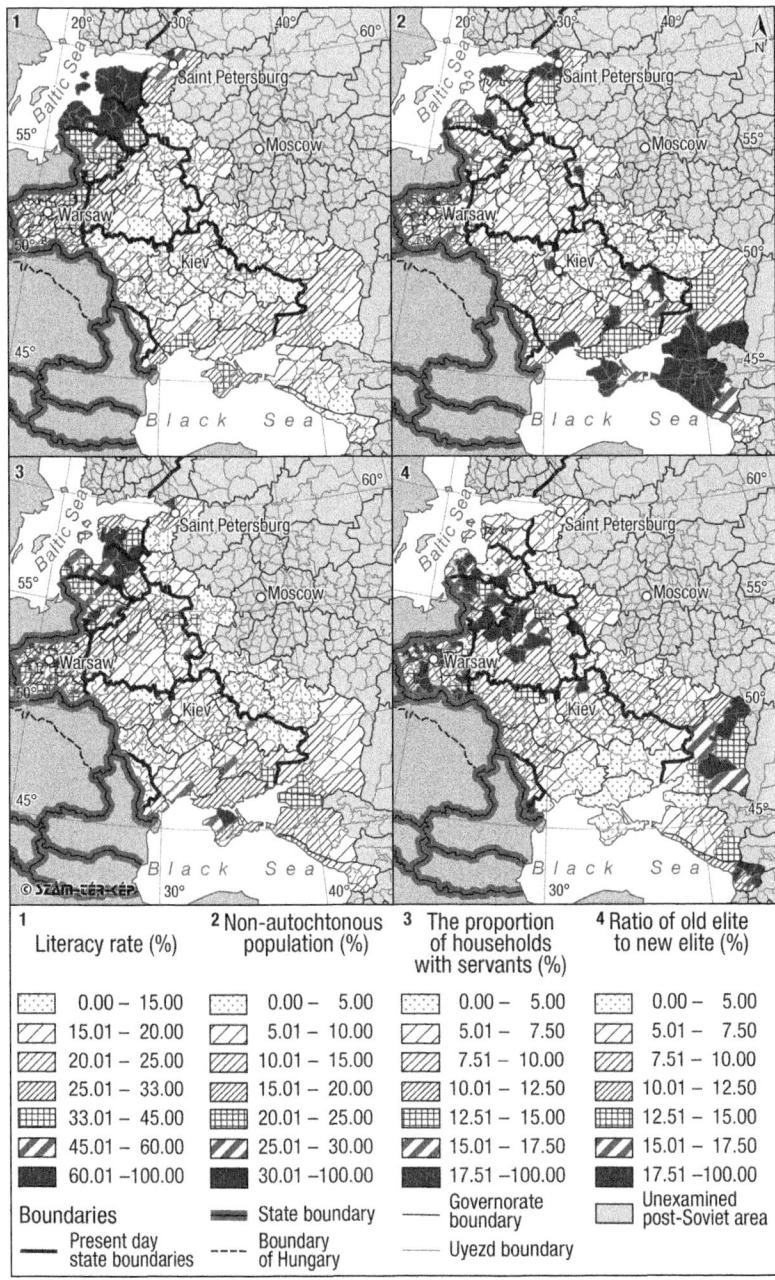

Figure 1.1.1. *Regional differences in the Russian Empire based on the variables of the 1897 census I (Source:* [29]*)*

cooperation and interdependence between the territorial constituents, therefore their features are heterogeneous and may vary within small distance), cluster analysis was carried out (Fig. 1.1.2-4). The historical regional structure appears distinct even at setting only five clusters (that refers to five predicted regions). The external and internal boundaries of old Poland (*Rzeczpospolita Polska*) were still visible 100 years after its dismemberment. The indicator values for Latvia and Estonia, which were under Swedish rule for centuries, were also different from that of the Polish-Lithuanian bloc in terms of characteristics. The Orthodox regions of the former Polish-Lithuanian Commonwealth also constituted a separate group (detached from the Polish core areas along the future Curzon line), and differed significantly from the Voronezh-Smolensk region located in the Russian frontier zone. The bimodality of present-day Ukraine was evident even at that time. If Crimea and its surrounding area is included, it was grouped into three clusters in 1897, which generally resembled the former Polish-Russian-Ottoman border prior to 1772.

The investigation was repeated by increasing the number of clusters (that is the number of predicted regions) to ten. This resulted not in large new patches (with the exception of Lithuania and the Don Cossacks), but rather caused fragmentation along the borders of the formerly defined clusters. In other words, a continuous buffer zone evolved along these "splinters" split off from the core regions. This means that the previously defined cluster (region) boundaries (when the cluster number was set at five) can be considered structurally stable. Thus these five regions have relatively stable and well-discernable borders.

In order to test the working hypothesis, the present-day boundaries and the map by Rónai in 1945, which illustrates the long-term stability of historical borders in East Central Europe, were overlain in Fig. 1.1.2-4. Present-day hot-spots were also marked. The result was clear: the boundaries of the pre-defined clusters for 1897 match present-day administrative-political boundaries only in Poland and the Baltic region. The boundaries of these clusters, which delineate the population of Crimean Tartars, the Don Cossacks, the Polish-Lithuanian Commonwealth, and Estonia-Livonia, coincide with older political boundaries. The pre-1772 boundary of the Polish Commonwealth coincided with the boundary of one of the clusters in 1897, and the boundaries of the developed Crimean cluster matched the old Ottoman boundary. It is also clear that the present-day fault lines in Ukraine, Crimea, and Belarus already existed in 1897.

Furthermore, the identified historical clusters not only varied in their characteristics, but there is also clearly a difference in their development levels as well (Fig. 1.1.2-3). Present-day

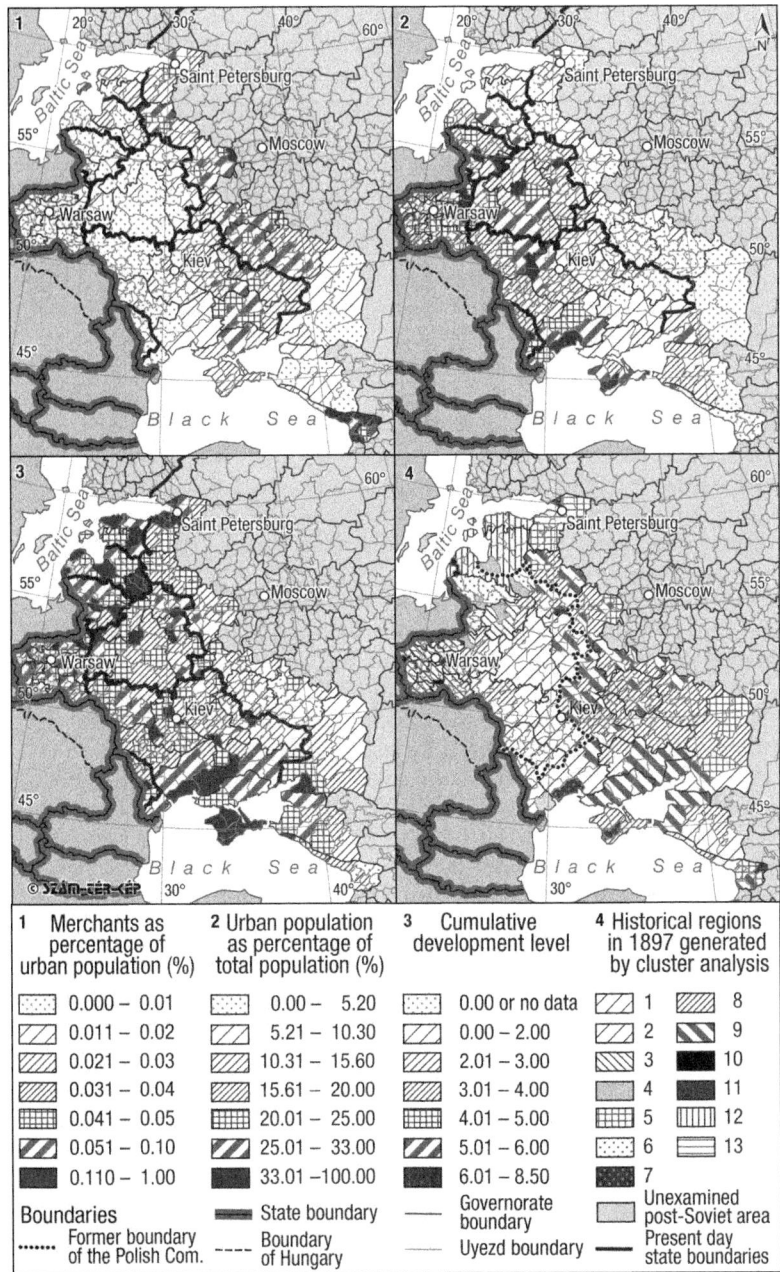

Figure 1.1.2 *Regional differences in the Russian Empire based on the variables of the 1897 census II. (Source: [29])*

southern Ukraine, which demonstrated five indicators with values above the regional average, as well as Crimea, were very developed then thanks to fertile lands, western demand for grain exports, and state intervention policies, which included the development of the military and heavy industry. Areas north of this region were found to be underdeveloped in 1897. The east-west division of the future Ukraine was evident with respect to development as well, but at that time eastern Ukraine was more underdeveloped. This situation only changed due to the industrial developments of the Soviet era. Furthermore, both zones extended beyond the present-day boundaries of Ukraine to the north, towards present-day Belarus.

The surrounding area of Warsaw showed a similar level of development to Crimea. The area of present-day Lithuania was also developed, but had only two indicators showing values above the regional average. The Baltic region demonstrated five favorable indicators, but had a low level of urbanization and a high ageing index. The area of Congress Poland was behind them, but demonstrated more favorable indicators than western Ukraine, whose development level was around the average. Present-day eastern Belarus, eastern Ukraine, and the Russian borderland were considered the most backward. In other words, the geographical peripheries of the Russian Empire experienced the highest levels of development, while the core areas were considered economic peripheries. As a result, it is not surprising that separatism grew within the peripheries, leading to the loss of these regions after 1920.

What were the main distinctive features responsible for the different characteristics in the 1897 clusters? In present-day southern Ukraine, for example, the proportion of migrants, merchants, and urban population was higher than in western Ukraine, where the low level of literacy and the low proportion of household servants was characteristic regionally, similarly to eastern Ukraine, but here three more indicators showed values under the regional average.

Internal inequalities: The urban-rural dichotomy in 1897

The census of 1897 can also be used to examine regional patterns of urban development. It is possible to calculate sub-regional differences, and to also measure inequalities within the uyezds. Cluster analysis can pinpoint typical differences and urban-rural relationships. An investigation of internal inequalities within districts is important because the dynamic and programmed urbanization of the Soviet era resulted in the increase, as well as the uniformization, of urban-rural differences, regardless of their original character and patterns of difference.

Indicators used to assess the development level and characteristics of towns were the same as those used in previous investigations. The literacy rate was seen to correlate with the proportion of migrants, as well as with social status (which was represented by the share of priests and noblemen from total earners). Strong negative correlation was observed between household size and literacy. The proportion of merchants did not correlate with religion. Calculations showed that greater household size in urban environments decreased the probability of migration. However, as migration was more characteristic for urban environs, this also suggests that household size in towns was smaller than in the countryside. The proportion of nobles and priests in towns correlated with the proportion of households with servants. In the case of merchants, a correlation with households with servants was not as evident. In other words, the connection between indicators in urban environments hardly differed from their connection at the sub-regional level. Only one remarkable difference was identified. As the literacy rate in towns was usually higher than in the district itself, it did not correlate with the number of households with servants, or with the proportion of non-Orthodox, which is in contrast to the situation observed during the investigations at the regional level.

The 500 towns investigated were not equally distributed throughout the region. Polish regions were characterized by high town-density, but in areas east of this region, in the moorland of Pripyaty, the population density was very low. The physical geography not only influenced the number of towns, but also their characteristics, though this was not always verified in our examinations. Based on their rich historical past, we supposed different urban types abundant in the Baltic region, from those that characterized the plains of Russia. We also assumed that the urban centres around the Black Sea (recently established or colonized) also constituted a separate type. These assumptions were tested through the analysis of the territorial patterns of single indicators.

With respect to literacy rates, the Pripyaty functioned as a real barrier towards the south (the future Ukraine), where literacy dropped below 40%, while this tendency in the east was not observable. However, the dispersion of values was great in the Polish areas. The regional pattern was colored further by the towns around the Black Sea, which were characterized by higher literacy rates again due to the economic and military functions of the towns. The differences in literacy rates between towns and their rural surroundings was small in the Baltic region and in today's southern Ukraine, while in the central and eastern half of the area studied, differences between towns and their hinterlands was great (Fig. 1.1.3).

The share of the non-autochtonous population in towns (those who migrated to their dwelling place in 1897) was the highest on

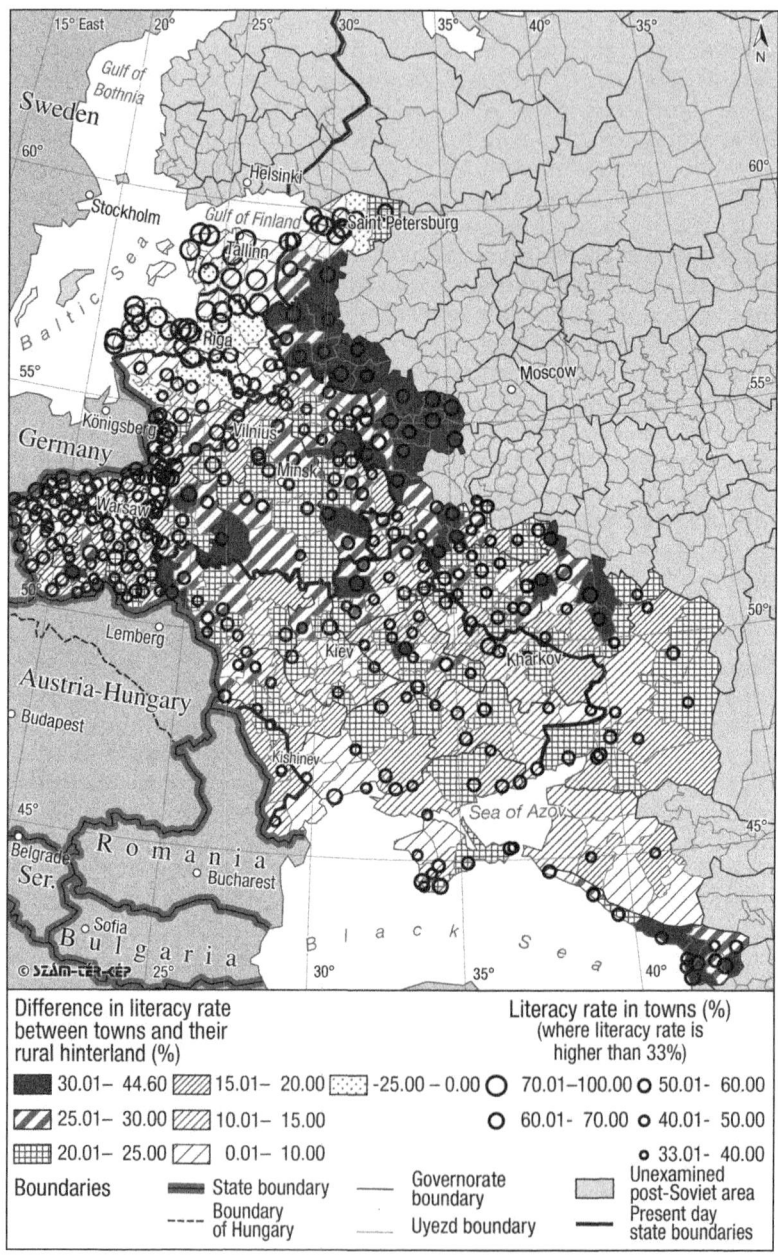

Figure 1.1.3 *Regional patterns of literacy rate — literacy in towns and difference between towns and rural areas (1897) (Source:* [29]*)*

the fringes, in southern Ukraine, and in Crimea. This was a result of attempts by the state to colonize the region. It was high in the Baltic region as a result of trade routes and proximity to the capital of St. Petersburg. It was also high in Poland as a result of the industrial revolution, although there were large local differences. In the central parts of the area studied, the proportion of migrants was lower, and there was less of a difference between the proportion of migrants in urban and rural areas. The same was true for the Caucasus. The difference between towns and rural regions was surprisingly high on the Black Sea coast, which suggests that colonization occurred in St. Petersburg and other urban areas first, as these areas were more appealing to settlers.

When considering the pattern of religious affiliation, the relationship between towns and their hinterland areas was very instructive (Fig. 1.1.4). In the Baltic and Polish areas, Orthodox urban dwellers were, not surprisingly, in the minority. However, in the central parts of the area studied, Orthodox inhabitants were in the majority in rural regions, while in urban areas, Greek Catholics (a heritage of Polish rule) constituted a relative majority of 40% to 50%, even in 1897, a hundred years after the dismemberment of Poland. This large contact area, which encompassed the future Belarus, was therefore characterized by an urban-rural dichotomy with respect to religion. Further east, away from the former area of the *Rzeczpospolita Polska*, the difference between the proportion of Orthodox urban dwellers and their corresponding rural population gradually lessened and Orthodoxy became predominant.

The ratio of the traditional elite, including nobles and priests, and the modern elite, including merchants, was similar in the rural and urban regions of Lithuania and present-day northern Belarus. In other regions, the traditional elite was more predominant in towns. This does not mean that merchants were absent from these towns (this variable gives the ratio of two layers), but rather that, in these regions, merchants were abundant in rural hinterlands too, while nobles were missing.

Considering the proportion of households with servants, the difference between rural and urban environments was small in the Baltic region, in the area of the former Congress Poland, and in Crimea. In the future Belarusian, Ukrainian, and Russian territories, the greater difference between urban and rural communities was a result of the weaker economic potential of the countryside in 1897.

When the values of the single variable are aggregated in order to obtain a general overview of the complex development level of towns (Fig. 1.1.5), the pattern we see is very similar to the pattern shown by the uyezds. The most developed towns in 1897 were found in the Baltic region area of Congress Poland, and in Crimea.

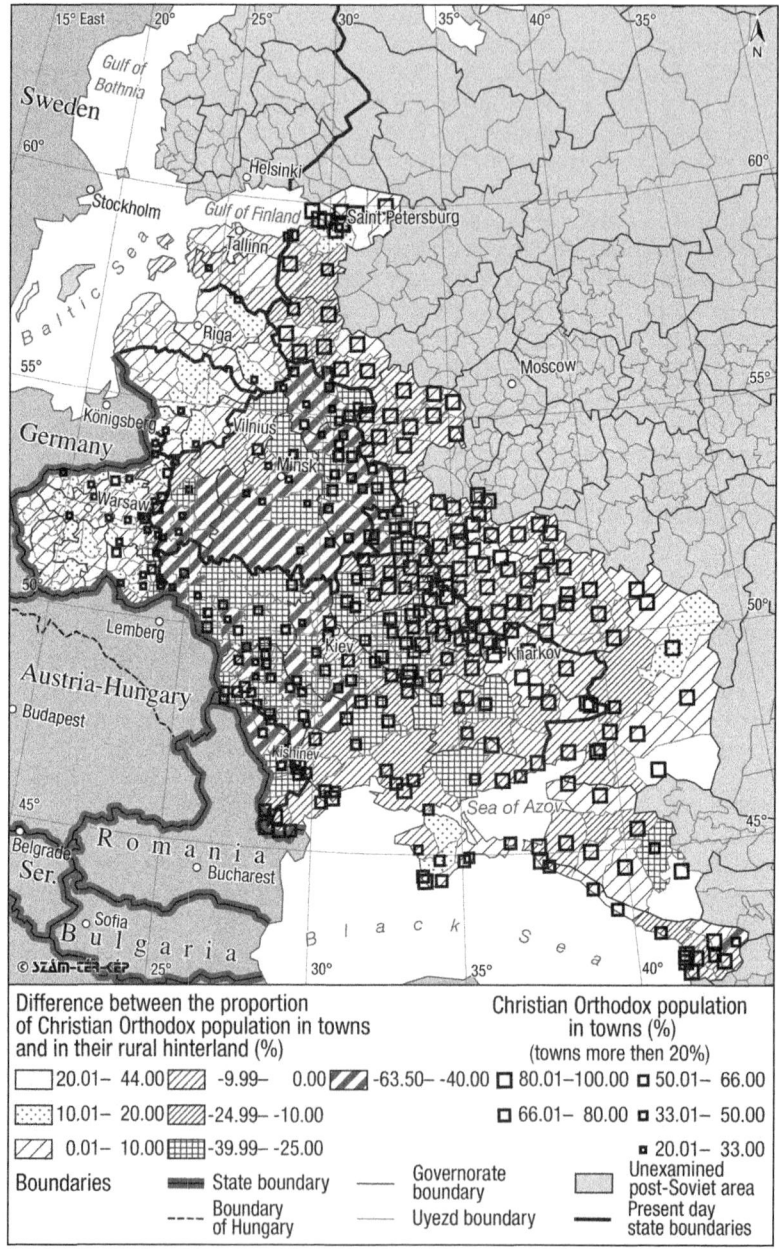

Figure 1.1.4 *Regional pattern of the Orthodox population in towns and the rural hinterland (1897); (Source:* [29])

Regional Inequalities, Peripheries, Conflict Zones

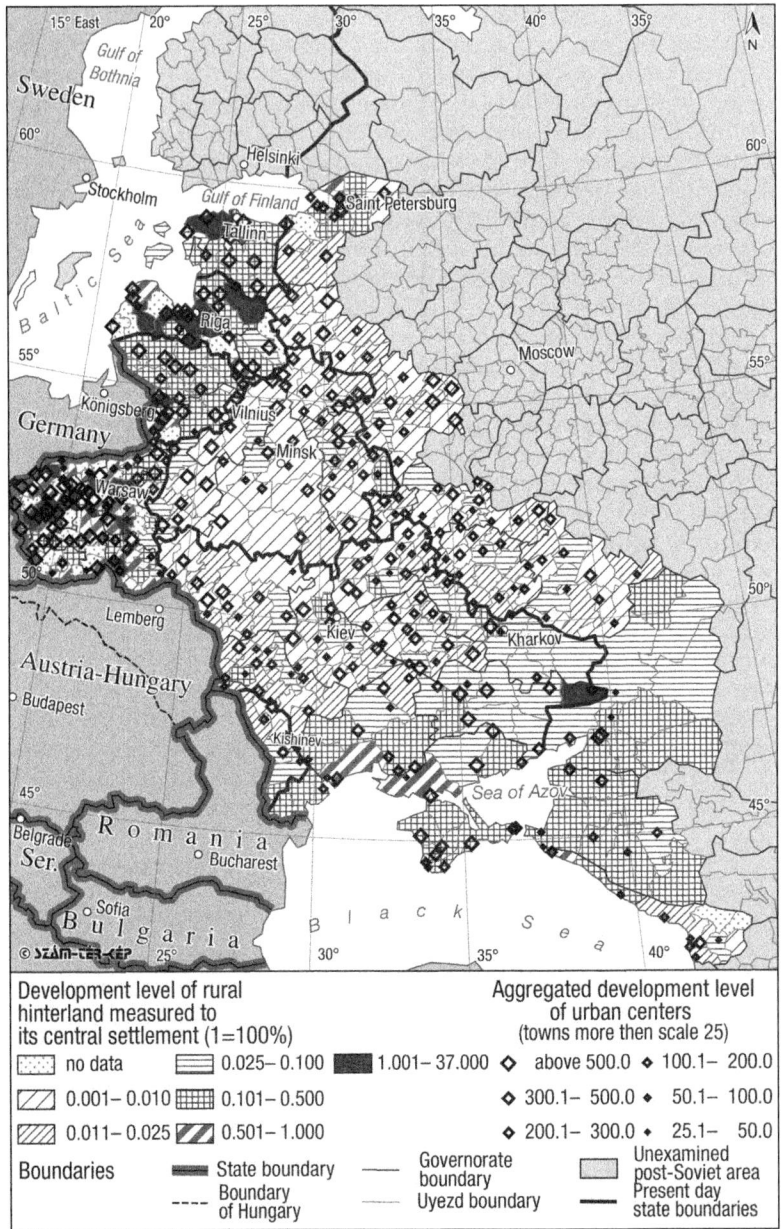

Figure 1.1.5 *Regional pattern of the aggregated development level of towns in 1897 and the differences of development between urban centres and their rural hinterland; (Source:* [29])

In the case of Crimea, targeted state intervention contributed to the favorable picture. In the case of the Congress Poland, it was the industrial revolution in the textile industry (primarily in Lódz), while in the Baltic region it was the closeness of the capital, in addition to historical traditions, that contributed to the high level of development. In the case of the Polish areas, the picture was very versatile: minor towns showed weak progress, and their level of development was similar to that of towns in eastern Ukraine and the Danube delta. With respect to the difference between the level of development of urban centers and their rural hinterlands (Fig. 1.1.5), the central areas displayed the greatest difference (where the countryside was characterized by Orthodoxy, but towns were not). In contrast, Polish, Baltic, and southern towns, were not only more developed, but the level of development of their hinterlands was similar to that of the towns.

If development levels are disregarded, and the focus is aimed at similarities in the value of indicators, and town groups are created according to this using cluster analysis (Fig. 1.1.6), then the group of "southern" towns was characterized by low levels of literacy, low migration rates, and the predominance of traditional elite over the capitalist formations, while the proportion of households with servants was low. In the "eastern" bloc these values were significantly higher. The proportion of households with servants was above the average, as was the proportion of merchants. These two groups overlapped in the southeast. In the third urban type characteristic for the "Polish areas", and for the future Belarus, the proportion of noblemen and merchants was low among urban dwellers, but the previous layer was more significant. This cluster was characterized by a low proportion of Orthodox people.

The "Baltic type" was characterized by high literacy rates. The numeric difference between the old elite of nobles and priests, and the new elite of merchants, was smaller than in Polish towns. The urban population was relatively old, whereas the population in the cluster of coastal towns was relatively young. The proportion of migrants was high in these coastal towns which suggested smaller households. The literacy rate was also high, and the proportion of priests and nobles was among the highest, as these two layers were the representatives of state power. The aggregated level of development in the Polish-Belarusian urban type in 1897 was above the regional average. The cumulative development value in the Lithuanian-Galician group and in southern Ukrainian towns was below the regional average.

The spatial pattern of urban-rural differences did not always follow the pattern of urban clusters (Fig. 1.1.6). The development level of the Baltic, Crimean, and Polish countryside was close to that of the urban cluster. However, the development level of the

REGIONAL INEQUALITIES, PERIPHERIES, CONFLICT ZONES

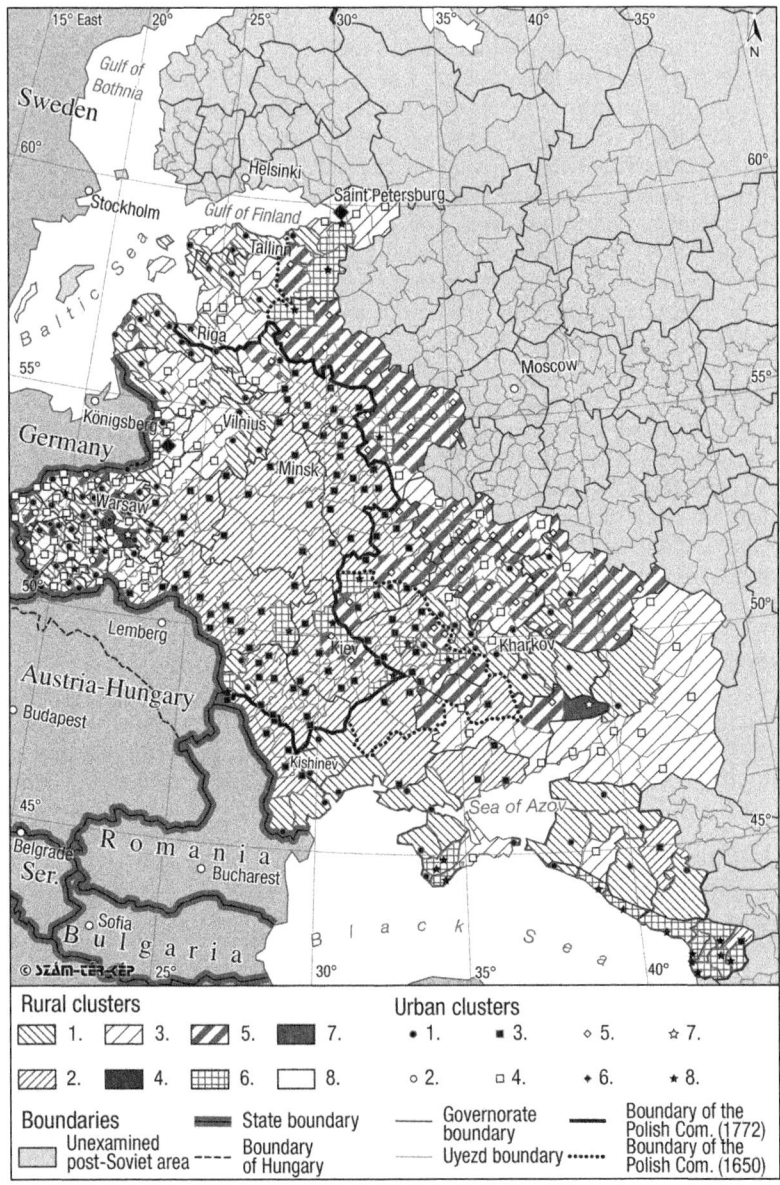

Figure 1.1.6 *Rural cluster types based on the character of differences between towns and their hinterland and urban clusters based on the difference in urban features; (Source:* [29]*)*

rural hinterland is always relative. The difference was small between developed towns and developed hinterland, but it was also small between underdeveloped towns and backward hinterlands. Clusterization made it possible to differentiate between them. Areas reclassed into rural cluster nr. 3, that was also abundant in the above described areas, was moderately developed measured to towns in its area, whereas rural clusters 6 and 7 were lagging behind the towns in their area. Their distinctive features (that separated clusters 6 and 7) were also well identifiable.

To sum up, at the beginning of the Soviet era, most of the old historical structures still prevailed despite the administrative reorganization of imperial Russia. The area encompassed by the former boundaries of the *Rzeczpospolita Polska*, the Baltic region, and Crimea were separate regions based on their general level of development, as well as on regional characteristics. The future Ukraine comprised three different historical regions that partly extended beyond the Ukrainian territories. The present eastern borders of Poland, and the present boundary between the Baltic states and Russia/Belarus, were drawn parallel to the "phantom" boundaries of the historical regions that were identified in 1897. The investigation of internal inequalities between urban and rural environs confirmed the existence of these regional phantom boundaries. Even the future area of Belarus correlated with the extent of the cluster that was characterized by great discrepancies between towns and villages in 1897. All of these cases support Osterhammel's theory (1997) that empires either refrain from attempting ethnic homogenization, or that their homogenization efforts ultimately fail.

The economic system of the Soviet Union and territorial inequalities after 1990 in the post-Soviet realm

Regional and sectoral development policies in the Soviet Union

Communism was utopian and teleological to a certain extent. Communist ideology saw world history as the consecutive series of production systems and social formations according to which the dictatorship of the proletariat would lead to the most developed social and economic formation. This would finally eliminate all inequalities and forms of exploitation, and would eliminate former structures, including the state itself, and ultimately put an end to history. Fukuyama offered a simple paraphrase of this concept in his famous work predicting the end of history, and a future in which democracy reined everywhere. While communism argued for "paradise to be realized on Earth," and not in heaven, it was in direct contradiction with its ideological rival, the Christian Church. According to communist ideology, a strong state, and a conscious and active elite, was required to realize these goals and reach the stage of communism. This would result in an asymmetric hierarchical system, because instead of building on civil cooperation and initiatives from the bottom, instructions from above would be required with little opportunity for feedback. The lack of political plurality meant a lack of control over the ruling party. This meant there was a dichotomy between the goals and instruments from the outset (to reach the dissolution of the state and full democracy through a centralized undemocratic system). This would mean a distortion of the ideas, and the system, itself.

Economic policy in the Soviet Union was characterized by central planning (*Gosplan*, *Goelro*), which initially utilized the experience of the German war economy (a system that never operated under peaceful conditions), and by forced industrialization, which also resulted in migration and urbanization. The cornerstone of the Soviet system was the belief that the (level of the) economy should determine the structure of society. This also meant that the maintenance of the dictatorship of the industrial proletariat required structural changes, as imperial Russia was not yet an industrialized state. It also meant that Russia was not an ideal location for the implementation of communism, because the social basis of communism, which included the industrial proletariat, was initially narrow. This, and the inimical international reception of the communist project, which compelled the Soviet Union to enforce autarchy, both urged for economic restructuring focused on industry. As a result of these factors, and a lack of capital, the Soviet system was characterized by forced industrial production. Capital was transferred from other sectors of the economy causing the neglect of non-productive (tertiary) sectors (the latter received only 6% of total investments around 1930) and partly also agriculture. This resulted in a decrease in consumption, while the lack of capital implied the minimalization of salaries because forced development required the immediate reinvestment of produced goods into the production cycle. During the first five-year plan, real wages fell by 6% despite the increase in output. This continued during the great economic crisis, when unit prices collapsed. Because of the low level of mechanization, full-employment was necessary, but it was cost-effective only if salaries were dramatically cut back. This policy was adopted, not only in the Soviet Union, but in other non-communist countries in Eastern and Central Europe as well. In the name of equality, the elimination of wage differentials between blue- and white-collar workers and the intelligentsia was achieved, not through the increase of the workers' wages, but through a cutback of the intelligentsia's earnings. This changed only in the 1960s, when the centre tried to encourage migration to the periphery by increasing local workers' wages. The 1.5 million imprisoned in GULAG camps supplied an additional cheap workforce, while also ensuring control over a possible political opposition. In this way, the Communist Party was able to decrease the gap between the GDP per capita in Western Europe and the GDP per capita in the USSR.

Beginning in 1926, the German war economy was replaced with economic planning. As a result of the changes discussed above, and the socialization of instruments and firms, the share of the private sector shrank to 18% of the industrial output by 1928, while the proportion of wealthy peasants fell from 38% to 13%, even though 90% of the grain production was still provided by private farms. As unit prices fell during the great crisis, the state had to export more and more to reach the same revenue levels it required to buy the machines for industrial development. The government increased pressure on private farms and peasants. Due to over-export, millions starved to death in the Ukraine and state farms (*kolhoz*) took over private farms. Thus, by 1940, the share of the private sphere fell to 27%, and then to 15% by 1960. The transformation of agriculture accounted for 50% of the total employed in 1954, but received only 11% of the investments (Pockney, B. 1991). Moreover, despite increasing mechanization, it was still characterized by extensive agriculture. This changed in the 1970s, when the share of agriculture from investments increased to 20%, while only 20% of the earners worked in agriculture. However, this change did not solve the problems in Soviet agriculture. After the 1970s, the state was unable to secure food supplies to sustain itself, and a huge amount of money was spent on food imports.

The development of industry was also ambivalent. Besides the neglect in the tertiary and the agrarian sector, 30% of capital investment was spent on heavy industry. Though the soviet system professed autarchy, most industrial developments — with the exception of development in military industry — were made possible by foreign aid. Germany, Italy, and even the United States, assisted in the industrialization of the Soviet Union. The share of industrial workers in the workforce increased from 3% in 1920, to 40% in 1980 (Krajkó Gy. 1987), while the USSR's share of world industrial output also increased from 3% to 40%. Sectoral preferences, such as the emphasis on energetics, was not surprising in a country that was suffering from the lack of capital. However, in the USSR, everything was realized in extreme ways and exaggerated forms. As a result of forced industrialization, the urban population grew 6.5% per year between 1924 and 1940. In contrast, the same process in England took place between 1776 and 1871 at a yearly rate of only 2.4% (Gyuris F. 2018). Rapid industrialization required extra investments in infrastructure, but as this would decelerate the pace of industrialization, only the most necessary networks were created. The quantitative approach — the preference of fulfilling the plan numbers at any cost — was realized at the cost of quality. This resulted in an elusive growth in living standards, whereas the consequence, the shortening life of products, accelerated the business cycle, causing an illusive GDP growth in the macroeconomy (the latter phenomena is frequent in capitalism too). An urban lifestyle brought higher standards of living, especially in access to public utilities, which increased demand to live in these areas (in 1993 80% of urban dwellings had drinking water, had access to the sewerage system, and had central heating, whereas in villages this was under 30%; Brade, I. and Schulze, M. 1997, Gyuris F. 2018). The resulting emigration from the rural countryside caused a shortage in the labour force required for the mechanization of agriculture. The large parcels of land created after the socialization of small farms also encouraged the implementation of mechanization.

In order to avoid distortions, regional planning after 1960 focused on the development of medium-sized towns, but these efforts were unable to mitigate rural-urban dichotomies. The situation was further exacerbated by interregional inequalities. In 1921, the eastern peripheries of the state produced only 3.5% of the production with 14.4% of the population. The regional structure was ultimately changed unintentionally, when during the Second World War, more than 1,300 factories were relocated east of the Ural Mountains, and a further 2,000 were newly established. This meant that 40% of investments were made east of the Ural Mountains (Gyuris F. 2018). During the Cold War, most developments in military industry were realized in the "closed towns" of Central Asia. Despite the decrease in the level of spatial concentration of industry, and the increase in outputs on the peripheries, regional differences between the centers and the peripheries were not eliminated. Central planning played a role in this, as it lacked feedback from the lower administrative levels.

The socio-political goals of *"homo Sovieticus"*, which were developed during the Soviet era, and became characteristic in the entire Eastern Bloc, were in sharp contrast to the picture of conscious, active, egalitarian, and equal citizens that was circulated by Soviet propaganda. Despite the illusory autonomies (see chapter 3 on the regional and ethnic policy in the USSR), and due to the high bureaucratization of the system, it was the lack of human relationships, and lack of consciousness and autonomous thinking, that characterized these types of citizens (beside their supererogation). Despite their lack of trust in centralized state institutions, these citizens looked to government for a solution to every kind of problem. The Soviet system destroyed "civic courage and entrepreneurship". Its lack of civil cooperation, moreover, resulted in an atomized society that lacked any cohesion besides loyalty to the Party. As a result, this society was unable to react to the new circumstances that emerged after the collapse of the regime. This is not an exclusively Soviet phenomenon. There were other systems in world history that produced conformist masses, and failed to provided alternative adaptation strategies.

Despite its huge size and raw material resources, new realities in the world economy did have an impact on the USSR. As the consequence of the oil price shock in 1973, western countries started to abandon investments in industrial sectors that depended heavily on energy and raw materials. This caused an economic restructuring. The Soviet Union was indirectly affected by high oil prices. Because of the transformation of western industry, the USSR had to abandon its export of processed goods and turned to the export of raw materials in order to increase its revenues in the form of foreign currency. By 1980, there was a decrease in the diversity of the USSR's exports. Half of all exports from the USSR were composed of energy, petrol, and gas (after 1990 in Russia these proportions were the same), which made the Soviet economy vulnerable to economic changes despite its increase in state revenues. During the 1980s, oil prices suddenly began to drop, forcing the USSR to increase its production in order to keep its revenues stable. This resulted in a spiral of over-export again. Soviet oil and gas rent was $270 billion in 1980–1981, but beginning in 1986, it dropped below $100 billion while output volumes remained mostly constant. At the same time, these incomes started to be spent outside of the country as the USSR depended more heavily on substantial imports of food.

Experts who believe the main reason for the collapse of the USSR was a result of its failure to operate its economic system look back to the 1970s and 1980s. Those who consider the Soviet constitutional system and its federal territorial organization and regional policies as the main reason of failure look back even further. Others, who draw attention to the growing distrust between member states blame the failure of Moscow's re-distributional practices. Others focus on growing ethnic and religious tensions (Sz. Bíró Z. 2018), even though the USSR was originally organized on the basis of large-scale ethnic autonomies.

Those who argue from the point of view of the worsening macroeconomic situation state that, whereas between 1951 and 1960, even post-Soviet researchers measure yearly 9% GDP growth (official propaganda claimed it was 10%), after 1980 this growth decelerated. Official statistics show a 3.6% per year increase in GDP; however, post-Soviet researchers have determined it was only a

0.6% per year increase. One of the reasons for this was the low productivity in agriculture, which was lower than the 20% agrarian productivity of the agrarian sector in the USA. At the end of the Brezhnev era, the number of harvesting machines under repair, and therefore out of usage, was 70 times greater than the yearly production of harvesters in the USA. It is not surprising that half of the often extreme incomes in currency after the oil-price shock in 1973 left the country immediately due to food imports (in fact the surplus itself was spent on alimentation). Although prior to the First World War Russia was the leading exporter of grain, accounting for 45% of the world exports, by 1970, it had become the world's largest grain importer at 16%. This resulted in rising investments in agriculture beginning in the 1970s. By the time Gorbachev became the first secretary of the Communist Party in 1985, the unsatisfied demand had grown from 4% of the GDP, to 8% of GDP (Sz. Bíró Z. 2018). This meant that the population was unable to spend even its meagre earnings, but the saved money was worth less and less due to inflation. Moreover, this money — which was fuel for the economy — was missing from industry and tertiary concerns. Although official propaganda stated the GDP per capita in the USSR had reached 66% of the value measured in the USA, in reality it was below 40%.

As Gorbachev came to power, it became evident that military expenses, which had reached 17-20% of the total budget, needed to be cut back if the new government wanted to realize its goal of increasing the standard of living. The US had initiated its "star wars" plan with the hidden hope that the USSR would be unable to keep up with the pace of the developments and that this would result in its collapse. However, a defeat in the arms race, and the halt of military investments alone (which fueled civil industrial developments also) would not lead to the collapse of the Soviet Union. The USSR could have survived for decades in a state of silent stagnation and decline, despite its economic problems and the low standards of living, because of the lack of internal or external pressure to transform the system.

The emergence of Gorbachev posed a serious challenge for the indebted state which was suffering from a shortage of financial resources, not only because of his social sensitivity, which was not characteristic of the former leaders, but also because he questioned the long-promoted belief in the moral superiority of the Soviet system over the capitalist West. After Gorbachev's first failures to increase productivity and increase work discipline through an anti-alcohol campaign, it became clear that the low productivity of the economy had been caused by external, non-economic factors. Therefore, his next series of reforms, perestroika, targeted the system itself. To gain support for this transparency, and the dissemination of information between hierarchic levels, the policy of glasnost was also necessary.

The attempt to override ethnic consciousness with the nationally indifferent archetype of the superior Soviet people was also unsuccessful. The supranational "Soviet" category did not even exist in censuses as a marker of national self-determination (contrary to the situation in Yugoslavia, which also fell apart). Examples of this are the 1978 student protest in Tbilisi over free usage of the Georgian language, and the dismissal of a local-born leader of the Party in Kazakhstan and his replacement with a reformer, who was nevertheless a Russian official. The student protest was important because the Soviet Union officially backed linguistic plurality and autonomous regions based on the principle of ethnicity. If this system had been functioning, no such event would have happened. The replacement of the local-born leader in Kazakhstan was a contradiction of the official practice of the Party, which usually promoted local-born people as local leaders. After Gorbachev had challenged this official practice, not even corrupt and anti-reformist leaders could have been removed without greater objection from the locals, because local leaders could play the "ethnic card". Regional policy failed in other areas as well. Although Soviet propaganda emphasized that differences in the development levels of member states had diminished, this was simply not true. Behind this false communication was the government initiative to finally put emphasis on sectoral development policies instead of regional action plans, in order to increase the rationalization of the economy by closing it to the market-economy.

Increasing ethnic tensions in the Caucasus also weakened state cohesion. Moscow hesitated to interfere in the deepening debate between the Armenian and Azeri SSR over Karabagh in 1988, as democratisation processes and local autonomy were taken seriously by the Gorbachev government. This hesitation, however, destroyed the authority of the central government in that region. The subsequent Georgian-Abkhazian incident in Sukhumi proved that these conflicts really did have ethnic roots, and were more than conflicts between the locals and the Moscovite party elite, or between Russians and non-Russians. Whenever the central power interfered in events as it did in 1989, when it put an end to the demonstrations in Chişinau, it usually weakened its position. And if the government chose not to intervene, as it chose to do during the 1989 pogrom against Armenians in Baku, this only proved its incapability in the eyes of the locals. In effect, the growing ethnic tensions were a manifestation of another type of social tension, similar to alcoholism. This is confirmed by the fact that none of these ethnic conflicts were separatist, nor were they a challenge to the system of communism.

In contrast to the situation in the Caucasus, separatism in the Baltic member states began not on the streets, but at the constitutional level in the Supreme Council of Estonia (the amendment of the constitution in 1977 maintained the legal possibility for secession), and had a more serious impact on the cohesion of the Soviet Union. As a result, the Moldovan-Transnistrian conflict and the Azeri-Armenian conflict also gained new interpretative frames. Each of these member states turned against the central government. This was a new phenomenon. Boris Yeltsin also did the same as the leader of the Russian SSR, when Gorbachev came up with the idea to use military coercion against the Baltic states. Military intervention was thus hindered, unlike in Yugoslavia. But the growing rivalry between the leader of the Soviet Union and its largest and strongest federal component destabilized the situation further. The protagonists of centralization considered this conflict between the interests of the central government and the Russian SSR to be the main cause of collapse.

In 1991, numerous member states chose not to participate in the plebiscite of the Gorbachev government, which was initiated in order to renew the "social contract" between the state and citizens, and to give a new form and content to the Soviet federation. Conservative communists, fearing that the decentralization and democratization process would weaken central power, planned a *coup d'etat* against Gorbachev, who wanted to give real rights to the states on the condition that they support the survival of the Soviet Union. Even though the coup failed as a result of Boris Yeltsin's intervention, it had weakened the authority of central power once and for all. After this, central state organs were not able to hinder secessionism, nor to secure minority rights. They also failed to modify problematic boundaries (Karabagh, Transnistria, Crimea, etc.) before the secession of federation members. In December 1991, after the failure of the coup, a new plebiscite was held in Ukraine. The coup underscored the member states' hidden fears and Ukraine voted for secession. The federation of the USSR soon transformed into the looser confederation of the Commonwealth of the Independent States (CIS), but without the Baltic States and an independent Georgia.

An atomized society, unsustainable economic structure, high indebtedness, oversized army, prevailing regional inequalities, growing environmental problems which were causing a decline in agricultural outputs, and increasing ethno-religious conflicts together stretched the frames of the USSR. Separatism was also a solution that was embraced in order to decrease indebtedness (most of the debt was undertaken by Russia), but in return successor states had to resign from the nuclear arsenal and deliver it to Russia.

Some of the seceding regions, such as the Baltic states, turned towards the West, while others, such as the states of Central Asia who were carrying the weight of Soviet heritage, did not fall apart, and continued to exist under authoritarian presidential dictators. A third group of states, such as those in the Caucasus, devolved into ethnic and religious conflicts, giving Russia plenty of space to regain its power and intervene in their internal affairs under the pretext of minority rights (see, for example, the Georgian-Ossetian war in 2006). A fourth group of post-Soviet states, such as Ukraine, Belarus, and the Moldovan Republic, began to function as a buffer zone between Moscow and the EU and NATO alliance. This ambiguous position did not help overcome the obstacles, or consolidate the internal and external situation of these newborn states. The presence of Russian armies in Sevastopol (Crimea) and in Transnistria under the aegis of the UN, coupled with the unilateral dependence of the region on Russian gas and petrol, were also barriers to stabilization.

Though Gorbachev initiated his reforms in order to increase social and economic welfare, the GDP per capita fell back to one-third after 1990 as a result of the collapse of the USSR, and thus state indebtedness reached the value of the yearly GDP of the country. The former level of GDP per capita was only achieved again in 2005. Due to the subsequent growth of the GDP, state indebtedness fell back to 17% (Gyuris F. 2018). In order to adapt to the world market economy as soon as possible, the President of the Russian Federation, Boris Yeltsin, initiated a policy of shock-therapy. Among the most important of these measures was the privatization of state property, deregulation, the liberalization of prices, the abandonment of central planning, and the loosening of state control. These measures were in line with the prevailing neoliberal economic policy of the US at the time, and the isolation of the region vanished quickly, probably as a result of this coincidence. The price of this economic restructuring was paid by the middle and lower-middle classes.

After the change of regime, regional polarization was strengthened both socially and economically. According to the population census of 2010, 73% of the population lived in the European parts of the country, which constituted less than 25% of the state, but accounted for 70% of the gross domestic product (Gyuris F. 2018). More than 20% of the Gross Regional Product (GRP) was produced in Moscow itself. Moscow's population increased by 38% between 1990 and 2016, while the population in the northwestern region decreased by 30%. As a consequence of the transition to a market economy, the development of many regions that enjoyed priority within the socialist regional and social policy had to be abandoned because they were no longer financially profitable. While larger towns with populations above 500,000 survived the transition to the market economy more easily, smaller towns fell behind. As villages were the losers of regional planning under communism, so were small towns the losers in the transition to a market economy. As a result of the economic collapse, the Russian population decreased by 0.5% per year between 2000 and 2010, and the average life expectancy fell from 69 years in 1990, to 65 years. It began to increase again only after 2000.

After 2000, the regional role of Russia began to increase again. In 1996, a customs union was established between Belarus, Kazakhstan, and Russia, which became the Eurasian Economic Community in 2000. In 2009, Russia became a permanent member of the BRICS-countries, as well as a founder of the New Development Bank, which serves as a counterweight to the IMF and World Bank. As a member of the G20, Russia now accounts for 2.8% of world exports and 1.8% of total imports in 2010, reaching the 10th and 16th positions respectively. Its former position has thus vanished, as only 2.1–2.4% of the global inward FDI stock is located in Russia, while its share of the outward FDI stock did not exceed 1.9% (Gyuris F. 2018). As a result of the overspecification in exports, and the narrow scale of exported goods which consist of mainly raw materials with low added value as opposed to manufactured goods, Russia remains very vulnerable to global economic trends.

Regional inequalities in the post-Soviet realm after 2000

In light of the observations discussed above, it is worth examining what happened to the regional disparities after 1945 and 1990 in the post-Soviet region. In the next sections we investigate whether the pattern of development levels changed in the last 100 years, or remained constant, and whether the actual pattern of inequalities coincided with recent fault lines and hot-spots or not. We have already seen that the historical regional boundaries we identified for 1897 often did coincide with present fault lines. In order to examine these questions, several indicators were created from the raw variables of Ukrainian and Belarusian censuses covering the period from 1979 to the 2010s. The area under investigation encompassed the territory of Belarus, Ukraine, and some environs from the Russian peripheries (in particular Bryansk) as a control area. First, the spatial patterns of the single indicators were identified as outlined in Table 1. The processes of ruralization and urbanization, which were accelerated by Soviet regional planning, are well defined. The first of these is seen in the historical areas of Galicia and eastern Ukraine, and on the Russian fringes. The latter is seen in western Ukraine and western Belarus along the Polish-Lithuanian border. The ageing index was high in the north, but low in Galicia and southwestern Ukraine. The natural population increase was also high in western and southwestern Ukraine, and in the Polesye. Migration could not compensate for

Table 1.1.1 *Indicators used in the investigations for 1897 and for the post-Soviet era*

Russian census of 1897	Indicators from 1979 and 2010
population of local birth, %	employment rate %, 2010
proportion of literate people, %	income/capita, 2010
proportion of merchants, %	migration rate, 2010
proportion of urban population, %	ageing index, 2010
proportion of pravoslavs, %	birth rate, 2010
(ratio of priests+bureaucrats+nobility to merchants)	death rate, 2010
households larger than 6 members, %	urban population change 2010/1979
proportion of households with servants %	
ratio of people between 20-59 / 60 years and older	

this population pressure because net emigration was seen only in the northern regions, whereas in western Ukraine, in- and out-migration was relatively balanced. As a result, western Ukraine experienced a population increase. The same was also true for Crimea, which experienced high immigration rates, as well as the Russian fringes outside urban environments.

In Ukraine, income per capita values, illegal activities, and exports per capita, all showed a regional distribution very similar to the linguistic-political-physical geographical division. However, other features such as life expectancy, employment rates, and death rates did not demonstrate this pattern. Instead, the spatial pattern of population growth showed a gentle east-west slope rather than a sudden fracture, which was dominated by a decrease in population in the east. Employment and migration values showed a similar slope. Furthermore, in some cases, reverse tendencies and patterns occur. In eastern Ukraine, higher income per capita values are measured after 2000 than in western Ukraine, which was facing a structural crisis, though the fault line itself persisted. In Belarus regional variability was even less observable. In the case of population increase, birth rates, and ageing index an east-west division reflecting the former Polish-Russian border (1920-1939) was observable, but other (especially non-demographic) indicators did not show this division. A new regional fault line evolved on the Belarusian-Ukrainian state boundary because of the political system in Belarus (the high employment rate can be considered as a relic of the Socialist era). Based on the income per capita, and the change in the population of urban areas, the Donets basin (the Donbas, with its heavy industry developed on coal and iron during the Soviet period) and the strip along the Polish-Lithuanian border was in a more favourable situation than other areas.

The aggregation of the single variables in a complex map illustrating the cumulative level of development (Fig. 1.1.7.) showed that western Ukraine, Crimea, the Donbas, and the Russian border areas were more developed than central Ukraine, which represented the average, while Belarus — due to the similarity of the employment rate in the raions, but differences in salaries and demography — was characterized by great disparities, with territories both above and below the Ukrainian average. Generally speaking, some of the fault lines, such as the one in western Ukraine along historical Galicia (which was a part of Austria-Hungary prior to 1920), the one along the present Polish-Lithuanian border or the southern Ukrainian fault, and the old fracture between east and west Ukraine are still traceable (these are not so evident as in 1897, though, because the communist regime and the changes after 1990 rearranged some of the former patterns). The finer resolution of the investigation — 740 entities instead of 360 — and the different set of variables might also contribute to this difference. Surprisingly, the socio-economic indicators did not correlate with each other, with the exception of employment rate versus income. For example, migration rates did not correlate with employment rates, nor with incomes, which was not an expected outcome, but can be explained by the differences in political systems and the creation of new boundaries.

After the examination of levels of development, an attempt was made to identify "homogeneous" regions with the help of cluster analysis (Fig. 1.1.7), as was done when studying the 1897 census. Cluster settings seemed to be ideal between eight and eleven (higher cluster number settings resulted in clusters with one or two raions, and such small entities cannot be considered as regions or sub-regions). The extent of formal regions generated by cluster analysis and that of the development regions did not match. For example, despite their similarity in development levels, the Russian areas and the Donbas were classified into three different but intertwining clusters. The same was true for western Ukraine and southern Ukraine with Crimea. In contrast to this, the Polish-Lithuanian frontier, and the region northeast of Kiev, were classified into the same cluster, despite differences in their development level, whereas 100 years ago they were grouped into different formal regions. A relatively new phenomenon was identified (and probably the finer resolution and the different set of variables are responsible for this): the central parts of Ukraine and Belarus were classified into two "interconnected" clusters (Fig. 1.1.7).

Surprisingly, the Polish-Lithuanian border strip was no longer among the most developed areas, unlike in 1897. Its aggregated development level was no higher than the value for the whole

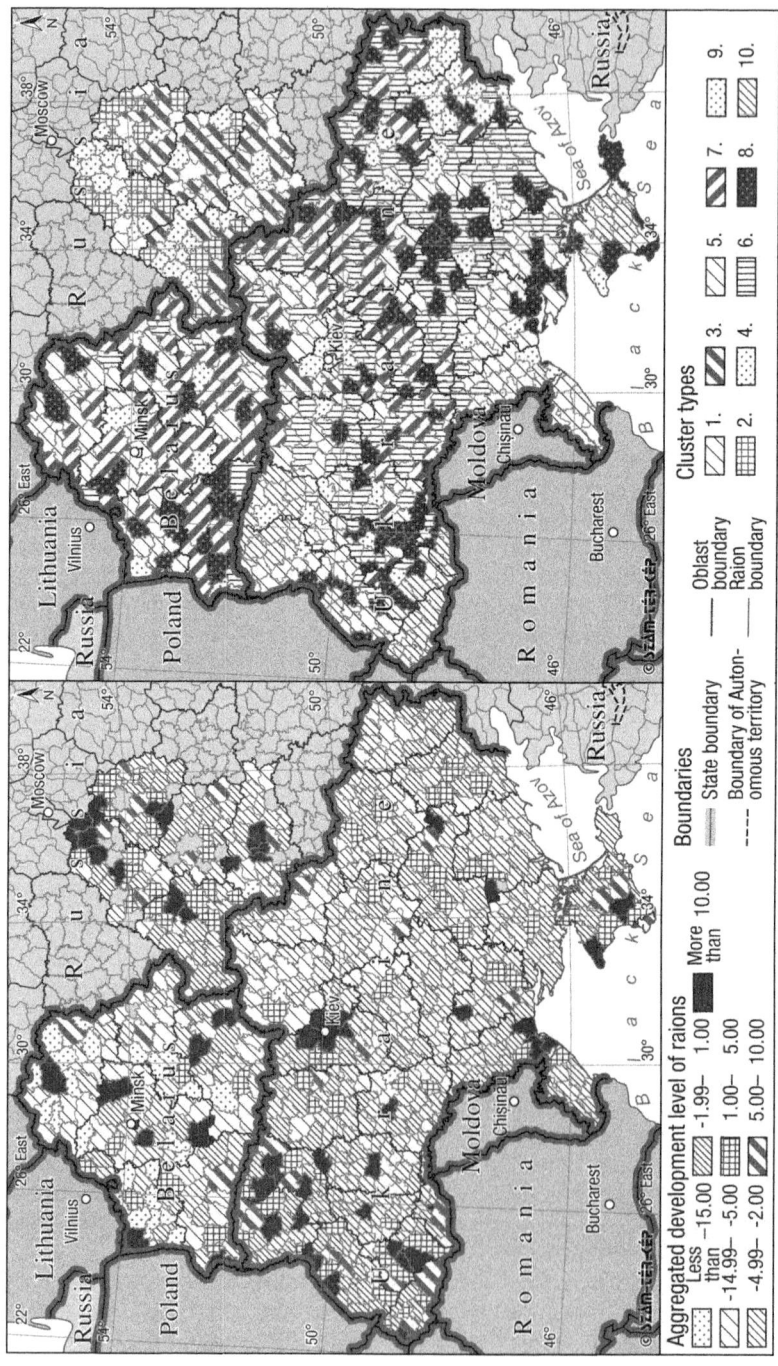

Figure 1.1.7 *Aggregated development level and the cluster types of raions in the post-Soviet realm; (Sources:* [30]; [39])

area. The only favorable indicators observed in this region were in the employment rate. Clusters 2 and 3 represented the Russian frontier zone, and both were characterized by higher levels of development than in neighboring areas. The distinctive feature between the two clusters/regions was their salary levels and birth rates. Eastern Ukraine (Donbas, Cluster 4) was also among the most developed areas and was characterized by high salaries and a positive migration balance. The fragmented-dispersed cluster of "urban areas" had the most favorable features, showing nine indicator values above the regional average. Central Ukraine (Cluster 6) was a backward region, with most values similar to the average. Cluster 7 was characterized by good employment rates, but low income and migration rates. Despite this, areas classified into this cluster were still in a slightly more favorable position when compared to areas in Cluster 6, even though they occupied nearly similar physical spaces. Cluster 9 and Cluster 10 recurred in two geographically distant regions, but their development levels, which were based on aggregated values, remained under, or near, the regional average. The main difference between them was that Cluster 10 showed six indicators above the average, whereas Cluster 9 had only two, but the low employment rate and low incomes diminished the progress observable in demographic features. The formerly developed historical Galicia, classified into these clusters, found itself in this poor position only after 1990, because the above-mentioned low employment rate and the regional differentiation of salaries was not characteristic during the Soviet period. Galicia and Zakarpatya still constituted separate clusters, and differ from the central and eastern Ukrainian zones as a result of their historical past. Their development level is not any better, however, than that of the Russian and eastern Ukrainian regions. Present-day hot-spots are located along the identified cluster boundaries and are also abundant where sudden drops in the development level occurred in 2010.

Conclusions

The quantitative investigation of the 1897 census proves that the Russian Empire, though it was able to integrate the acquired territories of Ukraine in 1654, Poland between 1772 and 1795, and Bessarabia in 1812, was unable to homogenize European Russia until the twentieth century. It is also important to emphasize that, unlike administrative-bureaucratic unification, ethnic homogenization for the empire was not a primary goal as it had huge costs. Loyalty was manifested in ways other than through "belonging to the same nation". As a result of the relatively low percentage of Russians (45%), the differences of cultural level (the incorporated areas had their own statehood and historical consciousness), and the extensive area (the Russian "colonies" — contrary to the European practices — were in physical connection with the core, which promoted administrative unification, but made ethnic homogenization difficult), nationalism in imperial Russia was not really successful.

The boundaries of historical regions correlated more closely to the old political boundaries than to the new ones. This proves that most of the "phantom borders" are "deep structural fault lines" that are not recreated and maintained by a short-term political-collective memory, but are instead determined by long-term differences in historical development, and are reflected mainly in socio-demographic, not economic, features. Therefore, the failure of the Soviet uniformization effort (which differed from the practices of tsarist Russia) is not surprising. (The term homogenization is admittedly somewhat improper here, as the USSR theoretically supported ethnic diversity). The new inorganic boundaries that were redrawn by Soviet regional planning, such as the incorporation of Crimea into Ukraine, lacked historical or ethnic content, and in fact remained vague. The problems of the new political entities stem from the distortions inherited from the Soviet era (Slovakia, for example, is a young state, and is ethnically heterogenous similarly to Ukraine, but socio-economically more stable). On the other hand, the census of 1897 implies that the nationalization of empires was a "mission impossible," (within the given timeframe — that is 30 years), especially if the empire's goal was to create a true nation-state, rather than a "citizenship-nation" (like the USA, for example).

Most of the present-day internal fault lines in Belarus, and in conflict zones such as Ukraine and Moldova, also coincide with old political boundaries. In the case of Belarus, this is the short-lived political boundary between Poland and the Soviet Union from 1920 to 1939. In the case of Ukraine, it is the eastern border of the former *Rzeczpospolita Polska* near Kiev, or with the boundaries of "historical regions" delimited by the quantitative analysis of the 1897 census. The traditional cultural patterns prevailed, partly because of recent political movements that were usually in opposition, or that have re-appeared in the form of regional, and partly ethnic, identities. Among the present-day borders, only the eastern political boundary of Poland and the Baltic region generally coincides with the historical cultural-economic fault lines.

The existing internal inequalities are not only the result of Soviet regional planning, or the collapse of the USSR. These inequalities already existed in 1897, though their pattern may have changed. The pattern of internal inequalities in 1897 also confirms the existence of historical regions. In the towns of what would become

Belarus the proportion of the non-Orthodox population was high, while towards the east differences between towns and their rural hinterland decreased together with the decrease of their general level of development. Some of the differences in 1897 identified in this study remained traceable even in 2010, despite the subsequent effects of Soviet regional policy and the turn in the economic policies of the post-Soviet states, both of which attempted to reprogram the old spatial patterns characteristic of 1897.

Some examinations not discussed here in detail also pointed to the fact that Soviet regions in 1930 differed remarkably from other parts of Central Europe based on the values of some socio-economic indicators (Rónai A. 1945). Based on the values of these indicators (representing development level in general), the Polish areas of 1897 that regained independence after 1920 were considered to be a part of East Central Europe, whereas East Central Europe — also based on these development indicators — was functioning as a buffer zone of the West (Demeter G. 2018, based on Rónai 1945). Present-day western Ukraine and western Belarus was a homogenous region in the 1930s based on the indicator values, and was separated from the core of the Polish territories, not only by cultural, but also by economic differences. At the same time, the Balkan Peninsula, which experienced different political circumstances, showed a similarity in its socio-economic indicators to the communist western Ukrainian and Belarus regions.

The regional inequalities after the fall of communism and the collapse of the Soviet Union have prevailed, but show a different pattern than in 1897. Though the cluster analysis still indicates the existence of historical regions that were identified in 1897, such as western Ukraine, eastern Ukraine, southern Ukraine, and the Polish-Lithuanian border strip, this does not mean there are significant differences in their development levels as was the case in 1897. The western fringes of the post-Soviet region, which were formerly characterized by higher levels of development when compared to the eastern regions, had lost their favorable position in many aspects by 2010. During the Soviet and post-Soviet eras, an economic levelling took place between the developing eastern Donets, and the stagnating-declining western and southern parts of Ukraine. The formerly backward Russian territories also showed significant advancement. The western parts of Russia now experience a higher standard of living than Belarus or western Ukraine. Fault lines observable in 1897 in both socio-economic and demographic indicators are observable now mostly in differences of demography. It is also worth mentioning that the pattern of clusters (sub-regions) was more mosaic-like in 2010 than in 1897. However, this might be caused by the differences in the size of territorial units and the indicator structure instead of socio-economic processes. Despite the changes in development levels and economic structures, the present-day "frozen conflicts" are still located around former and present socio-economic and cultural cleavages (Fig. 1.1.2-4 and 1.1.7).

As the examples show, spatial analysis — that is, the identification of backward, underdeveloped peripheries or regions of different characteristics — can contribute to a better understanding of historical questions, as well as the evolution of present-day conflicts.

The Faces of Russian Nationalism

Margit Kőszegi

The presence and growth of Russian nationalism has been palpable over the past few decades. Having hosted prestigious sporting events, such as the 2014 Winter Olympics and the 2018 FIFA World Cup, the Russian state has revealed itself to interested observers. Presidential declarations have emphasized Russian national interests and the protection of the Russian people, and the government agenda has been built exclusively on the idea of a national character. Following the collapse of the Soviet Union, Russia contemplated its own sense of nationhood, and emerged into the 21st century with nationalist policies that focused on the individual instead of the state. This was not a change dictated by power, but rather a response on the part of the political elite to perceptible changes in the community. As Pål Kolstø states in the first sentence of his book about Russian nationalism, "Nationalism is featuring increasingly in Russian society and in public discourse" (Kolstø, P. 2016).

This is an astounding phenomenon for older generations living in the countries of the former Eastern Bloc who can recall the loud voices proclaiming Soviet proletarian internationalism. It is a powerful signal that societies in the region have come a long way since the collapse of the Soviet Union in 1991, even in the most powerful society of all — the Russian community. The post-Soviet — whether this is interpreted spatially, temporally, or in terms of social or material qualities in the process of change — brought intense ethnic-based nationalisms. In the late 20th century, the West was shocked by the disintegration of the Soviet Union, and by the emergence of a series of nation-states on the periphery of what was previously considered an indestructible monolith. In the new millennium, attention has increasingly shifted towards Russia and the political direction it has taken.

The new Russia, emerging like a phoenix from the ashes of the Soviet Union, is now manifesting itself in terms of its ethnic identity. Freeing itself from its former shackles, it has joined the stream that Benedict Anderson described in 1991 as the "last wave" of nationalism. With the help of Anderson's theoretical work *Imagined Communities* (1991), this chapter explores the process that has given shape to Russian nationalism in the 21st century.

The nation as a horizontally imagined community

Anderson's influential work on nationalism was first published in 1983. Contrary to the conventional wisdom of the day, Anderson separated the concept of nationalism from other 19th-century "isms", identifying it as a phenomenon that had been taking shape for centuries. By reframing nationalism in this way, Anderson radically transformed the way scholars viewed and interpreted the "mindset" of societies around the world. He did not see nationalism as a product of the Industrial Revolution or modernization, but instead linked it to the Age of Discovery and the rise of capitalism. Anderson also highlighted the role that print itself played in the process, whereby people living under dynastic structures of power sanctioned by God began to imagine themselves as part of a community that coexisted synchronously across space and time.

A key component of Anderson's theory is his historicization of the emergence of horizontal thinking in the life of communities. As Anderson points out, prior to this fundamental shift in world view, vertical thinking dominated the political and social imaginary. Notions of the sacred characterized the relationship between celestial (divine) and earthly (human) phenomena, while the church and the dynastic monarch who received his/her power from the celestial sphere served as the connecting link between the two realms. During the Age of Discovery, however, a virtual explosion of new information distributed in print across vast spaces changed how people thought about the world. The notion of coexisting worlds became not just more common but also more imaginable as capitalism spread, and as pluralism became the norm. Geographic space began to play a central role in mediating one's relationship with the world, and boundaries became increasingly important as spatially larger geographic communities became imaginable.

Anderson's observations on the "national" transformation of multinational empires sheds important light on the emergent characteristics of Russian nationalism over the course of the nineteenth century. This national transformation of multinational empires can be interpreted as a special attempt to combine the vertical and horizontal ways of thinking outlined above. The phenomenon of "official nationalism", which was outlined by Hugh Seton-Watson in 1977, offered an explanation into how leaders of empires attempted to transform both their power and the state itself into a national framework. Perhaps ironically, this process of realigning imperial power within a national framework coincided with the suppression of nationalist movements. As Anderson notes, the attempt to give a special national character to the imperial state was like "stretching the short, tight, skin of the nation over the gigantic body of the empire" (1991: 86).

The process of "Russification" is an integral part of Russian "official nationalism". At the end of the 19th century, tsarist power assumed a distinctly Russian character, and built a Russian-speaking state administration with the related educational system. On the one hand, the tsarist leadership unified the language of power. On the other hand, they wanted to push other previously officially used languages into the background in certain (mainly western) parts of the Russian Empire. At the same time, tsarist power declared that knowledge of the Russian language and culture was the key to advancement.

Although these dynastic attempts had faded by the First World War, and an international framework of nation-states had become the norm by the end of the Second World War, the creation of the Soviet Union and the Second World nevertheless perpetuated and maintained the mechanism of influence described above. Building on the concept of "official nationalism", this chapter examines the imperial character of Soviet-type nation-building (a process that was similar to that of its predecessor, the Russian Empire) in the formation of Russian national consciousness, and reveals that "official nationalism" was only replaced in the 1990s by ethnic-based national aspirations. This delayed process, however, was characterized by its own phenomenon, one that Anderson suggests emerged in connection with the belated nationalism of the liberated colonies. As Anderston states, "in the 'nation-building' policies of the new states one sees both a genuine, popular nationalist enthusiasm and a systematic, even Machiavellian, instilling of nationalist ideology through the mass media, the educational system, administrative regulations, and so forth." (1991: 113-114). The ethnic-based nationalism of post-Soviet nations that emerged at the dawn of the new millennium was used by retrograde power elites to further strengthen their power through the expanded communication tools made possible by the information society. Russia has not been an exception to this phenomenon. This chapter approaches the ethnonationalism supported by the current government from different perspectives, ones that have themselves emerged over the centuries.

Characteristics of Tsarist Russian imperial thought

The idea of a strong Russian state is a central characteristic of Russian ethnonationalism in the 21st century, especially among more classical or orthodox nationalists (Kolstø, P. 2016). Rooted in the memory of the successful expansionist policies of the Russian imperial past, the ideological foundations of this key nationalist idea are linked in Russian historiography to the reigns of Ivan IV (Ivan the Terrible), Peter I (Peter the Great), and Catherine II (Catherine the Great). The image of a strong state whose expansion was unstoppable and even inevitable despite setbacks and failures is a powerful one. As Mikhail Heller notes in his monumental study on the history of Russia, "an interesting feature of Russian history is that even if the advance in one direction stopped, it could continue successfully in the other direction" (Heller, M. 1996: 224). Exercising its centralized power to dominate the smaller principalities that stood in opposition to Russian imperialism, the state invoked notions of internal unity against a perceived external danger, and therefore ensured the state's continued existence from the 15th century onwards (Heller, M. 1996). In addition to the constantly voiced defense against the threat from the east, the attack on the west was intertwined in this line of thought. As the area expanded, the symbolic meanings of the cardinal directions changed. After the unrestricted occupation of vast areas of Siberia, the perceived threat shifted to the south and southeast, thus helping to fuel the grandiose plans for world power of 18th century Russian monarchs. Whereas the struggle against a purported enemy drove expansionist ambitions in the south and southeast, necessity became much more of an explanatory factor in territorial growth to the west.

As the state of Muscovy became visible on the map of Europe in the 16th century — thanks in large part to European travellers such as the German diplomat Sigismund von Herberstein (who published a richly-illustrated travel diary) — the strengthening relationships with European states brought to the fore a pronounced Europeanism towards the east. This was reflected in the proclamation of Russia's Byzantine heritage. Moscow emerged as a new "third Rome," and Russian leaders positioned themselves as Christian defenders who stood against both eastern barbarism and Islam. Its most spectacular manifestations were the drastic measures taken by Tsar Peter I who, having returned from his journey to Europe, began to persecute people who practiced so-called Eastern customs. In the early 20th century, Vasily Klyuchevsky revisited this earlier trope, arguing in a popular work of Russian history that the mission of the Russian people was to serve as a bulwark against the east. As he wrote: "Fate has set our people at the eastern gate of Europe to protect the continent from the predator and invader Asia. For centuries She used Her power to stop the advance of Asians... Facing west, Europe with colonial supplies, cinnamon and clove felt that from the back, from the Uralic Altai East, nothing was threatening..." (quoted in Heller, M. 1996: 163). As Klyuchevsky's articulation of the Orientalist formulation of "us and them" illustrates, the Russian state was separated from the European-constructed east (Said, E. W. 1978). But Russia's relationship with Europe was nevertheless controversial in Klyuchevsky's formulation. He was well aware of Russia's need to remain vigilant against the Catholic and Protestant states of the West in defence of the Orthodox Church (Heller, M. 1996).

By the time of Tsar Ivan the Terrible's reign in the 16th century, a centralized state organization had been created with an eye toward growth at the expense of the dreaded eastern enemy, the Tatars. The word Tatar was used as an umbrella term by the Russian state, as well as by the Russian people, and was employed not only to refer to the inhabitants of the successor states of the former Mongol Empire (most of whom were not Tartar speaking), but also to denote the supposed otherness of the people who lived "beyond" the East Slavic principalities, people who were seen as the embodiment of barbaric antiquity, and even of evil (Heller, M. 1996). A crusade had been declared against them, in fact. At the same time the possession of the seas, one of the most important imperial aspirations of the Russian state, had already crystallized. The wars that broke out over control of the Baltic Sea (to the west and north), the Black Sea (first to the east and then also south), and the Caspian Sea (to the east) achieved lasting results after the issue of succession to the throne had been solved in the wake of the extinction of the Rurik dynasty, and in light of the ascendancy of the Romanov dynasty.

The expansionist policy linked to wars waged in three directions defined Russia in the 18th century. The first very spectacular, but less successful, attempts to realize these aspirations were under the reign of Tsar Peter the Great. The first lasting results, however, were achieved during the reign of Catherine the Great. Mikhail Heller describes this imperial policy as follows: "Without saving the lives of its soldiers, Russia sacrificed much to expand its territory in all directions where the obstacles were other countries, the military was the tool of its 'defensive imperialism'. In the endless areas of the steppe, taiga, and tundra, fugitives fleeing from the state had become the instruments of state policy. The fugitives seeking their freedom and fleeing because of power and landlords colonized the area in which the state appeared after them." (Heller, M. 1996: 314) Among the great armed military actions of Tsar Peter the Great, who harboured world-conquering dreams, the only lasting result of the Southern War for a Black Sea harbour was the destruction of the previously prosperous port city of Azov. Over the years, the Northern War secured for Russia the coveted Baltic Sea coast and the possibility of a Russian port. The Eastern War also brought short-lived success, as it was the first time Russia had ruled over the western Caspian coast and the city of Baku. The real agenda behind the Eastern War, however, was the "eastern plan" of the empire-building Tsar. He wanted direct contact with India and China. In addition to economic gain, which included the idea that brokerage trade should be in Russian hands, the Tsar wanted to give his empire a prominent place among the great European powers. This desire fuelled Russia's manifest destiny, which called for the expansion of European civilization to the east (Heller, M. 1996).

Tsar Peter the Great's successors continued to realize his grandiose plans. During the reign of Anna of Russia, a member of the ruling elite, Ivan Kirillov, became associated with the plan to connect

India and Russia. This plan called for the construction of a series of fortifications which would be connected by guarded roads. Russian settlers in the area would have to be relocated to secured lands. The dates these fortifications were founded during the 18th century can be used to trace the advancement of the expanding state. During the implementation of Kirillov's Eastern Plan, which took place during the reign of Catherine the Great, the so-called "*Novorossiya*" was realized to the south towards the Black Sea with the possession of vast areas of land at the expense of the Tatars and Cossacks. Catherine, however, was not looking towards India, but was instead looking towards Constantinople. She favoured the "Greek Plan" to conquer Istanbul, the former capital of the Byzantine and Ottoman Empires, in order to reach the Mediterranean Sea. Along with Russia's spectacular western and southern successes, the "Indian Plan" also achieved significant results, with the lasting conquest of the western basin of the Caspian Sea also taking place during the reign of Catherine the Great. Yet it was the 19th century that saw the emergence of the myth of the invincible army. A source of collective pride, this was the first step toward the creation of a Russian national identity. After the French invasion of Russia, the Battle of Borodino, and the shameful retreat and almost complete destruction of the French army, the Russian Empire was hailed as invincible by the European public. The indentification of an external threat, and the destruction of this enemy's army, had revived the Russian population's sense of togetherness and their need to join together against the conquering army, while expressing absolute loyalty to their ruler.

The myth of a strong state and a strong nation appeared both in the creation of a Russian identity, and in international public opinion. However, additional wars in the 19th century demonstrated the weaknesses of this "unbeatable" empire, and emphasized the backwardness that Russian intellectuals had so passionately articulated in that era. As a society undergoing transformation, tensions became increasingly obvious as capitalism spread throughout Russia. Faced with the strengthening concept of the nation-state, the vast empire became a symbol of an obsolete power structure. It was the geopolitical era of the Holy Alliance, an artificially maintained, volatile international system of conservative multinational empires guarding borders based on power contracts. No key player of the Alliance at this time was exempt from all of these internal transformations despite the efforts of powerful elites.

A multinational empire and national thought

While the European culture and way of life had become explicitly fashionable among the Russian aristocracy during the 18th century, the broader Russian population only became aquainted with the

European world during the 19th century. This was a result of the growth of print media, as well as Russian military actions in other European countries and attacks by Western states. At the same time, Russian society was developing its own distinctiveness, the main manifestations of which were seen by Russian intellectuals in Orthodoxy and the Russian language. The 19th century has come to be known as the golden age of Russian language because of education reforms, and the implementation of European-style higher ecucation. At the same time, Russian intellectuals also formulated Russian backwardness vis-à-vis Europe, calling it an urgent task to modernize society. In the debate between two groups of Russian intellectuals — on the one side the Westerners and on the other, the Slavophiles — the definition of moral superiority over the West that stemmed from Orthodoxy was also simultaneously articlulated alongside the need to overcome backwardness.

The importance of Orthodoxy can clearly be seen in imperial discourses of power (Fig. 1.2.1.) In order to strengthen the cohesion of the empire in the multi-ethnic realm during "the Age of Revolution" (Hobsbawm, E. J. 1962), the first step was the forced dissemination of Orthodoxy on the peripheries, especially among Greek Catholics and Islamic believers, less intensely for Roman Catholic and Protestant subjects in the Polish and Baltic region (Seton-Wattson, H. 1977). The conquered peripheries were continually characterized by the organized deployment of Russian settlers. With the 19th-century transformation of society and power, the deployment gradually became a means of enhancing Russian character instead of the local presence of trusted subjects. Another symbolic event in the formation of Russian national character was the long-delayed liberation of the serfs, which was ultimatrely prompted in 1861 by the shocking and disappointing failures of the Crimean War. Defeat was incompatible with the myth of invincibility, and therefore tsar Alexander II promoted the necessary social reforms in order to strengthen his power. This event marked the symbolic unity of the Russian people by eliminating the main obstacle to the promotion of the common interests of society. But loyalty to the the autocratic power of the Russian tsar proved to be a more cohesive force than Russian national consciousness. This regime changed its policy in the second half of the 19th century, trying to anticipate events in a society undergoing modernization prior to the period of national awakening, and seeking to strengthen its power on a national basis. The process of Russification, which translated to "becoming Russian", can be interpreted as an attempt to rescue the elite of a multi-ethnic empire (Anderson, B. 1991).

In his 1977 work *Nation and States*, Hugh Seton-Watson described the impact that Russification policy had on the development of Russia as a nation. According to Seton-Watson, the attitude

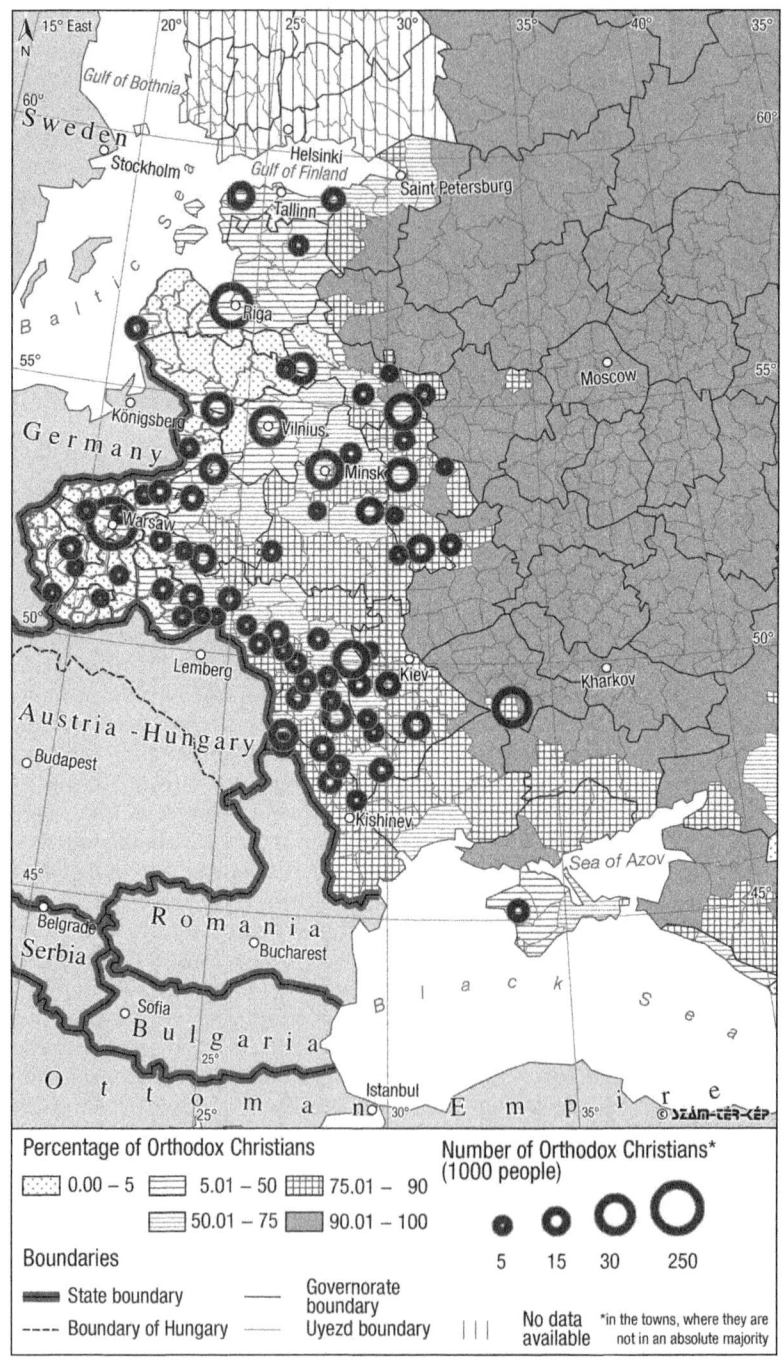

Figure 1.2.1 *The proportion of Christian Orthodox inhabitants in Russia in 1897; (Source:* [29]*)*

of power shifted in the 1880s, during the reign of Alexander III. This change was made manifest in the policy of Russification (*Rusifikatsiya, obrussenie*) which required that subjects of the empire declare themselves to be Russian, and that they see themselves as belongning not only to the tsar, but also to the Russian nation. In addition, Russian language and culture were placed above all other cultures in the empire. At the time, only about half of the population of the empire spoke Russian and lived in what was considered a Russian cultural environment (Fig. 1.2.2). The ideology of Russification had a dual purpose. On the one hand, it aimed to open up language and culture to all subjects of the empire through education. This would also provide people on the peripheries who spoke other languages, and practiced other cultures and religions, the opportunity to develop and become Russian over time. It offered the opportunity to participate in state administration, and to benefit from the advantages granted to the speakers of the dominant Russian language (that is why Seton-Watson called Russification "official nationalism"). On the other hand, this policy also aimed to strengthen their power by creating a homogeneous nation-state.

Russification was first implemented on the peripheries of the empire, where the educational and administrative system of the pre-Russian conquest had been in place for centuries. In the Baltic region, Russian was introduced in place of the German language; however, by making Russian compulsory at all levels of the public sphere, the state angered and ran the risk of alienating not only their German-speaking subjects, but also the empire's Estonian, Latvian, and Lithuanian inhabitants. The situation was similar in the neighbouring Finnish territories, as well as in Ukraine and Armenia, which was the most tsarist state in the Caucasus (Seton-Watson, H. 1977).

Russification can also be approached from a societal perspective, distinguishing its three types — namely spontaneous, administrative, and cultural Russification — on the basis that the term contains both the "conversion to Russian" and "becoming Russian" (Thaden, E. C. 1981, Weeks, T. R. 2004). The changing attitude of power fascilitated the rise of *spontaneous Russification* by providing opportunities for the reception of the Russian language and culture through the educational system. Use of Russian in the administration of the state required knowledge of the language, which led to *administrative Russification*. With the spread of literacy, and the emergence of written forms of other Slavic languages, including in print, *cultural Russification* made it possible to explore the similarities and power-driven convergence of different Slavic cultures.

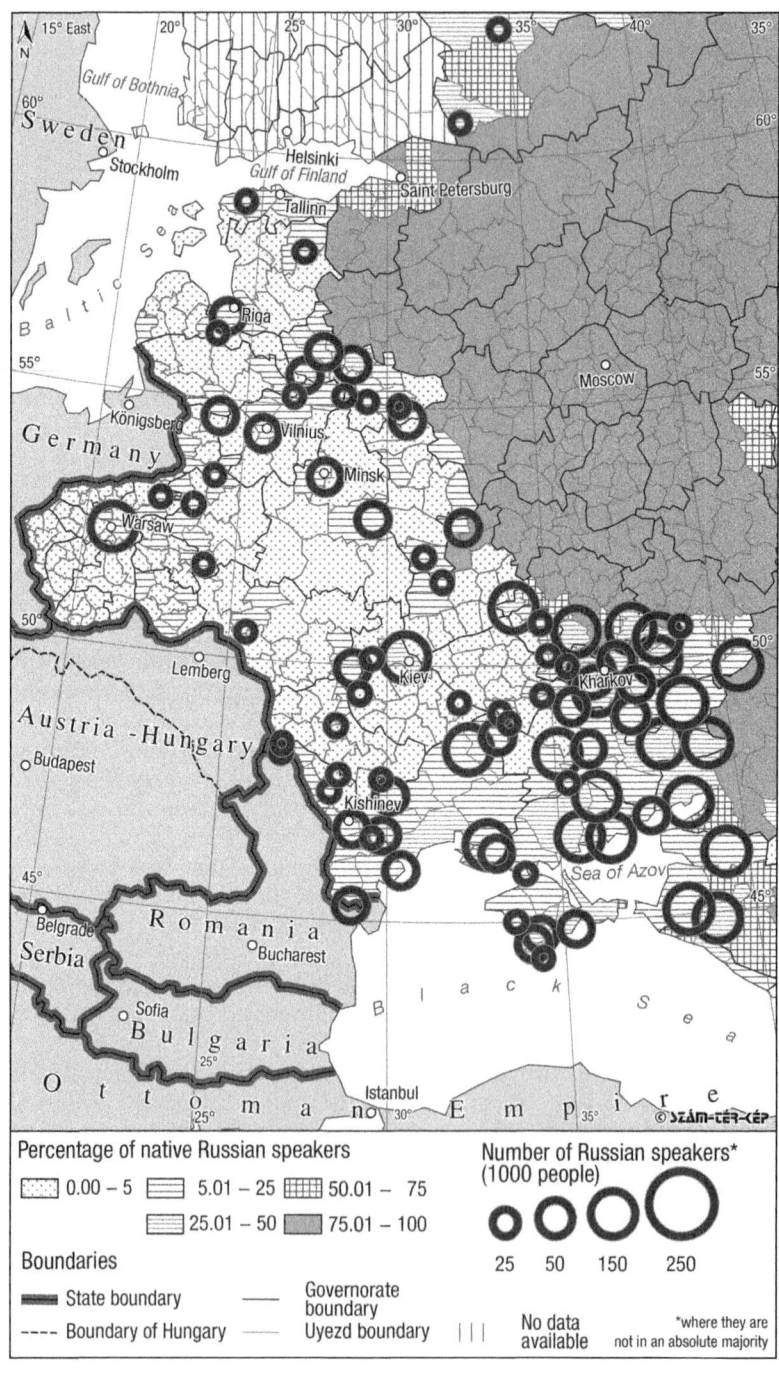

Figure 1.2.2 *The proportion and number of native Russian speakers in Russia in 1897; (Source:* [29]*)*

Theodore R. Weeks (2004) specifically links the emergence of this political attitude to the liberation of the serfs. With this symbolic event free subjects who differed significantly in language and culture from the dominant community became "visible" to Russian power. Weeks also emphasizes the Russian conquest of western territories that had European structures, where real power-control could take place by building a centralized, monolingual bureaucracy. Vasily Klyuchevsky described this dilemma in 1911, writing: "There is a contradiction connecting to the ethnic composition between European/Western and Asian/Eastern ends of the Russian state: there we have conquered peoples whose culture is much higher than ours, and over here a much lower culture. There we do not prosper with the enslaved because we cannot rise to their level, and over here we do not want to prosper because we despise them and we cannot raise them to our level. Also there and here, they are unequal to us, and so are our enemies" (Heller, M. 1996). The policy of Russification, therefore, can be interpreted as a response of power to this problem of peripheries.

As a result of its closed society, the people of Russia encountered many obstacles on their way to becoming Russian. For example, becoming Russian was especially difficult for those who differed in their outward appearance from the majority of the Slavic population, or had names that were indicative of their ethnicity, cultural affiliation and thus also of their social status as citizens (Seton-Watson, H. 1977). Being Russian was a privileged status, and the newly-emancipated peasantry found it difficult to fit in, something they slowly awakened to. For some social groups, it was impossible to become Russian. In addition to the Jews, Islamic believers were excluded, as it was generally understood that belonging to the Orthodox Church was a prerequisite (Weeks, T. R. 2004). Individuals living in the Russian Empire who wanted to become Russian, and who graduated from the state-run educational system into the ranks of bureaucracy, were actually trapped between two worlds. They were not Russian enough to be part of the Russian power elite, but because of their cultural affiliation, they were also alienated from their original ethnic community. These people experienced the same crisis of identity, and also forced career, as the local inhabitants of colonized areas did when they became functionaries in colonizing system (Anderson, B. 1991, Said, E. W. 1978, Fanon, F. 1952, 1961). These bureaucrats became enlsaved by official nationalism, and aligned with the representation of power.

Thus, spontaneous Russification actually achieved seeming success, but generally speaking, with the growing Russian cultural influence, administrative Russification in the target areas proved to be a fiasco. The failure of tsarist power to Russify its European peripheries manifested itself in the national character of the 1905 revolutionary upheavals. Movements of the poorer inhabitants (workers and peasants) were supported by educated intellectuals in the European peripheries. Their program addressed not only the necessity of social reforms, but also the ever-present Russian threat, and promoted the adoption of a self-identity different from the repressive power of the tsarist regime. The same was true for the revolutions that took place during the First World War, but with the collapse of central power, the possibility of independence opened up, albeit for a short period.

However, the majority of Russian society, especially peasants and the poorest urban inhabitants, still did not experience a sense of community with the privileged strata. They continued to experience isolation, oppression, and threats. Their revolutionary movements were cruelly suppressed, and so, in the same way as in France in 1789, the promotion of common interest proved elusive. Russian intellectuals welcomed Russianization, pronounced Orthodox unity, and supported the blending of Ukrainian and Belarusian culture in the spirit of Russian manifest destiny. This destiny, in particular, was expressed in the need to transform the peasant classes. As people who had "strayed," and who were under harmful Western, Catholic, or even Protestant influence, they needed to be integrated into Russian culture (Pavlenko, A. 2011).

Autocracy was considered a peculiarity of the Russian people, so most supported the existing order (Seton-Watson, H. 1977, Weeks, T. R. 2004). However, after a few years, the people themselves changed radically. Inflamed by the deprivations of war and mobilized by Bolshevik agitators, the masses rose to help destroy the old order. The awkward modernization and extreme negative effects of capitalism triggered the emergence of mass movements almost everywhere. As part of a European education system, intellectuals belonging to non-privileged groups had emerged and had begun to argue for change and the removal of the privileged strata, who had long been the opponents of change. According to these intellectuals, the privileged strata no longer represented the common interest, and therefore they no longer fulfilled their function. The repressed and then explosive societal processes fundamentally changed Russian society. The transformation was so intense that within a few decades after the death of the tsarist family, members of the privileged classes ceased to exist.

Russian nation-building in the Soviet Union

The Soviet nationality policies developed by Lenin and Stalin were first implemented by the Bolsheviks in the 1920s. As detailed by

Terry Martin in *The Affirmative Action Empire: Nations and Nationalism in the Soviet Union, 1923–1939*, all inhabitants of the Soviet Union had the opportunity to live according to their national consciousness. This approach was, in fact, part of an elaborate strategy implemented in order to control separatist nationalism (Martin, T. 2001). In order to keep the multi-ethnic empire together, the Bolsheviks had to sacrifice administrative Russification as a whimsical attempt to build a united Russian national consciousness. Administrative Russification was a kind of "official nationalism" (Seton-Watson, H. 1977) formed in the Russian Empire, striving for homogenization and prolonging the survival of former power structures. This was contested by the Bolshevik rhetoric of power, which defined itself as a stark contrast to the former system. Each community that was recognized as a nation received its own territory and was empowered to administer its state with its own elite, use its mother tongue as a state language, and promote its own culture. These policies were enforced within the multi-ethnic Russian Soviet Republic, where the use of the majority language was made mandatory, even for the Russian population living in non-Russian majority areas (Martin, T. 2001). The "internationalization" of the Russian Soviet Socialist Republic (SSR) was held up as an example of how communism could eliminate tsarist Russian chauvinism from the Soviet Union and give way to equality among its people. The policy of *korenizatsiya* (in Russian: коренизация, literally "putting down roots" or nativization, which was the Soviet version of indigenization) prevailed in the member republics (Bottoni, S. 2014). These republics aimed to adopt and integrate the Soviet system into the life of the officially accepted nation of the region, and to establish a local or "indigenous" nomenclature that mainatined roots that were specific to that place, but which remained faithful to the system.

The Soviet policy of *korenizatsiya* had mixed results. On the one hand, the existence of federal republics and autonomous territories suggested that the state had afforded its people a certain level of self-determination. This self-determination was evident in the use of local languages in primary education and print media. However, the ability of ethnic states to use their own languages served the purely propagandistic aim of widely disseminating the ideology of communism, which was strictly controlled by the centralized state. Communicating to the public in their mother tongue was the key to ensuring that the propaganda was effective in cultivating masses of people who were loyal to the new power. Western experts, on the other hand, based on secondary (mainly statistical) information obtained in the second half of the 20th century, perceived only the tolerance of the system in language use. Statistics showed that nearly fifty different nationalities were using native language in their public schools, and that print media and books were being published in seventy different literary languages during the 1950s and 1960s (Silver, B. 1974a).

Despite substantial social changes, certain manifestations of power remained unchanged. The framework of the federated Soviet Union held the vast former empire of the Russian tsars together, and the establishment of a party-state dictatorship concentrated supreme decision-making power in the hands of a new Russian power elite in a purely authoritarian manner. The rhetoric of communism ensured that orthodoxy was utterly neglected, but loyalty to power, the Russian language, and Russian culture remained a crucial component of leadership-mediated group consciousness. This was strengthened through the education system, administration, and bureaucracy (Bilinsky, J. 1981).

The contradiction between the above-mentioned Soviet nationality policy and the maintenance of the superiority of Russian culture was addressed and resolved by official rhetoric. In accordance with the idea of internationalism, there was a need for a mediating language among the peoples, which could only be Russian (the language of Lenin and the Bolshevik revolution). Teaching Russian was compulsory in all schools. Soviet doctrine, moreover, dictated that proletarian internationalism would soon need only the language of mediation, and as a result, national languages would die out leaving only Russian (Silver, B. 1974a). According to this line of reasoning, nationalist ideas would lose their significance as communism continued to develop. As a result, violent assimilation policies would not be necessary in the Soviet Union.

In his social criticism developed in the 1980s, Alexander Zinoviev reflected on the utopian nature of the Soviet approach outlined above, and undescored the ambiguous realization of the human ideal within the context of the construction of the Dictatorship of the Proletariat (Brom, L. 1988). In general, the often grotesque and negative image of the average, conformist inhabitant of the Soviet Union and the Eastern Bloc fell far short of the triumphant socialist ideals of Soviet ideologues. With the dissolution of the Soviet Union, Soviet inhabitants became the symbol of a people who could not prosper in capitalism because they lacked everything they needed to succeed in a market economy — the entrepreneurial spirit, initiative, risk-taking ability, and responsibility (Shiller et al. 1992). *Homo Sovieticus* was therefore interpreted not in an ethnic context, but rather as a model of behaviour that was adapted to authoritarian power, and economic necessity. Its indisputable feature, however, was its close relationship with the Russian language and culture (Govorukhin et al. 1989).

In spite of all appearances, it can be argued that Russification in fact did take place on some important levels in the Soviet period.

Although different ethnicities were given the opportunity to maintain, and even support, their own political framework, and to cultivate their culture, mastering the Russian language offered obvious benefits to the population; it was a pledge of social advancement and and a path to a more secure existence. However, the nature of Russification changed under Soviet leadership, though it shared some similarities in this light with pre-revolutionary processes. In the tsarist past, direct political will was the strongest element. Under Soviet leadership, power influenced personal decisions indirectly. In this way, the spontaneous character of Russification strengthened. According to this process, the non-Russian population became Russian in their way of thinking and lifestyle through a series of individual choices (Aspaturian, V. V. 1968).

As Brian Silver illustrated in his 1974 study, the process of urbanization and the rise of internal migration within the Soviet Union strengthened Russification (Silver, B. 1974a). The non-Russian population of the major Soviet industrial cities changed their mother tongue over several generations, then lost their original ethnic and cultural affiliation. Changing their mother tongue was the key to their prosperity, but the loss of their ethnic and cultural affiliation was interpreted as a loss of identity in the process of Sovietization. The forced Sovietization of official politics strengthened the Russian character of all the republics. Vernon Aspaturian (1968) called this phenomenon "Russianization" (becoming Russian). Because a radical transformation of society accompanied Sovietization, social mobility disrupted the old framework, and opened people up to embrace other, radically different, forms of socialization (Deutsch, K. W. 1961). The tools of mass communication and modern technology further facilitated this change in identity (Deutsch, K. W. 1966). Further arguments show that this process was much more intense in the lives of the urban population (Silver, B. 1974b). Migration of the Russian population during the Soviet period was also a factor. As the Russian population moved to areas inhabited by non-Russian ethnic groups in administrative centres and growing industrial areas, local communities in these places experienced direct contact with the Russian language and culture within their territory. At the same time, former traditional rural frameworks were destroyed by the Soviet system. As a result, forced industrialization strengthened urbanization, and an increasing number of people were directly affected by the process of spontaneous Russification (or Russianization). Silver also pointed out that, due to the relative limitations faced by women (who tended to stay home after work, and beyond raising children and running the household, often didn't have a career), Russification had a much greater impact on men (Silver, B. 1974a).

In a comparative study of quantitative methods, Anderson and Silver (1983) addressed the fact that the official nations of the republics, and the majority ethnicities of the autonomous territories, experienced a process of assimilation that was similar to Russification. Some of the minorities of these member states even identified with the state language and culture. This process was less intense and resulted in a significantly lower number of "converts" than Russification did. Examples include the Bashkirs becoming Tatars, Poles becoming Ukrainians or Belarusian, Ossetians becoming Georgians, Lezgins becoming Azerbaijanis, and Uighurs becoming Uzbeks or Kazakhs (Anderson, B. A. and Silver, B. D. 1983). However, mastering the Russian language and being open to Russian cultural influences was the catalyst for a much more marked social mobilization and, therefore, its impact was more pronounced.

The Russian national character of the Soviet Union's central leadership was also detectable in its late rhetoric (dating to the 1970s). According to this, the need for Russian as a mediating language was supported by economic interests and more efficient production. However, the superiority of Russian culture over other cultures was also formulated. According to this rhetoric, Russian was, on the one hand, Lenin's mother tongue, so the greatest thoughts of mankind were born in Russian. On the other hand, this language was the transmitter of the most advanced achievements (in particular the building of communism), and also the keeper of the most sacred values (for example permanent revolution and the Dictatorship of the Proletariat) (Bilinsky, J. 1981).

The consciousness of this superiority was not only articulated in the speeches and writings of the authorities. The Russian people themselves perceived their privileged position within the Soviet system, especially those living in the large cities of the republics. They had experienced the positive return of otherness in their lives very intensely. The discrepancy between Soviet citizenship and the forced display of ethnic group consciousness was not resolved in the equality proclaimed by Soviet ideology. It was embodied not only in the steady strengthening of purely nationalist movements against Russian hegemony, but also in the growing ethnonationalism of the Russian people who were "plunging" into ethnic pluralism (Lapidus, G. W. 1984). By the 1980s, the Soviet Union no longer existed as a model of communism under construction, but rather as the last multi-ethnic empire.

Features of post-Soviet Russian ethnonationalism

As a result of explosive nationalism and the crisis of the Soviet system, the Soviet Union eroded and collapsed along the borders of the Soviet republics. Among its successors, the Russian Federation is now the largest state in the world covering over 17 million square kilometres, and is home to nearly two hundred nationalities. The hegemonic state of the post-Soviet space is itself a multicultural state in which ethnic-based Russian nationalism has increasingly manifested in the form of pronounced government endorsements after the turn of the millennium (Kolstø, P. 2016). Despite broad-based ethnic diversity, the proportion of the Russian population rose to over 80% for the first time in centuries (it was 50% in the Soviet Union). Modern Russia, therefore, has entered a period in which it could form a classical nation-state for the first time (Tishkov, V. 1997).

The nationalists of the new millennium organize themselves around two different perspectives. The "statists" who adhere to historical traditions live in the spirit of a great and powerful empire, and are often called "imperialists" (Kolstø, P. 2016). Ethnonationalists, on the other hand, are focused on an ethnically-defined Russia, and have been triggered by changes in the intensity and nature of migration (Kolstø, P. 2016). Significant migration took place between the former member states when the Soviet Union existed, and after its dissolution. Large industrial centres and changing economic sectors continued to demand labour, so the migration of Russian-speaking, though non-ethnic-Russian, populations from poorer areas was continuous. However, by the turn of the millennium, the skilled workforce of the Soviet system had faded away. People from the backward regions of the Caucasus and Central Asia who were seeking a better livelihood continued to migrate to large centres, as they were able to cross the border without a visa and remained illegal workers in the Russian Federation. Their uneducated, poorly-integrated urban populations, providing the poorest social groups, have been a source of great tension for the local population. Xenophobia has increased (Kolstø, P. 2016), with Muslim immigrants being the main targets.

As a result of these social tensions, demonstrations were held against Putin and his government. An authoritarian politician renowned in the international press for his populism, Putin has transformed the rhetoric of power into nationalism. It was questionable whether he would ride the "statist" or "ethnic" trend discussed above. Due to the virtue of its power — he sought to preserve and strengthen Russian hegemony — it was easier to open up to "statist" nationalists who wanted a strong state (Pain, E. 2016). However, ethnic nationalism – which has been flourishing alongside xenophobia – was waiting for a different solution. The annexation of the Crimea was the solution to this situation. The Russian state demonstrated its power by launching military action, but officially did it "to protect the Russian people" on the peninsula. With this successful annexation, the Putin government once again gained enormous popularity with the Russian people (Kolstø, P. 2016).

Summary

The Russian state, which was formed from the once-insignificant small town of Moscow — and which has become the largest nation-state in the 21st century — is the product of continuous transformations. Having first united the eastern Slavs, the emerging Russian empire then defeated its great eastern adversary, the steppe nomads. Over the course of the 18th and 19th centuries, Russia developed at a snail's pace towards modernization and nation-state stature. The tsars, hoping to preserve their power over a vast multinational empire, embarked on a policy of Russification — what Seton-Watson called official nationalism — which centred on the primacy of Russian culture.

The failure of this project contributed to the decline of tsarist power, while the ill-fated modernization attempts on the part of the tsars ultimately led to the downfall of the entire Russian elite. In the Soviet Union, which assumed control of the territory of the multicultural empire, Russification was present in a different but more intensive form. This spontaneous Russification (often called Russianization) lent the party-state dictatorship a Russian national character. In the end, however, the Soviet Union could only delay, but not avoid, the process by which ethnonationalism developed in its territory.

Ethnic-based Russian nationalism appeared in this delayed process by the turn of the millennium. Its 21st century resurgence is closely connected to drastic changes in migration processes. This social phenomenon has been harnessed by the authoritarian Russian government in recent years, whose most successful and spectacular action in the name of Russian power was the military annexation of the Crimea in 2014.

Geopolitics and Language in the European Post-Soviet Realm

Zsolt Bottlik

Throughout the 19th century, in what is broadly understood as "In-Between Europe"[1] (*Zwischeneuropa*), local nationalisms were organized on the basis of language and culture. This process established an ideological basis for the political aspirations of ethnic groups with emerging identities. In the 20th century, this environment also served as a starting point for the spatial formation of local politics. Since the political change of 1989, the strengthening of regional identities and aspirations for political independence have continued to be articulated by various ethnic groups. These regional identities and aspirations may also serve as an expression of political attitudes in the self-definition, language use, and communication of different groups. The reverse may also be true: language choice, as expected by power, may be understood as the "adequate" form of behaviour. In many cases, an individual's relationship to language, as a channel of communication, is also manifested in the formation and occupation of space by groups of different languages and/or cultures. As a result, language use can serve as the subject of an explicitly geographical analysis.

Focusing on the European post-Soviet realm, this chapter looks in general at how Belarus, Ukraine, and Moldova were trapped in a kind of political vacuum that followed in the wake of the collapse of the Soviet Union. The analysis explores Belarus as a specific case study, interpreting it as a state that for centuries has figured as a peculiar geopolitical buffer zone in the region. Although centres of power failed in their attempts to integrate the region, their impact on local societies can nevertheless be seen. As a result, the external and internal narratives which determine local community identities in this buffer zone can be diverse. By providing an overview of these processes, this chapter will examine the role and importance of language use — either directly or

---

1 In geopolitical terms, In-Between Europe covers the nation-states that would later emerge in the pre-WWI buffer zone. In the broader sense, the belt from Finland to Greece is characterized by ethnic and religious diversity (despite the many attempts to change this in the 20th century), belated or incomplete development of parliamentary democracy, dependence on the Western and Eastern superpowers, and a semi-peripheral character. As a result, narratives on geopolitical orientation and national or ethnic identity are still a hot topic in these countries. In addition to the Baltic States, the Balkans, and Central and Eastern Europe, Finland can also be included within this zone.

indirectly controlled by politics — in shaping various social and economic processes.

Historical frames: The emergence of national languages in the region

The fundamentals: Geopolitics-oriented cultural influences and language

The vast majority of inhabitants of the post-Soviet realm speak one of the Eastern Slavic languages. The Republic of Moldova and Ukraine have relatively large populations that speak an Eastern New Latin language, although they are also bound to Church Slavonic by virtue of their orthodox religion. Language, culture, and political traditions have not always separated Eastern Slavic people from one another in later historical periods either. This is also true in the case of Russians whose identity was later predominantly shaped on an imperial basis. At the same time, Eastern Slavic groups show several characteristics since the regime change that serve as a counterpoint to the explicit societal (re)formation attempts of former empires.

During times of political uncertainty, various ethnic groups have been characterised by fluctuating identities, controversial separatisms, and different political interests. These have been seen along linguistic, cultural, and political fault lines. The pre-existing overlap, as well as the differences and contradictions between them, have not yet been resolved and integrated into a clear framework. Therefore, important political attitudes can often be identified by the choice and use of language, both from an individual, as well as a ruling-power perspective. The three countries of the European post-Soviet realm featured in this chapter emerged in different historical contexts, and were consolidated by the second half of the 20th century. For the most part, these regions lacked enduring state structures for the majority of earlier periods of history.

In much of this region, the first state formation was Kievan Rus', which was established in the 9th century by the integration of Eastern Slavic tribes. Mostly as result of its declining cohesion which began in the 12th century, Kievan Rus' eventually collapsed as a result of the Tatar invasion in the 13th century. Amidst the power vacuum that resulted from this geopolitical situation, much of the territory was initially occupied from the west by the Grand Duchy of Lithuania in the 14th century, and then by the Polish–Lithuanian state (united in personal union), and later on by the Principality of Moldavia (in the territory the of present-day Republic of Moldova). Following the collapse of Kievan Rus', the southern steppe regions — although they had been controlled by the Tatars for a long time — remained unconquered, and existed on the margins of Europe's great powers until the 17th century, when this area became a target of Russia's westward territorial expansion.

The founding prince of Kievan Rus' made the Byzantine-centred Orthodox religion dominant in the entire area. As a result, it was Eastern Christianity which provided the basic fabric of religious and cultural life. Among the predominantly Slavic speaking population even the aspirations of the Western Christian Poles failed to cause any fundamental changes in these circumstances, and the Tatars — having an utterly different cultural background — had neither military nor political power to radically transform these foundations.

Within the geographic region of this study, the early historical period was dominated by an Eastern Slavic-speaking population. The Slavic language used in the settlements with a Slavic population began to differentiate slightly in the 10th century, but at that time it was a rather dialectical continuum where the majority of ordinary folks used a local Slavic dialect. The further development trajectories of these dialects were mainly influenced by cultural attachment and power relations. Social organization, and the subsequent demand for a political power centre, resulted in the formation of a so-called "cultural dialect". This stemmed from various dialects and was established on the basis of power, politics, and language. The educated social groups of Eastern liturgical populations used the so-called Church Slavonic that was developed on the basis of Old Slavic language (Old Macedonian/Old Bulgarian), and spread as a result of the efforts of Cyril and Methodius. As the default language of the church and privileged social groups, it was based, not only on the mother tongue of the two monks (originally used in Thessaloniki, their home in historical Macedonia), but also on other locally spoken dialects (Figure 1.3.1).

On the periphery of the Kievan state, in the west and towards the steppe areas, several other predominantly-Turkic languages were spoken. In the Principality of Moldavia to the southwest, and especially after its geopolitical, economic, and social consolidation, a local dialect of New Latin languages started to serve as the basis of communication. In the western part of the area of our study, i.e. in the Polish/Lithuanian sphere of interest, the influence of the Polish language strengthened over time, including within the domains of public administration and culture. Polish was both the primary language of privileged social groups, as well as the official language of the chancellery. However, in places located far away from centres of power, particularly in rural settings, local Eastern Slavic dialects still remained the means of everyday communication.

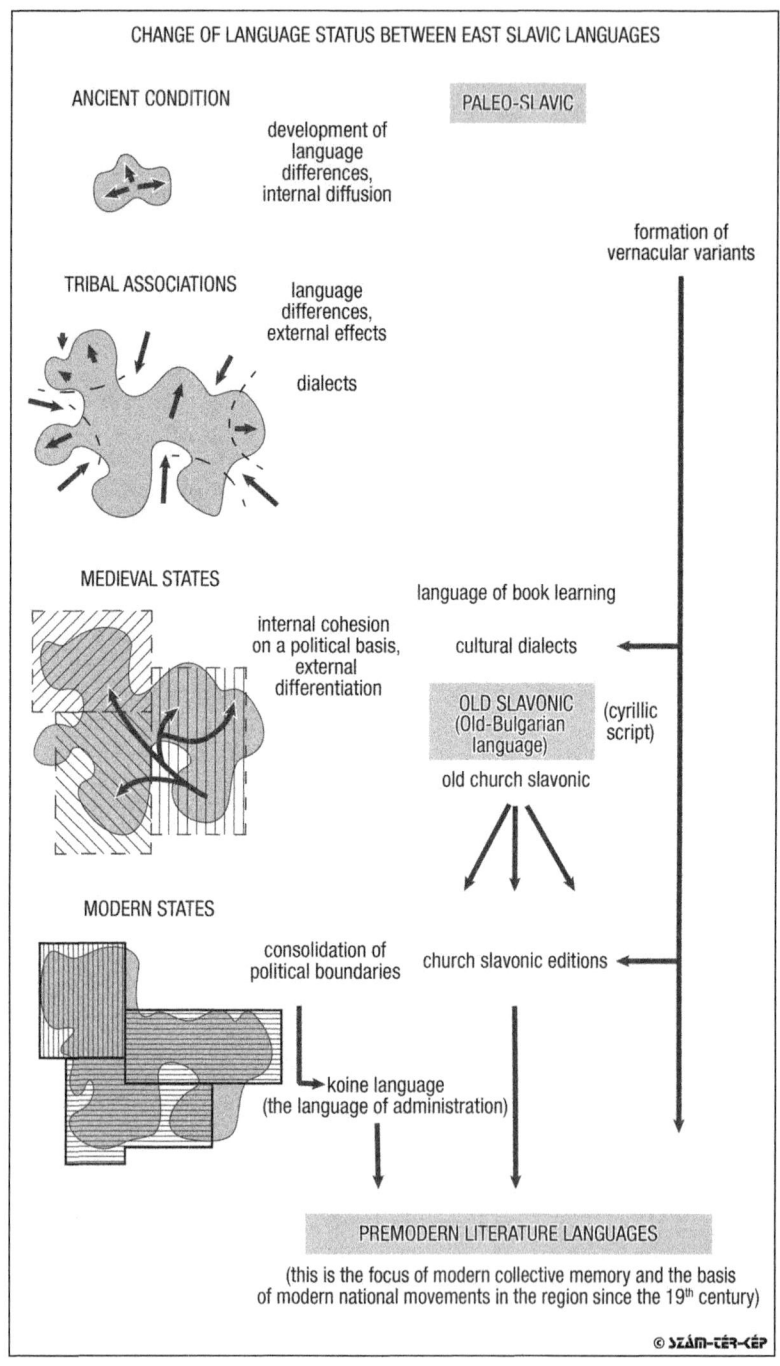

Figure 1.3.1 *The change of the linguistic situation among Eastern Slavic speakers*

The situation of language in early-modern local societies

The Medieval linguistic structure in the territory of present-day Belarus and western Ukraine changed as a result of the tightening of the personal union (which followed from the Union of Lublin in 1569) within the Polish/Lithuanian territories. This resulted in the strengthening of Polish culture in the eastern part of the new state formation, and in the so-called "Kresy" area as well. At the same time, the use of the Western Slavic Polish language was also expanding, especially among the nobility in the immediate vicinity of their estates and in towns. Consequently, the former local language based on older Eastern Slavic elements was gradually displaced from the chancellery, and hence, from the official sphere as well (this language is mostly referred to in the Anglo-American literature as "Ruthenian"). This meant that only its vernacular form survived among the peasant communities of agricultural settings (Dingley, J. 2001, Radzik, R. 2002). With the subsequent partition of Poland, present-day Belarusian territories fell into the sphere of power of the Russian state, which was expanding westwards dynamically. As a result, official language use in the region also drifted from the former local Eastern Slavic dialect, and also, later, from the Western Slavic Polish language (Ioffe, G. 2003a; 2003b).

Regarding the situation of language, this process was slightly different in some parts of the present-day territory of Ukraine. Over the 14th and 15th centuries, the emergence of Cossacks in the southern and south-eastern parts of today's Ukraine, long considered as a buffer zone on the periphery of Eastern European centres of power, proved to be a decisive moment in the formation of a later Ukrainian national consciousness. On the southern borderlands of the Polish–Lithuanian state and the constantly strengthening Russian state, and in a contiguous Slavic settlement area spanning from the Dnieper to the Oka River, their society was established in the shadow of competing powers, predominantly out of groups fleeing from feudal ties.

This area functioned as a kind of no-man's-land where local populations had to organize their own lives. This meant seeking protection from mostly external Tatar and Turkish attacks. Cossacks, who were made up of various groups, only managed to organize themselves as a formal state for a relatively short period of time in the 16th century, yet they maintained their particular way of life, culture, and customs for a significantly longer period, which certainly strengthened the cohesion of their community. The very existence of the Cossacks was a barrier, not only to the further eastern expansion of Polish culture, but also to the formation of a common Belarusian/Ukrainian language and identity. In 1654, in accord with the treaty which concluded the Zaporozhian uprisings, Cossacks joined the Russian state. This led to a gradual increase of tsarist influence, as well as to the limitation of their rights. However, it also facilitated the further differentiation of "Eastern Slavic language/identity".

The Principality of Moldavia, which was formed on the periphery of the Slavic settlement zone in the early modern period, became a vassal of the Ottoman Empire, and was characterised by a particularly dynamic foreign policy towards the Balkans and Crimea. Because of the relative tolerance of the Ottoman Empire towards different languages and religions, local societies in the area that were targeted for conquest (and thus recognized as military transit zones) usually had a mixed linguistic and religious character. This was the case in the territory of Moldavia, although the majority of its inhabitants spoke a dialect of the local New Latin language. However, the linguistic borderline could not be sharply drawn, so there was a gradual increase in the number and proportion of Slavic speakers from the west to the east. Despite this, New Latin speaking groups populated the western territories of low-density "*Novorossiya*", which was later conquered by Russia. Their presence can still be observed in oblasts beyond the Dniester River, namely in Odessa, Mykolaiv, and Kirovohrad.

Power frames: Language politics in the 19th and 20th centuries

Russia

Within the geographic region of our study, the geopolitical situation began to change in the 18th century when the gradually-strengthening Russian Empire — orienting towards its western and southern peripheries — became more and more influential in the area. As a manifestation of this process, and in particular with the partition of Poland between 1772 and 1795, a significant proportion of the speakers of the Greek Catholic Eastern Slavic dialect living in Polish territories fell under Russian authority. The spontaneous spread of the Polish language among those who previously held economic and political power ceased, and was replaced by state-controlled Russification. Running parallel to developments on Russia's western frontier, and as a result of another Russian–Turkish war waged by Russia to gain control over the shores of the Black Sea, the Principality of Moldavia was divided along the river Prut in 1812, with its eastern part, Bessarabia, annexed by the Russian Empire. This fundamentally determined the fate of the region during the period of modern nation formation and nation-building (Solomon, F. 2002).

In the second half of the 19th century, imperial Russia was confronted with a slowly-developing Ukrainian nationalism. In response, all forms of local language use, including book printing, education, and culture, were officially persecuted and banned (Lagzi G. 2001, Brüggemann, M. 2014). Among the Ukrainian territories with diverse historical and political traditions, it was the Habsburg authority over Galicia and Bukovina that turned these two areas into hotspots of the Ukrainian national movement. This nationalism was also fuelled by central modernization efforts, which provided a solid basis for the strengthening of Ukrainian language and self-awareness (Moser, M. 2000). A dense network of primary schools developed, and were aimed at eliminating illiteracy. This network helped to spread Ukrainian-language education, and improved the overall situation of the predominantly Ukrainian-speaking peasants. This era is considered one of the periods in which the Ukrainian language flourished. In the Russian territories, it was the conflict between Russian imperial politics and the formerly-strong Polish national movement that fuelled the Ukrainian national movement. Initially, the primary aims of the movement were not necessarily of a linguistic–ethnic character, but rather were aimed at social goals.

By contrast, the Belarusian national movement emerged relatively late. It emerged in the last third of the 19th century as a moderate movement, mostly to criticize the existing system (Mark, R. A. 2011). Following an intense wave of Russification, Russian authorities allowed people to use the notion of a Belarusian dialect, but gave no permission to have Belarusian-language schools. After the earlier direct attacks against local dialects, imperial language politics instead worked to degrade language construction efforts (based on local language variants) into mere dialects, particularly in non-Russian, Eastern-Slavic linguistic areas. By the turn of the 19th and 20th centuries, Belarusian territories were struggling for autonomy and self-government, and the very first product of the Belarusian-language press was published only in 1906. The Belarusians mostly articulated their identity against Poles, while towards Russians they tended to be more passive, and generally kept their distance. Nevertheless, we cannot speak of a solid, well-defined, local identity bound to the Belarusian language (Brüggemann, M. 2014).

For the population of Russian-controlled Bessarabian territories, tsarist politics initially promised tax breaks and a relatively favourable position amidst a generally unstable geopolitical situation (for example, by abandoning the practice of military conscription locally). However, from the late 1820s, especially through the retailoring of public administration and the adaptation of Russian customary law, the linguistically and culturally highly diverse local society was significantly limited (Bochmann, K. 1996). In order to strengthen the entire Empire, and particularly the peripheries, church organizations and school networks were also impacted by Russification. As a result, the influence of Russian language and culture increased in the region. Russian expansion had an impact on the language spoken in the eastern part of medieval Moldova as well. As a consequence, Moldavian was excluded from the 19th century modernization and standardization of the Romanian language, and this local variant was still written in Cyrillic letters (Ciscel, M. 2007). In the 1870s, use of the Romanian language was restricted, both in education and in church liturgy. Hence, its use was gradually limited to rural areas, while in towns, the Russian-speaking representatives of Russian political power and the economic elites (who were also Slavic speaking) turned out to be far more dominant.

In summary, the purpose of Russification was the marginalization of nearby Belarusian, Ukrainian, and local-Romanian languages, and the enforcement of Russian-language use in the school system. This resulted in a situation that contained enough Russian elements that they were simply considered as a dialect of the Russian language. In Bessarabia, the local language was pushed into the background by the universalization of Russian language use, as well as by the emphasis placed on differences between the local language and Romanian.

The Soviet Union

The language question was greatly influenced by the fact that in 1917, Russia — being in a weakened state due to losing its authority on its peripheries — was forced to renounce some of its territories. As a result, the Belarusian and Ukrainian languages started to follow diverging trajectories as they were incorporated into different political units. The westernmost territories became parts of Poland (this included the former Congress Poland with significant parts of western Ukraine and western Belarus), while Bessarabia became part of Greater Romania. The newly-formed Soviet Union sought to stabilize its power over its Belarusian and Ukrainian speaking peripheries in the 1920s. This manifested itself in the establishment of the Ukrainian Soviet Socialist Republic and the Byelorusian Soviet Socialist Republic, as well as in the formation of the Moldavian Autonomous Soviet Socialist Republic (MASSR) in the territory of the Ukrainian SSR, east of the Dniester River. At that time, local identity and languages enjoyed a higher degree of autonomy (Bieder, H. 2001). The introduc-

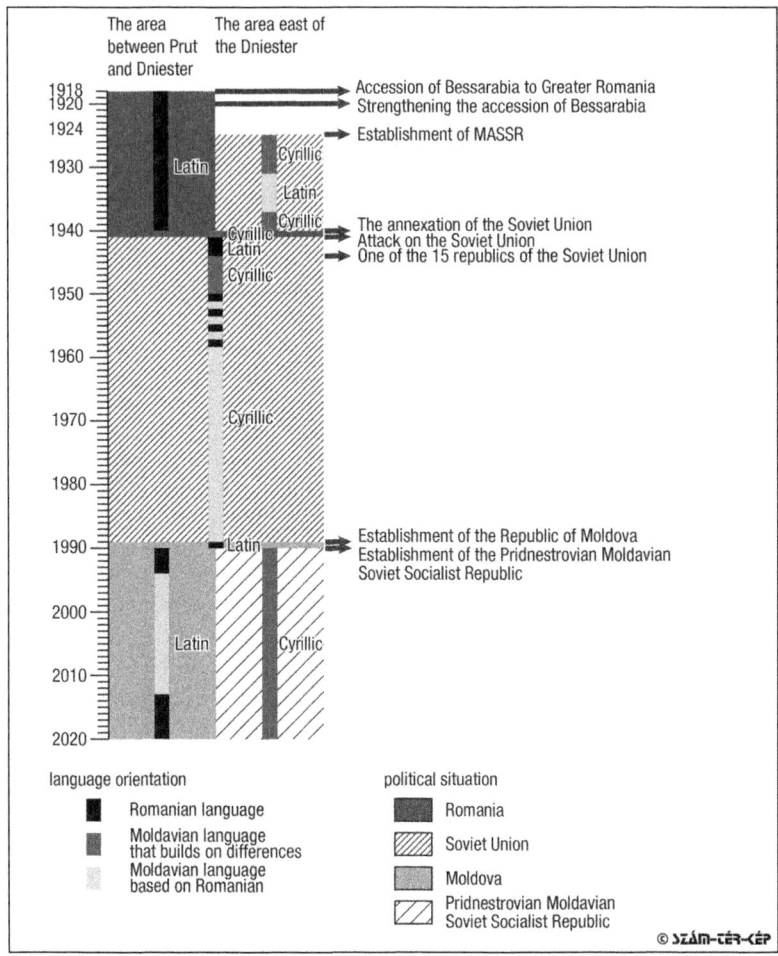

Figure 1.3.2 *The change of linguistic and political orientation in the territory of Moldova*

tion of local languages into school education was allowed, different types of media could be published, and the institutional framework of local-language education was established. All these measures allowed local languages to thrive. In the Moldavian ASSR, this was the beginning of the development of the standards for Moldavian language, which was based on a local dialect, written in Cyrillic letters, and emphasizing its differences from Romanian. This Moldavian language was revised in light of real language use in the 1930s, as it was written in the Latin alphabet for a few years (Figure 1.3.2).

With the strengthening of the Bolshevik system in the 1930s, the further development of local identities fundamentally changed in both the Byelorusian and the Ukrainian Soviet Socialist Republics. Stalin's nationality and language politics had become more aggressive towards minorities, while the forced industrialization of rural areas, and the persecution of kulaks, led to a severe weakening of the peasantry, who were the prime mediators of local language. In addition, local intellectuals mediating national-scale ideals had also been eliminated almost completely. The ruling power reinforced the presence of the Russian language, not only in the field of public administration, but also at all levels of education.

A parallel situation emerged in the case of Bessarabia, though with opposite effect. Whereas Russian language use grew in Belarus and Ukraine at the expense of emergent national languages, in Bessarabia it weakened and declined, and was gradually displaced by Romanian. After 1918, Romanian kin-state politics played a central role in defining the nation's origin and language, making it evident that the Romanian-speaking population of former Bessarabia was part of the Romanian nation. This was reflected in Romanian language politics as well, and the locally spoken New Latin language was undoubtedly considered as Romanian (Figure 1.3.2). The processes of the past 100 years also left a strong imprint on society at large, and in terms of language use the area has become generally Russian speaking, albeit not entirely. Romanian-speaking groups in rural areas were isolated from the literary language that had developed in the Regat area (i.e. the territory of the Kingdom of Romania between 1881–1913). This made it easy to label them as inferior citizens, and accuse them of not being loyal to the new regime because of their language (Dumbrava, V. 2006). The same was true for bilingual groups, who did not fit unequivocally into the official Romanian national definition, or who were living in mixed areas, or occasionally, in mixed marriages. It was mostly intellectuals who already had a close cultural relationship with Romania that benefited from the emergence and aspirations of Romanian authority.

During the interwar period, Poland faced a multidimensional problem as a result of the ethnic situation and the use of language. An enormous number of Poles remained beyond the borders of the reconstituted country, while a large number of Orthodox Ukrainians, Belarusians, and Greek Catholic Ruthenians lived within its eastern territories. In the spirit of the age, attempts had been made to violently resolve the situation by eliminating minorities who the authorities deemed dangerous. Between the two world wars, non-Polish nationalism, especially among Ukrainians, was also rising (Hasse, A. and Hudseljak, I. 2000). A fine example of fluctuating identity (and language use) is the category of *"język tutejszy"* (local language) in the 1931 Polish census, which was — according to official Polish interpretation — a non-codified local language (i.e., Belarusian) or dialect (Braunmüller, K. and Ferraresi, G. 2003). Most of the individuals who indicated on the census that they spoke this local language or dialect lived in Polesie/Podlasie, which in 1931 constituted the eastern part of Poland and can be considered a kind of contact zone between Polish and Belarusian dialects and culture. As a result of this fluctuating identity, people living in these areas sometimes claimed themselves to be Polish, and at other times, Belarusian.

After 1945, the historically-determined Ukrainian and Belarusian settlement areas, as well as the territory of historic Bessarabia, became parts of the Soviet Union. As the territorial identity of the population was mostly retained in the areas that maintained western traditions, the local culture and language use remained an integral part of everyday life into the 1950s. Despite this, the Soviet regime's nationality politics pushed Russification strongly, though they employed different methods and ideologies than officials had during the tsarist period. At the same time, this reinforced the historically-determined cultural and linguistic duality, which was particularly sharp in the Ukrainian SSR. The western part of the country had a more radical society and was exposed to a much stronger western influence over history. In contrast, the socially and economically different, almost continuously urbanized eastern territories, were successfully sovietised and oriented towards Moscow (Hrycak, J. 2000).

The Russification of official politics continued to intensify. The promotion of bilingualism, the agitation regarding the use of Russian language among non-Russian speakers, as well as the proclamation of the cultural "fusion" of the peoples of the Soviet Union, all emphasized the similarities rather than the differences between the two literary languages. Thus, due to the spread of Russian in education, so-called mixed languages — Trasianka in Belarus, and Surzhyk in Ukraine — also evolved (Golz, S. 2011, Kratochvil, A. and Mokienko, W. 2004). Their use did not help the development of the Belarusian and Ukrainian languages, however, and mainly served as local vernacular languages, especially in the case of Belarus, which significantly hindered their widespread use. As a result, differences between Eastern Slavic languages were blurred, and Russian was not regarded by the majority of the population as a foreign language, but instead as a more advanced form of their own dialect (Figure 1.3.3).

These processes were exacerbated by the Soviet leadership's ambition to create the ideal of *homo Sovieticus*. Privileging social cohesion over ethnic consciousness, this ideal fell on fertile ground in the majority of Ukrainian and Belarusian society, as both had

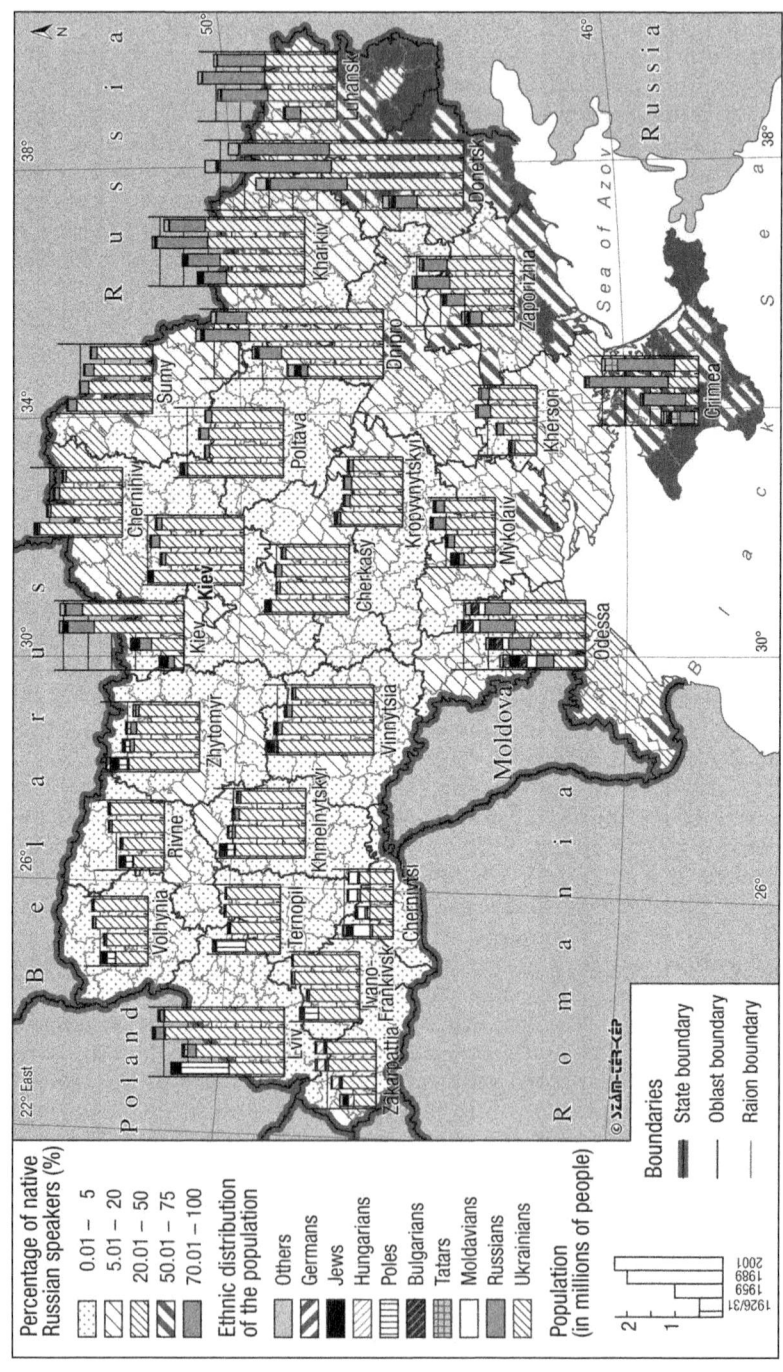

Figure 1.3.3 *The proportion and number of Russian native speakers in Ukraine in 2001; (Sources:* [26]; [27]; [28]; [38]*)*

fluctuating identities. The processes of the 1980s activated the suppressed national sentiments in various regions of the Soviet Union, and Belarusian was both recognised on a state level and also started to be taught at schools at the dawn of the politico-economic transition. However, local social changes were not primarily caused by internal processes, by the growing distance from the Soviet system, or by emphasizing local specificities, but rather were mainly ignited by external circumstances.

In the Moldavian Soviet Socialist Republic, the way was paved for the extraordinarily intensive spread of Russian by the massive influx of a mostly Russian- and Ukrainian-speaking population loyal to the regime. They stepped into a demographic vacuum that was created by the mass post-war population movements. This process was reinforced by the highly labour-intensive industrialization of the 1950s, and was further supplemented by the relocation of thousands of pensioners seeking a more pleasant climate. These newcomers did not feel the need to learn the local language and over time became alienated from the local cultural environment, which demonstrated that urban milieus were changing culturally as well (Posch, E. 2011). In addition, the use of the Russian language started to play a key role in upward social mobility, and shifted from being a mere "mediator language" to the second mother tongue of non-Russians. This process, as already demonstrated by the example of the Ukrainian and the Belarusian cases, also became a formal directive of domestic policy beginning in the 1970s. The local New Latin language was also considered "Moldovan", and similar to the language politics of the former autonomous region, started to be written with Cyrillic letters again. As this initiative was not fully and immediately followed by everyday language use, the official opinion changed very slowly, and in the official communiqué it was essentially regarded as a Cyrillic-written Romanian language as well (Figure 1.3.2).

Ideological frames: The "post-Soviet" problem of language use

It is apparent that even tsarist imperial Russification was unable to completely eliminate the linguistic, cultural, and political determinations that had evolved up to the early modern period. In the 19th century, however, it severely limited the awakening of local nationalisms which could have solidified distinct identities. Seventy years of communism — especially in the post-World War II period — further complicated the pre-existing cultural fabric of these societies.

As a result of Soviet modernization, groups with different linguistic and historical traditions jointly participated in the building of a cultural community. The imprints of common (for example, linguistic) experiences penetrated into society, and are still dominant in the post-Soviet realm today (Sapper, M. and Wagner, R. P. and Wagner, C. 2003).

The question of language has become an important symbol of the strengthening of local identities, and the relationship to this issue started to serve as an expression of political attitudes already during Gorbachev's perestroika in the second half of the 1980s. National revivals were typically thematised on the basis of local, mostly "lower-status", languages. Additionally, language functioned as a central element of local culture, and as a driver of resistance as well. At the same time, it portrayed Russified-elite culture as imperialist. Thus, language politics were placed into the broader dimension of power politics, since the "ethnicizing" of local elites also enabled a kind of re-positioning against central authority. This is how the language laws of the region became the primary manifestations of national revival in the year immediately preceding the regime change (Sapper, M. and Wagner, R. P. and Wagner, C. 2003).

The role of power in language use

In Belarus, the language use of the population has changed several times over history, mostly as a result of political intentions. Russian has had an official status since 1996, in addition to modern Belarusian. However, the difference between the current official forms of the two languages is not great, so ethnic identity is still not expressed primarily by mother tongue, a fact that is also reflected in the language use of the society (Savitzkaya, N. 2011). There are significant spatial disparities with respect to mother tongue and language use. In general, among those who claim themselves Belarusian, the number of Belarusian native speakers is greater than the number of those who actually use the language. There is a marked difference between rural areas and cities as well. In cities, Russian is preferred by the majority of the population, including those who claim themselves to be Belarusian. The reason for this can be explained not only by linguistic history, but also by the fact that the Russian language has had an official status in the country since 1996.

In Ukraine, the issue of language use is the subject of heated political debates (Höfinghoff, M. 2006). Ukrainians have emphasized that, even after gaining independence, there still exists a great deal of cultural and political assimilation pressure on their own language (not just on the similarly endangered Belarusian). As a result, declaring Russian as an official language is vehemently opposed.

Just as the Belarusian language is supressed by the Russian language in Belarus, Ukrainians argue that enforcing Russian as an official language would similarly endanger and devalue Ukrainian. Due to historical reasons, the language choice of Ukrainians living in the eastern parts of the country (and thus, occasionally speaking Russian better than Ukrainian) was, and still is, not free. On the contrary, in many cases it was based on the use of violence, not on a historically developed bilingualism (Kulyk, V. 2010, Zhurzhenko, T. 2001). By contrast, from the Russian side, the problem is seen completely differently. The Russian authorities have reacted with great sensitivity to the processes, and talk about a "Ukrainian absurdity" in connection with the "Ukrainian language death" envisioned by Ukrainians. They are referring to the constitutional freedom of language choice and to the protection of minority languages, as well as to the fact that Ukraine has not only signed but also ratified the European Charter for Regional or Minority Languages (Besters-Dilger, J. 2013). Russian authorities have been talking about a continuous "de-Russification" since the change of the political system, citing Switzerland or Spain as positive examples. Additionally, they also disagree with the political thematization of the importance of the language question. For example, they consider Mother Tongue Day (21 February) to be a pogrom against the Russian language (Besters-Dilger, J. 2000, Gasimow, Z. 2010).

In Moldova, the crisis caused by the political and economic transition led to a disruption within the Romanian-speaking population as well. As was the case of all former socialist countries, new conflicts emerged as the euphoria of the regime-change subsided. Moldova's unification with Romania was removed from the agenda as the Moldovan people put their confidence in the political forces that were promising a continuation of the relative peace of the Soviet era. This resulted in a process whereby the old-new holders of power harkened back to the idea of "Moldovenism", which aimed to establish a distinct, non-Romanian entity in the field of national ideology as well, even though this was definitely not according to its Soviet understanding (Zabarah, D. A. 2013). This required the rethinking of geopolitical positions. After abandoning the idea of unification with Romania, this change in political direction was not only aimed at calming ethnic minorities, but also at mobilising rural populations. The elements of this political program included, inter alia, an emphasis on linguistic independence, the continuity of the Moldovan state, and the recognition that the country had a multi-ethnic population. Other groups still maintain that there was a need to emphasize the characteristics that are in common with Romanian culture (the "Românists", who are advocates of another type of language politics). These two ethno-politically different but at the same time also politically competing streams are mutually exclusive, which is a result of the changing identity of the society and the establishment of different political strategies. It essentially expresses the opposition of a group more closely linked to the old system vis-à-vis nationalist circles. In the Pridnestrovian Moldavian Republic (i.e. Transnistria, separated from but not recognised by the Republic of Moldova) and in the Autonomous Territorial Unit of Gagauzia (Gagauz Yeri), both Russian and Ukrainian are preferred over Moldovan, partly because of the large number of Russian and Ukrainian native speakers, but partly also as a kind of political statement even among the majority of the non-Russian speaking (Gagauz, Moldovan) population.

The current situation of the Russian language in the European post-Soviet realm

Former Russian/Soviet imperial nationalism, and its accompanying language politics, can still be traced in the spatial patterns of the use of Russian language and its official status. These processes are well-illustrated by the number of people declaring themselves to be of non-Russian nationality, but who speak Russian as their mother tongue, and also by a per capita indicator calculated according to their differences (Figure 1.3.4). This indicates those groups whose linguistic assimilation is highly advanced, but as a result of other factors that indicate the strength of their ethnic identity, also still maintain the earlier/original identity of their family and/or environment. The status of the Russian language in any given region may also serve as a good indicator of the anomaly between the two viewpoints.

By mapping the indicator based on data derived from smaller-scale, subnational units of the European post-Soviet realm, we may be able to arrive at some conclusions. For example, these social groups are found in the largest number in capital cities and their broader environments, but also in larger urban areas, and especially on peripheries and in areas populated by traditional minorities. This may be the result of the Russian, and later Soviet, imperial language policy, and the effort to establish the ideal of *homo Sovieticus*. This is particularly true for the case of non-Russian minority societies.

In comparison with other countries, there is an extraordinarily large difference between the number of local non-Russians and Russian native speakers in Belarus, where the vast majority of the population — especially in the eastern part of the country — does not necessarily associate their identity with their mother tongue. Spatial disparities also reveal the dividing line between formerly Polish-controlled territories that had been more affected by Western

Figure 1.3.4 *The situation of the Russian language in the European post-Soviet realm; (Sources:* [2]; [3]; [4]; [5]; [10]; [21]; [28]; [38])

GEOPOLITICS AND LANGUAGE

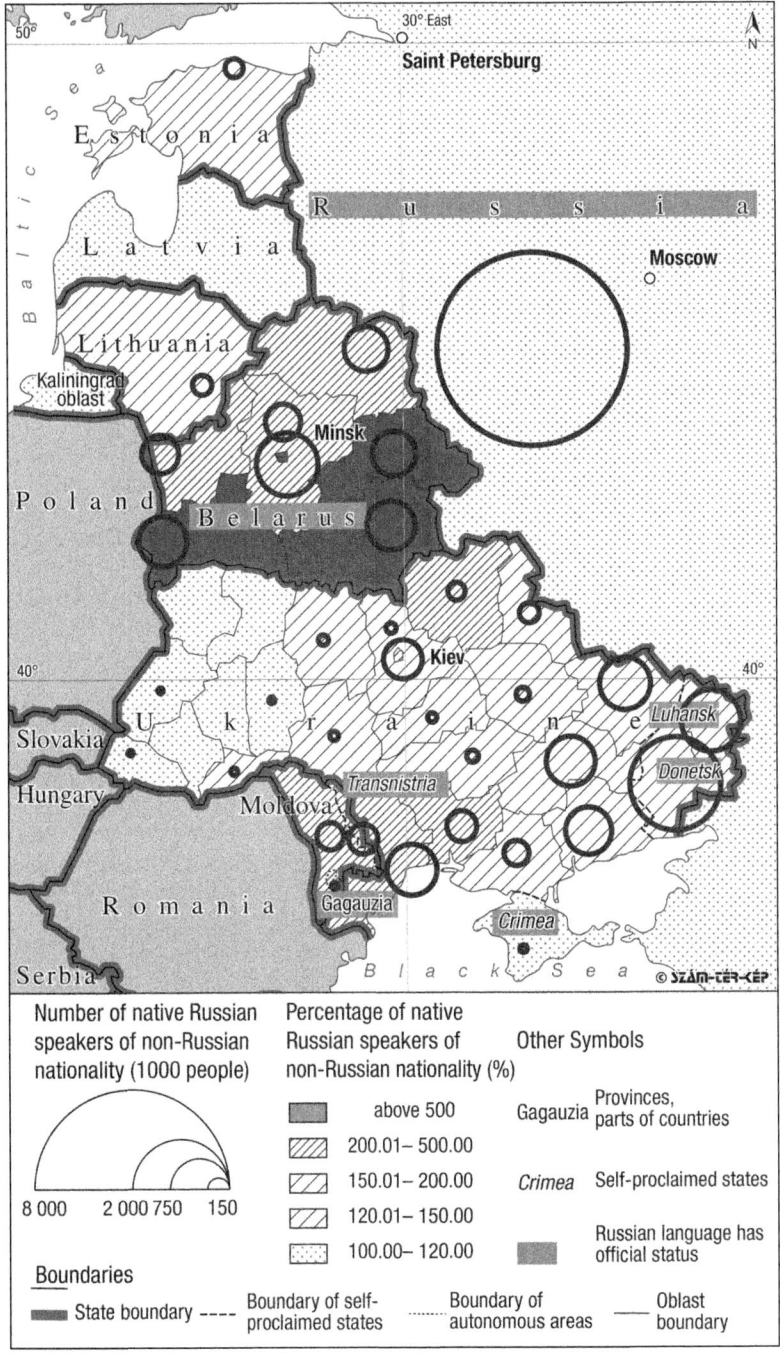

culture, and the territories located in an ethnic buffer zone that maintained a much more intense cultural relationship with Russia. Also, the fact that Russian is an official language in the country is also very significant.

The East–West cultural and political duality is even more apparent in the case of Ukraine, where there is a significant difference between the self-declaration of the population's mother tongue, and the ethnicity of the highly-urbanized eastern territories that were industrialized during the Soviet era. Southwest of this region, in the territory of former *Novorossiya*, the divide is widening towards more heterogeneous ethnic areas (the use of Russian language is becoming more widespread), whereas the central part of the country is a kind of intermediary area towards western Ukraine, the cradle of Ukrainian nationalism, where the linguistic and cultural difference between Ukrainian and Russian identity is the sharpest. In the territory of former Galicia (the true cradle of Ukrainian nationalism), the use of the Ukrainian language and strong self-identification is a general phenomenon. A similar if opposite trend is also true for the inhabitants of Crimea, where the identity of Slavic people is not determined by Ukrainian national movements but is traditionally tied to Russians and the Russian Empire, and articulated against Tatars, who were previously in power here. In Crimea, the use of Russian can be regarded as general and, therefore, the Russian language has official status in this currently annexed area as well.

The situation of the three EU-member Baltic States is also intriguing. In Lithuania, the number of people considering themselves to be of non-Russian ethnicity, but who speak Russian as their mother tongue, is high. This is a result of a large number of people from the Polish minority who are very organized politically, and who were supported by Soviet authorities against the local Lithuanian majority. Despite this linguistic assimilation, they have been more successful in preserving their national identity. In the case of Estonia, the data shows the rather high level of linguistic assimilation of Estonians. At the same time, the groups representing a significant proportion of the population that moved to Latvia from Russian speaking areas in large numbers after World War II retained their national identity and their separation from state-forming groups.

In the southernmost area of our study, which includes the western part of *Novorossiya* (around Odessa and in the Budjak), as well as the Republic of Moldova, the number of people who do not associate their identity with their mother tongue and who self-declare Russian as their mother tongue, is also significant. In this ethnically-mixed area, this "anomaly" is mainly a result of the use of the Russian language by minorities such as Gagauzians and Bulgarians, who live in ethnic contact zones (and thus were formerly supported by Soviet authorities), by a large number of Moldovans fluctuating between the two identities (especially outside present-day Moldova and in larger cities), as well as by the population of separatist Transnistria. Russian has an official status in both Gagauzia and Transnistria.

The development of language use from the 19th to the 21st century: The case of Belarus

This section outlines a more detailed case study of the processes that determine language use. The events of Belarus have been chosen, since the area is located in the eastern part of the long-standing buffer zone of "In-Between Europe" (*Zwischeneuropa*). This is an extraordinarily turbulent cultural and linguistic contact zone, where the imperial aspirations of neighbouring state formations have been attempting to influence the processes that have determined the identity of local populations for centuries.

The linguistic situation at the turn of the 20th century

As a result of historical events, the ethnic distribution of the population in the present-day territory of Belarus has always been very complex (Figure 1.3.5). The first all-encompassing census of tsarist Russia took place in 1897. The census also assessed the population's mother tongue and religion. At that time, the territory of present-day Belarus was almost entirely encompassed by the governorates of Minsk and Mogilev, and partly by those of Grodno, Vilna and Vitebsk. Due to the fluctuating identity of the inhabitants, it is difficult to reconcile mother tongue and religion-related data. In most cases, the respondents' social position also determined the language(s) marked in the questionnaires (Zeraschkowitsch, P. 2001).

In 1897, approximately 6.5 million people lived in the territory of present-day Belarus, of which the number of Belarusian speakers (4.7 million) and the number of Orthodox people (4.6 million) seem to correspond at first sight. However, after subtracting the number of Ukrainian and Russian speaking groups (287,000 and 281,000 people respectively) from the number of the Orthodox population, it can be seen that approximately 700,000 non-Orthodox — but Catholic — Belarusian speakers lived in the territory. Furthermore, the number of Roman Catholic inhabitants (880,000) was significantly higher than that of Polish speakers (156,000), which also included around 700,000 Belarusian speaking Catholics. Based on the above data, it seems that, due to their social position, a significant proportion of Catholics (i.e., the ones with Polish cultural background) did not declare Polish but Belarusian or Russian as their mother tongue in the census. This seems to be in line with the data of Polish statistician Włodzimierz Wakar as well (Wakar, W. 1917), who found that there were about 830,000 Poles in the area (with a ratio of 13%).

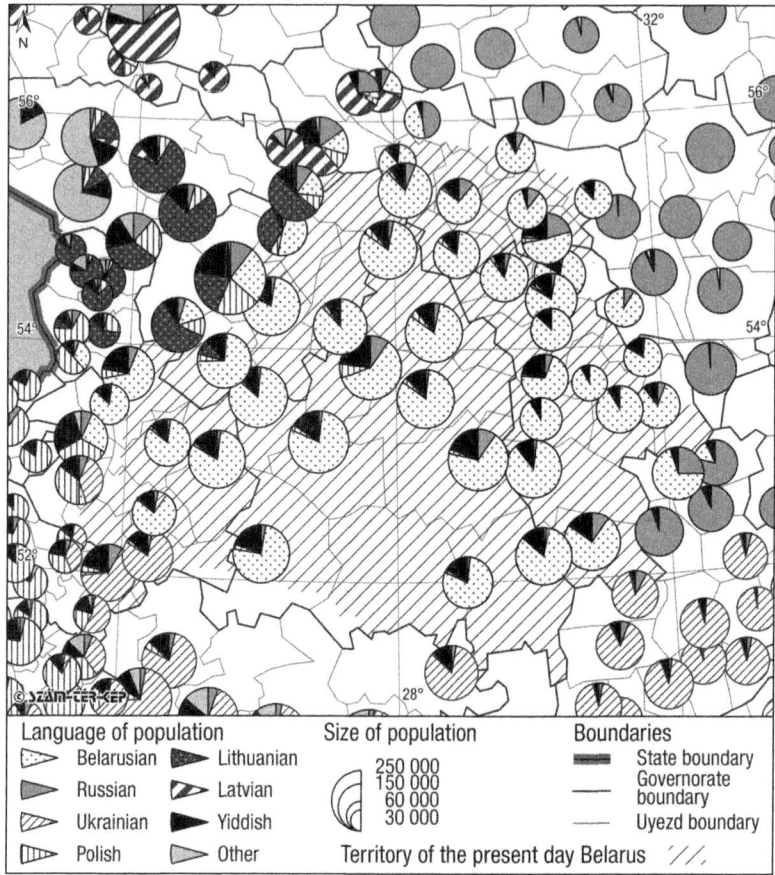

Figure 1.3.5 *Ethnic composition in the Belarusian-inhabited territories of the Russian Empire in 1897; (Source:* [29]*)*

Following the number and ratio of the Jewish population (910,000, or 14%), they constituted the second largest minority in the region at the turn of the century (Eberhardt, P. 2001).

Concerning the ethnic spatial structure, a significant proportion of the nobility and intellectuals, who were concentrated in cities, declared themselves to be Polish. The Jewish population was also constituted mainly by urban dwellers, just like Russian native speakers who were predominantly employed in public administration, and whose ethnic distribution was therefore quite even at a governorate level. Those having either a weaker or stronger Belarusian identity were living in less-densely populated agricultural areas. They were the ones who mostly defined themselves as "locals" (*tutejszy*) (Abushenko, V. 2004). When asked which religion they belonged to, in many cases they answered that they were of Polish or Ruthenian faith (Trepte, H-C. 2004).

In the western part of the region, especially in the hinterlands of larger cities (for example Hrodna and Vilnius), the process of Polonisation was also apparent in the local peasant society. As a result, the number and proportion of Poles was relatively greater in western governorates such as Vilnius and Grodno. Between Brest and Daugavpils, in the rural area along the Neman River, the Polish population formed a roughly contiguous settlement territory. At the same time, Russification turned out to be more prevalent in the eastern areas, which explains the slightly higher Russian presence in the eastern governorates of Viciebsk and Mahilioŭ. Although the lack of Polish statehood and a Polish school network, coupled with discrimination against the Polish language, weakened Polish cultural attachment, its presence and roots were still successful in slowing down Russification. However, this process also prevented the formation, and later the strengthening, of Belarusian identity in the eastern territories.

The emergence of modern Belarusian language variants — Taraškievica and Narkamaŭka

The evolving Belarusian national self-consciousness was given rather limited autonomy during the tsarist period, and was only revived in the first decade of the 20th century, with the dissolution of the tsarist empire (Smalianchuk, A. 2007). The Belarusian National Council was established in 1917, and when German troops occupied the western territories of present-day Belarus in March 1918, the long-standing and deeply-rooted local cultural duality was revived again. In the areas under German occupation, the formation of the modern Belarusian language could be observed (in line with the idea of linguistic pluralism), since the invaders were interested in strengthening the identities connected to non-Russian local culture (Bieder, H. 2001). Although the Belarusian-speaking Belarusian People's Republic was rather short-lived, all political forces had to deal with it, including the Bolsheviks. After the consolidation of the situation, the Byelorussian Soviet Socialist Republic was formed. After the Treaty of Riga, which was signed at the end of the Polish–Bolshevik War and split present-day Belarusian territories in 1921, the Byelorusian SSR covered only the former governorate of Minsk and later the Mahilioŭ and Viciebsk regions. However, it also integrated the population of the area for the first time in history by providing solid national-level frameworks for a relatively long period of time.

The attempt to establish a real national framework required the conversion of the local population's dialect into an official language.

The first codified version of today's modern Belarusian language is called Taraškievica. This standard was based on the Vilnius dialect, and the scholarly description of its grammar was published in 1918 (Knappe, E. and Wust, A. and Ratchina M. 2012). The editor of the volume, politician and linguist Branisłaŭ Adamavič Taraškievič, might accurately be regarded as the creator of the modern Belarusian language. He was born into a middle peasant Catholic family in 1892 in Mačiuliškės, which was then part of Russia, and is currently part of Lithuania. Like other speakers of the local Eastern Slavic language, he attended grammar school in Vilnius, which functioned as the cultural centre of the region. After grammar school, he pursued university studies in St. Petersburg, which is where he began developing and elaborating upon a Belarusian grammar.

Following the publication of the first Belarusian grammar in the first decades of the 20th century, some favourable tendencies further facilitated the development of the modern Belarusian language (Bieder, H. 2001). At that time, the present-day territory of the country belonged to two political power spheres. Its western half became part of Poland after the German occupation in World War I, and the eastern territories were annexed by the Soviet Union. By the end of the 1920s, the conditions for the further development of the Belarusian language were more favourable in the east. In the first period after the establishment of the Soviet Union, *korenizatsiya* (as explained in Chapter 1.2) was not only aimed at integrating non-Russian nationalities into the governments of their respective Soviet republics, but also became the official minority policy of the USSR. This also strengthened "albo-ruthenization" (Vaškevič, J. 2009), the policy of giving priority to the Belarusian language, and spreading Belarusian culture nationwide. Minority languages enjoyed a certain degree of protection in the country (Russian, Polish, and Yiddish were also official languages besides Belarusian), but Belarusian became the primary language of communication. However, in the 1930s, Russification returned, beginning with a new codification of the Belarusian language. The literary norm that consequently emerged was named Narkamaŭka, and it brought the Belarusian language significantly closer to Russian. The goal of domestic policy in the Stalinist era was the unification of the entire society of the Soviet Union, and Taraškievica — as a manifestation of Belarusian independence — simply did not fit in anymore. This language variant was completely rejected, and its inventor, Taraškevič, who had in the meantime stepped on the political stage, was murdered (Golz, S. 2011).

Even though the two language variants are not significantly different from one another, Taraškievica has since become a symbol of free Belarus (characterized by reforms, democracy, and a market economy), while Narkamaŭka is considered more neutral, although its use can be seen also as a pro-Russian symbol.

Geographical aspects of the use of the Belarusian language between the two World Wars

After the Treaty of Riga, Eastern Slavic people, including Belarusians and Ukrainians, were either assimilated or socially marginalized in the spirit of ethnic homogenization in present-day Belarus' western, then Polish-ruled, territory until its collapse in 1939. The Poles in power failed to mitigate the backwardness of their settlement area, and also failed to develop the local agricultural sector. Their national movement (which in many cases was actually backed by the Soviet authorities) was not strong enough either to influence the coming events.

By contrast, in the 1920s, the former Polish attitude — especially among urban intellectuals — was suppressed in the Soviet Union, and Belarusian identity significantly strengthened. The improvement of living conditions for peasant communities encouraged their widespread use of the Belarusian language, which was further facilitated by the establishment of schools, theatres, and libraries at the state level (Marples, D. R. 1999). A Belarusian-language university was founded in 1921, followed by the establishment of the Belarusian Academy of Sciences in 1926. As a result, the Belarusian language took precedence after 1927 over the region's other minority languages (namely Yiddish, Polish, and Russian). Nevertheless, albo-ruthenization was intertwined with Sovietization, which in turn distorted the belated process of Belarusian nationalization (Šibeka, Z. 2002). The reduction in the influence of the church and the weakening of Belarusian identity could also be observed, mainly among groups of lower social status (Bieder, H. 2000).

The intolerant nationality politics of the 1930s, the political sanctions against the mediators of local language dialects, and the exclusivity of the Russian language in education and administration combined to encourage the geographical and social marginalization of local languages. Between the two world wars, the Belarusian national movement did not receive sufficient impetus to make a stand for their goals or to formulate further aims, either culturally or linguistically (Ackermann, F. 2011).

In September 1939, according to the Molotov–Ribbentrop Pact, Western Belarus (i.e. the eastern territory of then-Poland) was annexed by the Soviet Union. Although the Belarusian-populated areas were completely united under Soviet occupation, the Stalinist repression immediately began in the western part of the country as well. 330,000 people were deported to Siberia, including Poles and Jews, but also Belarusian intellectuals who stood up for their own identity. Soviet authorities merely supported vernacular culture and folk traditions, in a very limited way and only up to a certain point. By the end of the 1930s, western Belarus — despite the process of Polonisation — was in a much better socio-economic position than Soviet Belarus. Interestingly, the border control between the two markedly different parts of the country continued to exist at Negoreloe (Nieharelaje), that is, within the internal boundaries of the Soviet Union as well, so that we cannot even speak of a true unification at that time.

After June 22, 1941, the present-day territory of Belarus became a background supply area for the Wehrmacht as a result of the German invasion of the Soviet Union, which began at the extended new border of the Soviet Union, the fortress of Brest (the symbol of the western gate of today's Belarus). At that time, the Jewish population of Belarus was almost completely exterminated by the Nazi Einsatzkommandos. Between 1942 and 1943, approximately half a million people fell victim to the Holocaust.

Belarusian identity was strengthened by the emerging wartime partisan resistance. Although it functioned only as an underground movement as a result of foreign occupation, it still enjoyed autonomy within Soviet power structures. Belarus turned out to be the main battleground of Soviet partisan movements, and the country's image of a "partisan republic" dates back to this period (Ioffe, G. 2006). On the other hand, Germans organized a Belarusian military government, and in 1943 established the Belarusian Central Council, which was a collaborationist puppet government. This movement did not have a broad social basis, but their flag was the same white, red, and white as that of the independent Belarus of the early 1990s. All this raises further questions in light of Belarusian identity.

Russification policy in the post-war decades

After the end of World War II, Poland was "pushed" by the Allies to the west, leaving its former eastern territories to the Soviet Union, and in particular to the Ukrainian and Byelorussian Soviet Socialist Republics. When compared to the boundaries in late-September 1939, the "west-shifted" borders of Belarus changed only in a few regions around Białystok, which became territories of the new Poland. Thus, the Belarusian settlement area fell almost entirely under Soviet authority.

Following the political consolidation of 1945, a Polish–Belarusian population exchange also took place as a part of the large-scale migration processes which fundamentally transformed the ethnic spatial structure of the new western Belarusian territories. The significant decline in the number of Poles living in Belarus was a result of the war and the subsequent repatriations (Lagzi G. 2001). It is estimated that during this exchange, nearly 400,000 Poles moved from western Belarus to the territory of the new Poland (officially only 275,000 Poles were displaced). In the first wave 37,000, and then a further 70,000 people of Belarusian identity found their new home in Soviet Belarus. In the 1950s, there was a massive influx of Russian native speakers into the demographic vacuum created by the casualties of the war. In line with the "Sovietization" of newly acquired territories, this meant migration into the major cities of the region (Eberhardt, P. 2000, 2002).

Following World War II, the official state opinion was that the aspirations of national movements were identical to those of the fascist aggressor, which was just another blow that the already weak independent Belarusian identity had to endure. In the territories formerly belonging to Poland, the increased industrialization of agricultural areas, the collectivization of agriculture, and the fight against religious social groups worsened the position of the mediators of local Belarusian dialects. In the western parts of Belarus, war losses were counterbalanced by higher fertility rates, leading to an increase in the number of Belarusian speakers. Nevertheless, their identities still remained fluctuating, and their communities became fragmented, as many of them migrated to cities that were by then mostly Russian speaking. After they arrived in the cities, and as a result of post-war Soviet industrialization, they became members of the urban working class, losing their identity and using the Russian language.

Post-war Soviet censuses (1959, 1970, 1979, 1989) show significant growth of Russians and Ukrainians, and a moderate increase of Belarusians (Figure 1.3.6). This might be explained partially by the significant "overlap" between these two groups. As Russification trends became firmer, emphasis was put on the similarities between the two literary languages (instead of their differences). As Russian-language education proliferated, a mixed language called Trasianka evolved. However, its use was not beneficial for the further development and widespread use of the otherwise official Belarusian standard. As a result, it is not surprising that the ratio of Russian-language speakers among Belarusians increased from 13% in 1959 to 28% by 1989.

Trasianka, a peculiar mixed language

Trasianka is a so-called "mixed language" used in Belarus, which combines Belarusian and Russian linguistic elements. This language has a distinctly lower prestige when compared to Belarusian, and especially when compared to the Russian language. The term Trasianka literally means "cattle fodder", which is made of a mixture of fresh grass and last year's hay. The word Trasianka has been used to refer to this language since the 1980s. There is a relatively long history of using mixed languages in Belarusian

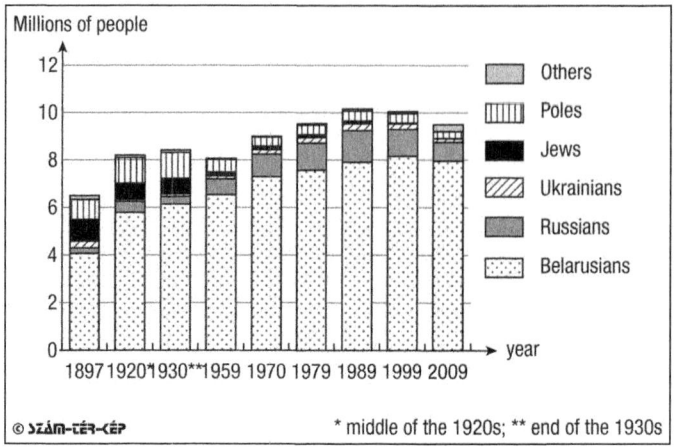

Figure 1.3.6 *The ethnic composition of the population in Belarus between 1897 and 2009; (Sources:* [5]; [28]; [29]; Eberhardt, P. 2000)

territories as a result of their buffer-zone position. The reason for this phenomenon is the opposition between local dialects and the official languages of various historical periods (Polish, and then Russian), as well as the different prestige associated with their use (Hentschel, G. and Kittel, B. 2011).

The emergence of mixed languages is a common phenomenon in multilingual societies. In the case of Belarus, it is mainly the outcome of post-World War II social processes such as the economic measures of the Soviet authorities that caused large-scale rural to urban migration. Intensive industrialization led to an increase of labour demand in the urban areas. This labour was partly recruited from the masses who had become redundant in rural areas as a result of the collectivization of agriculture. There were also large numbers of migrants moving from inner Russian territories to the peripheries. This meant that the people arriving from rural areas speaking local dialects were not always successful adapting to the use of the Russian language.

It should also be noted that adaptation was not reciprocal, and the prestige of the Belarusian and Trasianka languages fell behind that of Russian. The more similar two languages are to one another, the greater the likelihood a mixed language will emerge. This is particularly true in the case of the Belarusian and Russian languages. In the meantime, Trasianka has become standard, and is today the first language of many Belarusians. Therefore, its use is no longer determined by spontaneous processes, but has been spoken by several generations, based on more or less accepted conventions (Kittel, B. and Lindner, D. 2011). Until the 1980s, Trasianka was more of a symbol of the common fate of Russians and Belarusians, but since the regime change, it has become a manifestation of political orientation as well. For those who understand the language, it is a bit like reading Russian but with Belarusian pronunciation (Ioffe, G. 2006). Although the number of Trasianka speakers is difficult to determine, there is currently a gradual decline in the use of this mixed language, especially when compared to Russian, and it mostly remains the language of small-town intellectuals.

Among the processes determining language use, the endeavour to establish the ideal of *homo Sovieticus* — favouring social cohesion over ethnic consciousness — should also be mentioned. This has fallen on fertile ground in Belarusian society which has a fluctuating identity, especially in small-town environments (Šibeka, Z. 2011). At the same time, Jews and Poles, whose numbers significantly declined during the war, experienced immense linguistic assimilation, mainly due to their disrupted social structure and their narrow intellectual stratum (Ackermann, F. 2006).

The specific role of language in society after independence

Post-independence demographic conditions were characterised by a population decrease, which was also a general phenomenon throughout Eastern Europe. The decline in the total population was a result of the combined decrease in the Russian, Ukrainian, and Belarusian populations (Rowland, R. H. 2003). Formerly suppressed national sentiments erupted in many regions of the USSR as a result of the processes of the 1980s. The Belarusian language started to be taught at schools and was also recognised on a state level. These changes were not based principally on internal processes, the distance from the Soviet system, or on the emphasis on local specificities, but instead on the changing external circumstances (Lagzi, G. 2001).

The ethnic spatial structure after 1989

According to the nationalities-related data of the latest census in 2009 (Figure 1.3.7), Belarus is not a homogeneous nation-state, as only 83% of its approximately 9.5 million inhabitants belong to the state-forming group of Belarusians. Russians are the largest ethnic minority, with a population of nearly 0.8 million, which accounts for 8.2% of the total population. A considerable number of Poles (294,256; 3.2%) and Ukrainians (157,871; 1.6%) also live in the country. Slightly more than 300,000 people (3.2%) claimed they belong to the "other" category.

Concerning the ethnic spatial structure, Russians live in larger cities, whereas Poles live in the former territories of Poland, which have been strongly affected by Polish culture.

The distribution of the Russian population is relatively even, exceeding 10% of the population in nineteen raions of the country, out of which one is a city and six are urban-dominated regions. The largest Russian communities, with over 15,000 people, are exclusively found in cities. Ukrainians are concentrated in the Brest region, especially in two of its regions where their proportion is above 7% (Kamieniec 7.4%; Malaryta 7.2%); however, their

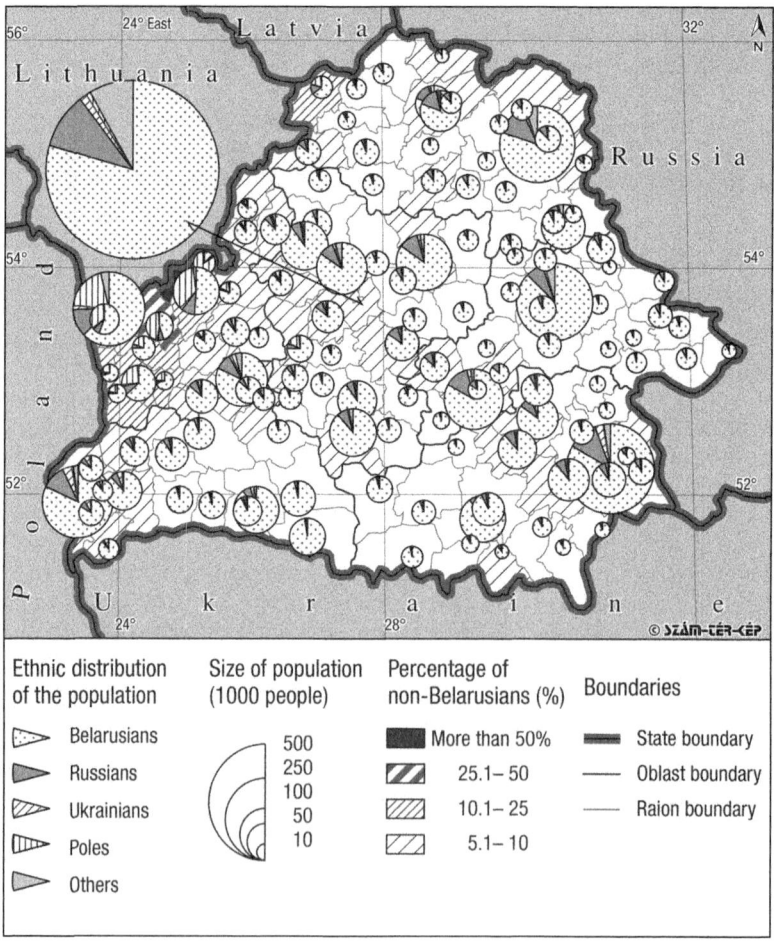

Figure 1.3.7 *The ethnic composition of the population and the proportion of non-Belarusians in Belarus by raions in 2009; (Source:* [5])

presence is also significant in the central cities of the regions. In two of them (Brest and Homieĺ), their number is above 10,000. Neither of these two minority groups constitute an absolute majority of the population in any of the regions.

The ethnic space of Poles is fundamentally different. It is characterised by a strengthening identity since the regime change (Iwanow, N. 1994). Among minorities, the concentration of Poles is the highest in the Grodno region, which forms an almost continuous settlement area (Eberhardt, P. 2000). Out of the 13 regions where the proportion is over 10%, only one is located in the Brest region and one in the Minsk region. Particularly along both sides of the Lithuanian border, their concentration constitutes a largely interconnected Polish territory, consisting of the Voranava and Ščučyn raions. In Voranava, Poles are in an absolute majority (80%), while in Ščučyn, they are in a relative majority.

The 12,000 Jews have been living here since the 15th century. There is also a significant number of Roma people (7,079), mainly located in the Homieĺ region, as well as Germans (2,474). Among the remaining groups, the number of inhabitants originating from former Soviet republics and having been living here for several generations is also considerable. In addition to the smaller communities of ethnic groups from the vicinity of Belarus (Lithuanians 5,087; Moldovans 3,465; Latvians 1,549), there is a significant number of people originating from farther steppe regions (Tatars 7,316; Chuvash 1,277), the Caucasus (Armenians 8,512; Azerbaijanis 5,567; Georgians 2,400) and Central Asia as well (Turkmens 2,685; Uzbeks 1,593; Kazakhs 1,355). In addition, there are Chinese (1,642), and Arab (1,330) communities, which further diversify the country's ethnic composition.

The spatiality of language use today

In the late-emerging Belarusian identity, local identity-building factors have remained the most significant. The wars and political cleansings which were fuelled by Soviet ideology not only suppressed or eliminated the mediators of national thought, but also actively influenced language use.

Over the course of history, the language use of the population has changed multiple times, predominantly in line with political intentions (Brüggeman, M. 2014). Since 1996, modern Belarusian, as well as Russian, have been officially recognized in the country. The population's fluctuating identity was also reflected in the differences between the results of the 1999 and the 2009 censuses. On the one hand, the data shows an increase in the proportion of the users of Russian. On the other hand, such a massive shift in proportions is completely unrealistic over the course of only one decade. This suggests that the

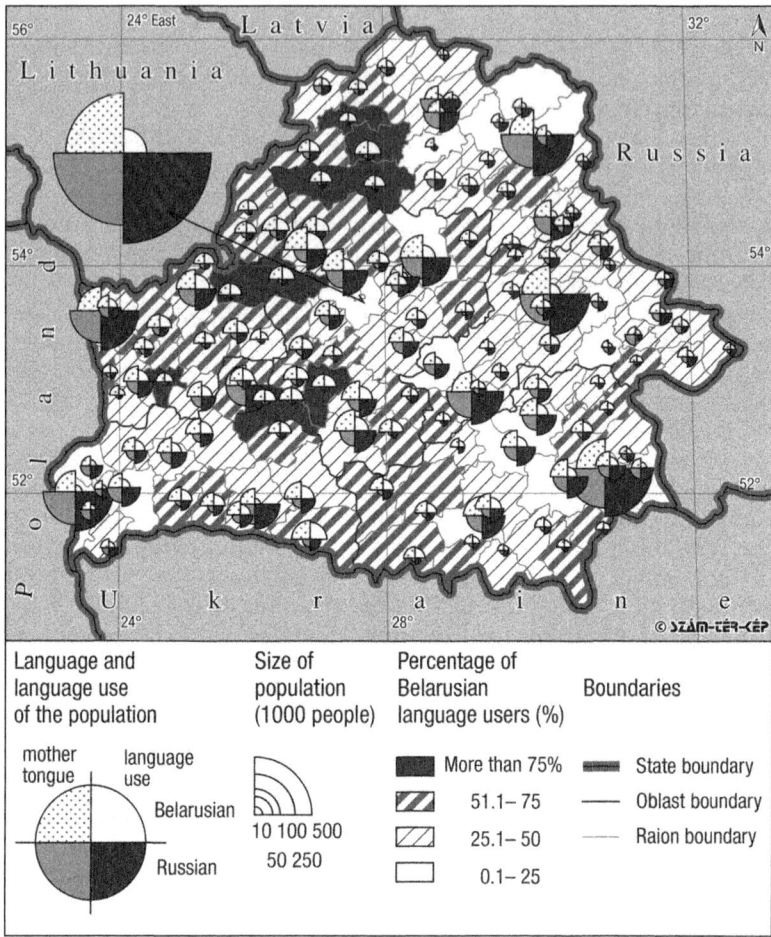

Figure 1.3.8 *The distribution of the population by native language and actually-used language in Belarus by raions; (Source:* [5]*)*

oft-cited fluctuating identity, or even current political reasons, may be the cause. Such a significant "change-over" was made possible by the proximity of the two languages. Since the differences between their current official forms is insignificant, the primary manifestation of ethnic identity is still not the mother tongue, which is reflected in the language use of the society as well (Burlyka, I. 2004).

When analysing data on mother tongue and language use, remarkable differences can be found across different areas of the country (Figure 1.3.8). Belarusian language use is more common in villages, where local linguistic specificities are generally more isolated from urban areas. Additionally, there are more people who specified Belarusian as their mother tongue than those who actually use the language. The proportion of Belarusian language users and Belarusian native speakers is essentially the same in cities, except in the Brest region. The majority of Belarusians apparently prefer to use Russian (Bieder, H. 2003, Törnquist-Plewa, B. 2005) (Figure 1.3.8).

The regions in which a majority of the population prefers to use the Belarusian language in their daily lives are mostly concentrated in the less-urbanized northwestern parts of the country, which had previously been more closely linked to the Polish centre of power, and belonged to Poland between the two world wars. These attitudes can be found in language use that functioned as counterpoints to Western — Polish — culture in earlier periods, and later to the Russification of the Soviet era. Today it is the differences in language use that mostly represent the country's cultural (linguistic and ethnic) transitional character (Savitzkaya, N. 2011). At the same time, the turning of Belarus towards Russia in terms of other social dimensions and economic orientations still does not allow the emphasizing of linguistic differences, and language use still generally remains a kind of political statement (Golz, S. 2011, Alexandrova, O. and Timmermann, H. 1997).

Russian and Soviet Censuses in Ethnic-National Context

Géza Barta; Tamás Illés; Zsolt Bottlik

Introduction

By the second half of the 19th century, political currents aimed at reorganizing the state on a national basis had strengthened in Russia. The intense political discourses emanating from the imperial centre had given way to a multiplicity of approaches, all agreeing that the establishment of a Russian nation-state required an inventory of peoples and ethnic groups living in the territory of the empire. The first census of 1897 was successfully implemented by Russia's imperial state apparatus. The census provided a firm basis for social debates on the issue of nationness which emerged after the 1905 revolution. However, despite serious preparations, World War I had thwarted the launch of a new census. Hence, the 1897 census remained the only one conducted in tsarist Russia. Thereafter, the collection of ethnic-national statistical data was of paramount importance for the Soviet system, since information on nationalities was indispensable for the establishment of an ethno-territorial federation. After the demise of the Soviet Union, the "national question" was once again at the forefront of political discourse in the newly-established post-Soviet states, and census data was considered a point of reference.

Power and the definitional aspects of the census

Despite the earlier reform efforts of Peter I and Catherine II, the Russian Empire's rigid social structure, based on despotic traditions, persisted into the 19th century. In a society characterized by a distinct development trajectory (and thus barely comparable to any of its European contemporaries), each sociocultural group had a specific identity, and lived separately from one another. A narrow elite considered a Western, European-style modernization process desirable, while the majority, in close alliance with the Orthodox Church, committed themselves to maintaining traditions (Wirtshafter, E. K. 2009). The nationalist discourse that emerged in tsarist Russia in the 19th century only impacted a narrow social elite. At this time, it was still not possible to speak of a Russian "nation", or national identity, as each clearly-defined group in society was characterized by an identity connected to its own community. Certain groups among the peasantry, who were not considered to be parts of the "nation" anyway, did not pay taxes to Russian-speaking nobles. Instead, they paid taxes to the Tatar nobility. The nationalist debate also raised the issue of social bonds. In this context, the old structure was embodied and defended by Orthodox leaders, who were opposed to the intellectuals who followed European patterns. In addition, a geographically explicit ideological divide also emerged, one which pitted the cosmopolitans of St. Petersburg against the traditionalists of Moscow (Lieven, D. 1998).

From the mid-19th century onwards, efforts to establish a Russian nation-state intensified, and a number of ideas emerged about how to unite Russians and non-Russians into one nation. Several hypotheses competed with each other for attention, ranging from aggressive cultural Russification, to the creation of a multi-ethnic nation-state. In addition, Russian Orientalists considered Central Asian and Siberian territories to be Russia's "own East". According to Orientalist academics, the local identity of the peoples living there had to be strengthened. This, however, could only be achieved by exporting Russian civilization, for example, by establishing local school systems (Tolz, V. 2005).

As scientists, intellectuals, and various other groups engaged in debate, the newly-crowned Russian tsar, Nicholas II, ordered a census of the Russian Empire in 1897. However, conducting a census on the basis of nationality was seen as a major problem, since feudal ties were strong in Russia even at the end of the 19th century. At that time, the identity-creating cohesion of traditional groups within society was so profound that the notion of "nationality" did not exist as a category for the imperial administration either. As a result, statisticians decided to collect data on language use, rather than nationality, which they considered to be the most objective indicator of nationality (Darrow, D. W. 2002). Their decision was greatly influenced by the Russification policy promulgated by the state, which was aimed at making Russian an official language. The aim was to create a united Russian nation, unified by language, that could then back-up the authoritarian leadership of the tsar (Anderson, B. 2016). From this perspective, an ethnically-based categorization was not justified, and thus a list of languages spoken in the empire was compiled. Based on the respondents' answers, data collectors chose the appropriate language to mark down in the census. In addition to language data, important information was also collected on age distribution, social status, well-being, and religion.

Given the vast size of the empire at the end of the 19th century, significant resources were needed to conduct the census. The data compiled by 135,000 interviewers took eight years to process, and the results were published in 119 volumes. Despite careful preparations, data collectors and data processors faced many challenges.

Even though the questionnaire attempted to transcend the rigid categorization of social groups that had solidified over centuries, in Siberia, for example, it was common among Yakuts to reply with the socio-cultural category "peasant" to the question regarding their mother tongue. There was also confusion between religion and mother tongue, especially among Muslim and Lutheran populations, who wanted to emphasize their religious distinctiveness in the language category as well. Those otherwise Great Russian- or Little Russian-speaking Jews who converted to Greek Orthodoxy were not categorized as Jews either. Since they were not connected to Jewry by either language or religion in this statistical system, they could not be assigned a Jewish identity by statisticians. Tatar leaders, in turn, disputed the proportion of Muslims, claiming that the number of Muslims living in the territory of the empire had been underestimated by tens of millions of people (Cadiot, J. 2005). By contrast, the Holy Synod in Georgia depicted their country as ethnically homogeneous, and, by counting Svans, Mingrelians, and other groups as Georgian, glossed over Georgia's ethnic diversity. Taken together, these examples draw attention to the complex relationship between power, statistical categories, and national identity.

The results of the 1897 census and the role of statistics in the nationalities question

In order to create a unified, Russian-language administration, the examination and categorization of the linguistic distribution of subjects living in the territory of the empire was considered to be of utmost importance for tsarist authorities (Anderson, B. 2016, Heller, M. 1996). However, the distinct cultural features of the regions, which were themselves characterized by diverging development trajectories, coupled with exposure to different socio-cultural influences, often made it impossible to distinguish ethnicity from mother tongue. Still, when trying to outline the macro-level ethnic spatial structure of the late-19th century Russian Empire, we can primarily rely on the mother tongue datasets of the 1897 survey.

A systematic analysis of the data reveals that 55.7 million of the total 125 million inhabitants of the Russian Empire — excluding the Grand Duchy of Finland — stated they spoke Russian as their mother tongue ("Great Russian", according to the survey's linguistic-ethnic classification). Despite the academic consensus on the overrepresentation of Russians — which according to Soviet historical demographers S. I. Bruk and V. M. Kabuzan, was 8% higher than the real figures, mainly to the detriment of Belarusians and Ukrainians ("Little Russians", according to the register) — the proportion of ethnic Russians did not reach 50% (Moon, D. 1996).

What might account for such a wide discrepancy? The explanation is embedded in the context of Russification, which was aimed at the cohesion and rationalization of the Empire. Since a positive answer to the question "Do you speak Russian?" that was asked during data collection stage was registered on the census sheet as "Great Russian as mother tongue", it gave the Tsarist establishment a false impression of the expansion of Russian culture (Darrow, D. W. 2002). Thus, the 1897 census was useful, not only for public administration purposes, but also as a key instrument for legitimizing authority over the western frontiers, where — just as in the Caucasus and Central Asia — the lack of Russians was the most apparent (Fig. 1.4.1). In contrast to these peripheral regions (from the Russian perspective), the highest concentration of Russian communities was found in the East European Plain. In total, 35 of all 89 governorates had a Russian majority.

With respect to mother tongue, the second largest group consisted of 22.4 million (or 17.81%) Little Russian (Ukrainian) speakers. Although Little Russian identity subsequently underwent several transformations, Ukrainian national identity was eventually based on this category. In 1897, however, Russian authorities made use of the census as an instrument of power to successfully marginalize the Ukrainian element by employing the Little Russian identity marker. Moreover, several demographers estimated that the real number of Ukrainians might have been closer to 25.3 million people (Saunders, D. 1995). In this case, too, the underestimation was driven by fears of the destabilization of peripheries, as Galicia — a part of the Habsburg Empire enjoying generous nationalities' rights (and thus, often referred to as the "Ukrainian Piedmont") — could set a dangerous precedent on the western frontiers. In addition, Ukrainians in Russia constituted an absolute majority in nine governorates, which may have provided a favourable breeding ground for Ukrainian national claims. Ukrainians also lived in considerable numbers in the governorates located far away from their central ethnic territory (e.g. in Blagoveshchensk, Khabarovsk). An even greater risk for the tsarist establishment striving for centralization could be posed by the growing collective national consciousness of the 8 million Poles living in the westernmost part of the empire. Poles were the absolute majority in all nine governorates acquired as a result of the partition of Poland, while the presence of their smaller groups was confined to the neighbouring regions (Figure 1.4.1).

With a total population of nearly 6 million, 91.5% of Belarusians lived in five governorates. Interestingly, Belarusian speakers

Figure 1.4.1 *The ethnic composition of the central and western territories of the Russian Empire and the governorates with a Russian majority in 1897; (Source: [29])*

CENSUSES IN ETHNIC-NATIONAL CONTEXT

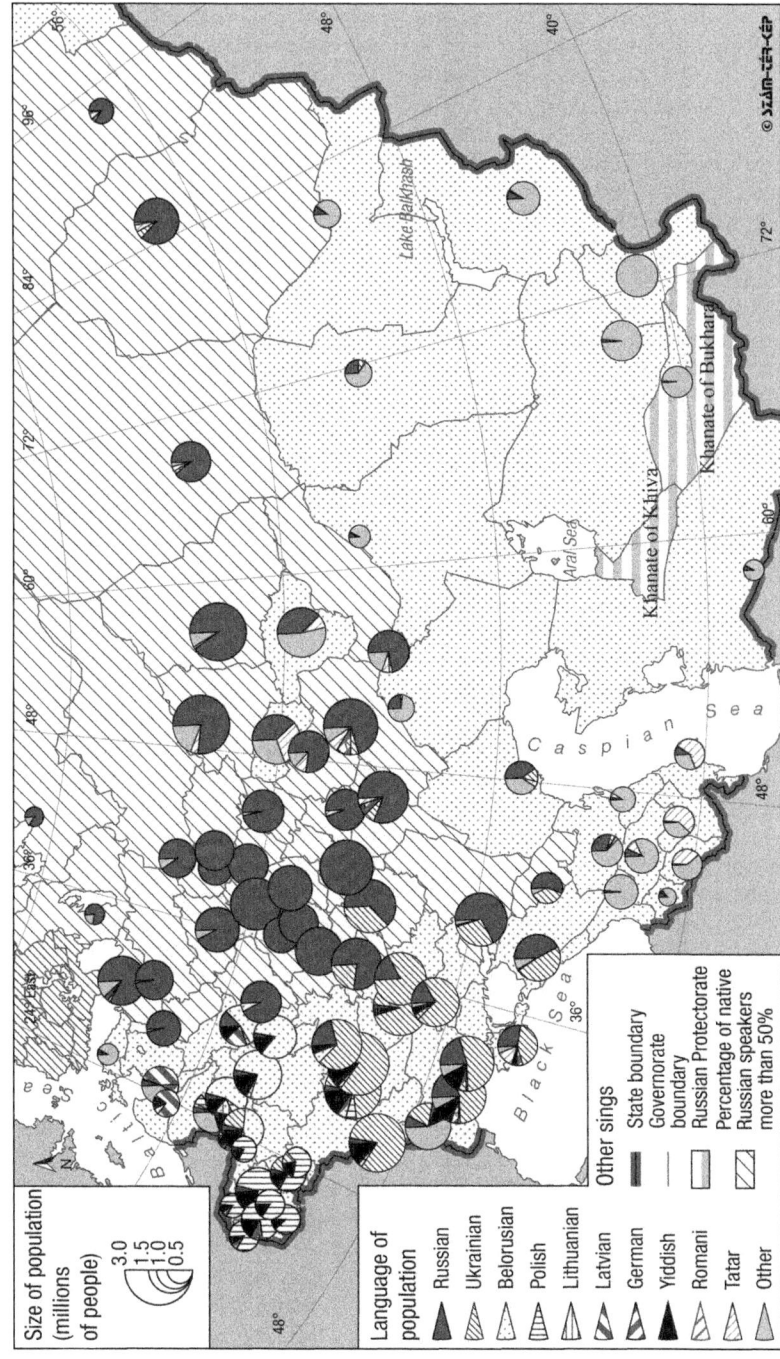

were the most populous group, not only in the territory of present-day Belarus, but also in the governorate that incorporated the capital of Lithuania. Concerning other groups of nationalities living on the western frontier, concentration may be regarded the most prominent feature of the spatial distribution of both Latvians (1.47 million) and Lithuanians (1.21 million) as well. 95.7% of the former and 92.9% of the latter covered only three governorates. The spatial patterns of Yiddish native speakers paint a much more sporadic picture. Although Yiddish native speakers mostly used the Russian language in everyday communication, their Jewish religion provided an important point of reference for delimiting their communities. This picture is rendered even more nuanced by the social groups who exercised their Jewish identities in parallel with their Russian and Orthodox identities, but who were categorized simply as Russians in the census; thus, their proportion was almost impossible to estimate. As a result of the spatial heterogeneity of people who can be considered Jewish by religion, their share exceeded 10% in twenty governorates situated exclusively on the western frontier; namely in Bessarabia, Ukraine, the Polish Plain, and the Baltics. They did not constitute a relative majority in any of these governorates, however.

The geographical distribution of 1.91 million native German speakers shared similar characteristics. A set of specific historical circumstances resulted in the geographic location, as well as the spatial segregation, of their communities. These communities included the autochthonous Germans of Poland; the Germans who were settled in the Baltics by the Crusader armies and the Hanseatic League; the Volga Germans who came at the invitation of Catherine the Great; and the German native speakers who started a new life in Ukraine and Bessarabia as a consequence of similar settler migrations.

In the census statistics, the number of Tatar native speakers was also noteworthy. Their total population of 3.74 million, accounting for 2.91% of the empire's population, can be divided into several groups. In the Caucasus, they were in the absolute majority in the Governorates of Elisabethpol (currently known as Ganja) and Baku, and represented a significant share (37.8%) in the Governorate of Yerevan. Similarly, in the Governorate of Kazan, a total of 675,000 Tatar speakers constituted 31.1% of the local population according to the 1897 census. Given the size of the Tatar population, it is perhaps no surprise that the Republic of Tatarstan, which covers much of the same territory as the former Governorate of Kazan, is part of the Russian Federation today. The centre of gravity for the population of the third group of Tatars can be identified with the Simferopol-centred Taurida Governorate, which also included the territory of Crimea, where 13.6% of the population were native

Tatar speakers. As a result of the multi-ethnic character of the empire, more than 16 million people belonged to a mother tongue group whose share did not reach 1% (Kőszegi M. 2016a, 2019).

The increase of Russification efforts in the second half of the 19th century, as well as the responses to Russification, were further intensified by the results of the census. The so-called "non-Russian element" became more visible than ever before. It also became clear that some of those using the Russian language were actually not Russian by nationality. As a result, nationalists created the category of "true Russian", although it was not used officially. In the early years of the 20th century, in addition to the national question, Russian society was also beset by its underdeveloped agriculture, unemployment, and several other problems. During these turbulent times, Russian nationalism took on an increasingly extreme form, with growing xenophobia and anti-Semitism, as well as increasing Russophobia among non-Russians. The 1905 revolution extended freedom rights, and the nationality question became an increasingly important part of public discourse. The revolution put an end to the primacy of Orthodoxy, as the secular state proclaimed free religious practice, and tried to eradicate the remnants of feudalism. The disintegration of the former social order led to the strengthening of national identity and nationalist movements, which also reinforced the need for a new census. Tsarist Russia prepared for the 1915 census within this turbulent social context. Together with other social scientists, ethnographers and statisticians attempted to formulate the definition of the nation, as it became clear that language could not replace nationality in the next census. During these preparations, statisticians constructed and translated the ideas of the authorities on the concept of nation, and together with ethnographers, played a mediating role between the state and individuals to establish a national identity. In this light, statisticians and ethnographers alike contributed significantly to the societal adaptation and acceptance of these "objective", science-based categories (Cadiot, J. 2005). World War I, however, and the demise of the Russian Empire, thwarted the announcement and implementation of the planned census. As a result, there was only ever one census completed in tsarist Russia.

The interfaces between Soviet statistics and "nationness"

19th-century Russian social democrats were deeply nationalistic, and, in accordance with the romantic approaches of that time, they found the essence of "Russianness" in the peasantry. Furthermore, they considered neither the hereditary monarchy, nor the Orthodox Church, as legitimate protectors of national identity (Lieven, D. 1998). The same ideas also emerged among the Bolsheviks, who drew on the results achieved by Russian statisticians and ethnographers in the early 20th century as evidence for their claims. Even though the Bolshevik Revolution had completely reshaped Soviet society, "nationness" still remained one of their central issues (Cadiot, J. 2005). In their view, according to the Leninist principles inspired by Marx, the proletarian dictatorship could only be assured by securing national self-determination. They also believed in a supranational category that existed above the nation that would bring together various peoples and nationalities under an umbrella that would allow them to "co-exist peacefully with an emerging all-union socialist culture" (cited in Tolz, V. 2005, p. 147). In their view, promoting Soviet ideology to the population through their own mother tongue could lead to a faster and more intensive transformation which would subsequently make the Soviet Union's proletarians cast off their national identity like worn-out clothes.

A total of seven censuses were conducted in the Soviet Union, the first in 1926, and the last in 1989. In 1926, there were relatively open debates about the categories, including one waged between the elites of the centre and officials on the periphery regarding the question of which nationalities and languages should be included in the questionnaires and which should not. Later on, however, as everything was controlled by the Communist Party, real dialogue ceased to exist, thus rendering the problems invisible (Arel, D. 2002).

For each Soviet census, an exclusive list of nationalities was compiled which revealed who was considered a distinct group by state power at the time. In 1926, the "Leningrad Finnish" category appeared, which created an "imagined community" among the Leningrad district's Finno-Ugric population. As a statistical category, however, this group existed neither before nor after the census. In the case of the Cossacks, linguistic classification was considered to be of primary importance, so for Soviet authorities a distinct "Cossack identity" did not exist (not least of which because many of them fought on the side of the Whites in the Civil War). The Bolsheviks expected to meet national demands through the establishment of ethno-territories. In a future, classless society, ethnic or national identity would lose significance, so that boundaries of linguistic–ethnic and autonomous territories would become irrelevant (Arel, D. 2002).

The nationality categories were significantly modified over the course of seven large surveys. A novelty at the time, the category of "Soviet" nationality was introduced in 1970, and the category of "second language" appeared in 1970 and 1979. The internal passport system, having been applied since 1932, recorded nationality data as well, which was registered in the case of all official events requiring administration. As a result, a kind of "official nationality" emerged, one that had a clear function within the matrix of Soviet administration, but was sometimes in contradiction with an individual's "statistical nationality" recorded during the censuses. Occasionally, census interviewers encountered unexpected problems. One example of this occurred during the 1959 and 1970 censuses, when female respondents from the Siberian *"even"* and *"evenki"* tribes were misregistered because of confusion over the feminine expressions of their respective tribe's name: *"evenka"*, or *"evenkijka"*. As a result, contrary to their actual numbers, more *"even"* and far fewer *"evenki"* females were included in the statistical data (Silver, B. D. 1986).

There is very little empirical evidence showing to what extent people modified their identity during the censuses (Anderson, B. A. and Silver, B. D. 1983), especially under the pressure of the nationality "politics" of the Stalinist terror, even though self-identification with the majority nation had proven to be an adaptive strategy. Though the similar logic and underlying methodological considerations of Soviet censuses render their data statistically comparable, we need to be cautious about their overall validity, and careful with our analysis. Based on the chart showing the change in the number of non-Russian groups living in the current territory of Russia (Fig. 1.4.2), it can be noted that up until the collapse of the Soviet Empire, and with the exception of the last decade, the number of minorities slowly increased. This is especially true for the Muslim Tatar, Turkish, and Caucasian peoples, who have traditionally high fertility rates. The tragic demographic consequence of the Stalinist terror is evident from the numbers of Ukrainians who were the largest minority group. Between the first two Soviet censuses (1926 and 1939), the number of Ukrainians was halved, which is closely correlated with the famine of 1932–1933. After this period, large numbers of Ukrainians migrated towards the target industrialization areas of the Sovietized peripheries and the newly cultivated agricultural zones, moving further away from their original ethnic settlement zone. Unsurprisingly, after the regime change, these allochthoon groups more likely assimilated into majority Russian-speaking groups. The population numbers of other minority groups that were statistically measurable but more peripherally located either stagnated (Finno-Ugric peoples), oscillated (Ossetians), or even decreased (Maris, Germans, Jews). Slightly increasing trends can be observed only in a few cases (e.g. Bashkirs, Chechens).

The post-Soviet period

In the territory of the former Soviet Union, the first post-Soviet censuses took place between 1999 (in Belarus) and 2002 (in the

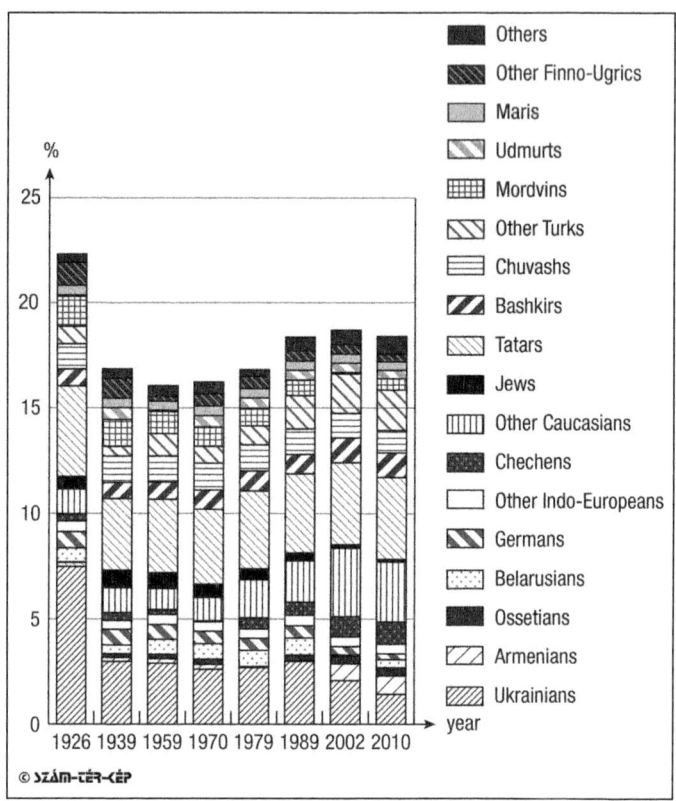

Figure 1.4.2 *The distribution of the ethnic minorities in Russia between 1926 and 2010; (Sources:* [25]; [26])

Russian Federation). In planning their own censuses, emerging nation-states had to navigate between several actors, and were compelled to consider a number of different factors. In addition to the demands of local politics and politicians, census planners not only needed to ensure some kind of statistical continuity with previous Soviet-era censuses, but also had to balance their projects against the suggestions of international consultants and the expectations of the scholarly community. Nationality, language, and their territorial aspects re-thematized public discourse, and have determined political discourses as well. Republics on the path to independence, and the newly established nation-states, formulated their right over their territory on the basis of the ethno-territory that was formed in the Soviet Union, which had become the home of the eponymous, "titular" nation. Where statistical data indicated a high proportion of the titular nation, for example in Lithuania, a less stringent citizenship policy was applied when compared to areas in which the share of minorities, especially Russians, was high, as in Estonia or Kazakhstan. The Kazakh example illustrates how important ethnic data was for successor states. During the Soviet era, ethnic groups that were deported from remote areas of the Soviet Union to Kazakhstan (predominantly Volga Germans) significantly reduced the proportion of Kazakhs. The process was further intensified by the immigration of Russians, so that by 1959, the share of the ethnic Kazakh population in the Kazakh Soviet Socialist Republic dropped to 30%. Despite a rise to about 40% by 1989, the independent Kazakh government was determined to increase the proportion of the titular nation above 50%. To this end, a support system was developed to help Russians and Germans move to Russia and Germany. The results of the census that justified these efforts received particular attention in Kazakhstan, since they could confirm the government's nationality politics and objectives on an "objective", scientific basis. Data from 1999 eventually confirmed these, as the proportion of Kazakhs rose to 53.5%. The data-distorting effects of over-compliance with political expectations have been pointed out by a Russian demographer based in Kazakhstan. In his opinion, there is no doubt that the share of Kazakhs was around 50%, but the number of the Russian-speaking population living in the northern parts of the country was underestimated. He calculated the proportion of Kazakhs to be around 48% (Arel, D. 2002).

The figure explaining the latest Russian census (Fig. 1.4.3), its legend, and its accompanying register, provide a good starting point for a macro-scale overview of the current ethnic spatial structure. The map on page 300 shows all the ethnic groups whose representation reaches the required minimum for such a scale. Importantly, the map indicates that the ethnic spatial structure did not change substantially over the course of a hundred years. In the 21st century, just as in the Tsarist era, Russian-dominated areas appear in economic centres and along major transport routes. The only exception is in the Ural–Volga region, where significant contiguous areas are inhabited by minorities. Such non-Russian ethnic areas are found on the peripheries of the country as well, in the north (with Finno-Ugric peoples), in Siberia (with dozens of smaller groups), and in the south (with Caucasian peoples).

With three exceptions, the map's legend lists groups larger than 5,000 people in a breakdown of language, regardless of whether or not they have their own territory shown on the map or a map symbol indicating their minority status. In the case of the Aleuts, Yupiks, and Sapsugs, who number less than 5,000, their extensive settlement size makes their mapping possible. It is also apparent from the grouping of the legend that the language categories may refer to groups of different numbers or sizes, where appropriate.

Géza Barta; Tamás Illés; Zsolt Bottlik

The six-page register (see pages 103-109 below) attached to this chapter allows readers to browse all categories of the 2010 Russian census in alphabetical order. We have provided the same breakdown of categories and the same detail that is in the Russian census data (in the register, nationalities that are shown on the map are in *italics*, while the categories with regular font are not featured on the map). By focusing on lower (subnational) scales in the following chapters of our book, we will also provide a detailed overview of ethnic spatial processes in the post-Soviet realm.

Summary

The linguistic, national, and ethnic categories of Russian, Soviet, and post-Soviet censuses can be considered as imprints of contemporary power relations, scientific endeavours, and societal discourses. At various times they were capable of discriminating against particular social groups, while at other times, these easily-identifiable ethnic categories served as prerequisites for advancing on the social ladder. Political expectations had, and continue to have, an influence on national statistics in the post-Soviet period as well. However, the nature of these expectations, their depth, and their embeddedness in exercising power, are significantly different in the Soviet Union's successor states.

As nationality statistics are inseparable from power representations and aspirations, actual data are worth analysing only in a given space and time, and in the context of an interactive system of relations between the individual and society. This book is not aimed at exploring the technical and theoretical problems related to the collection of statistical data, and the interpretation of results. However, it should still be pointed out that statistical data is not suitable to descriptive "reality," but may provide certain clues for a kind of contextual approach to social phenomena and events. Therefore, the maps and graphs featured in this book are mere visual representations of census data from tsarist Russia, the Soviet, and the post-Soviet realm, and are provided to help perform macro-scale analyses.

Figure 1.4.3 *The ethnic composition of the Russian population in 2010 (see page 300) (Sources:* [23]; [24]; [25]; [28])

INDO-EUROPEAN
SLAVIC
Belarusian	1)	⊖
Bulgarian	2)	
Polish	3)	⊕
Russian	4)	○
Ukrainian	5)	⊙

BALTIC
Latvian[1]	6)
Lithuanian[1]	7)

GERMAN
German	8)	◠

IRANIAN
West
Kurdish	9)	
Tajik	10)	▽

East
Ossetian	11)	
Pashto	12)	●

GREEK
Greek	13)	◐

ARMENIAN
Armenian	14)	◐

OTHER INDO-EUROPEAN
Roma	15)	◓
Moldovan	16)	◑

CAUCASIAN
NORTHWEST
Abaza	17)	⋏
Abkhazian[1]	18)	
Adyghe	19)	
Circassian	20)	
Kabardian	21)	
Shapsug	22)	

SOUTH
Kartvelian[1]	23)

NORTHEAST
Aghul[2]	24)
Avar	25)
Chechen	26)
Dargic[2]	27)
Ingush	28)
Lak[2]	29)
Lezgian[2]	30)
Rutul[2]	31)
Tabasaran[2]	32)
Tsachur[2]	33)

ALTAIC
TURKIC
Oghuz
Azerbaijani	34)	⬥
Gagauz[1]	35)	
Turkish[1]	36)	⊕
Turkmen	37)	◇

Kipchak
Balkar	38)	
Bashkir	39)	
Karachay	40)	
Kazakh	41)	◈
Kyrgyz	42)	◆
Kumyk	43)	
Nogai	44)	
Tatar	45)	◇

Uighur
Uzbek	46)	◆

Oghur
Chuvash	47)

Siberian turkic
Altai	48)	⊕
Chakas	49)	○
Dolgan	50)	⊖
Shor	51)	
Tuvan	52)	⊕
Yakut	53)	⊕

MONGOLIAN
Buryat	54)	●
Kalmyk	55)	

MANCHU-TUNGUS
Even	56)	◐
Evenki	57)	◑
Nanai	58)	♠

URALIC
FINNO-UGRIC
Ugric
Khanti	59)	◨
Mansi	60)	⊠

Finno-Permic
Estonian	61)	□
Finnish	62)	⊞
Karel	63)	◪
Komi[3]	64)	◧
Mari	65)	
Mordvinic	66)	
Udmurt	67)	
Veps	68)	◫

SAMOYEDIC
North[4]	69)	⊡

AFROASIATIC
SEMITIC
Arabic[1]	70)
Assyrian[1]	71)
Yiddish	72)

PALEOSIBERIAN
CHUKCH-KAM-CHADAL
Chukchi	73)	▲
Gilyak	74)	
Koryak	75)	△

ALL OTHER
Chinese [1]	76)	
Korean[1]	77)	
Yupik	78)	
Vietnamese	79)	▽

[1] *not on the map*
[2] *on the map like avar*
[3] *together with Permians*
[4] *especially Nenets*

Name	Language f.	Area	Population
A			
Abazins,	Caucasian,	N-Caucasus,	43341
Abkhazians,	Caucasian,	N-Caucasus,	11249
Adyghe people,	Caucasian,	N-Caucasus,	124835
Adjarians [3],	Caucasian,	N-Caucasus,	211
Aghul people[1],	Caucasian,	N-Caucasus,	34160
Akhvakh [2],	Caucasian,	N-Caucasus,	7930
Aleuts,	Eskimo-Aleut,	Far East,	482
Altai,	Altaic,	Siberia,	74238
Chelkans,	Altaic,	Siberia,	1181
Telengits,	Altaic,	Siberia,	3712
Tubalars,	Altaic,	Siberia,	1965
Americans,	Indo-European,	European Russia,	1572
Andi people [2],	Caucasian,	N-Caucasus,	11789
Arabs,	Afroasiatic,	N-Caucasus,	9583
Archi people [2],	Caucasian,	N-Caucasus,	12
Armenians,	Indo-European,	N-Caucasus,	1182388
Assyrian people,	Afroasiatic,	N-Caucasus,	11084
Avars,	Caucasian,	N-Caucasus,	912090
Azeris,	Altaic,	N-Caucasus,	603070
B			
Bagvalal p. [2],	Caucasian,	N-Caucasus,	5
Balkars,	Altaic,	N-Caucasus,	112924
Bashkirs,	Altaic,	Volga region,	1584554
Belarusians,	Indo-European,	European Russia,	521443
Besermyans,	Uralic,	Volga region,	2201
Bezhtas [2],	Caucasian,	N-Caucasus,	5958
Bulgarians,	Indo-European,	European Russia,	24038
Botlikhs [2],	Caucasian,	N-Caucasus,	3508
Buhara Jews,	Indo-European,	Volga region,	32
Buryats,	Altaic,	Siberia,	461389
C			
Chamalal p. [2],	Caucasian,	N-Caucasus,	24
Chechens,	Caucasian,	N-Caucasus,	1431360
Akhin Ch.,	Caucasian,	N-Caucasus,	76
Cherkess,	Caucasian,	N-Caucasus,	73184
Chukchi people,	Chukchi-Kamch.,	Far East,	15908
Chulyms,	Altaic,	Siberia,	355
Chuvans,	Chukchi-Kamch.,	Far East,	1002
Chuvash people,	Altaic,	Volga region,	1435872
Cossacks [4],	Indo-European,	Volga region,	67573

Name	Language f.	Area	Population
Crim. Karaites,	Altaic,	Volga region,	205
Czechs,	Indo-European,	European Russia,	1898
D			
Dargins [1],	Caucasian,	N-Caucasus,	589386
Kajtakok,	Caucasian,	N-Caucasus,	7
Kubacsik,	Caucasian,	N-Caucasus,	120
Didoic p. [2],	Caucasian,	N-Caucasus,	11683
Dolgans,	Altaic,	Far East,	7885
Dungans,	Sino-Tibetan,	Siberia,	1651
E			
English people,	Indo-European,	European Russia,	950
Enets,	Uralic,	Siberia,	227
Estonian,	Uralic,	European Russia,	17875
Setuk,	Uralic,	European Russia,	214
Evens,	Altaic,	Far East,	21830
Evenkies,	Altaic,	Far East,	38396
F			
Finns,	Uralic,	Northwest,	20267
Inkeri Finns,	Uralic,	Northwest,	441
French people,	Indo-European,	European Russia,	1475
G			
Gagauz people,	Altaic,	European Russia,	13690
Germans,	Indo-European,	Siberia,	394138
Godoberi p. [2],	Caucasian,	N-Caucasus,	427
Greek Urums,	Altaic,	N-Caucasus,	1
Greek,	Indo-European,	N-Caucasus,	85640
Georgians,	Caucasian,	N-Caucasus,	157803
Georgian Jews,	Caucasian,	N-Caucasus,	78
H			
Han Chinese,	Sino-Tibetan,	Far East,	28943
Hemshins,	Indo-European,	N-Caucasus,	2047
Hinukhs [2],	Caucasian,	N-Caucasus,	443
Hungarians,	Uralic,	European Russia,	2781
Hunzibs [2],	Caucasian,	N-Caucasus,	918
I			
Indians,	Indo-European,	European Russia,	4058
Ingiloys [3],	Caucasian,	N-Caucasus,	98
Ingush,	Caucasian,	N-Caucasus,	444833
Name	**Language f.**	**Area** **Population**	
Italians,	Indo-European,	European Russia,	1370

Itelmens,	Chukchi-Kamch.,	Far East,	3193
Ingrians,	Uralic,	Northwest,	266

J

Japanese,	Japanese,	Far East,	888
Jews,	Afroasiatic,	European Russia,	156801

K

Kabardians,	Caucasian,	N-Caucasus,	516826
Kalmyks,	Altaic,	South,	183372
Kamchadal,	Chukchi-Kamch.,	Far East,	1927
Karachays,	Altaic,	N-Caucasus,	218403
Karakalpaks,	Altaic,	Volga region,	1466
Karatas [2],	Caucasian,	N-Caucasus,	4787
Karels,	Uralic,	Northwest,	60815
Kazakhs,	Altaic,	South Russia,	647732
Kereks,	Chukchi-Kamch.,	Far East,	4
Kets,	Paleosiberian,	Siberia,	1219
Yughs,	Paleosiberian,	Siberia,	1
Khakas,	Altaic,	Siberia	72959
Khantys,	Uralic,	Ural,	30943
Khwarsis [2],	Caucasian,	N-Caucasus,	527
Komi-permyaks,	Uralic,	Northwest,	94456
Komis,	Uralic,	Northwest,	228235
Izsmaiak komis,	Uralic,	Northwest,	6420
Koreans,	Korean,	Far East,	153156
Koryaks,	Chukchi-Kamch.,	Far East,	7953
Krymchaks,	Altaic,	Volga region,	90
Kubans,	Indo-European,	European Russia,	676
Kumandins,	Altaic,	Siberia,	2892
Kumyks,	Altaic,	N-Caucasus,	503060
Kurds,	Indo-European,	N-Caucasus,	23232
Kurmanjis,	Indo-European,	N-Caucasus,	42
Kyrgyz,	Altaic,	Moscow,	103422

L

Laks [1],	Caucasian,	N-Caucasus,	178630
Latvians,	Indo-European,	European Russia,	18979
Latgales,	Indo-European,	European Russia,	1089
Laz people [3],	Caucasian,	N-Caucasus,	160
Lezgins [1],	Caucasian,	N-Caucasus,	473722
Lithuanians,	Indo-European,	N-Caucasus,	31377

Name	Language f.	Area	Population
M			
Mansis,	Uralic,	Urals,	12269
Mari people,	Uralic,	Volga region,	547605
Hill Maris,	Uralic,	Volga region,	23559
Meadow Maris,	Uralic,	Volga region,	218
Mennonites [4],	Indo-European	Volga region	4
Meskhet. Turks,	Altaic,	N-Caucasus,	4825
Mingrelians [3],	Caucasian,	N-Caucasus,	600
Moldovans,	Indo-European,	European Russia,	156400
Mongols,	Altaic,	Siberia,	2986
Mordvins,	Uralic,	Volga region,	744237
Erzya-mor.,	Uralic,	Volga region,	57008
Moksha-mor.,	Uralic,	Volga region,	4767
Mountain Jews,	Indo-European,	N-Caucasus,	762
N			
Nanays,	Altaic,	Far East,	12003
Negidals,	Altaic,	Far East,	513
Nganasans,	Uralic,	Siberia,	862
Nivkh people,	Paleosiberian,	Far East,	4652
Nogais,	Altaic,	N-Caucasus,	103660
Karagash	Altaic	N-Caucasus,	16
Nenets,	Uralic,	Siberia,	44640
O, Ö			
Orochs,	Altaic,	Far East,	596
Oroks,	Altaic,	Far East,	295
Ossetians,	Indo-European,	N-Caucasus,	528515
Digorons,	Indo-European,	N-Caucasus,	223
Irons,	Indo-European,	N-Caucasus,	48
P			
Pashtuns/Afghans,	Indo-European,	Moscow,	5350
Persians,	Indo-European,	N-Caucasus,	3696
Poles,	Indo-European,	European Russia,	47125
R			
Romani people,	Indo-European,	South,	204958
Romani in Asia,	Indo-European,	Volga region,	49
Romanians,	Indo-European,	European Russia,	3201
Russians,	Indo-European,	Whole country,	111016896
Pomors,	Indo-European,	Northwest,	3113
Rusyns,	Indo-European,	European Russia,	225
Rutuls [1],	Caucasian,	N-Caucasus,	35240

Name	Language f.	Area	Population
S			
Sámi people,	Uralic,	Northwest,	1771
Selkups,	Uralic,	Siberia,	3649
Serbs,	Indo-European,	European Russia,	3510
Shapsugs,	Caucasian,	N-Caucasus,	3882
Shors,	Altaic,	Siberia,	12888
Slovaks,	Indo-European,	European Russia,	324
Soyots,	Altaic,	Siberia,	3608
Spaniards,	Indo-European,	European Russia,	1162
Svans [3],	Caucasian,	N-Caucasus,	45
T			
Tabasarans [1],	Caucasian,	N-Caucasus,	146360
Tajiks,	Indo-European,	Saint Petersburg,	200303
Talysh,	Indo-European,	N-Caucasus,	2529
Tatars,	Altaic,	Volga region,	5310649
Astrahan t.,	Altaic,	South,	7
Crimean t.,	Altaic,	European Russia,	2449
Krjasen t.,	Altaic,	European Russia,	34822
Nagaj t.,	Altaic,	Urals,	8148
Siberian t.,	Altaic,	Siberia,	6779
Tats,	Indo-European,	N-Caucasus,	1585
Tazs,	Sino-Tibetan,	Far East,	274
Teleuts,	Altaic,	Siberia,	2643
Tindi people [2],	Caucasian,	N-Caucasus,	635
Tofalars,	Altaic,	Siberia,	762
Tsakhur p. [1],	Caucasian,	N-Caucasus,	12769
Turkmens,	Altaic,	N-Caucasus,	36885
Turks,	Altaic,	N-Caucasus,	105058
Tuvans,	Altaic,	Siberia,	263934
Tuvan-todzs,	Altaic,	Siberia,	1858
U, Ü			
Udeges,	Altaic,	Far East,	1496
Udis,	Caucasian,	N-Caucasus,	4267
Udmurtok,	Uralic,	Volga region,	552299
Uighurs,	Altaic,	Siberia,	3696
Ukrainians,	Indo-European,	European Russia,	1927988
Ulchas,	Altaic,	Far East,	2765
Uzbekhs,	Altaic,	Moscow,	289862
V			
Veps,	Uralic,	Northwest,	5936

Vietnamese,	Austro-Asian,	Moscow,	13954
Votes,	Uralic,	Northwest,	64
Y			
Yakuts,	Altaic,	Far East,	478085
Yazidis [4],	Indo-European,	N-Caucasus,	40586
Yukaghirs,	Paleosiberian,	Far East,	1603
Yupik,	Eskimo-Aleut,	Far East,	1738

The table above shows, in alphabetical order, the nationality categories and subcategories of the 2010 census in the Russian Federation(Национальный состав населения российской федерации 2010). Larger communities on the map on page 300 are in italics (Figure 1.4.3; page 300). Groups that are difficult to locate do not appear on the map but are listed in the table. The second column of the list shows the linguistic classification of the language of the given group. The third column shows the federal district (федеральные округа) of their typical settlement area. The last column shows their population according to the census.

Groups marked with a number:
[1] Classified in the Avar category on the map
[2] The official census classified the dialects of the Avar language in separate categories, but they are represented in one category on the map
[3] The so-called Kartvel-speaking peoples were classified in the Georgian category in the official census
[4] Residents classified according to religious and cultural categories, rather than ethnic or linguistic

Local Identities under Russian Rule

The Layers of Post-Soviet Central Asian "Nations"

Margit Kőszegi; Zsolt Bottlik

Introduction

In the immediate wake of the disintegration of the Soviet Union, the Central Asian publicist and military correspondent Ahmed Rashid looked to the future, and asked: "Islam or nationalism?" His question was not surpising. The Central Asia region includes some of the former religious centres of Islam, but its territory had been under Russian, and later Soviet, rule since the 19th century. The impact that these different societal factors would have on the further shaping of their communities was a big question for newly-independent states in the 1990s. Given the dominance of the nation-state organizational model globally, nationalism has proven to be an obvious answer to Rashid's question. However, traditional local frameworks are proving stronger, at least for the time being, and have been able to neutralize the nation-building aspirations of the central power.

The territories formerly ruled by the Kazakh Ordas, Mongols, Uzbeks, and Tajik clans gained independence in the early 1990s within the borders that had been established by the Soviets. The lives of their inhabitants had been shaped by the partial modernization that had been achieved during Sovietization, as well as by the Soviet-style framework that had been established to ensure the functioning of society. Since the collapse of the Soviet system, the rhetoric of emergent authoritarian leaders throughout the region has had strong nationalist overtones, which in many cases are motivated by the desire to preserve their positions.

This chapter examines the centuries-long processes behind this national rhetoric. A key role in this is exerted by external (imperialist) influences that have sought to reshape the former social frameworks by force. In addition to Russian colonization efforts, the British-Russian colonial rivalry, Russification, and awkward modernization by the tsarist empire and the Soviet system, forced identity constructions specific to the Soviet period have all played a foundational role in the formation of the Central Asian "nations" of the 21st century.

The interpretation of Central Asia

In the 19th century, Turkestan was the name given to Central Asian territories by Western geopoliticians. 19th-century colonization, which was known throughout Europe as "the Great Game," played a key role in placing Central Asia on Western maps. Aside from the northern frontiers of the Ottoman Empire, the Anglo-Russian colonial rivalry spilled over into the interior of Asia. The actual events of "the Great Game", mediated as they were by romantic exaggeration in works like Rudyard Kipling's *Kim*, remained obscure and even distorted to many Western observers (Hopkirk, P. 1990). Chinese interest in the region added a yet another layer of geopolitical complexity, and in this light it is important to keep in mind that Central Asia was a space in which three different intentions and interests met (Vakar, N. 1935). The fate of the Turkestani people in the 20th century, therefore, was shaped by rather different sets of political aspirations.

By the end of the 19th century, eastern Turkestan had come under Chinese rule. Western Turkestan, along with the northernmost settlement of nomadic Kazakhs, had been annexed by the Russian Empire, and the southern territories, which are now Afghanistan, belonged to British interests (Allworth, E. 1989). As a result of the changed geopolitical situation, the name Turkestan has largely been forgotten. In the 20th century, the label "Central Asia" was assigned to the territories of the four Soviet republics in the region. Since the end of the 20th century, the former Soviet Union member states of Uzbekistan, Turkmenistan, Tajikistan, and Kazakhstan (which itself was not originally part of Turkestan), have generally been referred to as Central Asia (Gammer, M. 2000). In geographical terms, this represents a shift to the northwest of Kazakhstan's vast steppes and semi-desert areas when compared to the original concept of Turkestan. This chapter uses the term Central Asia based on this interpretation.

Prior to its colonization, the Western world (and even the Russian conquerors) had very little information about the population of Central Asia. The northern territories had previously been organized under the auspices of the General Governorate of the Steppe during the 19th century. The military-governed General Governorate of Turkestan was created after the Russian occupation in the late 19th century. In the southern part of Central Asia, the Kahantes of Khiva and Bukhara existed at that time as vassal states of the Russian Empire. According to the statistical surveys conducted in the 1880s, as well as the accounts of foreign travellers and Russian military intelligence, the estimated population was 6 million, which was later confirmed by the 1897 census (though the census did not cover the whole area).

As the name Turkestan suggests, Central Asia was considered to be the home of Turkish-speaking peoples. This collective term covered communities in which a great variety of languages were spoken. Authorities attempted to identify ethnic groups based on spoken language in the 1897 census (see Chapter 1.4 for more details on the results of the census). Nomadic inhabitants were at that time called Kyrgyz, and those who lived in permanent settlements, in the southern so-called Central Asian oasis belt, were called Sarts. The census of 1897 used not only "Kyrgyz" and "Sart", but also other terms. Therefore Russian authorities had created the ethnic categories of the area by the beginning of the 20th century. Nevertheless, all the peoples of Central Asia were united under one religious category: Islam.

Central Asia in postcolonial discourse and nationalism theories

Tsarist Russia emerged as a colonial — or what the Soviets would later call "imperialist" — power in Turkestan in the 19th century. In a way this was not unlike the process identified by Edward Said as "orientalism," in that the Russian state created its own "East," and in the nomadic people of the steppe — a people the Russian elite identified as "Tatars" (see Chapter 2.2 for the complex meaning of the term "Tatar") — the Russians discovered their own "Other." Representing Russian Orthodoxy, the authorities declared a holy war against the Muslim Tatars, and extended their enmity to all Islamic believers to the east and south (Heller, M. 1996). The manifest destiny of the conquering Russians was to spread both the Orthodox faith and the achievements of European civilization to the eastern "barbarians."

In effect, Central Asia was colonized twice. After the Bolshevik takeover, the Soviets, who were driven by colonial goals that were similar to those of their tsarist predecessors, also worked to reshape the societies of the region, albeit on different ideological grounds (Gammer, M. 2000). As a result, the nation-states of the region, which were modernized in the process of Sovietization, have features similar to those of third-world colonies. Like the former European colonies in the Global South, Central Asian states had export-oriented, monoculture economies, and were generally dominated by non-indigenous elites who exercised considerable power over industry and state administration, a reality that characterized the unequal relationsip between Moscow and the local elites. The forced ethnonationalism of post-Soviet authoritarian leaders, therefore, can be interpreted in a postcolonial context, and with regard in particular to Benedict Anderson's Last Wave concept (2016). In this light, the contemporary process of top-down identity-buliding is a response to the colonial legacy of the Soviet system, which of course couched the modernization of Central Asia in communist terms.

With the implementation of *korenizatsiya* the officially-recognized and defined ethnicities of the member republics were given the opportunity to strengthen their identities through the use of language and cultural features, independent of religion and historical traditions that had been preserved in the collective memory. With the persistence of Russification and official nationalism (Seton-Watson, H. 1977, also described in detail in previous chapters), the Russian education system produced generations of loyal employees who filled positions in both the administrative and corporate bureaucracy (Anderson, B. 2016). The "national" elites in the new nation-states were increasingly able to convey this national attitude to their citizens through the rapidly expanding information technologies introduced by globalization. However, for the time being, the clan systems exert a much stronger influence over the identity of individuals (Collins, K. 2003).

Layers of Central Asian national identities

Before colonization: traditional Central Asia

The Silk Road, which once crossed the vast Asian continent and linked Europe to the luxuries of the East, was quickly replaced by the ever-expanding process of colonization that was made possible by the discovery of sea routes in the wake of the Columbian voyages. Given the dramatic shift to oceanic trade, Central Asia was largely ignored by the emerging capitalist states of the West. Shielded as they were from the forces of Western modernization, Central Asian practices persisted well into the 19th century, and traditional frameworks were thus preserved.

It is important to note that these traditional frameworks and practices were themselves dynamic. Structures that had existed for centuries, in fact, had provided the basis for a multicultural world. Central Asia was, after all, the meeting point for different languages, philosophies, and technological and artistic innovations. For centuries, the Turkic and Iranian peoples living in the region had been affected by a number of external influences. The numerous conquests of White Huns and Mongols from the East, for example, and the invasions of Persians, Greeks (Macedonians), Parthians, and Arabs from the West, had a significant social and cultural impact on the people living here. The ability of regional culture to adapt to this blending of different influences has been key to its survival (Mandel, W. M. 1942).

The Hungarian Ármin Vámbéry was one of the first Europeans to travel to Central Asia in 1863. His detailed itinerary served as a valuable source of information for English diplomacy at the time (Vámbéry, Á. 1873). In his detailed work, Vámbéry outlined some of the key "peculiarities" that characterized 19th-century Central Asia, at least according to the Western gaze. Fixated on the coexistence of many different influences, Vámbéry noted that Central Asian society showed a marked divide in lifestyle. Settled Iranian peoples engaged in agriculture, commerce, and handicrafts, and lived in oases, river valleys, and mountain ranges in the southeast (Whitman, J. 1956). The Turkic peoples, who engaged primarily in nomadic herding, were mainly inhabitants of the northern steppes and southern deserts. Borders were not distinct, and people practicing different lifestyles were in constant contact with each other. Some Turkic-speaking groups, for example, lived in permanent settlements in the Central Asian oasis belt, but maintained economic and cultural ties with nomadic peoples as well (Mandel, W. M. 1942).

Common cultural features also figured into the identities of peoples who, though they lived side by side, nevertheless practiced different lifestyles. The Mongolian legacy figured prominently amongst these shared characteristics. Whether nomad or a city dweller, for example, the ruling family in a particular area was definitely derived from Genghis Khan, who united the territory in a vast empire in the 13th century. Everyone saw the legitimacy of power under Mongol rule, which united the whole territory. This sort of attitude also prevailed in Europe, where the legacy of the Roman Empire had similar legitimacy, even in the 20th century. The parallel is both apt and instructive. Napoleon, in fact, crowned himself emperor after bringing an end to the Holy Roman Empire in 1801, and by doing so saw himself as inheriting the Roman legacy. Little more than a century later, Hitler would claim that his Third Reich was the successor of the Holy Roman Empire.

As in many other Asian and African societies, the collective identities of Central Asian peoples were tied more to clan structures than they were to the territory-based political formation of the nation-state. Clan identity is based on the extended network of kinship relations, the informal social organistaion of which include a web of vertically and horizontally related families (Collins, K. 2003). Because the bond between patriarchal families was based on a patron-client relationship, each clan included both elite and nonelite members. The most influential family held the title of khan. The khan was the head of a system based on absolute loyalty and responsibility. In the case of nomadic people, the genealogical kinship determined the social structure. In settled communities, the place of residence was also important in collective identity.

This complex social structure untimately led to the appearance of state formation within settled communities. The khan of the Central Asian oasis belt brought together the inhabitants of the area with a high level of organization, while nomadic cavalry accounted for much of their military potential. The Khanates of Bukhara, Khiva, and Kokand were located in what is now Kyrgyzstan, Tajikistan, Uzbekistan, and the northern border region of Turkmenistan. North of them were the Khazar hordes, and to the southwest the Turkmen tribes. The Khanates, which brought together a multitude of ethnicities, functioned under the leadership of a prominent ethnic group. In the most prominent Khanate of Bukhara, leadership was in the hands of the Uzbeks.

In addition to a high level of trade and craftsmanship, slavery — which is itself a product of the relationship between settled (sedentary) and nomadic peoples — was also characteristic among these communities. The nomads took "human goods" to the slave markets of the big cities where those interested purchased them, primarily to serve their domestic needs. The slave markets in the large city centres of Bukhara, Samarkand, and Khiva can be found in literary works and also in various travel descriptions. For example, a Central Asian slave market appeared in Dumas's famous novel, *The Count of Monte Christo*. In Dumas's fuctional account, the female character, Haydée, serves as the symbol of the mysteries of 19th-century Central Asia. Saved from slavery by the protagonist, a sincere European man, her fate is a classic example of orientalism. The story shows at once both European prejudices with respect to the East, and also the sense of mission that many Europeans felt towards the East.

The main factor that united the region and influenced the daily lives of the inhabitants was Islam, which was brought to the region by Arab people in the 7th and 8th centuries. In particular, the Hanafi school of the Sunni branch was strongly orthodox among the settled population, who followed religious protocols strictly. Influenced by Persian practices, the ceremonial system was transmitted for centuries by the schools in the great cities of Bukhara and Samarkand, not only to the inhabitants of the region, but also to more remote Islamic countries. Intense contact with the remote parts of the Islamic world ceased in the 15th century as a result of the consolidation of the neighbouring southern states and their constant wars, which made the long pilgrimage routes to Mecca uncertain. However, relations with immediate neighbours, such as Iran and India, remained intact. Among the nomads, religious syncretism was much more prevalent. The incorporation of local customs and the preservation of the rituals of shamanic belief characterized their Islamic faith.

Russian expansion and its effects in Central Asia

Running parallel with the construction of the Russian Empire more generally, the plan to conquer Central Asia was conceived after the dissolution of the Tartar yoke in the 15th century, but was only finally realized in the second half of the 19th century (Heller, M. 1996). After the defensive policies of previous centuries, the Russian territories were united when Moscow began a successful and spectacular process of expansion at the expense of the Golden Horde, which was formed on the ruins of the Mongol Empire. Russian troops occupied Kazan's fortress in 1552, and Astrakhan in 1554. The merger of the two khanates resulted in enormous territorial growth. Instead of the Oka River, which was a few hundred kilometres away from Moscow, the Russian influence extended an additional thousand kilometres to the Caspian Sea.

Leaders of the new Russian state, however, wanted first and foremost to be European. So for a long time, they focused their power on their western territories and neighbours instead of on Asia. Nevertheless, Russian expansion to the east and south was almost continuous. The Siberian conquest began in the 16th century, and proceeded without great efforts. As vassals of the Russian tsar, the Cossacks acquired territories at the expense of the Ottoman Empire already in the early 17th century.

The plan for the conquest of the southeast — which was termed the "Eastern Plan"— was first conceived during the rule of Tsar Peter I (Peter the Great) (Heller, M. 1996). This plan had two primary drivers. On the one hand, Peter was forced to divert his attention to the region due to rebellions in the Khanates, and he thus mobilized his army to restore order. On the other hand, Peter was motivated by the desire to expand both the power and territory of his empire in the East (Cheshire, H. T. 1934).

The extension of the frontiers (which aimed at realizing the "natural" borders of the empire), was an essential part of the eastern policy of the Russian Empire (the idea of natural borders first appeared in Europe; the typical example is the French hexagon between the Pyrenees and the Rhine). In the heart of Asia, these efforts led to the establishment of a direct relationship with China and India, and compelled the Russians to build cooperative alliances with peoples who were constantly threatened by the Ottoman and Persian Empires (Heller, M. 1996). At the same time, a long-standing ideology of manifest destiny was formulated within the Eastern Plan. During this period, Russian manifest destiny meant nothing less than the transmission of the achievements of European civilization to the East. This idea later became an integral part of Russian identity and appeared even in the rhetoric of communist elites during the Soviet era.

The principle of "graduality" was central to the implementation of Russia's grand plans. Tsar Peter the Great first wanted to bring the Khanates of Khiva and Bukhara under Russian control and to station Russian troops as patrols on their territory. However, military action was only partially successful at that time. After the war with the Persian Empire in 1723, the tsarist empire acquired the entire western and southern Caspian coast, as well as the city of Baku. His successors soon lost control over much of the conquered territory, but the Caspian Sea remained part of the Russian sphere.

The practical implementation of Peter the Great's plan was developed by Ivan Kirillov, an influential figure in the state apparatus during the reign of Peter's successor Anna (Heller, M. 1996). Kirillov launched the conquest of Central Asia from the Bashkortostan region by establishing fortifications from which Russian garrisons could penetrate further and further into the continent (Cheshire, H. T. 1934). According to Krillov's plans, the cities of Orsk and Orenburg were established along the Ural River. Kirillov called the conquered territories *Novorossiya*, or "New Russia", a term that would be used in the second half of the century, and which became a reality following the conquests of Tsar Catherine II (Catherine the Great).

By the end of the 18th century, the ideological background of the conquests had changed. After reaching the eastern sea, Russian settlers appeared in Alaska and California, and the state could no longer justify Russian expansion as the realization of "natural" borders. A new explanation formed at that time for further expansion: the need for new, arable lands. The Russian state enjoyed immense territorial growth for more than 30 years during the reign of Catherine the Great. This was also a period of significant social transformation, and the formation of imperial thought. In addition to her "Greek Plan", which achieved brilliant success, Catherine also pursued the "Indian Plan" inherited from her predecessors, and as a result, Baku was once again in Russian hands by the end of the 18th century.

The conquest of Central Asia ultimately took place in the second half of the 19th century, though in a different geopolitical situation. By the end of the 1850s, and in the wake of the Russian defeat during the Crimean War, the importance of Central Asia had grown to such an extent that it had become more than just the scene of the dreams of the tsars and statesmen. Nikolay Pavlovich Ignatyev, a diplomat during the reign of Tsar Alexander II, revived Ivan Kirillov's plan, and with the help of the Russian military machine, began to systematically implement it (Heller, M. 1996). At that time, the Indian subcontinent became a part of the British sphere of interest, from which the British carried out commercial and military actions in Central Asia (Cheshire, H. T. 1934). For the first time,

Central Asia took on a supporting role in expansionist policy with the beginning of the Russian-English colonial rivalry known as the "Great Game" (Hopkirk, P. 2006).

Within a few years, Russian troops had occupied the Kazakh steppes. By 1854, the city of Verniy, later Alma-Ata/Almaty, was founded, and over the next two decades, Russian troops defeated the three khanates of the Oasis Belt (Khiva, Bukhara, and Kokand), and occupied their largest cities (MacKenzie, D. 1974). Two of these Khanates, Khiva and Bukhara, did not become part of the Russian Empire, and continued to exist as vassal states. During the reign of Tsar Alexander III, Turkmen nomads in the southern deserts were overtaken by Russian conquest, which eventually stopped at the border of Afghanistan, thus avoiding confrontation with the English troops. General Konstantin Petrovich von Kaufman organized the Turkestan territories under Russian rule (Mackenzie, D. 1967).

Though the effects of Russian colonization were later dwarfed by the party-state dictatorship of the Soviets, this period was still an important precursor to the radical transformation of the 20th century. The Russian administration made only minor changes to the hierarchy of power in the region, and in fact left the system of clans untouched. The khans, however, who were formerly the supreme power, became local representatives of the Governor General, who directed the whole region (Russian Tatarstan), and who himself was the representative of the "Great White Tsar", the head of the Russian Empire who ruled from a distant centre (MacKenzie, D. 1974). Russian colonization also introduced the local population to a radically different culture. The new sights of cities, which introduced locals to banks, train stations, trading houses, hotels, churches, hospitals, and theatres, were alien to the traditional Central Asian landscape. At the same time, the Russian elite articulated the economic importance of the Turkestan territories, noting the abundance of raw materials (mainly cotton), in addition to trade advantages (MacKenzie, D. 1974). The subordination of the local economy to Russian needs began with colonization. The rise of cotton production, the construction of railway lines, and the emergence of a new entrepreneurial stratum linking local and Russian traders, was a springboard to monocultural farming during the Soviet era (Whitman, J. 1956, MacKenzie, D. 1974, Morrison, A. 2006). The effect was substantial. On the one hand, this transformation was hostile to traditional forms of farming. On the other hand, cheap, mass-produced goods transported by the railways led to the decline of the regional craft industry (Morrison, A. 2006).

The official policy of Russification under Tsar Alexander III, and his successor Tsar Nicholas II, had a significant impact on the Russian-influenced Islamic territories of Turkestan. In addition to the introduction of Russian as the official language, conversion to the Orthodox faith and the compulsory introduction of the Russian education system brought about dramatic changes, especially to everyday urban life. A manifestation of this policy was the presence of large numbers of Russian settlers who immigrated in the early 20th century, which thus ensured that the revolutionary upheavals in western Turkestan in 1905 were markedly anti-Russian. While in the former khanates of the oasis belt the prominent Russian presence was perceptible in the larger centres, in the northern steppes, which had long been under Russian rule, the intensification of colonial practices led to the marked reduction of the pastures of nomadic shepherds and the closure of their traditional grazing paths. The exploration for, and subsequent exploitation of, copper, coal, and oil deposits, which in many cases was facilitated by funding from Western European and American investors, also disrupted traditional ways of life. The suppression of uprisings, in turn, contributed to the awakening of ethnic identity and nationhood. Given the diversity of peoples, sharpening divisions between ethnic groups was a powerful tool in the fight against revolutions.

The ethnic diversity of western/Russian Turkestan was gradually becoming apparent to the conquerors. In the late 19th century, attempts were made to make the Muslim-believers visible to Russian power. Authorities carried out experiments by creating the categories of sedentary and nomadic ethnic groups in statistical surveys. According to the 1897 census (Fig. 2.1.1), the most populous group in the area were the Kyrgyz. However, the term "Kyrgyz" employed in the census does not correspond to the ethnicity known today as Kyrgyz. It was a collective term at that time, and referred to the nomadic communities of Turkestan. Since nomads living in the north of the Turkestan territories (north of the oasis belt) were named as Kyrgyz, they were later identified with the Kazakh people (Matley, I. M. 1989). The population of the Kyrgyz people in the 1897 census can be identified on a similar territorial basis as the ethnicity later called Kyrgyz. Most nomadic communities living south of the oasis belt were added to the Turkmen and Karakalpak categories of the census. The oasis belt, and in particular its most densely populated area, the Fergian Basin, provded to be a more difficult case for the census commissioners. The census data conveyed an ethnically complex picture. Among the categories was the still-forgotten Sart term, which had previously been generally applied to the sedentary people, therefore it was a very populous category. The term Tajik has functioned as a similar concept for a long time, but there is a linguistic difference between the two. Most of the people living in permanent settlements in the oasis belt spoke

Figure 2.1.1 *The ethnic composition of the Turkestan population and the proportion of Russians in 1897; (Source:* [29]*)*

Post-Soviet Central Asian "Nations"

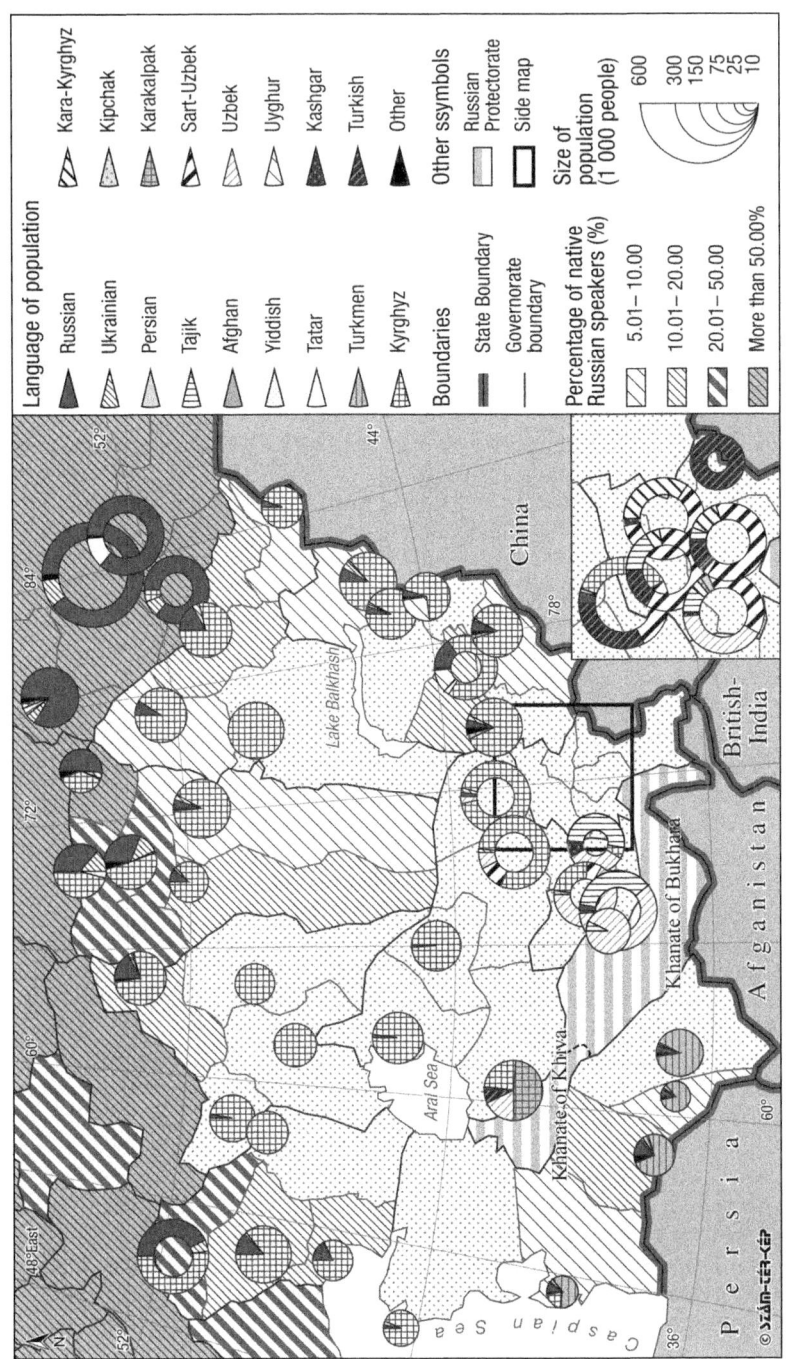

some dialect of the Persian language. In terms of numbers and proportions, the Tajiks were the dominant inhabitants. In the oasis belt, however, there were also groups of people of Turkish origin living in permanent settlements known by the name Sart. Because of the Uzbek nomadic clans who organized the political control of their settlement, the Sarts were later merged into the Uzbek category (Matley, I. M. 1989).

Ethnic identity and Russification in the Central Asian republics of the Soviet Union

The revolution of 1917, the Soviet military takeover, the civil war, the invasion of the interventionist armies, and the period of bitter war waged against the peasants created very entangled conditions in the former Russian Empire. The inhabitants of Central Asia, and especially the nomads living in the northern area, fought against the Russian settlers who had made their traditional livelihoods impossible. For them, Bolshevik claims about working class-struggle and the Dictatorship of the Proletariat rang empty, and did not provide answers to the social problems generated by Russian colonization. By comparison, Russian settlers, railway workers, and soldiers were more sympathetic to communist ideology. In November 1917, a Soviet state was proclaimed by the Russian workers of Turkestan. Established in May 1968, the Soviet Socialist Republic of Turkestan was likewise supported and led by the local Russian population. Having served the former colonial power, this group acted as a self-conscious organizational factor in the newly-formed republic.

However, this transformation, which was led by Russian and non-native cadres, did not coincide with Moscow's ethnic policy. Taking advantage of the gap between the Slavic settlers and the local population, the Bolshevik leadership organized a group of cadres from local inhabitants to serve central Soviet power in the 1920s (Yaroshevski, D. B. 1987). By embracing local nationalist movements in the first half of the 1920s, Uzbek, Tajik, Karakalpak, Turkmen, and Kyrgyz states were organized as Soviet republics. However, the relationship to central power was clearly reflected in their hierarchy. While Uzbekistan and Turkmenistan were formed as Soviet federal republics, Tajikistan and Kazakhstan received only autonomous Soviet federal status, while Kyrgyzstan and Kara-Kalpakistan were established as autonomous territories (Bacon, E. 1947). The borders and status of the five Central Asian Soviet republics were settled upon in the 1930s.

During the period of *korenizatsiya*, the peoples of "titular nations" were given the opportunity to develop their national identity, completely independent of Islamic religion, in order to cultivate local cadres who were loyal to the centre. This process included the forced creation of their own literary language and literacy, and also gave rise to a new national culture in education, which was promoted and facilitated by the widespread use of print media and mass communication. However, the spread of Soviet ideology was promoted in order to cultivate masses loyal to the party, the state, and the Soviet Union. The nomenclature "adapted" to the bureaucratic state machinery of the Soviet system, and was the link between central power and the local population. Being a member of the Soviet Union meant being in a position of permanent vulnerability for the republics, which was achieved by arrests, purges, and deportations at the hands of the Russian elite of the centralized system.

World War II gave rise to a difficult situation in Central Asia. After the German attacks, a significant proportion of the evacuated Soviet population was resettled there, and with the commencement of deportations, so-called collective criminals were expelled, and ethnic mixing took on even greater significance. To satisfy war needs, Central Asia was transformed into a new economic base, where cotton production, non-ferrous metal production, and exploration for raw materials was dramatically increased. These changes strengthened the dominance of the Russian population, as they had become increasingly important in public administration and industry, not only within management, but also as a skilled workforce. Russification had a pronounced and even spectatuclar impact on the Central Asian republics, with the Russian language and Russian culture penetrating these previously closed societies. Despite ideological Soviet commitments to the equality of people, the Russian settlers throughout the 20th century continued to act as colonizers in the region, and remained separate from the local population. They lived mainly in urban areas, which only served to reinforce the differences between rural and urban areas.

One of the central elements of Soviet ideology was the overcoming of backwardness through the abolition of peasant societies. They wanted to transform societies by means of industrialization, and in so doing achieve a classless society for workers based on equality through modernization. Much like earlier expressions of manifest destiny, this process reproduced the project first articulated during the reign of Tsar Peter the Great: to spread the achievements of civilization to the backward east. Announcing a radical transformation for all non-Russian peoples, the Soviet leadership proclaimed: "We want to help the working masses catch up with Russia" (Heller, M. and Nyekrics. A. 1996). The results speak for themselves: illiteracy decreased drastically, health services improved, electricity was brought to the entire region, intensive industrialization was introduced, and transport and telecommunications systems were developed. Mass communication opportunities were also expanded, as were employment opportunities. Modern culture was spread to the masses within this context, and modern state institutions were established.

In 1924 and 1925, the new nation-states of Kazakhstan, Uzbekistan, Turkmenistan, Kyrgyzstan, and Tajikistan were added to the map of the world. They had no historical antecedents, and they were artificially created on a linguistic basis. The boundaries were drawn in such a way that a prominent language group dominated the territory of each state. These divisions did not reflect real identities, but instead created oppositions between the dominant group and the minority. The new territorial divisions, and the emphasis on linguistic differences, worked against previous social structures. They produced national myths, along with national symbols and institutions, which was accompanied by powerful propaganda that shaped the newly-constructed modern nations of Central Asia (Fig. 2.1.2). At the same time, the strengthening of Soviet identity was industrialized, resulting in a hierarchical structure for the artificial construction of identity. The Soviet level represented the state, and relations with the outside world could only be accessed at this level. The army and diplomacy, not to mention popular sportsmen, were all Soviet. At the same time, the elites who exercised power in the member republics transmitted an official national character to the public.

A precondition for successful ideological change was the radical transformation of the education system. The introduction of Soviet education, completely independent of religious institutions, provided the basis for the organization of adult training in addition to primary education. Education was considered key to the development of Central Asian peasant societies (Bacon, E. 1947), as it would result in a drastic reduction of illiteracy, and would contribute to a growing number of skilled workers. As a result of the Soviet emancipation model, women also participated in the educational system, and later in the workforce. The effects of the emancipation model were seen mainly in the cities. One spectacular sign of this was the change in what women wore. The abandoning of traditional clothing, and mainly headscarves, was more typical in the cities, while the traditional closed lifestyle continued in the countryside.

The advent of large-scale nature conversion plans brought the process of collectivization to the region. In the southern cotton-growing areas, the process was completed in the early 1930s, but in the northern-most nomadic regions, nationalization was implemented with great sacrifices on the part of the local population. To break the resistance of populations forced to settle and grow

Figure 2.1.2 *Changes in the ethnic composition of former Soviet Central Asia (1926-2010); (Sources:* [14]; [16]; [17]; [19]; [26]; [34]; [35]; [36]; [37])

Post-Soviet Central Asian "Nations"

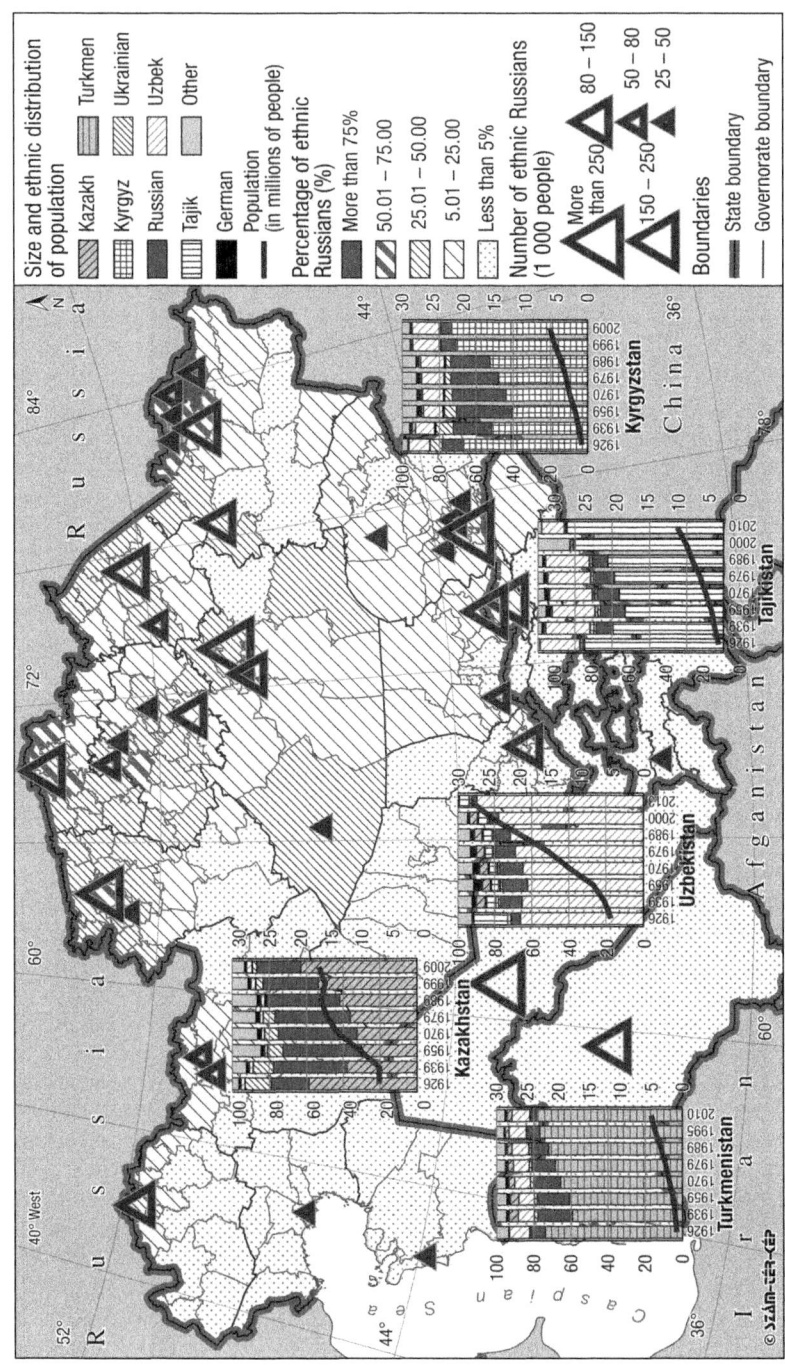

crops, agents of the state destroyed their basis of life, the livestock. Massive losses in livestock led not only to famine, but also to the cleansing of more than 2 million Kazakhs, many of whom escaped deprivation by fleeing to neighboring countries. Agricultural production in the Soviet period underwent significant changes through mechanization and technical innovation.

Urbanization had begun in Central Asia during the period of tsarist colonization. This earlier process was accelerated under the Soviets, however, and occurred on a much more spectacular scale as industrialization transformed the spatial and social structure of society. Not only did the proportion of the population living in towns and cities increase, but the towns themselves were also transformed, and took on a Western character. However, it was not just the mobility of the local population that was behind the trend towards modernization. The overwhelming majority of the settlers, mainly Russians coming from other parts of the Soviet Union, lived in the central settlements of Central Asia. These places were converted into socialist industrial cities in a short period of time.

The anti-clerical Soviet system also attacked and sought to undermine the foundation of local identity, namely the Islamic religion that determined everyday life. As a result of the transformation of the educational system, early liquidation of religious institutions and mosques began in the second half of the 1920s. In the 1930s, only a few mosques could operate, but only with permission, and under strict control. Anti-religious propaganda did not spare Muslim intellectuals, and many religious leaders and teachers were imprisoned and liquidated. The pilgrimage to Mecca and the use of the Arabic alphabet was banned and replaced by the Latin and then the Cyrillic system. Employing every means to break the rhythm of the Islamic way of life, the Soviets pushed for cultural modernization, which meant spreading the European/Russian way of life in terms of behaviour, clothing, body language, speech, and architectural styles.

Despite these oppressive measures, a continuity can nevertheless be detected, especially given the survival of traditional structures and the noticeable overlap between the old and the new system. On the one hand, family networks strongly influenced the structure of everyday life; it was the space where traditional frameworks were maintained, and an inner sphere where the essential features of society with centuries-old traditions were preserved. The identity network of clans persisted in spite of modernization and the Soviet-style transformation of society (Collins, K. 2003). These netorks remained deeply embedded in the culture and local economic framework, primarily because they were not formally institutionalized, and could therefore function in parallel with the Soviet administration. The leading clans thus maintained their position during the Soviet era by serving central Soviet interests. This process was particularly successful in Turkmenistan, Kyrgyzstan, and Tajikistan. However, in the case of Uzbekistan, the most artificial state formation, the attempted consolidation of power resulted in a constant rivalry between the three regional centres: Fergana, Samarkand, and Tashkent. In the case of Kazakhstan, there was no force that could bring the whole territory together because of its large size. As had been the case in previous centuries, the influence of local clan leaders remained intact in the region.

The post-Soviet transformation

As a result of the collapse of the Soviet Union, states that had been created artificially under Stalin became independent entities in the 1990s.These remarkably hybrid societies, which had been modernized by the Soviet system but also preserved traditional clan relations, were thus left without their "creators". The drastic Soviet-era transformation of society had occurred over a relatively short period of time. The disappearance of the Soviet project as an external modernizing force therefore led to the strengthening of (partially modified) traditional structures. For this reason, political transformation in the region echoed political conditions that had prevailed a hundred years earlier. What was different, however, was that politics were conducted within a nation-state framework, and within the state apparatus created during the Soviet period.

The leading elites of the Soviet era (who were from the most influential clans) continued to enjoy legitimacy after the dissolution of the Soviet system. They not only represented continuity amidst the uncertainty of transition, but also simplified the structre of power. Supreme power no longer resided in the hands of a distant leadership based in Moscow, but was once again in the hands of native leaders. The most prominent families who had benefitted from the Soviet-era patronage system inherited centralized state structures, and the authority of the former Soviet system. Accordingly, each of the new and, on the surface, democratic states is constituted as a presidential republic where the supreme leader, the president, has exceptional power. While power is today exercised through the modern institutional framework established during the Soviet era, there is a clear parallel between the traditional khans and the current presidents of contemporary Central Asian states.

The traditional patronage system based on loyalty is interwoven with modern bureaucratic frameworks, so that power and administration are the scenes of constant rivalry, which is why individuals rotate quickly, in most cases with a complete lack of experience in the field. In the new presidential republics, the only sure point of power is in one person, as in the khanates. The clan system also offers the potential for stability, which spared most of the population of Central Asia from wars rooted in nationalist, or even radical religious, tendencies (Collins, K. 2003). The clan-related group consciousness, and the traditional, pre-colonial characteristics of the society, have proven to be stronger in the region than the "ethnic" (ethnic-based) nationalisms (Collins, K. 2003).

Economic restructuring, deteriorating living standards, and increased criminal activity accompanied the transformation in the 1990s. The transformation allowed for the emergence of a new entrepreneurial class who gained significant influence through the establishment of international trade relations, and the operation of major economic concerns. At the same time, there was a renewed struggle for power at the regional level within each state in order to control the local administrative apparatus and to control resources such as oil, gas, and gold. In the 1990s, these rivalries led to civil war in Tajikistan.

Independence allowed for mobility, which resulted in the emigration of hundreds of thousands of people who came to Central Asia during the Soviet period (Fig. 2.1.3). However, due to the drastically declining standard of living, many native inhabitants have also left their homes in hopes of pursuing a better livelihood. Profiting from the knowledge of the Russian language, skilled labourers in particular left Central Asia and moved to the largest cities of Russia (their main target was Moscow). After the turn of the millennium, masses of people migrated to more prosperous regions of the former Soviet Union in order to escape poverty and poor living conditions. Their presence caused a migration crisis in Russia, similar to the crisis faced by the European Union, which has increased social tensions and has contributed to Russian nationalism.

However, internal mobility is still not common. The vertical links within society have weakened, but the horizontal solidarity has grown stronger because of the great social divide between the urban elites, who adopted European/Russian characteristics, and the "traditional" population of the villages. Rural society has changed significantly, though. Reduced to modest living conditions, the basis of their livelihoods remains questionable.

The states of Central Asia joined the Commonwealth of Independent States created after the dissolution of the Soviet Union. As members of the Defense and Integration Association, they continue to maintain close ties with Russia, but have also had the

Figure 2.1.3 *The ethnic composition of former Soviet Central Asia in 2010; (Source:* [18]*)*

Post-Soviet Central Asian "Nations"

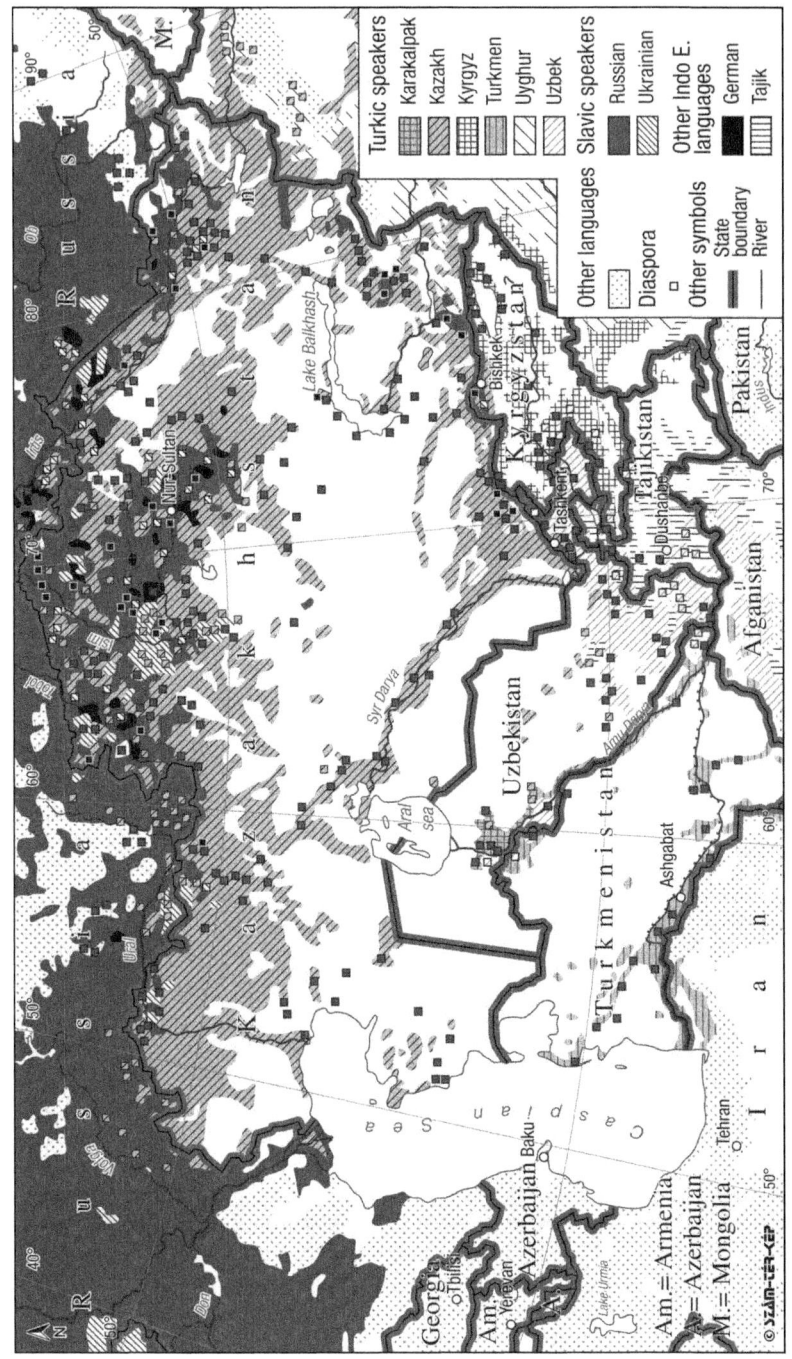

opportunity to open up internationally as independent states (Carney, C. P. and Moran, J. P. 2000). Renewed relations with southern neighbours also meant contact with the Islamic world (Hann, C. and Pelkmans, M. 2009). In a society returning to old traditions, the revival of Islam is of great importance in revitalizing these relationships (Karim, M. 2005).

Summary

Central Asia, which includes the former Soviet republics, was brought to the attention of the Tsarist Russian Empire by colonialist efforts in the 19th century. This semi-desert and desert extreme climate that characterizes the environment of former western/Russian Turkestan is home to the oasis-dwelling, sedentary Iranian peoples, and nomadic/semi-nomadic Turkic peoples. Their most important settlements were the holy centres of Islam, the centuries-old keepers of Islamic culture. The last "unknown" territory of the "mysterious" East became visible to the West as a result of the Russian conquest, while local inhabitants were forced increasingly to accept the conquering settlers, as well as their culture and Western-style modernization.

The Soviets, as the second colonizer, brought about a more powerful transformation in Central Asian societies. While they pushed Islamic culture almost entirely into the background, they also assigned national identities to the majority of ethnicities of the newly-founded republics through the process of nativization (*korenizatsiya*). The main instruments employed to create "titular nations" in Central Asia were the Russian model of education, the bureaucratic state machinery, and the native language press. At the same time, in order to cultivate cadres loyal to Soviet ideology and the Soviet system, a process of Sovietization defined by Russian culture was conducted through these channels. The large-scale Russian migration in the context of industrialization intensified the process of Russification. In addition to the strong Russian presence after the Second World War, the region's ethnic spatial structure became even more complex due to deportations.

In post-Soviet Central Asian societies at the beginning of the 21st century, different cultural strata coexist (Collins, K. 2003). The national line conveyed by the authoritarian elite, which is of a purely ethnonational nature, is more the result of Soviet-era identity constructions than it is a bottom-up initiative of the societies themselves. The migration of mass number of people from Central Asia to Russia (and especially Moscow) is also an important legacy of the transformational process initiated by the Soviets. That being said, local factors are also important to take into consideration. Religious renewal in particular has provided an opportunity for Islamic culture to flourish again in the region. However, in the end, it is the cultural influences most closely associated with clans that intersect with and inform the lives of societies at the level of micro-communities.

Tatars in Russia and the Post-Soviet Realm

Margit Kőszegi

Introduction

Having been the subject of much discussion in recent years, and especially in the wake of the Crimean conflict, it is no exaggeration to say that the Tatar people of Eastern Europe are well known. History books portray Tatars as formidable barbarian steppe warriors who made their way to central Europe during a series of raids in the 13th century. This picture is similar to the one in collective Russian thinking. For Russians this name means centuries of oppression under the Tatar yoke. However, the Turkish-speaking Tatars were a minority among the people of the vast Mongol Empire of Genghis Khan. Their most populous communities lived closest to the European territories, making their name synonymous with the nomadic peoples of the eastern steppe.

The majority of Tatars today live within the territory of the Russian Federation. The Tatar language, which is now estimated to be spoken by 6 to 8 million people, belongs to the Turkish group of the Altaic language family. Tartars became followers of Islam in the 14th century under the rule of the Golden Horde Mongol Empire. Close to 6 million Tartar people live in Russia, including in Crimea, but they also live in Uzbekistan and Kazakhstan. In addition to living in the Soviet successor states of Central Asia, they also live throughout the territory of the former Ottoman Empire, and in European countries bordering Russia.

In Russia we can distinguish between three large Tatar communities. These include the Volga and Siberian Tatars, as well as the more well-known Crimean Tatars. The largest population of Tartars can be found in Tatarstan and Bashkortostan, which is part of the Russian Federation at the southwestern foot of the Ural Mountains along the Volga River (Fig. 2.2.1). The Tatar population of these internal territories adheres to a different identity and harbours a different attitude towards the Russian state than the Crimean Tatars, who will be discussed in more detail in the next chapter. The focus of this chapter is on the specific identity of the Volga Tatars and, to a lesser extent, the Siberian Tatars in Russia.

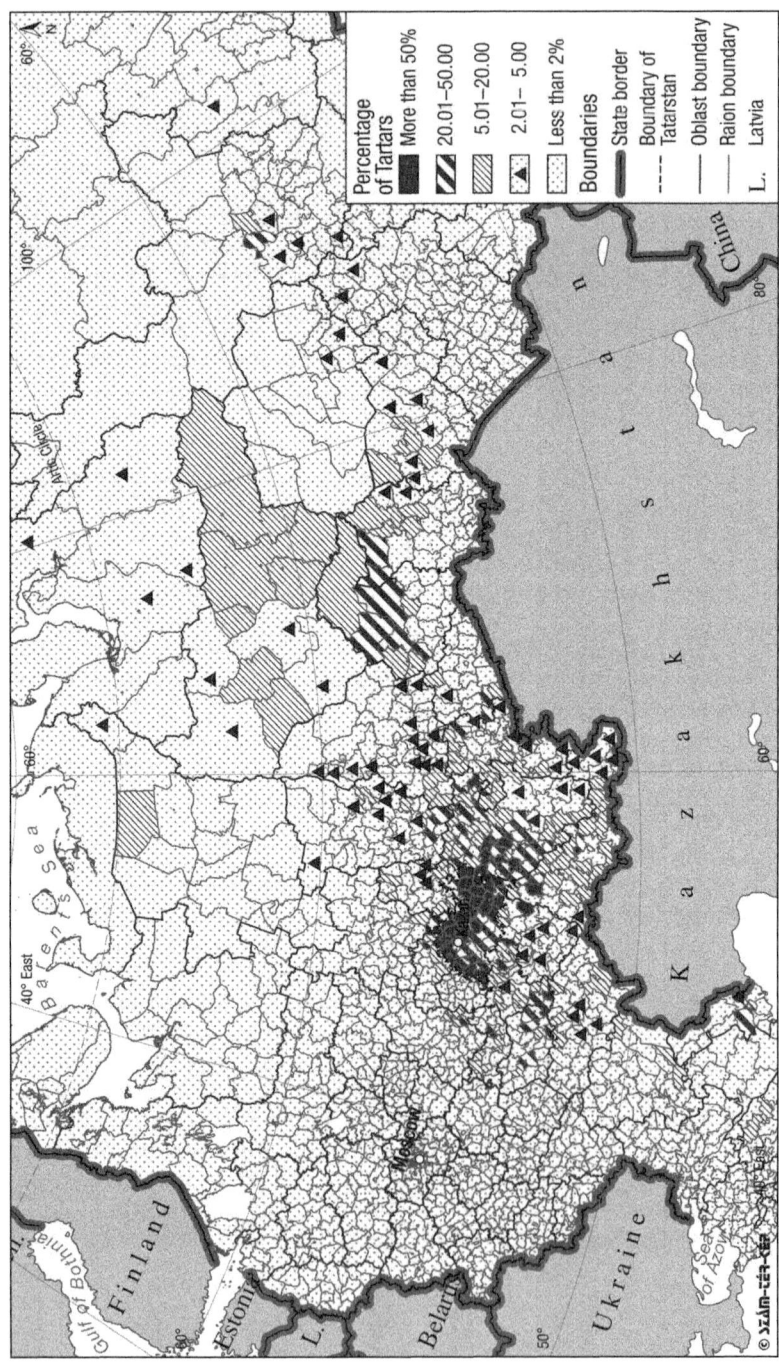

Figure 2.2.1 *The territorial presence of Tatars in Russia in 2010; Source:* [25])

Tartars as nomadic peoples of the steppe

In the Middle Ages, the Tatars represented the Mongol conquerors more generally. They played a crucial role in the formation of Russian principalities under the Tatar yoke, which is the term that is commonly used to indicate the period of dependency on the Mongol Empire and its successor states. Tatars were a constant source of danger to the shifting small state formations of East Slavs (Heller, M. 1996). With the disintegration of the Mongol Empire of the Golden Horde, the Khanates of Kazan and Astrakhan along the Volga River, and the Khanate of Crimea on the northern shores of the Black Sea, became the best-known and most populous communities among the Tatar khanates. In Russia today, we can find smaller groups to the east, but as a result of their remoteness from Europe, and the isolation of the Siberian landscape, they are not as well known.

During the Tatar period from the 13th century to the 15th century, a special relationship developed between western Tatars and Eastern Europe. As a result, a Tatar population can still be found in Poland (Bohdanowitz, L. 1942). In the Middle Ages, their military power was often mobilized by rival Eastern European states, such as the Poles and Lithuanians, against the Teutonic Order of German Knights. In return, they were given land and settlement opportunities in the Grand Duchy of Lithuania (Danylenko, A. 2006). The presence of the Tatars in Lithuania, Poland, and Belarusia is reflected in the census results. Even the Russian principalities suffering under the supposed Tatar yoke called on the Tatars, their sworn enemies, during their armed struggles with each other and later with their western neighbours.

The military potential stemming from their way of life was one of their main identity-defining features. The other was not so much their non-Slavic Turkish language, but rather for centures has been their Islamic religion. While their way of life has radically changed as a result of modernization, their Islamic belief is still their main distinguishing feature for the outside world, and especially for current Russian power. Although the presence of Islam in Russia is tied to the Tatars, it came relatively late, and only in the 14th century, when Islamization reached their western communities. The Tatars living in the territories beyond the Urals became Muslim even later, with some communities adopting Islam during the period of Russian rule (Frank, A. J. 2000). Communities in the central territory of the Siberian Tatars along the Irtysh and Tobol Rivers converted to Islam immediately before the Russian conquest. From there they transmitted their religious ideals to their eastern neighbours (Frank, A. J. 2000).

In the Russian collective memory constructed by Russian power, Tatar refers to all negative things. The word Tatar means "enemy," "pagan," and the embodiment of evil. The era of the Tatar yoke, therefore, is widely viewed as a period of alien rule, bondage, violence, and arbitrariness (Halperin, C. J. 1982, Heller, M. 1996). Two hundred years of purported Tatar oppression, moreover, has become the explanation for a course of development that was different from that of the West, and is also evoked as a justification or explanation for backwardness both in historical narratives and in narratives of power (Heller, M. 1996). In fact, however, during most of that time, Russian principalities paid taxes to Genghis Khan's offspring in order to preserve their sovereignty.

By the 15th century, Russian principalities were consolidating and uniting through the centralization efforts of the Grand Duchy of Moscow. Following the disintegration of the Mongolian Golden Horde, Russian rulers viewed the southern and south-eastern neighbouring lands as areas of expansion. In the context of Russian political intent, the time had come to strike back. During the 16th century, the expansion into Tatar territories began with the occupation of the Khanate of Kazan in 1552, and ended by placing the Khanate of Crimea under Russian rule in 1783. The dissolution of the khanates, in addition to the substantial territorial growth of the Russian Empire, resulted in a considerable number of Muslim subjects living in the orthodox tsarist empire.

The gradual establishment of an administrative structure followed the quick Russian expansion in Siberia, which was met with almost no resistance. As a result, smaller Tatar and Chuvash Turkish communities living scattered throughout the area became visible to the authorities. Tatars living in the southern part of the Western Siberian Lowland, near the present-day Kazakh-Russian border along the Irtish, Tobol, Ishim, Ob, Tom, and Yenisei Rivers, migrated from Central Asia to the northern edge of the steppe, and moved further and further east in response to the Russian advance (Tomilov, N. A. and Frank A. J. 2000). The term Siberian Tatar is a collective term for Tatar and/or Islamic communities without significant state formations that existed scattered across southern Siberia (Tomilov, N. A. and Frank A. J. 2000).

Tatars in the Russian Empire

Although Tatar subjects were limited in many ways by tsarist power, the mass conversion of the conquered was not an explicit goal of the Russian imperial authorities, and Islamic-based communities continued to function within the new state framework. As religion was the leading indicator of their otherness in the eyes of the authorities, the exclusionary policy of power was expressed along these lines and not because of their language. This attitude made their faith the primary source of their ethnic identity that was beginning to form (Devlet, N. 1991). The geographical location of Tatar communities had a strong impact on the social status of Islamic subjects in the Russian Empire. More precisely, political ideas formed from different territories determined the formation of the social system and the building of power and economic bodies. Depending on the strategic importance of the newly conquered territories, especially in regard to their proximity to the centre, and proximity to Europe and the Ottoman Empire, political intent brought to life various forms of relationship with Tatars and other Islamic believers. However, the conquered Tatar communities themselves differed in many respects, as those located closer to Europe and thus to centres of power, as well as those located in modern cities, had a different mindset than members of the closed Tatar communities in Siberia and Central Asia.

The number of Tatar communities on the Black Sea and in the northern foothills and valleys of the Caucasus fell sharply following successive Russo-Turkish wars, as many Tartars chose to emigrate to Ottoman territories in the 18th and 19th centuries. The most influential community of survivors were the Crimean Tatars, though they had fallen significantly in number. They were the westernmost Tatar community, and therefore had a more intensive relationship with other Slavic communities. Because of this they showed a greater openness to European and Slavic culture, and sought to adapt to the changed circumstances. The 19th century cultural reform efforts, and the nationalist movements that followed them, also spread to the Eastern Muslim communities through the Crimean Tatars. However, the lives of the members of these Muslim groups were severely restricted by centralizing Russian power.

During the period of expansion in the second half of the 18th century, Catherine II decided to guarantee the functioning of religious communities in the former Khanates of Kazan and Astrakhan, and to lift restrictions on their economic activities and establish a central organization of Islamic subjects in Ufa as well (Devlet, N. 1991). Propelled by commercial necessity, Russian imperial authorities not only saw the Tatars as an important economic link, but also regarded them as a foundation for further eastern conquests. The resulting religious tolerance facilitated the flourishing of Tatar Islamic culture under Russian rule. A dense network of mosques existed in the 19th century, and some people reconverted from Christianity back to Islam (Devlet, N. 1991). Volga Tatar traders travelled to the newly conquered eastern Muslim-populated territories more willingly, and with more bravado, than their Russian counterparts.

Therefore they gained massive wealth in the 19th century and invested in industrial facilities which flourished in Kazan and other areas along the Volga River. Under the leadership of the ulema (the collective name for Islamic scholars) sitting in Orenburg, the Volga Tatars were able to establish an autonomous social system based on religion. Their positions made them both believers and supporters of the Russian Empire. The influence of European culture was also apparent in their communities.

As a result, a distinct Islamic culture developed in the areas of the Russian Empire that were east of the Volga. The strong influence among Volga Tatars of the Sunni orthodox religious centres of Bukhara and Samarkand was increasingly reflected in their habits and attire. One of its garments, which has become a symbol nowadays, is the headscarf. Because of the orthodox Sunni Islam influence from Central Asia, the Tatar women began to wear the headscarf again in the 19th century. In order to maintain both good relations with the central power and economic benefits, Tatar leaders also integrated Russian influences into their educational system and their daily lives. Taking advantage of capitalist systems of commerce, they organized Arabic-language book printing and spread their doctrines widely (Devlet, N. 1991). The effectiveness of this project was reflected in the mass conversion to Islam among Tatars after the promulgation of the Tsarist Manifesto of 1905, which guaranteed civil rights to all subjects (Devlet, N. 1991). The adoption of the modern methodology of the Crimean Tatar reformer Ismail Gaspirali (in Russian, Ishmail Gasprinsky) in education can also be interpreted as an indirect influence of Russian and European culture (Gaspirali's reforms and their Russian/European features are discussed in Chapter 2.3). This methodology, in addition to reforming the teaching of Arabic, also brought secular curricula into Muslim schools (Kirimli, H. 1993).

As a result of Catherine II's more open policy towards Muslims, the Obi, Tomsk, and Baraba Tatars in Siberia also converted to Islam (Frank, A. J. 2000). Turkish-speaking ethnic groups living in Siberia were not necessarily Tatars in terms of their language, but after conversion to Islam, they were regarded as Tatars (Frank A. J. 2000). In Siberia, Turkish-speaking ethnic groups, as well as Finno-Ugric peoples then under Russian rule, converted to Islam (Frank A. J. 2000). The assimilation of Turkish and Finno-Ugric folk elements into Tatar communities began in the 19th century on the basis of mutual religion. These groups, officially considered pagan, could gain Muslim religious status in the Russian Empire only through long bureaucratic battles (because pagans were traditionally considered as falling under the sphere of influence of the Orthodox Church). This is the reason why mass conversion was associated with periods when Russian power was more lenient towards Muslims.

The 19th century was the period of "national awakening" in European history (Hobsbawm, E. 1962). Societal transformations related to modernization, coupled with the processes linked to the formation of nations as the new types of communities, did not leave the western Tatar population of the Russian Empire intact. This disruptive set of interconnected processes manifested in the need for joint action by Sunni Islamic and Turkish-speaking peoples on Russian territory. The formulation of these claims found expression in the westernmost Tatar community. Crimean Tatar intellectuals studying European ideas at Russian universities were in the best position to cast a critical eye on the extent to which the Russian imperial state restricted the exercise of liberties in their communities. This was not only due to the fact that they had acquired different views on society, but also because Crimean Tatars were living in areas where repressive politics were most prevalent because of Russia's geopolitical aspirations (ruling the Black Sea was one of the most important goals of Russian expansion in the 19th century).

The need for joint action — and in particular joint action that responded to new types of common interests — brought to life the pan-Turkish idea. Pan-Turkism was the product of the cultural reform movement of Crimean Tatar intellectuals, and was accompanied by the emergent pan-Islamism of the early 20th century. Pan-Islamism targeted all Muslim believers in Russia, and called for unified action in regard to their rights (Kirimli, H. 1993). However, the congresses initiated by the Crimean and Volga Tatars failed to establish a unified program. A large number of non-Turkish-speaking believers were aware of the initiative but did not join the congresses. Because of this widespread lack of interest, these movements did not go further in formulating the claim for autonomy of the various peoples, which, a few years after the Communist takeover, remained unfulfilled. The movements started by western Tatar communities reached Central Asian Muslims, but they were not taken up by Siberian Tatars, who were more affected by the intensifying relationship with the Russians and the transformative effect of modernization on their lives (Tomilov, N. A. and Frank, A. J. 2000).

Tatars in the Soviet Union

The years of the Russian Civil War and the consolidation of the proletarian dictatorship marked a tragic turning point in the lives of the Tatars in the western Europen areas of Russia. With the collapse of former economic systems, famine struck almost the entire country. The most critical areas were the Volga region, the Ukrainian-populated regions, and the Crimea (Kirimli, H. 2003). With the impossibility of agricultural production, a massive famine broke out in these areas. The epidemics that followed in the wake of famine were particularly devastating because of neglected infrastructure, a complete lack of medicines, and the vulnerability of entire populations of people weakened by hunger. In light of such conditions, there were a million deaths among Volga and Crimean Tatars alone (Kirimli, H. 2003).

As Soviet power solidified, anti-clerical leaders had to face the role of the Islamic religious factor affecting millions in the Soviet Union. In the early years of the Soviet regime, Islam was seen as a movement with political potential, but after the consolidation of Soviet power, anti-Islamic rhetoric guided decision making. Before the Stalinist takeover, the ideas of communism also had an impact on Muslim believers in the West. The most well-known Muslim Bolshevik was Mirsay (Mirza) Sultan-Galiev, a Bashkir Tatar and the founder of the Muslim Communist Party. In his particular interpretation, the class struggle did not occur within the Muslim community in Russia, because Islamic believers were living under collective repression in Tsarist Russia. He made communist revolutionary ideas a national ideology by considering the repressed Tatars as the ideal vehicle for the transmission of revolutionary ideas to the Islamic world in Asia. As a result of his views, which were considered dangerous by the Russian communists, he was imprisoned in the early 1920s, and executed in 1940.

After centuries of cultural flourishing since the 1930s, the atheist, anti-clerical ideology of communism brought significant change to the communities of western Muslim Tatars. In the early years of communism, all religious property was confiscated and all religious institutions were eradicated in the name of anti-religion. The closing of these institutions impeded the most fundamental community-organizing power of Muslim communities. Schools could not function, and Arabic writing was banned, as was religious law and traditional clothing. Volumes of the Qur'an were collected and publicly burned. Ulema members were slandered, imprisoned, or deported to labour camps. Common prayer was also banned. According to official statistics, there were only 1,312 functioning mosques in 1942, compared with 24,562 in 1914. The Soviets strove to suppress the ideas of pan-Turkism and pan-Islamism by slandering, imprisoning, and removing the advocates of these movements from the community. All activities aimed at preserving Muslim culture were classified as reactionary.

Following the removal of Muslim communist leaders, the closure of mosques that functioned as educational institutions, and the dissolution of the Islamic press, the policy of *korenizatsiya*, or "putting down roots", had come to the fore also in Tatarstan. The Tatars were encouraged by powerful propaganda to leave rural areas, or to become involved in modernizing urban life, or to study. As a result, the mobilization of Tatar society began. Within a few generations, they became part of the Soviet elite and were linked to power, corporations, and intellectuals within the autonomous region (Giuliano, E. 2000). Within the Russian-style educational system, anti-clerical and Russian culture-oriented identity formation developed (Devlet, N. 1991). The Tatars, who were educated in the Russian system and attended Russian higher education institutions, used the Russian language in their work and integrated Russian cultural influences into their lives (Giuliano, E. 2000). At the same time, the construction of the new educational system was also a means of rethinking Tatar ethnic identity, which had been separated from Islam. The incorporation of Tatar history written by Russian historians into the syllabus contributed greatly to this (Lazzerini, E. J. 1981). The reinterpretation of Russian–Tatar relations, and the convergence of culture and communication between the two peoples were also characteristic at that time (Lazzerini, E. J. 1981).

At the same time, there was a systematic "weeding out" of Islamic cultural influences from Tatar society. The number and diversity of anti-religious, atheist publications in Tatarstan was much higher than in the Muslim republics of the Soviet Union, or in the eastern Siberian Muslim communities (Devlet, N. 1991). Anti-religious movements were also organized much more intensively than in other more remote areas of the Soviet Union that were far-removed from Moscow (Devlet, N. 1991). During the Stalinist dictatorship, although their communities were not spared from religious persecution, their autonomous minority rights were severely restricted, and they did not become the collective enemy of the homeland like their Crimean counterparts did in official propaganda. With the death of Stalin, direct and administrative attacks on Islam ceased. Even the limited and controlled operation of Islamic communities was accepted. Still, the vigorous activity of the anti-religious propaganda machine remained directed against the Volga Tatars until the disintegration of the Soviet Union, leaving a profound impression on their religion (Devlet, N. 1991).

Systematic anti-religionism also provided an opportunity for Russification to become more prominent. This was facilitated by the large number of Russian settlers moving into the cities, the adoption of the Russian language (which meant the potential for upward social mobility), the acceptance of cultural influences, and the growing number of mixed marriages. Therefore a significant proportion of Tatar society had adapted to Russian-dominated Soviet rule. However, rural communities retained more of the religious features of their everyday lives because they were generally less open to change. One of the peculiar features of surviving Islamic practices in the region is that Islamic believers have established their own local places of pilgrimage. The most important of them were ruins of a former Bulgarian city on the Volga. This place was the first in the region to adopt the Islamic faith in the 10th century (Devlet, N. 1991).

For the Crimean Tatars, communism and World War II marked the most significant moments in their collective memory, especially in light of the deportation of their entire community to Central Asia and Siberia. Following the end of German occupation in 1943-44, Muslim groups in the Black Sea and the Caucasus were declared to be collective traitors. Stalin used this accusation as an excuse to solve a geopolitical problem: the presence of non-Russian inhabitants in a border region of particular importance to Russians. The principle of collective guilt was applied to all ethnicities along the Black Sea coast and in the Northern Caucasus. The massive Soviet propaganda campaign which accused the Crimean Tatars of treason, forged the public's negative attitude towards them (Williams, B. G. 2002). As a result, there was little public sympathy when Crimean Tatars were deported to Central Asia and Siberia. Those who survived the cruel journey were mobilized by the state to help build the socialist economy as workers in the special camps established for the deported. Forced to live in an environment unfamiliar to them, they nevertheless found themselves in a region that may have been similar in religion, but was certainly alien in mindset (Uehling, G. 2001). The severe trauma caused by this deportation became part of the community's consciousness as displaced peoples, and fueled their opposition to the Soviet Union, and to the Russian people more generally. The tragedy of the Crimean Tatars was more severe than it was for other deportees from the Black Sea coast and the Caucasus. They were not allowed to return to their homes even during Khrushchev's period of relief. Crimean Tatars, therefore, waited for decades for their fate to change.

Tatars in post-Soviet Russia

The disintegration of the Soviet Union affected Tatar groups in different ways, though in 2020 their largest communities remain within the territory of the Russian Federation (Fig. 2.2.2). Siberian Tatars, far from the great urban centres, endured the collapse of the Soviet system and the political transformation that followed without significant changes. In the 1990s the Crimean Tatars were given the opportunity to return to their original homes from Central Asia. Half of them had returned to independent Ukraine, to a region that has been the subject of an ongoing debate between Russia and Ukraine. However, based on current power relations, Crimean Tatars belong to the population of the Russian Federation. Half of the Crimean Tatars returned to Crimea from Central Asia, and they

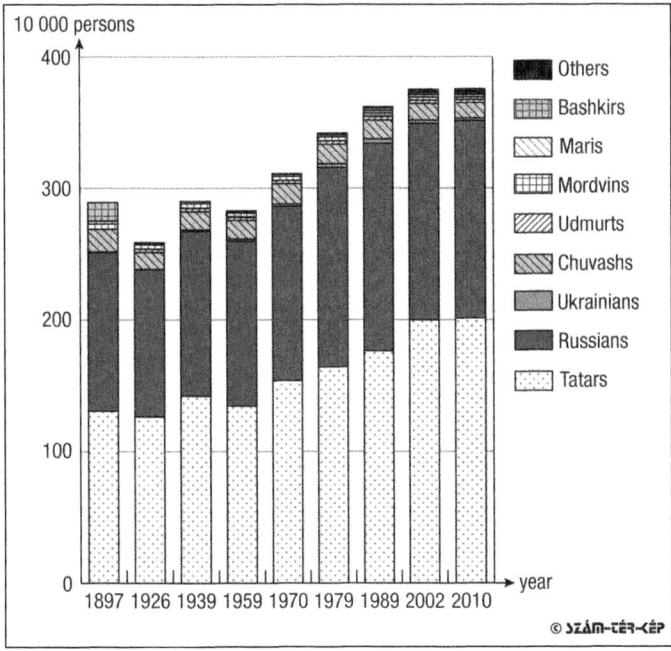

Figure 2.2.2 *Changes in the ethnic composition of Tatarstan (1897–2010); (Sources:* [25]; [26]; [27]; [29])

now comprise almost 10% of the inhabitants of Crimea with their community of 230,000 people. The specific situation of the Crimean Tatars is presented in the next chapter.

Unlike the Crimean Tatars, the millions of people who make up the largest Volga Tatar communities experienced different changes. The Volga Tatars are residents mainly of the Autonomous Provinces of Tatarstan and Bashkortostan. According to census data, they account for nearly 50% of the 4 million people of Tatarstan, and for roughly 23% of the 4 million people of Bashkortostan. Within both political units, the former communist elite remained in positions of power. In addition to persistent administrative and corporate structures, social processes influencing identity also demonstrate continuity, with Russification continuing after the disintegration of the Soviet Union (Graney, K. E. 1999). In the 1980s, strong nationalist political movements emerged in Tatarstan advocating for the protection of the Tatar culture and language, and also demanding full independence. Tatar political forces articulated their demands on a purely ethnic basis. However, despite all efforts, these movements could not create a mass base so that they could act as a significant force against Russia. In the 1992 referendum on independence, over 60% voted to break away. Following the conclusion of the Russian–Tatar bilateral treaty in 1994, divisive nationalist groups became irrelevant in the political life of Tatarstan, and the Russian Federation rejected their independence. In Tatarstan itself, Tatar is the official language alongside Russian (Cashaback, D. 2012).

Behind the failure of nationalist politics lies the duality of the Volga Tatar community. As a result of the significant transformation process that took place during the Soviet period, Tatarstan is an economically developed, urbanized area of the Russian Federation. Russification dramatically influenced the lives of those who live in Tartarstan (Giuliano, E. 2000). When comparing the capital of Tartarstan with the countryside, the difference is striking. While the majority of the population of Kazan Tatars claim Russian as their first language, the Tatar language is typically dominant in the countryside. This duality is also present in lifestyle and social status. Urban, Russian-speaking politicians who seek to instil a sense of nationality, and promote the dangers of Tatar culture, have not found a way to communicate with rural society or to address its problems. Because of the lack of consensus and internal social divisions, initiatives originating from the capital fizzled within a short period (Giuliano, E. 2000).

The rebirth of Islam in the Russian Federation has been relatively slow. Muslim believers were cautious about their religious affiliation during the 1990s, but put a greater emphasis on their religious beliefs following the turn of the millennium. In the North Caucasus, this issue gained prominence within a climate of escalating conflict, but the Tatar population of the inner territories view religious affiliation as a much more personal and non-communal issue (Karimova, L. 2013).

A critical moment in the reorganization of religious communities has been the operation of mosques. In 1917, mosques numbered more than 12,000 in the territory of present-day Russia, but only 3,500 at the beginning of the 2000s. Islamic education was also reorganized in the 1990s, when it was already possible for young people to study at renowned institutions in other parts of the Islamic world, such as in Turkey, Pakistan, and Arab countries. As a result, community organization has been accelerated in the 21st century. For the first time, with the intensification of foreign relations, spectacular religious building complexes appeared in the modest communities of Volga Tatars. This also represents a shift in attitudes among Tatar Islamic believers, one that is not only linked to an internal reorganization after decades of forbidding politics, but also represents a growing attachment to the more modest and influential centres of the Islamic world (Karimova, L. 2013).

Summary

For many people in the eastern part of Europe, "Tatar" is used as a collective historical term rather than a name of an existing ethnic group. In the early history of the Russian state, the phrase "Tatar" was employed as a symbol of barbarity and backwardness. Over the centuries, it has evolved into an umbrella term referring to Islamic communities in general in Russia. Today, Tatar communities can still be found scattered across Russia's vast territory.

Much like the Bosnians in Bosnia and Herzegovina, Tatars in the Russian Federation are widely recognized as a large Muslim community that has long lived within the European cultural sphere. This is especially true if we focus specifically on their most populous territory, the Volga region with its millions of Tatars, and the Autonomous Republics of Tatarstan and Bashkortostan. The Volga Tatars, who were in contact with Europe indirectly by means of their connections to Orthodox culture and the Soviet system, have become even more Western in character as a result of the globalizing world economy, thanks to their natural gas assets. Capitalism, a modernized society, and the possibility of self-government have also sparked ethnic movements within their circles. But internal social fractures between urban and rural areas and between richer and poorer social strata proved to be stronger than the national myths created by Russian historians. The failure of national movements amongst these Tatar communities is a product of the ideological effects of the Soviet period and the still existing Russification that has persisted after the ambiguous transformation in the 1990s.

The 20th-century tragedy of the Crimean Tatars makes it impossible for them to assert their national identity. Siberian Tatar communities are scattered, and national movements have not appeared within their groups. In addition to the linguistic and religious communities of the Crimean, Volga, and Siberian Tatars (who are thousands of kilometres apart), very different societal factors shape the lives of their communities in the 21st century. Russian power, and its relations with individual Tatar communities and their settlements, plays a crucial role in this.

In the Net of Power: Small Nations and Ethnicities on the Black Sea Coast

Margit Kőszegi

Introduction

In addition to being a region of new beginnings and dynamic change, European post-Soviet space has also been a region of war in Europe in the new millennium. For years now, media attention has been focused on this part of Eastern Europe where a civil war is raging in Ukraine, a state immediately adjacent to the European Union. Borders have changed as a result of Russian military intervention, and Russia considers Crimea a part of its territory. In many ways, none of these recent developments are new or even unexpected. The region, in fact, has been plagued by conflict since the change of regime. In addition to the example of Transnistria (the Pridnestrovian Moldavian Republic), which is a contested region despite being recognized internationally as a part of Moldova, armed preparedness has been ongoing in the Caucasus since the 1990s, and conflict characterized in part by ethnic tensions has created repeated war situations.

The Black Sea coast has been a source of tension and competition between powers for many centuries. As a result, the population living here is not only caught in a linguistic, religious, and cultural transfer zone but has also been affected by waves of migration. Given the diversity of small ethnic groups and minorities who are cut off from their majority nation, it is not surprising that existing power relations, coupled with political developments and military events (including war) have significantly influenced the shifting identities in the region. Following the specific ethnic patterns and the flourishing nationalisms among small peoples, this chapter outlines the main aspects of the ethnic and national identities of the communities living on the north Black Sea coast, and in so doing also examines the advocacy efforts that have helped determine conflicts in this region.

Theoretical background: ethnic and national identity, and ethnic nationalism

Identity, ethnicity, and nation are terms commonly used not only in social practices and political rhetoric, but also societal research (Brubaker, R. and Cooper, F. 2000). Because the meaning of these words can change according to the context within which they are employed, it is very important to conceptualize them clearly. The use of the term "identity" in this chapter refers to a collective phenomenon, or what Brubaker and Cooper identify as "a fundamental and consequential sameness among members of a group" (Brubaker, R. and Cooper, F. 2000: 7). By applying the phrases "ethnic" and "national identity", we point to the nature of these groups. These terms are sometimes used as synonyms in scholarly works (Özkirimli, U. 2010), but in our case we separate them, emphasizing the differences between the two social phenomena. In Europe, the traditional source of the nation as an idea is ethnic identity, a concept that refers to and articulates the common values associated with the unifying force of culture (Cox, K. R. 2002). Ethnicity-related expressions may, therefore, play a key role in interpreting nationalism (Martin, J. 2005, Smith, A. D. 1986). In this volume, we interpret *ethnic identity* as a group construction based on real or perceived common origins; that is, the manifestation of a group's essential worldview, one which includes the classic distinction between "us and them". Ethnicity presupposes both inclusive and exclusionary behaviour, wherein members of an ethnic group believe that a common origin and culture connect the community and, at the same time, makes them different from others. This social construction of difference is deeply embedded in the discourses of science, public opinion, and politics (Bressey, C. 2011).

In addition to the formulation of common values, *national identity* has a very strong territorial dimension (Herb, G. H. 2018). Its attachment to a specific area increases the significance of history and collective memory (Wiebe, R. 2000, Murphy, A. B. 2002, Saphiro, M. J. 2003, Williams, C. H. 2003). In this context, the boundary between ethnic and national identity is given by the need for self-government and autonomy, and the existence of an independent state. One of the major trends in nationalism theory approaches national identity as a social phenomenon on an ethnic basis (Smith, A. D. 1986, Eriksen, T. H. 2010 [1993], Atatürk, S. 2012, Kennedy, J. 2016), which is usually characteristic among scholars of the eastern half of Europe (A. Gergely A. 1997, Schöpflin Gy. 2003, Romsics I. 1998, Kocsis K. 2002). According to this approach, ethnic groups and nations coexist in space and time, and the difference between them is a result of their relative ability to assert their interests. The manifestation of this advocacy is their aspiration for independence and their own territorial entity.

As we can see, ethnic and national identities present different collective phenomena. If we foreground the meaning of these terms in scientific research, the feeling of "sameness" is fundamental in both cases. National identity has a strong ability to assert common interests; therefore, it has a dynamic connection to power and its identity-making processes (Gellner, E. 2008 [1983]). The most spectacular manifestation of this advocacy is the existence of the *nation-state space* (Calhoun, C. 1993, Herb, G. H. 2018).

But this statement needs to be refined. The *image of a collective homeland* is indispensable to national identity, but this image does not necessarily refer to a currently existing nation-state framework. Moreover, it does not necessarily correspond to the current place of residence. It is also important to emphasize that the existence of the nation-state is not a precondition for national identity (Aydıngün, I. and Aydıngün, A. 2007). However, the process of transforming power frameworks generated specific situations in the eastern half of Europe. Therefore, in some cases, it was ethnic rather than national identity that became a more definite community-forming factor in the identification of groups living further away from the nation-state.

Focusing on three ethnic groups located on the Black Sea coast, this chapter examines the factors that have shaped the collective identities in the "buffer zone" of Eastern Europe. The chapter begins with a comparison of the Crimean Tatars and the Gagauz, two ethnic groups whose ethnic and national character have been differently shaped by their historical experiences in the modern period, and who have pursued nationalist aspirations and have engaged in national identity formation in the absence of a nation-state space. As a counterpoint to this, the chapter also examines how the same factors have resulted in the emergence of an ethnic identity for the Bulgarians living in Budjak, an ethnic group located outside the Bulgarian nation-state.

Ethnic groups on the Black Sea coast

On the northern shore of the Black Sea, in the former Russian-Ottoman buffer zone, several ethnic groups have suffered historically from the turbulent events that have consumed the region over the centuries. Despite constant migration following the wars, many of these groups remained, and have been included continually in this strategically significant area. Though perhaps much diminished, their communities are still present in the region, and are today undergoing somewhat of a revival. Current events coupled with the aspirations of centralized power have reenergized some of these groups, and have breathed new life into the politics of national identity amongst them.

The most well-known ethnic group in this region are the Crimean Tatars. Previously a formidable enemy, Tatars became the victims of the disruptive and often violent events of the 20th century. In addition to the Tatar language, which is considered a branch of the Turkish language group, their Sunni Muslim religion, coupled with their collective attachment to the Crimea, form the basis of their ethnic and national identity. Stigmatized in part because of their grievances against both Russian and Ukrainian power, they remain conspicuoulsy isolated from the mainly East Slavic-speaking majority on the peninsula.

Less well-known are the Gagauz people. Also of Turkish origin, the Gagauz nevertheless remained culturally separated from the Ottomans during the period when the region was controlled by the Sublime Porte, in part because of their use of the Oguz Turkish language, and also because of their adherence to the Orthodox Christian faith. Their fate was tied directly to the events of the Russo-Ottoman wars in the 18th and 19th centuries. The Gagauz people moved to the southern part of today's Moldova at the turn of the 19th century at the express call of the Russian authorities. The image of the Orthodox Tsar who had "rescued" them was very strong among their communities, and served to solidify their positive attitude toward Russian power. The events of the 20th century, therefore, resulted in dramatically different changes and living conditions for the Gagauz than they did for the Crimean Tatars.

The ethnic composition of former Bessarabia, which is the area between the Prut and Dniester Rivers, was significantly altered by tsarist Russian rule in the 19th century. The main factor in the development of ethnic diversity in the region was the migration from Ottoman territories organized by the tsarist administration. The Ottoman authorities, who had been put on a defensive footing as a result of a series of defeats in the 19th century, were less tolerant of non-Islamic peoples living on the Black Sea coast. Therefore, in addition to the Gagauz people, large numbers of Bulgarians from Ottoman territories settled in Bessarabia. Today, the majority of the Gagauz population live in Moldova, while the majority of the Bulgarian immigrant communities in Budjak are residents of Ukraine.

Against the grain: the Crimean Tatars

The ethnic identity of Crimean Tatars

At the heart of Crimean Tatar identity is a common sense of origin rooted in notions of legitimacy connected to the former Mongol Empire of Genghis Khan (Voitura, E. 2014). The legacy of Genghis Khan is an essential feature among the nomadic communities of the Eurasian steppe. It is also the basis of the hierarchy of origin even among the most distant (and westernmost) people, the Crimean Tatars. The khans, who lead the community, trace their lineage to Genghis Khan, the leader of a former nomadic state who united the most extensive area. Although Mongolians and Tatars are synonymous both in European public consciousness and in medieval sources, the Tatars are not identical to the Mongol tribes united by Genghis Khan. The Tatar language they speak, which is estimated to be spoken today by six to eight million people, belongs to the Turkish group of the Altai language family. Tatars became proponents of Islam in the 14th century when they came under the rule of the Golden Horde (one of the Mongolian state formations after the death of Genghis Khan). Inhabitants of the Crimean Tatar Khanate were very heterogeneous in terms of their origin. Before the establishment of the Khanate, various Turkish-speaking tribes from the north settled there, in addition to people of Greek and Roman origin, and Turkish Anatolian tribes (Aydıngün, I. and Aydıngün, A. 2007).

The Crimean Tatar Khanate was formed in the 15th century as the Mongol Empire of the Golden Horde disintegrated. Several factors played a role in shaping their specific identity, and in determining their separation from other Tatar communities. While other Tatar ethnic groups gradually became subordinate to tsarist Russia beginning in the 16th century, Crimean Tatars were taxpayers of the Ottoman Empire. In exchange for their military service, they enjoyed a high degree of internal autonomy in the organization of their communities up until the second half of the 18th century. As a result, in addition to their language and religion, some aspects of their traditional nomadic way of life, such as the military strength of their infamous cavalry and their fruit, grape, and tobacco growing — enterprises that strengthened their territorial ties — gave them a unique character. Their connection to the Ottoman Empire also ensured a degree of connection to European culture and to the innovative approaches of religion.

For centuries, Crimean Tatars were a formidable enemy of the Russian principalities to the north. They had raided these Russian territories many times. Because of their tremendous military strength, Crimean Tatars were often hired by the Russian principalities in their struggles against each other (Katchanovski, I. 2005). Tsarist Russia, which had durable central power and pursued an intensive expansionist policy, gradually reversed this situation, eventually occupying the Crimean Tatar Khanate in 1783 as part of one of the episodes of the Russo-Turkish wars. The Russian conquest resulted in negative changes in the lives of Crimean Tatars, and, as a result, their collective memory continues to be imprinted by this era.

Crimean Tatar territory, which includes the Crimea and part of the northern shores of the Black Sea, was of strategic importance to the new conquerors (Hellie, R. 2005). The ultimate goal of the "Greek Plan" to acquire the Black Sea was to occupy Istanbul (former Constantinople). This plan was reinforced by the widespread view among the power elites that the Russian tsars were the heirs of the Byzantine rulers. The idea of Byzantine (Roman) heritage came to life in the Russian quest for Crimean Tatar settlements, which were assigned classical names reminiscent of the Hellenistic past. The city of Akmechet, for example, became Simferopol, which is now the largest city in Crimea, and Akhitar became Sevastopol, a city made infamous during the Crimean War in the mid-19th century, and that continues to serve as the seat of the Russian Black Sea Fleet. Of the larger cities, only the capital of the Crimean Tatars, Bahchiserai in the southern part of Crimea, has retained the name given to it by the Tatars.

The number of Crimean Tatar communities declined sharply in the wake of the Russo-Turkish wars, as many people chose to migrate to areas that were under Ottoman rule. Migration and Russification efforts significantly changed the ethnic composition of the peninsula. By the beginning of the 20th century, the proportion of Crimean Tatars had fallen from 80% to 21% of the total population that had been present in the region in the middle of the 18th century (Fig. 2.3.1). The estimated number of emigrants was 1.8 million (Aydıngün, I. and Aydıngün, A. 2007). The remaining inhabitants of this area were able to maintain their relative cultural independence until the end of the 19th century, when positive changes in the lives of their communities began to occur. The Crimean Tatars, in fact, became an influential Islamic community in Russia, primarily because they were more open to European and Slavic culture and sought to adapt to changed conditions. Their 19th-century cultural reform efforts illustrated the strengthening of their national identity. These reforms and the national movements that followed them also spread to Muslim communities in the East. Their actions, presented below, achieved significant results even though their communities were limited in many ways by the forces of Russian centralization.

The national identity of Crimean Tatars

The idea of pan-Turkism emerged as a result of the cultural reform movement of the Crimean Tatar intelligentsia, mainly through the writing of Ismail Gaspirali (Ishmail Gasprinsky) in the 1880s. Although he focused on cultural renewal, education reform, and enlightenment in his work, he also articulated the need for "unity of language, faith, and deeds" of the Islamic Turkish peoples of Russia, which was the slogan of pan-Turkism. The need to unify different Turkish languages drove him in his novel linguistic work, in which he sought to minimize the pho-

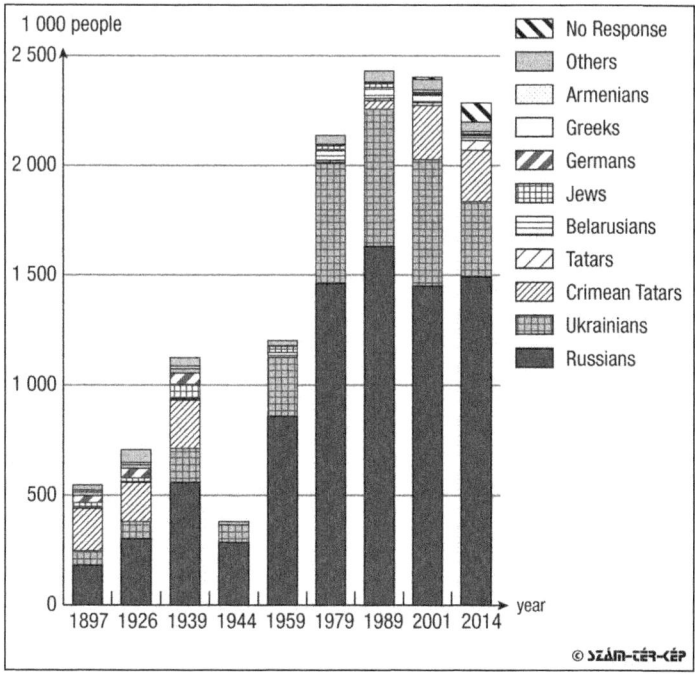

Figure 2.3.1 *Changes in the ethnic composition of Crimea (1850–2014) (Sources:* [10]; [26]; [29]; [38])

netic differences between different Turkish styles. In his journal *Tercüman* (Translator), he utilized a unified Turkish language that was understandable to all Turkish-speaking peoples in the Russian Empire, which resulted in the journal being distributed over a vast area.

In addition to reforming the teaching of the Arabic language, the new methodology developed by Gaspirali for renewing education also introduced a secular curriculum to schools beyond the borders of the empire, and not only in Turkish-speaking Islamic communities. Instead of embedding Arabic Quranic texts incomprehensible to students into the curriculum, Gaspirali's methodology introduced learning through interpretations of the Quran in the mother tongue. However, the tsarist administration did not allow the changes to take effect; the strengthening Russification efforts stood in the way of the benevolent transformation of Crimean Tatar education.

At the beginning of the 20th century, the idea of pan-Turkism was connected to pan-Islamism, which addressed all Muslim believers in Russia, and called for united action in support of their rights. However, these congresses initiated by the Crimean and Volga Tatars failed to create a unified program, and non-Turkish-speaking believers were indifferent to the initiative from the outset. Participants did not go any further in articulating the need for autonomy of the various peoples, which remained only empty words a few years after the communist takeover.

Following Lenin's establishment of the Soviet Federal Republic of Crimea, Crimean Tatars were able to exercise significant cultural autonomy rights. In the Stalinist era, Soviet centralization dominated from the 1930s onwards. Rights that had previously been granted were gradually curtailed, and Crimean Tatar communities were exposed to religious persecution. Anti-clerical measures resulted in the abolition of basic community-organizing institutions, the disintegration of community frameworks, and the complete loss of their previous achievements.

The defining moment in the collective memory of Crimean Tatars was the tragedy that befell the community during World War II, and which radically transformed their lives. At the outbreak of the war, Crimean Tatars fought alongside the soldiers of the Soviet army, and as a result, many became prisoners-of-war as the Nazi German army advanced during the opening stages of Operation Barbarossa, which was launched in June 1941. In their attempts to consolidate their military gains, the German occupiers mobilized non-Russian peoples to help them achieve their goals. It was in this light that Crimean Tatars were allowed to establish national institutions, and prisoners of war who were willing to cooperate with the Nazis were organized into a Crimean Tatar legion. After the Stalinist tribulations of the 1930s, there were many Crimean Tatars — and indeed other minorities in Russia — who regarded the Germans as liberators. Perhaps not surprisingly, they therefore agreed to cooperate with the Nazi occupiers. The Soviets renounced these prisoners of war as Nazi sympathizers, branding them as traitors, and thus making it impossible for them to return to their communities.

The accusations of treason cast by the Soviet leadership applied not only to actual collaborators, but also to the entire population of Crimean Tatars. Their punishment was deportation. Almost all non-Russian populations were removed from the Black Sea coast, including Crimean Tatars and Crimean natives, as well as Greeks, Bulgarians, and Kurds (Williams, B. G. 2002). Residents were herded into cattle cars and moved east. According to various estimates, the number of Crimean Tatars in 1944 was estimated to be approximately 180,000 to 200,000. Approximately 150,000 of these people were scattered among the various provinces of Uzbekistan, with the largest community in Tashkent being in excess of 50,000 people (Williams, B. G. 2002). A small number, approximately 30,000 mainly male prisoners of war, were deported to Siberia and the Urals. As a result of these deportations, the Crimean Tatar community was eliminated from Crimea.

The wartime deportees, who were primarily women, children, and the elderly, generally suffered a horrific fate. Many did not survive the journey of thousands of miles, while the survivors, who were referred to as the so-called "spec-settlers," lived in isolation and worked in industrial facilities (Williams, B. G. 2002). As a result of Stalinist propaganda, local Muslims viewed the new arrivals as enemies, though within a few years their shared faith and common cultural roots aided in the reconciliation process. There are devastating stories, for example, of locals who helped wounded and often mutilated veterans who had come in search of their wives, children, or parents (Uehling, G. 2001, Williams, B. G. 2002). Given the scale of the tragedy, however, many families never met again, while local Muslim men later adopted Crimean Tatar widows.

The first years after the deportation proved extremely difficult for Crimean Tatars, in part because of the unusual climate and their exposure to new diseases, but also as a result of the inhumane working conditions on industrial sites (Williams, B. G. 2002). For the predominantly rural population, who were previously engaged in agriculture, this new life required a radical change in their lifestyle. After leaving the "spec-settlements" (which was permitted in 1957), their integration into the community was not easy, despite a shared religion. The Central Asian Muslim communities they had been relocated to were much more traditional from a religious point of view, something which was was alien to the "Western" perspectives of the displaced Crimean Tatars (Uehling, G. 2001).

Following Stalin's death, deported peoples, which included Chechens, Ingush, Balkars, Karachays, and Kalmyks, were officially allowed to return home. In November 1956, a decision was made to restore the ethnic autonomy of these groups, but not of the Crimean Tatars. They were not very welcome at home. In 1954, in order to commemorate the 300th anniversary of the unification of Russia and Ukraine, Ukraine received the Crimea as a gift, and its politicians explicitly opposed the return of the Crimean Tatars. Only a fraction of them could return home after 1956, and so their share of the peninsula's population was only 1.5% on the eve of the regime change (Aydıngün, I. and Aydıngün, A. 2007). Between 1989 and 1995, however, the population grew from 35,000 to 260,000. According to the 1995 census, the proportion of Crimean Tatars within the whole population reached 10%. According to the 2014 census, with a population of just over 232,000 Tatars continue to account for 10% of the Crimean population (Fig. 2.3.2).

The national identity of Crimean Tatars, which had evolved in the 19th century and was the foundation for increasingly significant cultural achievements, fundamentally changed as a result of the deportations in 1943-44. Positive attitudes towards pan-Turkic and pan-Islamic aspirations disappeared. During the period spent in Central Asia, religious and linguistic ties lost their significance, and the territorial attachment to the homeland became a determining factor in Crimean Tatar identity (Aydıngün, I. and Aydıngün, A. 2007).

The ethnic nationalism of Crimean Tatars

Although Crimean Tatars could not return home, they nevertheless remembered the "Green Island" in their collective memory, and held annual commemorations on the day of the deportation. "Nothing is forgotten, nothing will be forgotten" became their motto (Williams, B. G. 2002). The changes of the last two decades of the 20th century also paved the way for them: in 1989, the repatriation of Crimean Tatars was officially allowed. Roughly 250,000 people (half of the community of nearly 500,000) chose the long trip. Decades of romantic daydreaming, however, ended in great disappointment (Uehling, G. 2000).

Born in Central Asia, the generation that has returned had never actually seen the Crimea prior to their repatriation. Far from being welcomed back, the returning Tatars were met with fierce resistance from the local communist nomenklatura, and destroyed villages (Uehling, G. 2000). Crimean Tatars were not allowed to settle on the south coast, which was previously densely populated, which is why their proportion in this region of Crimea is currently the lowest. As a result of their exclusion from Soviet collectivization, they were also unable to benefit from privatization in 1999 (Wilson, A. 2013). In addition to their economic, cultural, and political marginalization, they are also widely disliked. The xenophobia that they are subject to has resurrected old sayings and slander. Monuments and cemeteries have been desecrated, while Nazi swastikas and the word "traitors" dominate the graffiti in places associated with the Crimean Tatars (Voitura, E. 2014).

In 21st-century Crimean Tatar national identity, the image of stolen territory (the region where they lived before the deportation) represents the experience of the homeland. The 20th-century Russian aspirations and the ill-considered Soviet minority policy transformed the 19th-century movements for the legal experiments of the cultural community: they turned to violated nationalism, because of the lost homeland. Their return to the Crimea has resulted in their segregation, and they remain marginalized

Small Nations on the Black Sea

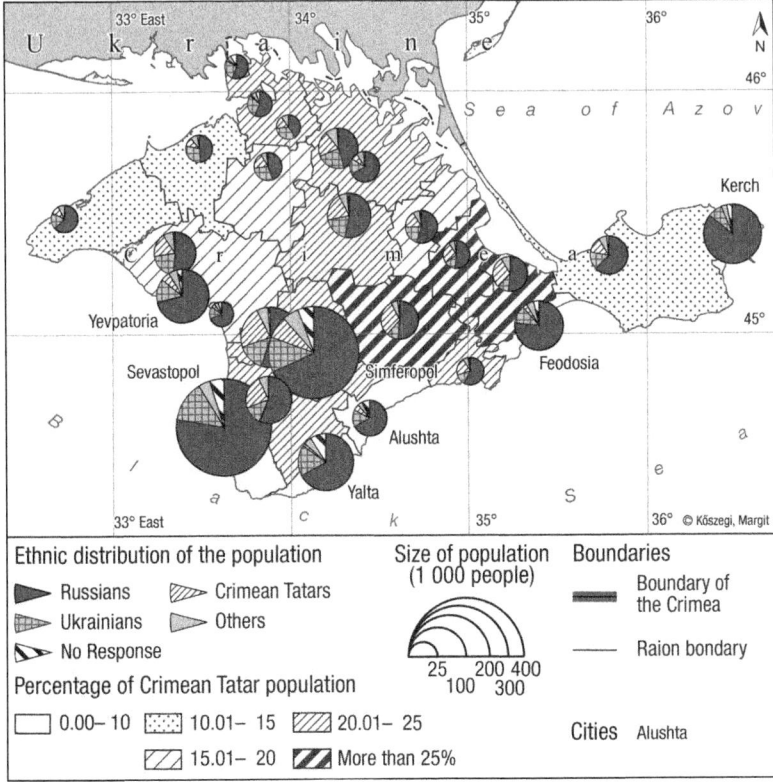

Figure 2.3.2 *The ethnic composition of the Crimean population by municipalities in 2014; (Source:* [10]*)*

among the Russian and Ukrainian majority. Their unclear legal, economic, and political situation in the state make peaceful coexistence impossible. Their future has been made even more precarious by the Russian annexation of the peninsula.

Under the protection of Big Brother: the Gagauzes

The ethnic identity of Gagauzes

Unlike the Crimean Tatars, the Gagauz population of nearly 200,000 on the northwest coast of the Black Sea is not as well known. Their most populous communities, totalling approximately 150,000 people, are located in Moldova, in the Autonomous Region of Gagauzia, and also in the Odessa region of Ukraine. According to the 2004

159

Moldovan census, Crimean Tatars, numbering 147,500, account for 4.4% of the total population. According to the 2001 Ukrainian census, nearly 32,000 people claimed to be Gagauz, with the most significant communities living in Budjak, which is part of the former region of Bessarabia. A smaller group of approximately 3,000 people is located in Bulgaria. Their common sense of origin, which forms the basis of their ethnic identity, is determined by the transmission of a mystical past; myths of origin that are obscured by legends. Their language is part of the Oguz Turkish group of the Altai language family, and their origins are disputed. Considered to be descendants of several Turkish peoples, they presumably entered the southeast corner of Europe in the wake of the Mongol conquests.

For Gagauz people, language and religion play an essential role in their identity. The Gagauz, unlike their Turkish-speaking relatives in the area, are Orthodox Christians. They lived on the western shores of the Black Sea for centuries, located mainly in the Dobruja (in Romanian Dobrogea) region, and as a result of Byzantine influence, they adopted the Orthodox faith in the Middle Ages. They were tolerated by the Ottoman Empire, as were other Christian peoples in the Balkans, but were subjected to special taxation, including the infamous child tax. The Gagauz language separated them from the other Christian communities in the Balkans, and their religion separated them from the Muslim subjects of the Ottoman Empire. This marginalized situation became critical in the 18th century when a series of Russian-Turkish wars broke out in the region. Given their strategic position and Russian propaganda aimed at activating Orthodox Christians living in the empire, the Ottoman leadership took a tougher stance against Gagauz communities. Ottoman concerns were not necessarily misplaced, as the Russian tsar referred to the Gagauz as the forward bastion of the Orthodox faith, even though they were not Slavs. After the Russian occupation of Bessarabia, the Russian Empire offered them lands in the newly conquered territory. As their situation worsened in the Ottoman Empire, a significant proportion of the community chose to emigrate, and thus came under Russian rule at the turn of the 18th and 19th centuries.

As a result of this history, the ethnic identity of the Gagauz people took a peculiar turn. The population remaining in Dobruja after the Ottomans were driven from the Balkans had to face the negative attitude of Bulgarian nationalism that prevailed in the 20th century after the Ottomans were driven from the Balkans. The Gagauz people were different from the majority of society, not in their faith, but because of their language, which was of Turkish origin. In the first half of the 20th century, the official Bulgarian position favoured the principle voiced by the Pomaks, according to which these communities were in fact inherited Bulgarians who had to be "returned" to their original identity (Brunnbauer, U. 2002). Because of their language, the Gagauz people were targets of Bulgarian national sentiment in later decades. In an effort to avoid discrimination, older generations adopted an assimilationist lingustic strategy that had become commonplace among young people in Bulgarian schools. As the use of Bulgarian became more and more widespread among them, their mother tongue waned (Kvilinkova, E. 2013). The assimilation of their population of 10,000 into the majority society continued into the 21st century, and was intensified as a result of globalization.

As new inhabitants of Bessarabia, the identity of Gagauz communities developed differently. Their Turkish language and Orthodox religion which followed the Byzantine Greek rite was not a source of tension with other people in the area, but it did signal a cultural dissimilarity from the others. Gagauz communities approached the Orthodox liturgy in religious life and in writing, but they were able to carry on their mother tongue undisturbed (Kvilinkova, E. 2013). Their small rural communities became the basis of their identity in later decades, and they continue to be inhabitants of rural settlements to this day (Katchanovski, I. 2005).

The national identity of Gagauzes

The experience of the new homeland for the Gagauz people in Bessarabia was connected to the Russian state and to the power exerted by their Russian hosts. For the Gagauz people, the Russian tsar provided a space for their interests, thereby legitimating their national identity. The period of Russian rule between 1812 and 1918 provided decades of calm and independence for Gagauz communities and resulted in a positive attachment to the Russian leadership in the collective memory of the Gagauz people. Subsequent events reinforced these positive feelings, ones that were later applied to the Soviet Union. After the First World War, the territory of Bessarabia became part of Romania, and thus the Gagauz homeland was effectively transferred to a new "owner". This "Romanian period", which lasted from 1918 to 1940, resulted in a marked change in their situation. They did not matter, nor did they factor into the evolving Romanian national identity. The Romanian state put the Moldovans, who they considered to be of Romanian nationality, in the foreground. In the Soviet Socialist Republic of Moldova, which was created after 1940 from almost the entire territory of former Bessarabia, the majority nationality found itself in a challenging position. Stalin, who played the "nationality card" successfully against his opponents, strengthened the rights of the Gagauz people in order to weaken the Moldovans.

The Gagauz were spared the deportations ordered by the Soviet leadership at the end of World War II, and so for them, the negative collective experience that is remembered as part of their identity is not related to this event, but rather to the discriminatory measures the Gagauz suffered in Romania in the interwar period. The hardship they endured after their territory was reclaimed by the Soviet Union, and in particular, the famine that ravaged Moldova, was not blamed on the Soviet state, but rather was seen as a negative consequence of the war itself. As a result of the above mentioned Stalinist partition policy, the situation for the Gagauz people improved, even though Moldova remained one of the most backward federal republics in the Soviet Union (Crowther, W. 1991).

The borders that divide Bessarabia separate some Gagauz communities from other communities in Moldova. Gagauz people living in the Odessa region of Ukraine, including Budjak, also had a positive view of the Soviet regime. According to a 1995 survey, 35% of Gagauz people declared themselves to be residents of the Soviet Union, while 22% regarded themselves as Gagauz, and only 12% indicated they were citizens of independent Ukraine (Katchanovski, I. 2005).

Given the nature of Gagauz collective memory, the positive attitude towards the Russian leadership is of paramount importance to their national feeling. The existence of their common homeland has been confirmed throughout history by the tsarist Russian administration, Soviet power, and most recently the Russian state, which provided assistance to the Gaguz after the regime change. A sense of friendship with the Russians, coupled with their nostalgia for the Soviet state framework, renders the Gaguz unique within the region. Their friendly relationship with the Russians, which is reflected in election results, is fueled by neighbouring Russia in every possible way, most notably through concerted propaganda campaigns. The growing use of Russian alongside their mother tongue in recent decades is an obvious result of their positive attitude towards the Russian people and the former Soviet system. However, economic coercion sometimes overrides the orientation dictated by national feelings. In the migration from highly disadvantaged rural areas, specifically for employment opportunities, the direction arising from linguistic relations can also be observed. It is evident, for example, in the tendency among Gagauz women to look for employment as domestic workers in Turkey (Keough, L. J. 2006).

The ethnic nationalism of the Gagauz people

Following the transition, and even after 2000, the positive attitude of the Gagauz people towards Russia and the former Soviet Union remained. Investigations into election results confirmed that Russian friendship as well as nostalgia for communism permeated their communities (Katchanovski, I. 2005). In a 1991 referendum, 83% of Gagauz people in Moldova supported membership in the Soviet Union. The proportion in Transnistria was 93% (Katchanovski, I. 2005). According to a survey conducted just before the turn of the millennium, Gagauz affinity with Russia surpassed even that of the Russian population in Moldova, where 58% of respondents supported the joint government with Russia, compared to 43% of the Russian population (Katchanovksi, I. 2005).

With a territory of just 34,000 km² and a population of 3.5 million, Moldova neverthess decided on independence after the collapse of the Soviet Union. As a result, its territory was torn apart by separatist forces. The Russian influence remained stable in the de facto independent Transnistria (Pridnestrovian Moldavian Republic). Like people in Transnistria, during the turmoil of the 1980s, the Gagauz people also defended their rights, which resulted in the creation of an autonomous territory in southern Moldova in the early 1990s (King, C. 1993). In 1990, the Gagauz people boycotted the creation of an independent Moldova and proclaimed the Soviet Socialist Republic of Gagauz. In December of the following year, a census in the area decided in favour of Gagauzia's independence. The Moldovan leadership was only able to prevent civil war in the region by establishing a military presence, in which the Transnistrian leaders also played a role (Katchanovski, I. 2005). An agreement was finally arrived at in 1994, with the creation of the Gagauz Autonomous Region (Gagauz Yeri, Gagauzia) (Fig. 2.3.3). In addition to gaining autonomy, the Gagauz people, who live in deep poverty, also reserve the right to declare their independence and their intention to join the Russian Federation in the event of the unification of Moldova and Romania, or in the event of Moldova's accession to the European Union.

The "shelter" of the Balkan Slavs: Bulgarians in Budjak

Breaking away from the emerging nation

The efforts of the former Russian Empire to settle Christian peoples living in the Ottoman Empire on the shores of the Black Sea — the so-called *Novorossiya* — was a long process that played out over several centuries. After a long series of Russian-Turkish wars spanning centuries, Russia's territorial demand for the Black Sea, and even for its largest city, Istanbul (Constantinople), had become increasingly apparent. The fact that the Russian state considered itself the heir of Byzantium, and at the same time, of the Roman Empire, was demonstrated through the renaming of settlements, and the

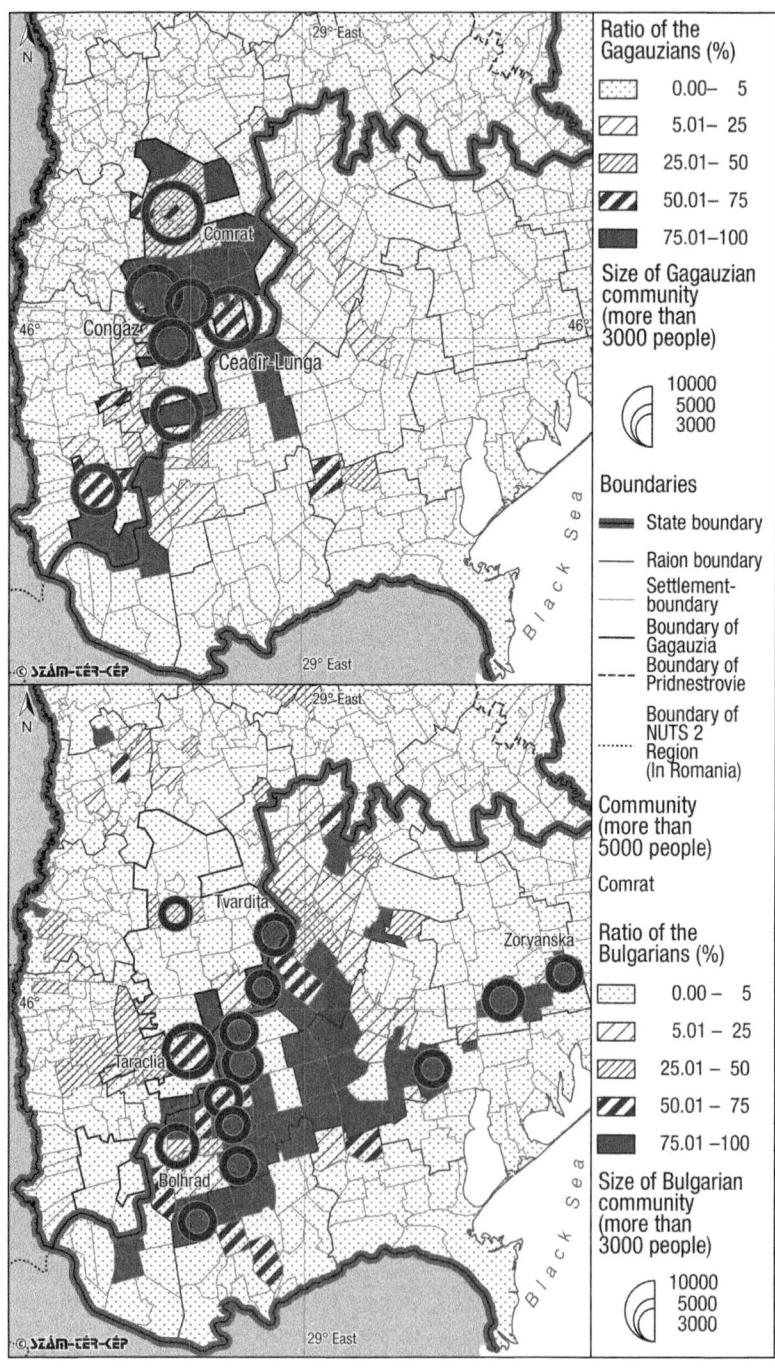

Figure 2.3.3 *The proportion of Gagauz inhabitants and their larger communities in Budjak and Moldova 2001/2014; (Sources:* [21]; [22]; [38]*)*

assigning of Greek-sounding names to newly founded cities such as Odessa and Kherson. With the territory conquered from the Ottomans as a result of the wars, *Novorossiya* became increasingly expansive along the Black Sea (Heller, M. 1996). Christian peoples living in the territory of the Ottoman Empire were called the "forward bastions" of the Orthodox religion in government rhetoric. The Russian authorities saw them as a means of taking action against the Ottomans, so they tried to win them over. One element of this was to provide them with refuge from the threatening Islamic power. It also meant a strengthened border region on the frontier with the Ottomans.

In the early 18th century, the tsarist administration provided land in *Novorossiya* for Christian soldiers from the Balkans, primarily as recognition for their military service. The consequent small-scale immigration into the southern territories of the empire changed during the reign of Catherine II, with the Peace Treaty of Küçük Kaynarca in 1774. The Russian ruler officially gained the status of protector of Orthodox Christians living in the territory of the Ottoman Empire, which provided an opportunity to increase the intensity of relocations. Several soldiers from Balkan ethnic groups who had fought with the Russians in the multi-year war settled in the newly-acquired lands. The Russian–Turkish wars continued for centuries, and all peace agreements were followed by significant Christian immigration into the Black Sea areas of the Russian Empire. One of the most significant waves of migration followed the treaty of Bucharest, which ended the war that had raged between 1806 and 1812. According to this treaty, Russia occupied Bessarabia, where more than 4,000 Bulgarian families had settled, most of whom had assisted in one way or another in the Russian war effort (Bitis, A. 2005). The tsarist leadership saw the economic benefits of Bulgarian peasant families who had arrived in Budjak, which had previously been inhabited by the Tatars (Fig. 2.3.4).

The number of Bulgarians living under Russian rule also increased in the 19th century, during the reign of Nicholas I. In 1829, a small number of Bulgarians, as well as Greek immigrants, were settled directly on the Black Sea littoral. But the majority of Bulgarians were settled in Bessarabia. More than half of the nearly 50,000 Bulgarian immigrants eventually migrated back to independent Bulgaria in the second half of the 19th century. Their dissatisfaction with the quantity and quality of the land received in Bessarabia did

Figure 2.3.4 *The proportion of Bulgarians inhabitants and their larger communities in Budjak and Moldova 2001/2014 (Sources:* [21]; [22]; [38]*)*

not correspond to what they felt they were promised (Bitis, A. 2005). The more self-conscious members of the community returned to the confines of their nascent nation-state.

Under the temporary protection of ethnicity

Bulgarian inhabitants of Budjak lived almost exclusively in rural areas and engaged in traditional agricultural activities. Far from the noise of the world, preserving their traditional linguistic and cultural frameworks, they were even left out of the Bulgarian nation-building process, and managed to adapt to the changes introduced by a central power far away from them, thus preserving their identity. This state of affairs persisted until World War II, when the violence of war swept through their territory, changing their previous life.

At the end of World War II, the people living on the shores of the Black Sea were judged to be collectively guilty, and the deportations carried out as punishment did not spare them. Having once been protected by the Russian state, the Bulgarians of the Budjak region were treated cruelly by the Soviets, so much so that the Russian-dominated state relocated their Slavic relatives not to their former homeland, but to remote areas in Central Asia. Based on conflicting sources, it is difficult to say how much the deportations affected Bulgarian communities. It can be stated that not everyone in the community was affected by the deportation. Bulgarians living closer to the coast were the primary victims of Stalin's purges. In this area of strategic importance, increasing the Russian population was the main goal of Stalin's Soviet policy, which was pursued at the expense of Bulgarian communities (Williams, B. G. 2002). The tragic events of the 20th century drastically reduced the numbers of ethnic Bulgarians in the region, and by the 21st century their population was a fraction of what it had been in the previous two centuries. The assimilation of their small communities into the Ukrainian and Russian majority has accelerated since the late 20th century. According to the 2001 Ukrainian census, nearly 205,000 Bulgarians lived in Ukraine, of which 151,000 were located in the Odessa region (Fig. 2.3.5).

Summary

Nationalist aspirations in Europe's post-Soviet regions have standard features that outline a characteristically post-Soviet nationalism. Behind the common traits, the most dominant is Russian nationalism, which has had the greatest social potential, and as the

Figure 2.3.5 *Linguistic composition of the population of Budjak 2001/2004; (Sources:* [20]; [38])

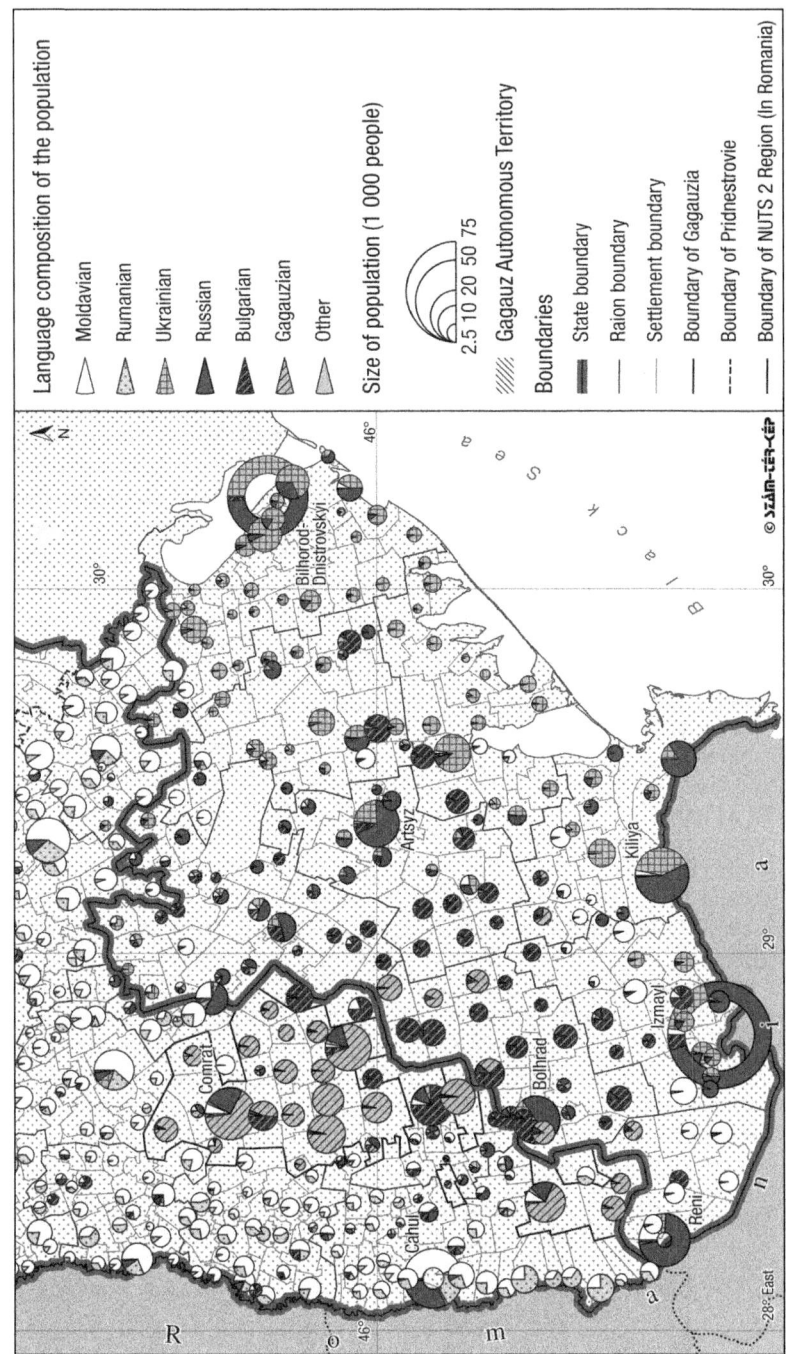

holder of power in the region over centuries, was the main driver of events that determine collective memory. It feeds at the same time on previous tsarist imperial aspirations and the subsequent Soviet mission to save the peoples.

Over time, Russian politics has had a marked influence on the identity of the peoples living in the region. The Soviet policy of *korenizatsiya* helped especially to strengthen the national consciousness of small groups of people. Soviet policies reinforced nationalist aspirations, which have, in turn, generated ethnic-nationalist conflicts in the region.

For the Crimean Tatar community, the rule of Russian tsars meant both the loss of independence and the opportunity to encounter modern European ideas and cultural influences. As a part of the Soviet Union, the Crimean Autonomous Soviet Socialist Republic provided an opportunity for the formation of Crimean Tatar national identity in the first part of the 20th century. But the deportations during World War II, coupled with the abolition of the autonomous territory and its annexation to the Ukrainian SSR, drastically changed the positions of Crimean Tatars. Because of these events their collective attachment to their homeland became the most important feature of their national identity in the 21st century.

In the case of the Gagauz people, the tsarist Empire was the source of their collective homeland, which resulted in a positive attitude towards the Russian authorities. Soviet central power strengthened the position of the Gagauz in the Moldavian Soviet Socialist Republic. It is perhaps no surprise, then, that Gagauz national sentiment stresses ties to the Russian leadership, even in the 21st century. In simple terms, they see Russia as a primary defender of their autonomy. Their particular dependence is given a distinctly positive place in their identity, so the pro-Russian nature of their nationalism has meant a separation from, and also a source of conflict with, the Moldovans, who are the majority national group in the region.

In the case of the Bulgarian communities along the Black Sea, which were left untouched by the nation-building process in the Balkans, ethnic segregation proved to be stronger than territorial and national ties. Groups that managed to survive the vicissitudes of World War II locally have remained loyal citizens of the Ukrainian nation-state in the 21st century.

Living on the Edge: The Origins and Evolution of the Kalmyk Ethno-Religious Enclave along the Southern Russian Frontier

Tamás Illés

The Kalmyks are most often referred to as the only Buddhist group within Europe, but their history has also served as one of the most dramatic examples of collective guilt under Stalin. At the turn of the millennium, however, Kalmykia owes its reputation primarily to its eccentric leader, Kirsan Ilyumzhinov. Known for his brash and often colourful personality, Ilyumzhinov once reportedly stated that: "A wealthy president is a safeguard against corruption" (The Guardian 2006). He has also declared: "If the People need a Khan, then I will be that" (Birtalan Á; Rákos A. 2002: 20). Beyond exploring these newsworthy pronouncements, this chapter will focus on the key events that led to the establishment and survival of this Mongolian population near the Caspian Sea. It will also consider the processes that contributed to the institutionalization of the present-day, ethnically defined Republic of Kalmykia, as part of the Russian Federation.

Secession and settling down

Kalmyk history coincides with the origin of the Oirat people, whose homeland was located in the southern part of the Eurasian forest belt, stretching between Lake Baikal and the headwaters of the Yenisei River (Birtalan Á. and Rákos A. 2002). During the reign of Genghis Khan and the rise of the Mongol Empire, the Oirats were still at a low level of social cohesion and mostly lived in forests (Lee, J-Y. 2016). Before migrating to the steppe, their semi-nomadic hunter-gatherer lifestyle distinguished them from equestrian nomad groups. By the 14th century, the Oirats had transformed into a community with a strong tribal system, which was capable of maintaining a balance of power in the region in opposition to the successors of Genghis Khan (that is, the Genghisids). Despite belonging to the broadly-understood Mongolian languages, their geographical location did not make the Oirats a western Mongol community. This distinctiveness was manifested over the course of three centuries of constant warfare between the Northern Yuan Khaganate (i.e. the Mongolian state organization displaced from the Chinese imperial throne) and Oirats, which goes beyond the oversimplification of a conflict between eastern and western Mongols (Lee, J-Y. 2016). Due to their relatively weaker position, the Ming Dynasty favored the Oirats. However, the Oirat tribes were engaged in inner conflicts as well over the dominance of the pastures. Not surprisingly, the entire population (roughly 200,000 to 250,000 people) of one of the Oirat tribes, the Torghut, emigrated in several waves during the early 17th century to the lower reaches of the Volga River (Birtalan Á. and Rákos A. 2002). The main reason for the mass exodus is debated among historians. The most likely explanation is that the sudden western emigration was driven by the desire for new, and thus larger, pastures (Perdue, P. C. 2005).

Bringing Mongol military tactics and organization with them, the arrival of the Torghut people was not met with enthusiasm from the local Nogai Tatars, who had been gradually squeezed to the foreground of the Caucasus, and towards the Crimean Khanate (Khodarkovsky, M. 2004). The Russian tsars were more likely to see the emergence of the Oirat ethnic group, which they referred to as the Kalmyks, to be like the Cossacks. As a result, they strove to bind them to the empire by military alliance (Perdue, P. C. 2005). The Russians did not have the necessary resources to stabilize the region of the Caspian Sea. However, securing trade lines with China was in the interest of the emerging Russian economy. As G. Kendirbai (2008: 265) puts it eloquently, rather than describing frontier politics in terms of domination/submission or divide and rule, the tsars felt more inclined to establish a pragmatic patronage system compatible with the nomads' extensive land use, thus contributing to the emergence of a relatively porous buffer zone along the Central Asian frontier (Kendirbai, G. 2018). Kalmyks needed Russian trading capacity as well as support against the intensifying Kazakh invasions. This less than harmonious interdependence led to the establishment of Kalmyk control over a vast territory, stretching from the Ural River to the Don, and from Tsaritsyn (later Stalingrad, now known as Volgograd) to the foot of the Caucasus, in a north-south direction (Grousset, R. 1970). As a further benefit of the long-standing interdependency, Peter the Great formally acknowledged the khanate in 1664, when approximately 270,000 Kalmyk people enjoyed the trust of the tsar (Grin, E. 2000). In exchange for their combat services, Kalmyks received autonomy, tax exemptions, and free trade rights, while the tsars sought to ensure the khans' allegiance by bestowing various honours and generous gifts (Kendirbai, G. 2018).

With Russian power increasing over the southern peripheries, the Kalmyk khans' tendency towards self-governance had become a serious obstacle to the empire's planned extension. Successive tsars tightened conditions for military cooperation, and over time, began to treat Kalmyks as subordinates, and even as an irregular part of the Russian army (in a way very similar to the Don Cossacks) (Khodarkovsky, M. 2004). By 1718, the so-called Tsaritsyn Fortified Line had been built up between the Don and Volga Rivers, cutting off the Kalmyks from their summer grazing areas. Thus, it was not only trade that came under Russian control, but also the free pastureland upon which the nomadic lifestyle depended, and which had become threatened from almost every direction. From the west, the expanding Don Cossacks, from the east escalating Kazakh raids, and from the south the heavily populated Caucasian region together constricted the Kalmyk autonomy, though to a lesser extent. The idea of a homogeneous Kalmyk space was also challenged by immigration from Russian and Cossack territories (Birtalan Á. and Rákos A. 2002). These increasingly hostile circumstances triggered a desire to move back to the homeland. However, because the Dzungar Khanate was in constant battle with the Kazakhs and the Manchu Qing Dynasty that came to power in China, the conditions for this were not favorable (Perdue, P. C. 2005).

The relationship between the Oirats who remained in Dzungaria, and the Kalmyks who moved to the lower Volga region, was facilitated by related ecclasiastical affairs, since the Tibetan branch of Buddhism was considered to be the predominant faith of both groups. Mongolian leaders regarded Buddhism as indispensable for the restoration of the mighty empire of Genghis Khan, which they believed would eventually reunify the rival Mongol tribes (Kitinov, B. U. 2016). The Tibetan-Mongol alliance was not only the result of a constellation of certain historical circumstances, but was also firmly established by the extension of the Dalai Lama's politico-religious power over Tibet, which was overwhelmingly supported by Oirat tribes.

The Lama also gave Oirat leaders the title of Khan (as the great protector of the religion), which previously had only been extended to Genghisids on the basis of blood (Birtalan Á. and Rákos A. 2002). It is not surprising, therefore, that during the 17th and 18th centuries all of the Kalmyk leaders sought to obtain a seal of authority from the Tibetan religious leadership (Bormanshinov, A. 1998). No matter how long the pilgrimage to Lhasa took, in the eyes of the Kalmyk subjects, earning a superior spiritual authorization invalidated any appointments made by the Russian tsars (Kitinov, B. U. 2016). Kalmyk-Tibetan relationships began to deteriorate from the mid-18th century onward, however, due to the harassment of pilgrims by Russian and Chinese authorities (Bormanshinov, A. 1998). Hence, living on the edge of both Europe and Asia, the Kalmyks found themselves caught between two realms as the Oirat relatives also moved further and further away from each other symbolically (Kendirbai, G. 2018).

Integration into the Tsarist framework of nationalism

As a result of power negotiations along the Russian Empire's frontier, Kalmykia evolved into a peculiar territorial entity. Yet the fragile status quo had been threatened seriously as the Tsaritsyn Fortified Line shifted further to the south with the emergence of Russia's expansive endeavors. This act necessarily caused the depletion of livestock, which served as the primary source of income for the Kalmyk population. Looking for other means of subsistence, a significant proportion of Kalmyks settled in nearby Russian cities (Khodarkovsky, M. 2004). The worst, however, was yet to come. Catherine the Great's excessive demands for military service during the Russo-Turkish wars proved to be the last straw for the Kalmyks. Taking advantage of the Russian army's engagement against the Ottoman Empire, Ubashi Khan decided to resettle in Central Asia with 150,000 to 170,000 Kalmyks (roughly three-quarters of the whole population) (Perdue, P. C. 2005). At that time, the Volga was a dividing line as roughly three-quarters of the Kalmyks were living east of the river, with the others basically on the western side of it. In January 1771, Ubashi had been waiting for the Volga to freeze in the hope of joining Kalmyks from the eastern bank of the river, but in the meantime the Russian governor of Astrakhan had been informed about the planned expatriation. Hence an earlier departure had to be settled upon. The rest, however, remained in place for such prosaic reasons. Known as the last great Eurasian exodus, this journey ended disastrously due to epidemics, raids by Kazakh tribes, and persecution by Russian authorities who were provoked by illegal desertions (Grousset, R. 1970). The approximately 50,000 survivors found refuge in China, where they were welcomed by Emperor Qianlong of the Manchu Qing dynasty. This was the same emperor whose name is associated with the so-called Dzungar genocide, which has been identified by historian Mark Levene as "the eighteenth-century genocide par excellence" (2008, p. 183). Although the Manchu leaders made room for the Kalmyks, they were settled hundreds of kilometers apart in areas of Xinjiang, currently the westernmost and largest area of China, that had been depopulated as a result of the genocide (Perdue, P. C. 2005). Guided by rigid geopolitical considerations, the story can also be interpreted as old Oirats replaced by new, obedient ones.

The unexpected exodus urged the surprised Russian authorities, who identified the sudden demographic vacuum as threatening to southern border protection, to take more aggressive steps toward centralization. To this end, the Kalmyk steppes were integrated administratively into the Muslim-majority Astrakhan governorate, while the Russian legal system was extended to the 11,000 Kalmyk households remaining in the empire, and the colonization of Kalmykia with peasants from inland Russian territories intensified (Khodarkovsky, M. 2004).

The subsequent period brought some easing of tsarist rigidity as Kalmykia once again enjoyed some level of subsidiarity. However, with the emergence of a modern absolute monarchy from the mid-19th century, Kalmykia — similar to other areas in Russia — lost all its former privileges and became fully integrated into the highly centralized state administration (Maksimov, K. N. 2008). As a result of these measures, the social hierarchy of the Kalmyks, which was based on kinship and a relatively stable tribal system, began to unravel (Birtalan Á. and Rákos A. 2002). Acculturation was also forced by Russification under the guise of religious freedom, whereby the Kalmyks who converted to Christianity became free peasants, and were eligible for state benefits (Maksimov, K. N. 2008). Although local Buddhist clergy suffered from centralization policies as well, the Dalai Lama enjoyed at least as much symbolic power as the reigning Russian authorities (Kitinov, B. U. 2016).

The first and only census in the Russian Empire was held in 1897. Census data concerning the distribution of native tongues indicates that the Kalmyk Steppe uyezd (which was part of the Astrakhan governorate) was inhabited by almost 129,000 people, 95.3% and 97.4% of whom considered themselves to be Kalmyk and Buddhist respectively. The data also show that practically no Kalmyk inhabitants within the Astrakhan governorate lived in any of the cities, which, in spite of tsarist endeavors, was the consequence of the persistent dominance of traditional nomadic herding (Richardson, C. 2002). Although even at the time of the 1897 census social engineering played a crucial role in the formation and delimitation of ethnic groups, the following period, which was determined by Sovietization policies, had a more profound impact on the acceleration of this process.

Institutionalization of the Kalmyk identity

Initially, Soviet ideologists discredited the idea of nation-states based on ethnicity, as these were regarded as the result of a capitalist, and thus temporary, stage of production. However, the realpolitik of the early Bolshevik period did not enforce Marxist theory, but instead created regional autonomies in order to gain the support of the peasantry and non-Russian nationalities, thus making Soviet Russia the first modern state to base its federal system on the basis of the social category of nation (Suny, R. G. 1993). Following this principle, in 1935, Kalmykia obtained its republic status in the form of the Kalmyk Autonomous Soviet Socialist Republic (KASSR). With this generous move, the party leadership simultaneously institutionalized ethnic autonomy, and made a gesture toward the

Kalmyk people, who, because of their origin, were thought to be a useful ally in mobilizing the Mongolian peoples for the forthcoming proletarian world revolution (Maksimov, K. N. 2008).

The Soviet leadership designated national regions and divided them into two groups: 1) less developed territories and 2) territories where "bourgeois" nationalism and "mature" social classes were already present. Regions taking part of the former category — encompassing all the 97 ethnic groups apart from Russians, Germans, Jews, Ukrainians, Georgians, and Armenians — had also been treated as culturally backward, justifying the need for immediate interventions (Martin, T. 2001). In the Marxist reading of historical epochs, nationalism was seen as an undesirable, yet inevitable, catalyst for moving societies from the feudal order, through the capitalist stage of development, to the coveted end goal of socialism and communism (Hirsch, E. 2005). Thus, Soviet nationalities, even without having any common attributes with modern nationalisms, promised a more appropriate starting point than tribal categories did, because the communist-evolutionist approach interpreted the nation as a post-feudal phase closer to socialism.

The new cultural policy launched during the Leninist era was referred to as *korenizatsiya*. Reversing tsarist practices of Russification, the policy aimed not only to strengthen the language, education, and culture of ethnic majorities within the autonomous regions, but also to enhance the political power of local elites. However, in many places, the implementation of *korenizatsiya* was hampered by the almost complete lack of white-collar workers and, in a broader sense, nationalist intellectuals (Martin, T. 2001). In the case of Kalmykia, for instance, it remained difficult for the local administration to translate Russian texts into the so-called Clear Script vertical script, which was created in 1648 by the Buddhist monk Zaya Pandita, who is now venerated as a national hero. In light of the difficulties, Kalmyk intellectuals opted unilaterally for the Cyrillic script. *Korenizatsiya* also gave further impetus to the development of local educational infrastructure, which reinforced a person's ethnic self-determination. The results spoke for themselves. While in 1913 there were 31 schools attended by 302 students in Kalmykia, by 1939 these numbers had risen to 674 and 44,000 respectively (Richardson, C. 2002). Accordingly, levels of literacy among the Kalmyk population increased from 2.6% to 59.2% between 1897 and 1939 (Statiev, A. 2005).

Favorable cultural processes could not offset the severe material and human losses caused by the First World War and the subsequent Russian Civil War. During this period, livestock, which was the main source of livelihood in Kalmykia, decreased by 87%, and the droughts of 1921–1922 almost resulted in a widespread famine (Maksimov, K. N. 2008). Negative population growth was also exacerbated both by the low natural increase in population that had already been observed in the tsarist period, as well as by the forced migration of thousands of Kalmyks fighting the Bolsheviks (Richardson, C. 2002). Not surprisingly, the 1926 census showed that just over 107,000 Kalmyks were registered in Kalmykia, as their share fell to 75.6%. Moreover, the number of Kalmyks living outside the KASSR declined to 22,000 (Fig. 2.4.1). This showed that the geographical distribution of the Kalmyks had become more concentrated, in accordance with the efforts of top-down social engineering.

In the Soviet Union, the desire to "purify" society (which was not foreign to the West, see, for example, the popularity of eugenics) entered a new phase beginning in the 1930s. In a speech delivered in 1934, Stalin openly blamed nationalist views, and the ethnicization of Soviet society, for the delay in the realization of the communist utopia and its world revolution (Weiner, A. 1999). This marked a new turn in Soviet nationality politics. Suddenly, at the expense of minority rights, Russian nationalism — marking a continuity with the tsarist era — became a central element of cultural policy. Despite the state's abandoning of *korenizatsiya*, the legacy of its policies continued to provide a coherent and far-reaching framework for national revival along ethnic lines, the results of which could not be abolished even by Stalinist terror (Suny, R. G. 1993). Furthermore, the possible rise of capitalism in the peripheries

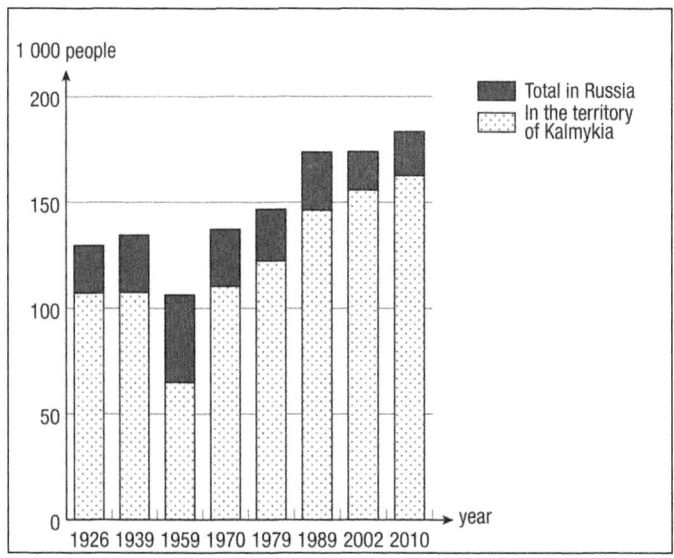

Figure 2.4.1 *The change in the number of Kalmyks between 1897 and 2010; (Sources:* [25]; [26])

generated concern among the Soviet leadership, which in turn led to mass deportations of "dangerous elements", paradoxically fueling the group-consciousness of ethnic minorities even further (Martin, T. 2001). In Kalmykia, the decline in the proportion of the titular ethnicity to 48.6% in the period between the 1926 and 1939 censuses was clearly related to the eradication of the kulaks (Maksimov, K. N. 2008). However, the true trials of the Kalmyks' unique story came only afterwards.

German occupation of western regions of the Soviet Union during World War II provided Stalin with an ideal opportunity to expel social groups suspected of collaboration against Soviet society based on the principle of collective guilt. Thus, deportations informed by the ideology of purification not only targeted certain social classes of the border regions, but also affected all stigmatized ethnicities (Weiner, A. 1999). According to contemporary records, most of the Kalmyk people remained faithful to Moscow during the German occupation, though the presence of some level of cooperation with the Nazis (which hardly differed from the local Russian population's attitude) provided Stalin with sufficient evidence to support a further step towards a purified Soviet society (Nekrich, A. M. 1978, Statiev, A. 2005). Shortly thereafter, within a few weeks in December 1943, the whole Kalmyk population was deported to Siberia. The NKVD (the People's Commissariat for Internal Affairs, which was responsible for the deportation) reported that 93,000 Kalmyk civilians were relocated along with 23,000 Kalmyk soldiers who had been withdrawn from the battlefield and transported to Siberia (Grin, E. 2000). While 1,300 people had already lost their lives in the cattle wagons, 20 to 30% of the settled population (ranging from the Urals to Sakhalin, predominantly in the Far East) died during the exile (Pohl, J. O. 2000). KASSR itself was dissolved, the names of the towns were Russianized, and primarily Russians were settled in the almost totally deserted area. Despite these massive atrocities, Guchinova (2005) has pointed out that, rather than embracing a perspective of victimization, expelled Kalmyk people perceived their years of exile to be almost tolerable under the circumstances.

Unfolding de-Stalinization marked a turning point for the Kalmyks as they had the opportunity to move back to the re-established KASSR. However, mitigating measures towards the ethnic groups did not mark the resolution of the national question in the Soviet Union. On the contrary, the concept of social class became so irrelevant for central administration that no matter how outdated the national approach was considered, it remained the basis of social engineering (Brubaker, R. 1994). Thus, though with softer methods, Russian as the cultural fabric of the national communities continued to receive special attention. One tangible sign of this endeavor was that Russian became the language of instruction in all schools of the Soviet Union by the end of the 1970s. After such a centralized cultural agenda, it is not surprising that the use of the Kalmyk language has been increasingly overshadowed. In 1985, 93% of Kalmyk people living in urban areas, and 87.2% of those living in the countryside, were able to speak, write, and read Russian. The corresponding figures for their ancestral language was only 27.3% and 45.8%, respectively (Tishkov, V. 1997). The lack of literary traditions and the higher social prestige of the Russian language has resulted in a further decline of the Kalmyk language.

According to 1989 census data, Kalmyk ethnic affiliation has also been losing ground, as just 146,000 people defined themselves as such (45.5% of the population), while 121,000 Russians (37.7% of the whole) were found in the KASSR. However, the two censuses that followed marked a dynamic increase in the numbers of titular ethnicity, and an enormous decline among Russians (Fig. 2.4.2). The 163,000 people surveyed in the Republic of Kalmykia in 2010 accounted for 88.7% of the Kalmyk population within the Russian Federation. Ethnic distribution in Kalmykia reflects the general migration trends of the Soviet Union. Russians and other nationalities tend to be concentrated in cities, while titular ethnicities dominate rural spaces (Figure 2.4.3).

The most tangible sign of the national renewal of the Kalmyk people today is undoubtedly religious. The burgeoning practice of Buddhism is all the more remarkable if we take into account

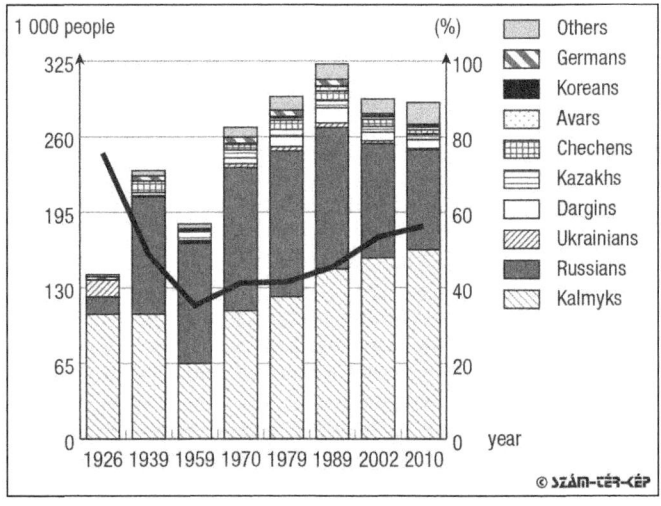

Figure 2.4.2 *The change in the ethnic composition and population of Kalmykia between 1926 and 2010; (Sources:* [25]; [26]*)*

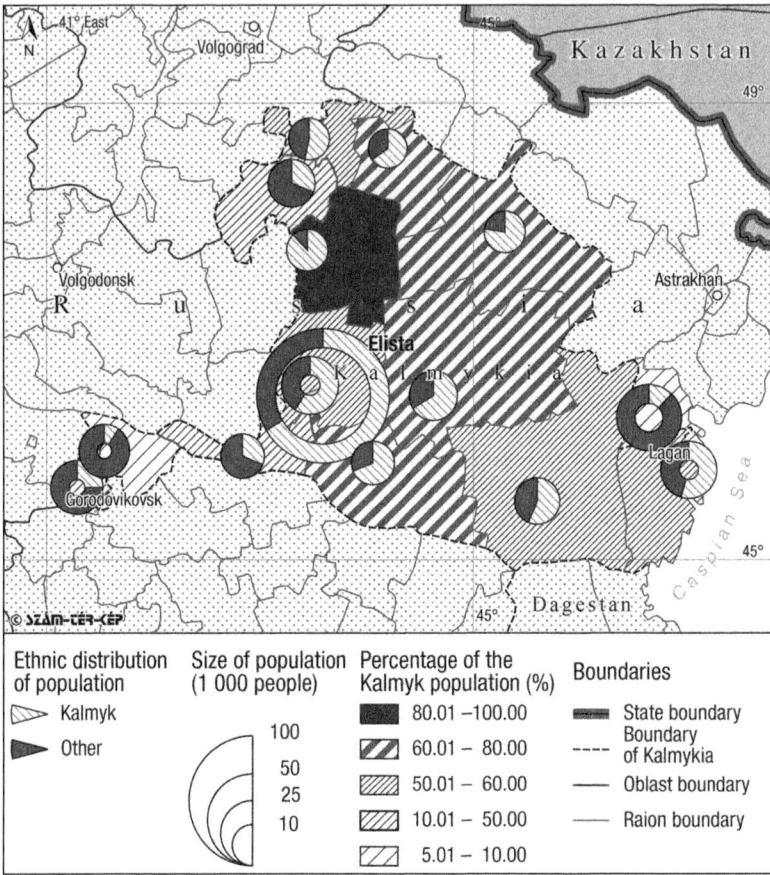

Figure 2.4.3 *The settlement area of Kalmyks in 2010; (Source: [25])*

that during the systematic persecution of the church in the 1930s, Buddhist khurul monasteries were not only closed, but also destroyed and razed to the ground. Until the implementation of glasnost, which was promoted by Gorbachev in the mid-1980s, Soviet religious policy was defined by a peculiar faith in scientific atheism (Froese, P. 2004). For decades, Buddhist clergy had been working to nurture religious traditions through secret gatherings and Sunday schools (Richardson, C. 2002). Following the collapse of the USSR, the Kalmyk republican apparatus, especially under the presidency of Kirsan Ilyumzhinov, supported the institutional development of Buddhism by supplying considerable financial resources, and by supporting the building of new khuruls, stupa, and pagodas (Sinclair, T. 2008). In 2004, for example, with the blessing of the Dalai Lama, the president opened up the Golden Temple complex in Elista, which contains one of the largest Buddha statues in Europe. The rapid development of ecclesiastical infrastructure also had an impact on local religiousness. According to a 2004 survey, 69% of local youth were active in their religion, and more than half of the respondents visit Khurul at least once every six months (Nuksunova, A. M. 2009). Another study underlined the importance, but not the exclusivity, of Buddhism to a sense of Kalmyk identity, and also pointed to the superficiality of religious renewal, the lack of immersion, and spiritualization (Holland, E. C. 2015).

Conclusion

Kalmyks have come a long way symbolically and factually, and their group consciousness has transformed into a modern ethnic identity. Leaving Dzungarian tribal rivalries behind, and wandering along the Central Asian frontier, the Kalmyk people inhabited the wider area of the Volga Delta, a region defined by a political vacuum and ideal living conditions. With the majority of the Kalmyk people residing on the left bank of the Volga opting for repatriation in the 18th century, Kalmykia later shifted to the west geographically, and its survival was ensured by integration into the tsarist system. Although the Russification of the area during the tsarist era led to the limiting of rights in a politico-cultural sense, the real violation of the Kalmyks took place as part of the massive deportation that defined Stalinist purification. De-Stalinization brought an end to years of exile in Siberia, and in the ensuing period of relative peace, the Kalmyk people were able to strengthen their social position in the KASSR.

While hundreds of years of Russian and Soviet influences resulted in a certain degree of acculturation (affecting especially the Kalmyk language and the traditional way of life), from the Soviet era, *korenizatsiya* and other policies promoting ethnic-based subsidiarity became the main pillars of Kalmyk identity. Harnessing the political turmoil of the 1990s, Kirsan Ilyininov's presidential career adequately demonstrates the degree to which local elites, through a flexible interpretation of the legal framework, were able to establish a self-governing milieu, and personally determine the cultural revival of the Kalmyk people.

A question remains regarding whether those who remained on the Kalmyk steppe, or those who emigrated in 1771, were more successful in preserving their culture and group identity over the last 250 years. As this chapter shows, returnees who succeeded in reaching the borders of the Chinese Empire have since merged into the Mongolian nation, and no longer appear as a distinct ethnic group. On the other hand, Kalmyk people stranded on the eastern bank of the Volga have been the subject of successive waves of cultural repression. Today, however, they are witnessing a real renaissance in Kalmyk culture, especially in the form Buddhism, in an autonomous republic.

"Constructed" (Soviet) Ethnicities

In the Contact Zone of In-Between Europe and the Post-Soviet Realm
Notions of Karelian Spaces

Géza Barta

Introduction

Karelia has never been an independent nation-state. Since the 14th century, it has been caught in a conflict zone created by the geopolitical aspirations of Sweden, Finland, and Russia. The geographical definition of Karelia has never been clear. Evolving in tandem with an ethnic, national, and regional identity shaped by intense, and sometimes violent, influences, the Karelian space-conception has often shifted. Discussions about Karelia inevitably include an analysis of both Russian/Soviet and Finnish approaches to this region, as well as the politics of history, culture, and memory.

Naming Karelia as a territorial unit remains both relative and controversial to this day. From the Russian perspective, the common and simple term "Karelia" refers to the "Karelian Republic" (the Republic of Karelia was an autonomous region of the Soviet Union, and is now a part of Russia). From the Finnish standpoint, however, this very same territory is named "Eastern" or "Russian Karelia". The Finnish perspective of "Karelia", which is broader than the Soviet notion and can be distinguished from "Eastern" and "Russian Karelia", extends to the entire region of Karelia. This Finnish conception refers to a compound unit comprised of four units: North and South Karelia (the two small Karelian regions in Finland), as well as the Karelian Isthmus and half of Lake Ladoga (both had been "lost" to the Soviets during World War II). According to the Finnish perception, "Karelia" and "Russian Karelia" overlap, since the southern counties of the Republic of Karelia (Ladoga-Karelia) together with the Karelian Isthmus belonged to Finland before the Second World War (Figure 3.1.1). This overlapping of spatial terms further complicates the definitional question.

As a region, Karelia played a special role in the construction of the Finnish nation-state. In the 19th century, the Karelian landscape became an essential part of Finnish romantic nationalism, which ascribed Karelia and the Karelians' transcendental values as a symbolic source of the nation's purity and originality. The ethnic kinship between Finns and Karelians became unquestionable, not only in historical, but also in cultural context as well. Finnish expansion in the east, the ambition to create "Greater Finland," and the clashes with the Russian Empire and Soviet Union, were real events in Karelia, and caused distress and misery for the vast majority of local people, especially in the 20th century.

Since the northwestern expansion of the medieval Novgorod Republic, the Russian cultural-religious influence on the Karelian lands has been more intense and unavoidable. Successive Russian regimes regarded the Eastern Orthodox Karelians as their own subjects, while in the Soviet era identity politics endeavoured to create an institutional context (which included ethnoterritorial enclosure as well as state support for local language and the preservation of regional folk heritage) within which Karelian identity could be developed and thrive. The results were mixed, and the sense of alienation between Finnish and Karelian people living in Russia became more and more obvious by the end of the 20th century.

However, after the dissolution of the Soviet Union, a slow convergence has been evident as a result of changes in the international socio-political environment, and the permeability of borders. Finns on the western side of the border, and the relocated Karelians living in Finland, have rediscovered the landscapes and settlements left behind in Eastern (Russian) Karelia. As a result of their visits, places of national remembrance have been created in conjunction with the intensely assimilating Karelian population (and with the Russian majority). Thus, dynamic processes of "rediscovery" have contributed to a reassessment and reinterpretation of the ethnic, national, and territorial dimensions of Karelianness.

Karelian territories and Karelian ethnogenesis

Finnish tribes settled in the territory of present-day Finland and Karelia c. 1000. Whereas the southernmost area of the region was occupied by the Finns, the Karelians occupied the east, and the Häme tribe settled between the two. Together, the three groups were trapped in the conflict zone of two rival northern powers, the Western Catholic Kingdom of Sweden, and the Eastern Orthodox Novgorodian Rus. In 1323, the Treaty of Nöteborg drew a relatively clear border between the Russian and Swedish spheres of influence. This division had a significant impact on the Karelian region, and resulted in "Western" and "Eastern" spheres of social and historical development (Wilson, W. A. 2006). The boundary drawn by the Treaty of Nöteborg proved to be so permanent that it continues to delimit the boundary between Eastern and Western Christianity in Northern Europe to this day (Figure 3.1.1). The great-power rivalry lasted for centuries. The Treaty of Teusina, which put an end to the Russo-Swedish War (1590–95), strengthened the borders of Nöteborg, but also secured the northeastern borders of Sweden. Further Karelian areas were annexed to Sweden after the 1616 Treaty of

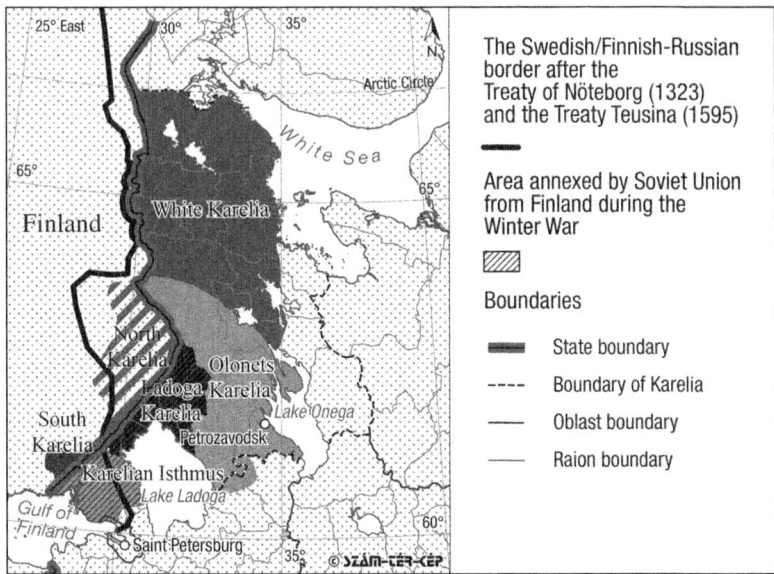

Figure 3.1.1 *Regions of Karelia and significant territorial changes of the region (Source:* Kirkinen, H., Nevalainen, P. and Sihvo, H. 1994*)*

Stolbovo, such as Ingria, the former Finno-Ugric region between present-day Estonia and Lake Ladoga along the Southern shore of the Gulf of Finland (Siikala, J. 2006). The occupation of this region by the Swedish Empire, which by then was Lutheran, forced the largely Orthodox population to flee, and because they settled in Tver, they became the ancestors of the "Tver Karelians", creating the easternmost Karelian territory in Russia. Under Swedish rule, the Lutheran faith was spread to what became known as West-, Swedish- or Finnish-Karelia, while in Eastern- or Russian-Karelia, the Orthodox religion was solidified (Horváth Cs. 2010).

Karelia was first mentioned as a distinct territorial unit in the *Novgorod First Chronicle* (1016–1471), and also in Sebastian Münster's *Cosmography* (1544). However, it is unclear what exact territorial unit the medieval documents were referring to. The core of Karelian culture was in the north of Lake Ladoga according to archaeological and historical documents, but visitors to the region in the 19th century did not see much evidence of it. According to the British traveller, John Scott Keltie (1879), both the population and the villages in Eastern Karelia looked Russian. The unstable border area rendered the region similar to the Balkans, and was even referred to by some as the "Macedonia of Northern Europe" (Mead, W. R. 1952). According to Nordenskiöld's early 20th century analysis, the eastern border was ethnically incorrect and, in a significant area of Russia, almost entirely inhabited by Finns (Nordenskiöld, E. 1919). The above examples illustrate the uncertainty around the ethnic classification of Karelians at that time: they could easily be assumed to be either Russian or Finnish.

As part of the Russian Empire, the Grand Duchy of Finland (1809–1917) enjoyed considerable autonomy, and the Finnish national movements associated with this period lay the groundwork for the growing national interest in Karelia. The 1897 census ordered by Nicholas II did not count the population of Finnish Karelia within the territory of Grand Duchy of Finland, but counted only the Karelians of Eastern Karelia. As a result, it appeared that the Eastern Karelian settlement area from Lake Ladoga to the Kola Peninsula was ethnically uniform. Subsequent censuses revealed that this homogeneous linguistic area was divided into islands, and that the proportion of Karelians was decreasing. In 2010, according to census data, the proportion of Karelians was only 7% in Eastern Karelia. Thus, the assimilation of the "labelled" ethnic group of the Russian autonomous Republic of Karelia was significant. Only two tiny areas had a considerably higher Karelian population: Olonets Karelia, on the northeastern shore of Lake Ladoga, and in the central areas of White Karelia around the city of Kalevala. In the first case the proportion of the Karelians exceeded 60%, and in the Kalevala region it was 36% (Figures 3.1.1 and 3.1.2).

In Finland before the Second World War, Karelian was an autochthonous, definable language, but this linguistic unit disintegrated after the war as a result of the large number of migrants arriving from different regions. Today, the Karelian language has no special status in Finland, and was spoken by only five thousand people in 2016. The declining rate of Karelian speakers provides quantifiable evidence regarding the progress of linguistic assimilation in the region (Sarhimaa, A. 2016).

It has never been easy to distinguish Karelians from those surrounding groups whose languages belong to the Balto-Finnic branch of the Uralic language family. In-Between Europe provides several similar examples of this phenomenon. In many cases, neighbouring ethnic groups are hardly distinguishable. Ethnoculturally, the Finnish–Karelian relationship can be interpreted in terms of Serbian–Croatian, Czech–Slovakian, or Csango Hungarian–Hungarian relations. Though each of these group-pairs have been separated from each other (with the degree of segregation fluctuating over time), they nevertheless display numerous linguistic and cultural similarities. Similar to the two South Slavic groups – namely the Orthodox Serbians and the Roman Catholic Croatians – a significant number of Karelians are affiliated with the Orthodox Church, whereas almost all Finns are affiliated with Western Christianity.

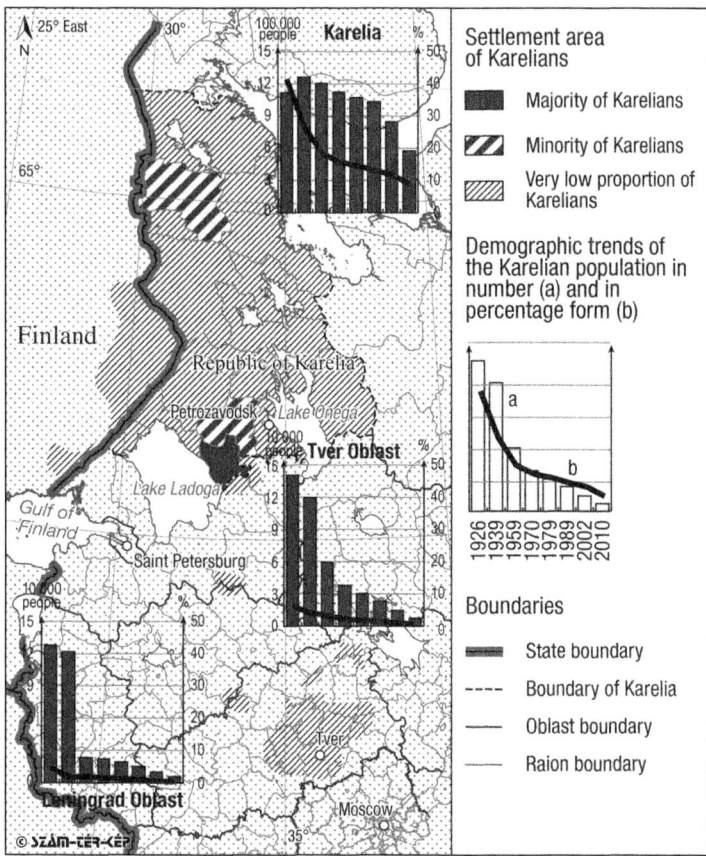

Figure 3.1.2 *The settlement area of the Karelians and population changes between 1926 and 2010; (Sources:* [25]; [26]*)*

Much like the Czech and Slovak case, by the 19th century, the inhabitants of Eastern Karelia had become a part of the Russian Empire in the same way that Slovaks at that time were integrated into Hungarian society. In the case of the Slovaks, the "parent state" was the semi-autonomous Bohemia-Moravia, which was part of the Austro-Hungarian Monarchy. The emerging national movement amongst Czechs and Moravians had a noticeable impact on Slovaks as a "kindred" nation. Similarly, the Finnish national movement, which formed within the Grand Duchy of Finland as part of the Russian Empire, had a significant impact on Karelian ethnic and national identity. In both cases the idea of unifying the imagined nation was powerful, as it was hoped that Czechs, Moravians, and Slovaks would constitute one nation, much in the same way that

Finns and Karelians would. The Csango Hungarians in the Romanian region of Moldova have always lived outside the political borders of Hungary, as did the Eastern Karelians outside of Finland. The accelerated process of assimilation within a distinct linguistic, ethnic, and national environment was characteristic of both areas (Horváth Cs. 2010). However, these comparisons are only suitable for macro-generalizations. Amongst other factors, the division of Finns and Karelians on the basis of religion does not take into account the Lutheran Karelians. In fact, there is no unambiguous territorial or ethnic boundary between the Finns and the Karelians. Although Karelians in Russia and Finland have diverse historical and cultural backgrounds, the role of Karelians in 19th-century Finnish nation-building, and their linguistic-regional similarity, justify their consideration as a characteristic group.

The role of Karelia in the geopolitical orientations of the Finnish nation-state

In the 19th century, the population of Finland had already identified itself as a national entity, and Finnish lands had become a well-defined, separate territorial unit without the Eastern frontier. Since then, Finnish leaders have been attempting to imagine and define Finland, placing the country in an international environment aligned with the incessantly altering geopolitical surroundings. Within this context, Finland has been associated with changeable geopolitical notions and cardinal directions. Narratives of the relative position of Finland on the world political map — occupying an "Eastern", "Western" or "Northern" position — have intersected with identity politics and have influenced social representations of Karelia. The association of cardinal directions with Finnish identity have changed throughout history, but have left impressions on new generations. As in the other countries of in-between Europe, it is perhaps no surprise that the East-West orientation has received special attention in Finland.

Marco Antonsich (2005) has identified five distinctive narratives in this regard. The first of these narratives refers to the idea of "belonging to the West". Linked closely to notions of modernity, "belonging to the West" has played an exceptional role in the historiography of the Finnish nation-state. According to this conceptual paradigm, the modernization and westernization associated with the Swedes created an intellectual force field in the southwestern centre of the country by the end of the 18th century. Finland (Suomi) was named after this southwestern region (which was known as Varsinais-Suomi or "Finland Proper"), and the dialect spoken became the basis of the Finnish literary language. The emergence of the modern Finnish nation-state can be interpreted as a cultural, military, and linguistic expansion of the southwest region.

The notion of Finland's western orientation also found partial expression in a parallel counter-narrative regarding the "East." Cast against images of Soviet barbarism, Finland was portrayed as a "bastion of the West," and as a defender of Western values, especially between the two world wars when the Finns fought several wars with Russia. For the independent nation-state, the establishment of territorial and national unity became particularly important in 1918. The ideology of separation from neighbouring Soviet society was crucial in this respect. According to this narrative, a stable, free, peace-loving, and democratic Finnish society faced the oppressive, unstable, and war-loving Soviet system of the East. This resulted in a strong sense of Russophobia in Finland, which only subsided in the post-World War II period (Luostarien, H. 1989). The construction of the "Eastern Other" helped to strengthen western-oriented conceptualizations of Finnish identity, and provided an ideological background for the "liberation" of Karelia, allowing Finland's Karelian brethren to join the "civilized" world. Westernizing discourse re-emerged in the 1990s when it became obvious that Finland, which was ripe for EU membership, was not only capable of progressive development, but also had reached a level at which Western values like democracy, freedom, and rule of law had become unquestionable and axiomatic (Antonsich, M. 2005).

By contrast, coming up with a clear definition of the eastern border remained problematic for the Finns, as the eastern border with Russia was ambiguous, and more ambitious notions of the nation envisioned a frontier that extended further to the East. In the 19th century, the Swedish-speaking Finnish historian, professor, and journalist, Zachris Topelius, introduced the rather bold "Finland as an island" concept. Contrary to the view of Finland as a peninsula, the island-nation concept argued that state borders should correspond to natural features formed by bodies of water, and in particular rivers, lakes, and seas. In the east, the border was therefore constituted by the White Sea, Lake Onega, and Lake Ladoga, and the watercourses connecting them (Mead, W. R. 1952, Horváth Cs. 2010). According to this conceptualization, the resulting "Greater Finland" would have almost completely covered the Karelian language area, and the Kola Peninsula would have been under Finnish control as well. But the establishment of "Greater Finland" proved to be a utopian idea (Figure 3.1.3). Geographer Väinö Auer, and historian Eino Jutikkala, played a major role in creating the ideology of Finnish "living space". Their 1941 book, *Finnlands Lebensraum*, which was published in Berlin, established the "scientific" background for the ethnocentric utilization of the Eastern territories. After the Second World War, the eastern border became a material and symbolic dividing line as part of the Iron Curtain, and its definition became a symbol of the separation from "Eastern Otherness". Furthermore, the boundary between the "Orthodox East" and the "Lutheran West," coinciding roughly with the prevailing Finnish–Russian border, was also an important element of cardinal directions-oriented distinctions (Paasi, A. 1996).

Running counter to notions of Finland's Western orientation, some 19th-century advocates of the Finnish nation-state began to turn East (this is the second narrative identified by Antonsich). The Fennoman movement considered the essence of the Finns to be in Karelia: an area unaffected by Western influences. The ancestors of the Finns lived freely in the mythical past in Kalevala-land, beyond alien influences (Antonsich, M. 2005). Eastern origins, an ancient land full of myths, and romanticized national identities were the most important ingredients of the Eastern Orientation, which provided the ideological backdrop for eastward expansion.

A "Neither West nor East" conception of the Finnish nation is a third narrative identified by Antonsich. This conceptualization of the nation not only promoted sovereignty and independence in the "choice of direction", but also emphasized Finland's distance from both Russian and Swedish influences, thus reinforcing specific Finnish features (Antonsich, M. 2005). This self-affirming ideology, which served as a catalyst of cultural identity, was summed up succinctly in the 19th-century adage: "We are no longer Swedes, we will not be Russians, so let's be Finnish!" (Richly G. 2010).

As a result of the geopolitical discourse during the long

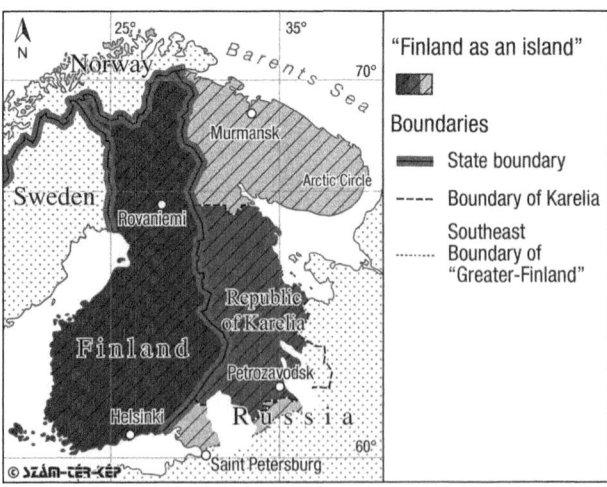

Figure 3.1.3 *The concept of "Finland as an island" as the modest version of Greater Finland notions (Source:* Manninen, O. 1980*)*

presidency of Urho Kaleva Kekkonen, which determined Finnish Cold War policy, Finland placed itself on the map of world politics "between East and West" (this is the fourth narrative identified by Antonsich). Kekkonen, who consciously built a bridge between the USA and the Soviet Union, promoted a "rediscovery" of Eastern identity domestically, which counterbalanced the dominance of Western orientation. A large number of Karelian refugees also made the development of an eastern partnership crucial, while this Soviet relation had significance in realpolitik, economics and world politics (Antonsich, 2005). The Cold War policy of "equal distance" led to a reduction in Russophobia and the fading of the idea of the Soviet enemy, which later facilitated the development of cross-border relations and opening up to Russia (Luostarien, H. 1989).

The fifth narrative identified by Antonsich embodies the idea of Finland's "northern orientation". Advocates for this notion of Finnish identity aimed to transcend the East-West dichotomy, and instead focused on Finland's northern expansion, and in particular the conquest of Lapland, as activities pursued independently of the great powers. The idealized national landscape, replete with pine forests and lakes, in addition to the elements of traditional folklore, such as everyday tools, food, rituals, or songs, became noticeable markers of the Finnish character, and located Finland squarely in the North (Antonsich, M. 2005). In this context, the sparsely populated pine forest, which covered northern White-Karelia (Figure 3.1.1), was embodied as a unique place within the collection of national epic songs. The symbolic role of Karelia itself, which became significant in the narratives of Finland as both "Northern" and "Eastern," was thus revalued in the process of national identity formation. This role was strengthened from the second half of the 19th century until the first part of 20th century, and as a result Karelia achieved a self-sufficient and essential position in the Finnish national movement. What is more, the oppositional character of Karelia was gradually reduced; thus, Karelia did not stand in contrast to "Western" values.

The Fight for Souls: Finnification, Russification, and Sovietization in Eastern Karelia

During the reign of Nikolai II Alexandrovich Romanov, Russian nationalist movements, and the Russification of non-Russian territories, caused an increasing number of conflicts. In this light, Karelia became an arena of conflict as the Russian state attempted to reduce Finnish influence in the region. Alongside the pan-Finnish idea, the Karelian autonomous movement and the increasing independence of the Lutheran Church opposed the process of Russification, while the Finnish national movement in general faced off against its Russian counterpart in the Karelian region. Emergent Russian nationalism likewise found strong support amongst the Russian elite, the Orthodox Church, and The Black Hundred, a violent, far-right, ultra-nationalist Russian organization that was secretly backed by the Imperial Court. The rise of Russian nationalism triggered resistance on the part of Karelians, while aspirations for independence became more pronounced (Vitukhnovskaya, M. 2001). During the Russian Civil War, a post-revolutionary, sovereign Karelian government was formed in Uhtua (in Russian: Ukhtua/Ухта), a town in White Karelia that the Soviets renamed Kalevala in 1963 after the title of the Finnish national epic. The Bolsheviks did not appreciate or approve of the creation of the Karelian "nation" without the consent of the revolutionary centre. As a result, in early 1920, the government of the Republic of Uhtua was disbanded, and its members were arrested (Baron, N. 2007).

On the other side of the border, the victorious Whites in the Finnish Civil War of 1918 did not give up the dream of the Finnish annexation of Karelian territories under Russian rule. After 1918, vigorous propaganda campaigns were carried out in Eastern Karelia in preparation for war with Soviet Russia. The Finnish name given to this struggle was the difficult-to-translate "Heimosodat," which in general terms referred to the military assistance given to "kindred peoples" in their fight against the Soviets. Encompassing more than just a series of battles, the meaning of the term was understood quite literally, and was associated with positive connotations. Finnish nationalism, however, ignored Karelia's historically multicultural heritage, and neglected Karelian attempts at self-definition. During the Heimosodat (1918–1920), smaller territories of Karelia, such as Repola and Porajärvi, were successfully annexed, and Russians living there were considered enemies. Most of them were forced into camps surrounded by barbed wire.

The Treaty of Tartu signed in 1920 ended the war, and the occupied territories had to be returned to Soviet Russia, though a lane with an ice-free harbour (Petsamo) was obtained by Finland in order to ensure access to the Arctic Ocean (Tepora, T. and Roselius A. 2014). Although the Treaty secured Karelian autonomy within Soviet Russia, the purpose and end goal of the Karelian movement had shifted by then. This was indicated quite clearly during the uprising against Soviet rule in 1921-22, a revolt that had been sparked by a desire to unite Finland. Though the uprising was suppressed, the autonomous powers granted to the Karelians by the Treaty of Tartu were nevertheless further extended by the Soviet authorities (Horváth Cs. 2010).

In 1918, the Finnish Orthodox Church was established, and independent Finland officially declared the religious self-determination of Eastern Christian Finns. Finnish Orthodox, like the Lutherans, celebrate the most important ecclesiastical holidays according to the Gregorian calendar. Its introduction, especially in the Eastern Karelian territories annexed between 1918 and 1920, caused conflicts. Karelian religious leaders, still attached to the Russian Orthodox Church, frowned upon the integration of Western Christian ideas and practices (Mead, W. R. 1952, Alasuutari, P. and Alasuutari, M. 2009, Kupari, H. 2016)

After the collapse of the Russian imperial administration, the Bolsheviks implemented an ethnic and spatial rearrangement of Soviet Russia on a scientific foundation. According to their dialectic approach, the Soviets attempted to apply both absolute and relational space theories. To put it another way, they could give consideration to space as a container and as a social phenomenon at the same time. The Bolsheviks assumed an evolutionary relationship between space and society. "Spatial Emancipation" was an important program for the Bolsheviks, and embodied their goal to clear space of oppressive feudal structures. Such a process would break outdated and repressive social bonds, and would liberate productive social resources, and hence allow for the creative energies of the societies in the Soviet Union to build a new communist world. They sought to achieve the organic unity of space and society through the humanization of nature, and the naturalization of space. The discourses of early Soviet regionalization were thus based on ontological and epistemological foundations that were different when compared to the former imperial division of space. Soviet interpretations and categorizations were more complex, while the structure and source of knowledge were built on scientific foundations.

During the reign of Catherine the Great, the macro spatial structure of the Russian Empire had been described (or simplified) on the basis of a centre-periphery model. In the case of the periphery, border protection as well as colonial or military aspects were taken into consideration, while economic, developmental, or ethnic concerns were irrelevant. According to Lenin, rigid, feudal spatial structure did not recognize the peoples' legitimate demands for self-determination. Imperial Russia was the "prison of the nations", as he declared in 1914. According to Soviet thinking, natural, economic, and human factors therefore had to be taken into account in newly created regions. In areas with ethnically mixed populations, Soviet authorities argued that the "national component" should be treated on the same level as economic and other social components (Baron, N. 2007). However, the ethnic-national affiliation of a community was unclear in many cases, and these groups were categorized, defined, and identified with the assistance of ethnographers.

In the case of Karelians, classification was based on language and ethnocultural understandings, but these categories themselves did not necessarily guarantee unambiguous interpretations (Minescu, A. and Poppe, E. 2011).

As a result of national movements, multilingual and multi-religious Imperial Russia had been transformed into a multinational state by the end of the 19th century, but the multinationality of the Empire, with the exception of the Grand Duchy of Finland, had not become institutionalized. The Soviet system endeavoured to remedy this deficiency by introducing new institutions, but these measures were highly controversial. The codification of the "nation" at the sub-state level was a speciality; in other words, the ethnic-national level was given different status and was separated from the state as a subarena of the ethnic or national identification process. Furthermore, the Soviet state was represented as a supranational category over everyone. Although "Sovietness" was formed as a new identity at this level, it was not thought to apply in place of nationality. The state, or citizens as a whole, were not defined in national terms, but the components of the state were already defined in this way. Nor did they try to organize the Soviet Union into a nation-state, and strongly opposed "Great-Russian chauvinism". Great Russian (Velikorossy/Великороссы) had been the official linguistic category for ethnic Russians in imperial Russia. As an exemplar of the emerging ethnic-national opposition in the Russian Empire there was a terminological and identification war around Russian-considered communities during the first decades of the 20th century. Besides Great Russian there was the Little Russian (Malorossy/Малороссы) category, but they were frequently considered "Russian" which was equal to Great Russian, as a simplification. Similar processes took place in the case of White Russians (Belorossy/Белороссы). From the perspective of All-Russian Unity, which was an imperial ideology unifying the three subnations (Great, Little, and White Russians), these confusions were not problematic. However, local national movements attempted to distinguish their nations from Great Russians, a process that was strengthened under Soviet Rule. As a result, Little Russians were officially considered Ukrainian (agreeing with local national movements) and with White Russians were administered differently. The tangible evidence of these processes were the ethno-territorial units established as the Ukrainian and Byelorussian Soviet Socialist Republics.

The resulting ethno-territorial federalism was complemented by an individualized national policy. The latter assigned a legally binding ethnic, or national, status for individuals. This ethnic-national category was also included in personal papers and official documents, and was used in state statistics. Certain national or ethnic groups were given their own territory. These "titular" nations became the eponymous group of the autonomous Soviet Republic or region, such as Georgians in the Georgian Soviet Socialist Republic (Georgian SSR), Karelians in the Karelian Autonomous Soviet Socialist Republic (Karelian ASSR), or the Adyghe people in the Adyghe Autonomous Oblast (Adyghe AO). The two conflicting definitions of nationhood or nationness (that is, the territorial-political and individual-ethnocultural definitions), became the source of conceptual and political tensions. The usage of local language, coupled with the ability of members of titular nations to more easily climb the social ladder, increased the number of conflicts for non-ethnic minorities and non-titular groups, who were mostly Russians, living outside of their ethno-territory. Authorities sought to solve these problems by prohibiting nationalism and broadly endorsed supranational Sovietization (Brubaker, R. 1996).

Lenin and Stalin (who was himself in charge of national affairs as People's Commissar for Nationalities between 1917 and 1923), thought that setting up autonomous regions needed to be carried out on the basis of nationality. This reality would be temporary, since national identity would be transformed into proletarian internationalism. However, nationally-organized groups were assumed to be a good springboard to a classless society. In the 1920s and 1930s during the *korenizatsiya*, the institutions of ethnic-national groups were strengthened and established, and were represented in local administration and legislation, using positive discrimination where necessary.

This process proved tricky in the case of Karelia. In fact, Karelian autonomy, as embodied by the Uhtua-government established during the Civil War, complicated the process of *korenizatsiya* in Karelia. Bolshevik leaders, in turn, were not at all pleased with this "state". According to Anatoly Lunacharsky, who was the first People's Commissar for Education, collective creativity was not equal to the spontaneous emergence of the will of the masses. He believed the masses must be taught a higher level of revolutionary awareness, and some kind of instinctive compliance was desirable (Lunacharsky, A. V. 1918). As elsewhere in national territories in Soviet Russia, Bolshevik authorities reorganized the Karelian region after the failed, poorly prepared attempt at independence. But *korenizatsiya* was not carried out in cooperation with the local Karelians. The communist Finns, who emigrated from Finland to Soviet Russia, had good relations with Bolshevik commanders. One of their leaders, Edvard Gylling, a former professor at the University of Helsinki, argued that Karelia should be made a prototype of a communist governorate, and offered his services to this end. He was entrusted by the Soviet leadership, and became the leader of the Karelian Autonomous Soviet Socialist Republic, which was formed in 1923. In order to achieve swift results, Gylling believed that intensive inter-Karelian campaigning was needed (Baron, N. 2007). The purpose of the Karelian revolutionary campaign was to export the communist revolution to Finland, and later to Scandinavia as a whole, in order to establish the "Scandinavian Soviet Republic." Thus, reunification with Finland was on the agenda again; however, Gylling's idea of "Great Red Finland" did not take Karelia's historical, cultural, and ethnic complexity into account, as he imagined the Karelians within the Finnish nation. In cooperation with the State Planning Committee, commonly known as *Gosplan*, (which was considered — at those times — an organization for the equitable spatial distribution of productive forces in the Soviet Union), ethnic situations, as well as economic and natural conditions, were taken into account in establishing the Karelian region. In 1923, the newly created area had significantly extended beyond the ethnic boundary in the east. Thus, Karelians became an indigenous minority in the Karelian ASSR (Figure 3.1.4).

Gylling was a nationalist in terms of spatial organization, but a communist in terms of social-political arrangement, calling his own ideological concept revolutionary nationalism compatible with Bolshevik aspirations. Several protests erupted in response to Gylling's attempts to enhance the "Finnishness" of Eastern Karelia, in part because people were forced to use the Finnish language, but also because Finns were overrepresented in the emergent local elite. Finnification politics were crucial to Gylling, as he thought the reunification with Finland was imminent. Challenging Karelia's earlier peripheral position, he considered it both as a "dual periphery" and a center. He envisaged that Karelia, as a dual periphery of Scandinavia and the Soviet Union, would play a central role in exporting Leninist ideas from the Karelian revolutionary kernel to Scandinavia, bearing in mind that the ultimate goal was "World Revolution". Nevertheless, communist considerations for the function of the boundary lines were a "vestige" of imperialism, and Gylling regarded the border between Karelia and Finland as an anachronistic artificial formation that would be swept away by the upcoming World Revolution. According to his interpretation, this border did not separate nations from each other, as it had no national status, and merely formed a temporary economic and ideological barrier between the two countries (Baron, N. 2007).

The Finnish project in Karelia could have been remarkably successful because in the 1920s approximately 25,000 ethnic Finns, most of them adherents of left-leaning ideologies from North America and Finland, emigrated to the Soviet Union. Gylling tried to offset the penetration of Slavic migrants with the implementation of economic programs, and convinced the Soviet government

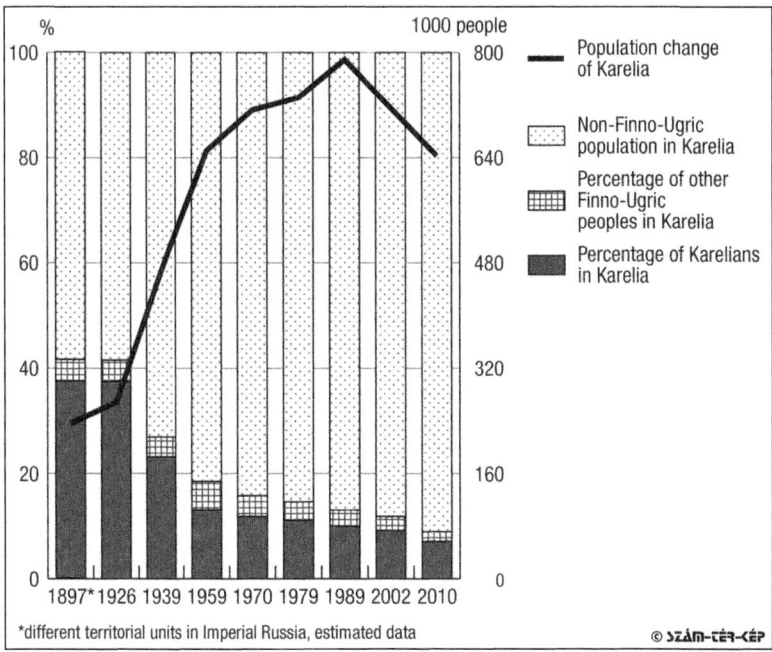

Figure 3.1.4 *Changes in the population of ethnic groups in Karelia between 1897 and 2010; (Sources:* [25]; [26]; [29])

to develop Karelia's economy with the assistance of qualified Finns abroad. Recruitment agencies were so successful that even Finnish businessmen with substantial capital were attracted to the Soviet Union. The "Karelian fever" had infected many, though immigration was also fuelled by the unemployment caused by the global economic crisis. It also contributed greatly to the boom in the Soviet wood and paper industry, which made use of Karelian forests (Gelb, M. 1993). Under Stalin's autarchy, the notion of emancipated spatial structure was forgotten and became the victim of total centralization. The theory of organically developing regions, and cooperation with one another, turned into a reality of isolated spatial units controlled from the center (Baron, N. 2007).

A specially administered zone was established around the White Sea Canal, which was being built by the "enemies of the system", and at the time was under constant construction. This forced labor was also intended to boost Karelia's economy. The territory of the so-called "Karelian Gulag" increased continuously, and by the middle of the 1930s, there were forced labor camps in one third of Karelia with a special central administration. As a result, a huge part of Karelia was not under local control.

Ultimately, the remaining self-governed territories were abolished by Stalin (Baron, N. 2002).

The beginning of the Stalinist terror was linked to Stalin's speech in 1928, in which he communicated visions of an intensification of class struggle, and stigmatized national "deviation" as bourgeois nationalism. Furthermore, he was determined to transform the agricultural sector in his Soviet Empire, establishing collective- and state-controlled farms. The collectivization of agriculture began with the dekulakization, and as a result of this "policy", approximately 11 million kulaks were deported from throughout the Soviet Union[1]. This affected Russians, Karelians, and Finns equally in Karelia, and thus had no ethnic connotation. Rather, during the unveiling of "counter-revolutionary conspiracies" and "spy activities" between 1932 and 1938, the majority of ethnic Finns were arrested, sent to labor camps, or executed. After 1937, the Stalinist purges were extended to all Finns in the Soviet Union, and not just those in Karelia. Ethnic Finns were expelled (if they had a foreign passport) or deported (if they were Soviet citizens). Gylling himself was unable to escape this fate: he was abducted and executed, presumably in 1938. In addition to the Finns, the "finnified" Karelians became enemies as well.

The new passport system, introduced in 1932, was an administrative tool for authorities who aimed to tie Soviet people to the land, and enforce ethnic segregation. The document, which contained nationality data, was used to restrict migration and travel within the country. Furthermore, based on this dataset, applying collective punishment against ethnic communities was not difficult for the authorities. Under the Stalinist terror, entire ethnic groups were deported from one end of the vast territory of the Soviet Union to the other (Gelb, M. 1993). As a result of this forced migration, there is even a Finnish community in Kazakhstan to this day.

Karelians living along the border of "capitalist Finland" were deported as "suspicious elements" to remote areas of the Soviet Union such as Siberia or Central Asia. It is estimated that 25,000 to 50,000 Karelians were killed during the Stalinist terror. Others were imprisoned, deported, or humiliated, or otherwise had their professional careers destroyed. Finnification was labeled as a national deviation. Attempts were also made to isolate Karelia from

---

1 *Kulak* (кулак) was a Soviet term for a higher-income farmer who had a larger farm than other members of an identified peasant subclass. Stalin's goal was to eliminate kulaks as a "class" and establish newly constructed collective farms without them (and thus not making use of their knowledge). The procedure of the liquidation of kulaks was called *dekulakization* (раскулачивание), while the process linked to the organization of collectively-controlled farms was named *collectivization* (коллективизация).

Finland linguistically by putting an emphasis on the linguistic uniqueness of the local language, and by stressing the gap between the Finnish and Karelian languages. New leaders, in turn, urged the Karelianization of Karelia (Gelb, M. 1993, Bartha A. 1996, Kostiainen, A. 1996).

In 1937, the Finnish language was banned, and the first official language of Karelia became Russian. The second official language was "authentic" Karelian, which was in itself an attempt to standardize the Tverian dialect (Laitila, T. 2001). This particular dialect was spoken by Karelians who had been living for more than 350 years next to the Russian city of Tver, which was far from Karelia proper. Surrounded by ethnic Russians, Tver Karelians had managed to preserve their archaic dialect, mixing it with the Russian language. Tver Karelian was therefore considerably different from "proper" Karelian. In spite of this, Dimitry Bubrikh, a Finno-Ugric scholar from Leningrad (now: Saint Petersburg), insisted that the Karelian literary language had to be developed on the basis of the Tver dialect. Although he was later arrested and charged with counter-revolutionary activity, Bubrikh enjoyed broad support from the Soviet leaders, and the Tver dialect was adopted as the official literary language of Karelia. Given that it was rendered in unfamiliar Cyrillic characters and included Russian vocabulary, Tver Karelian was often incomprehensible to Karelians. Perhaps not surprisingly, the half-Karelian, half-Russian language formation did not live up to expectations, though children's books and newspapers were printed in "the only socialist language in the world" (Austin, P.M. 1992). The Tver Karelian project in the Karelian ASSR did not last long, and the upcoming World War altered almost everything.

Three months after the outbreak of World War II, during the so-called Winter War, Stalin pushed the Finnish-Russian border further west to protect Leningrad, and annexed much of Finnish Karelia to the Soviet Union. The occupation of Vyborg (Viipuri), the capital of the area, was represented in Soviet propaganda as a Red Army "liberation" of the old Russian city that was part of the Russian Empire under Peter the Great. The opportunity to Sovietize Finland was once again anticipated by Soviet leaders (Austin, P. M. 1992, Paasi, A. 1996). To this end, a puppet state, officially named the Democratic Republic of Finland, was established in the city of Terijoki, which was located in the occupied Karelian Isthmus, with the aim of winning over Finnish workers, and converting Finland to communism. The Finnish project in Karelia was strengthened again, and the official Karelian language introduced a few years earlier was disgraced. The Karelians living in the occupied territories fled from the Red Army, and many Russians moved to the evacuated settlements (Laitila, T. 2001, Taagepera, R. 2011).

During the Continuation War between 1941 and 1944, Finland, with the help of Germany, attempted to recapture the areas lost during the Winter War, and re-annexed Eastern Karelia. Despite initial successes, the action eventually failed.

After the war, Stalin did not give up on the Sovietization of Finland, and Karelian Finnification was continued. In 1940, the official name of the Karelian ASSR was changed to the Karelo-Finnish Soviet Socialist Republic (Karelo-Finnish SSR), which signaled that the region had reached the top of the ethno-territorial hierarchy. As a new SSR, it became a separate entity from the Russian Soviet Federative Socialist Republic, or in abbreviated form, Russian SFSR (Austin, P. M. 1992). During and after World War II, the Finnish project was enhanced again in Eastern Karelia, a process which continued until Stalin's death. In 1956, the privileged status of the Finnish language ceased to exist, and the Karelo-Finnish SSR once again became an autonomous region as part of the Russian SFSR. Radical ethnic-national projects had been replaced by quiet assimilation, resulting in a steady decline in the number of Karelians, and the enhancing of Russian language use among ethnic Karelians (Austin, P. M. 1992, Laitila, T. 2001, Taagepera, R. 2011). It was also emblematic in the 1950s that, during the censuses, many people identified themselves as ethnic Russians (Anderson B.A. and Silver; B.D. 1983), which, considering the history of the Karelians in the 20th century, proved to be an adaptive strategy.

After the Second World War, the newly occupied Karelian Isthmus, and the Karelian ASSR, were treated differently by Soviet authorities. By the end of the war, the Isthmus had an entirely altered ethnic population as a result of Karelians who had fled and Slavs who had since been resettled there. In this light, there was an attempt to change the Finnish-Karelian legacy of the Isthmus by identifying the region as an inalienable part of Russia, and by emphasizing its Russian historical heritage. The Isthmus was not granted autonomous status, as it was attached to the Leningrad Oblast (region), and the re-denomination process of the geographical names was based on Russian terms. Some exceptions had been made, including the Vuoksi River (Vuoksa) or the Karelian Isthmus itself (*Karelsky peresheyek*). However, in the Karelian ASSR, despite the growing dominance of the Slavic population, the retention of Karelian-Finnish names was supported explicitly (Hannula, M. 2006, Ackermann, E. and Urbansky, S. 2016).

Representations of Karelia and the Karelians

Karelia has been associated with a variety of ideas throughout Finnish history. At certain times, it was the focus of attention for public life and politics, and at other times it was just forgotten. This astonishing duality can also be observed in relation to the Karelian people. They could be considered essentially Finnish, but also "aliens" living on the periphery. Building on the work of Dennis Cosgrove (1989), Maunu Häyrynen (2004) distinguishes three stages in the historical development of the way Karelia has been perceived. The region first appeared as an alternative national landscape, offsetting the dominance of the southern areas. Later, Karelia played a central role in the construction of the national landscape, and after Finland lost much of its territory during the Winter War, it appeared as a national periphery. Since World War II, the forgotten territory had lingered like a ghost frozen behind the Iron Curtain. Following the collapse of the Soviet Union, this condition dissolved, and a Karelian revival process emerged, one that resulted in the perception of Eastern Karelia as less peripheral.

According to Häyrynen's first phase, the territorial extension of the "alternative landscape" was ambiguous, as Karelian borders were not outlined on mental maps in the first part of the 19th century. As the historian Zachris Topelius noted, the Karelian landscape may have become increasingly attractive nationally because the owners of urban and rural properties and estates were members of the Swedish social elite. The natural landscape was "common" and "Finnish", whereas property and land ownership were more Swedish. Patriotic Finns retained "nature", which was the essence of Finnishness. The Romantic image of Karelia was also considerably stimulated by a textbook written by Topelius and introduced into the Finnish school system. According to *The Book of Our Country* (Boken om vårt land), written in Swedish, Karelia (the area between the Gulf of Finland and Lake Ladoga), was a place where one could encounter wildlife and ancient poems. Karelians were the most positively-depicted Finns: they were regarded as open-minded, neighborly, and content. They were also seen as having beautiful songs, and beyond merely retaining the memory of their forebears, showed respect for their ancestors (Häyrynen, M. 2004).

The popularity of the epic poem *Kalevala*, which its author Elias Lönrot had based on songs he collected (mostly in Karelia) during fieldwork conducted between 1831 and 1833, as well as the stereotypes from Topelius, developed into the Karelianism of the late 19th and early 20th centuries. Finnish literary, linguistic, and ethnographic research already occupied a prominent position in national sciences in the 19th century, the collaborative convergence of which culminated in the *Kalevala*. The Finnish national epic was consumed by the general public, and people became emotionally saturated in their attachment to the national past. Though it was set in Finnish-Karelian cultural surroundings, the *Kalevala* followed an ancient Greek pattern, and its literary structure was based on *The Iliad*. Following Homer's example, Lönrot's epic explored universal ideas, such as love, endurance and heroism, though the Finnish-Karelian cultural surroundings rendered this a quintessential Finnish story. First published in 1835, the expanded and better-known version of the *Kalevala* was published in 1849 (Siikala, J. 2006). The success of the *Kalevala* had a "magical" effect on Finns, as they felt part of the "civilized" world, and their historical epic made them comparable to other Europeans with great traditions, such as the Greeks. All of this not only boosted national self-esteem in overcoming the inferiority complex they felt when compared to the great powers, but also gave new impetus to the spread of the national language press. The Finnish national anthem was also based on a Karelian song. The literary scholar, Yrjö Hirn (1870-1952), called Karelianism the intellectual stream in which artists sought inspiration. Similar to the Swedish Dalecarlia, the Norwegian Telemark, or the American Appalachia, Karelia was regarded by writers and intellectuals as a treasure trove of premodern world-views, and as the quintessential embodiment of national culture (Wilson, W. A. 2006).

19th-century tourism, national romance, and contemporary photographs or paintings, solidified the portrayal of Karelia as a prototype of the national landscape. Prominent tourist sites were linked to nature (Sortavala, Imatra), religion (Valamo Monastery), folk traditions (Koli) or historical monuments (such as the fortifications of the Karelian Isthmus). In the last decades of the 19th century, the consumer habits of the Finnish middle class changed considerably, and Karelia provided ideal places for tourist activities, such as hiking, sport, and recreation (Häyrynen, M. 2004). Karelianism attracted interest in Karelians and the "alternative" national landscape became more and more dominant. Later, Finnish nationalists between the two world wars began to regard it as an inalienable part of the country as the Eastern region of Greater Finland.

During the Cold War, Finnish and Russian interests in a divided Karelia had subsided, and the eastern border became both distinctive and mysterious. However, the specially-managed frontier zone caused inconvenience for the inhabitants living next to the Iron Curtain, as there were strict limitations related to free movement (Paasi, A. 1996). After the collapse of the Soviet Union, the Finnish rediscovery of Karelia began. Eastern Karelia proved to be an ideal field of reconstructed history, a process in which memory played an important role. Privileged sites that were often (re)visited provided therapeutic treatment for individuals who wanted to rethink and assimilate the past. As a result, Finnish tourists, as well as the formerly expelled Karelians and their descendants, created a new interpretation of the past filled with both emotion and affection. These newly constructed memories had tight links with particular sites in Eastern Karelia. Framing this in terms of Pierre Nora's conceptualization of *lieux de mémoire* ("sites of memory"[2]), the memories developed around privileged sites have become symbolic points of self-identification for visitors from Finland (Nora, P. 1996, K. Horváth Zs., 1999).

Karelians from Finland have used war memorials, abandoned family houses, and other remembrances to create a utopian image of Karelia. A special relationship has developed between residents and visitors, further modulating the depths of human interactions when locals are non-Karelians (Fingerroos, O. 2006). An example is the divided city of Värtsilä (Вяртсиля). The western part went to Finland after the Second World War, and the larger eastern part to the Soviet Union, along with its ironworks. Most of the local Karelians fled to Finland from the Red Army during the Winter War. After 1991, visits began, and many Finnish tourists who had local roots (re)constructed their territorial identity by recounting bitter stories and reminiscences (Paasi, A. 1996). Tearful interviewees spoke of their Karelian visits, their accounts filled with emotion and affection. These visits can be considered a pilgrimage of sorts, while the memories of Karelia as a utopian space have been nationalized (Alasuutari, P. and Alasuutari, M. 2009).

The spatial representations and imaginations of Karelia can be organized according to scale and performativity. The Karelian landscape, as the homeland of the *Kalevala* and the territory hiding the mythical treasures of the Finns, is the source of national identity, embodying a homogeneous space that can be interpreted from the macro-perspective, and that reaches transcendental heights. It is not bound to performativity, but rather replaces it. National memorials, museums, and political or religious centers break the homogeneity of the space, and take possession of their own past as privileged sites and new localities. These smaller-scale, unrelated heterogeneous space-fragments are brought alive by performativity. The personal stories are replete with individual emotions related to micro-scale intimate spaces. These micro-spaces, such as a house, a lakeshore, or a tree, can be imagined as invisible bubbles which can overlap with each other because of their links to individual memories and rituals. The performativity of remembrance, which

---

2 Defining *lieux de mémoire* is not a simple task. Pierre Nora attempted it in the preface of his famous book's English edition: "... a *lieu de mémoire* is any significant entity, whether material or nonmaterial in nature, which by dint of human will or the work of time has become a symbolic element of the memorial heritage of any community. [...] The narrow concept had emphasized the site: the goal was to exhume significant sites, to identify the most obvious and crucial centers of national memory, and then to reveal the existence of invisible bonds tying them all together." (Nora, P. 1996. pp. XV)

can only be obtained through subjective manifestations, saturated the Karelian landscape. Marc Augé's non-places (Augé, M. 1995), outside the Karelian memory-generated association of ideas, are not related to Karelianness, nor are they associated with rites, actions, or myths. The intensively transformed Soviet-Karelian space produced these symbolically neglected spaces or, in other words, the counter-places of privileged sites of memory.

Karelians on both sides of the border during the Cold War and after the turn of the millennium

Most of the Karelians living in Finland today are descendants of World War II refugees from the Karelian Isthmus and Ladoga-Karelia. In the winter of 1939–40, most of the settlers moved back to their homes, and then left in the summer of 1944 after the end of the Continuation War. Karelians dwelling in North and South Karelia have been living in the inland territory of Finland, and simply call themselves Karelians. Furthermore, the Finnish terminology distinguishes "resettled Karelian" (*siirtokarjalainen*) who were evacuated during World War II, from "Karelian refugees" (*Karjalan pakolainen*), who came from Russian Karelia (Hannula, M. 2006, Alasuutari, P. and Alasuutari, M. 2009). Consequently, three Karelian groups can be distinguished in Finland. Along with the autochthonous Finnish Karelians, who live in North and South Karelia, there are resettled and refugee Karelians. The latter two groups are difficult to locate because they are also settled in southern and western Finland, not only in the traditionally Karelian-inhabited North and South Karelia.

The largest cultural barrier was between the Orthodox settlers and the "indigenous" Lutherans, but the post-war environment favored national unity, and thus conflicts were not allowed to escalate. During the Cold War period, the "Russian-sounding" Karelian language was more likely to be considered a disgrace in Finland, but today it is more often regarded as a curiosity (Kupari, H. 2016). Despite the fact that North Karelia is one of the least economically developed regions, and that cardiovascular disease is interpreted as a Karelian curse by locals (Honkasalo, M-L., 2009), Karelia is regarded as an exotic, eastern province of Finland, which is increasingly visited by tourists.

After the Cold War, the "Karelian question" became part of public debate again, but there was no serious political basis for attaching Eastern Karelia to Finland. The boom in tourism and the permeability of borders have also contributed to the fact that Karelia and Karelians have become fashionable and unique in Finland (Alasuutari, P. and Alasuutari, M. 2009). Karelians have always played a central role as the subject of the "Inner Other" image, but while they were previously perceived as "Inner Alien", they are now more visible because of their local dialect and their distant but familiar traditions and customs, all of which have remained fascinating to Finnish visitors to this day.

In post-transition Russian Karelia, demands for autonomy were related to nationality rights, language protection, and the preservation of local culture. As inhabitants met with state power in regional or local institutions, the tension between the rights and the reality of everyday life became apparent. Goals included the partial gaining of political power and the establishment of their own elite in agreement with the federal government (Minescu, A. and Poppe, E. 2011). In the 1990s non-titular minority groups, who responded to what they felt was a lack of community law, prepared for cultural autonomy all over Russia. These communities were predominantly comprised of Russians and small ethnic groups living in an autonomous region of a titular nation, but the Russians living in Karelia did not embrace any autonomous movement (Prina, E. 2016). This is obviously due to the fact that the proportion of Karelians is below 10%, and Russians feel at home within the Republic of Karelia. According to a survey, Russians' perception of the titular nation in Karelia is not unfavorable at all, and Russian-Karelian intergroup-actions take place without conflict (Hagendoorn, L. and Poppe, E. and Minescu, A. 2008). The Karelian language enjoys state support under the 2004 law, although Karelia is the only republic in Russia where the language of the titular nation is not official. This is likely due to the growing decline of the ethnic Karelian population and the widespread usage of Russian in the republic (Austin, P.M. 1992). Everyday problems are caused by the lack of teachers, lack of opportunities for higher education in the mother tongue, and lack of money for community building (Varfolomeeva, A. 2014). After the collapse of the Soviet Union, Russia and Finland also supported the development of cross-border trade, as well as cultural and economic relations. Today, more students are studying Finnish in Karelia than Karelian because parents have realized that Finnish language skills will be useful to their children both locally, where they can employ Finnish in the tourist industry, or in Finland itself. If similar trends persist, the disappearance of the Karelian language is perhaps likely, along with the strengthening of the Finnish language and Russian hegemony (Allen, D. 2015).

The identity process in the formerly Finnish Karelian Isthmus exhibits considerable differences when compared with Eastern Karelia, as its original population was exchanged during the Second World War. For the resettled, non-Karelian, predominantly Russian population, attachment to the region became increasingly important after the dissolution of the Soviet Union. The newly-established Karelian Society has played a major role in the construction of "Isthmus Identity". The term "Karelian" refers to the region and regional identity, and has no direct connections with Karelian ethnic groups. The members of the Society show a special interest in local historical events and sites, and have begun to rediscover the territory where they are living. Good examples of this include the interest they have shown in memories of the medieval Novgorodian Rus that are related to the Karelian Isthmus or Finnish-Karelian traditions of the region and the accurate history of the Winter War. In addition, these groups have acquainted themselves with old Finnish settlements and geographical names. As historical facts have been re-learned, the locals have built new knowledge, which has changed their earlier conceptions. According these new recognitions, which were considerably different from the official interpretations, Soviet Russia had wrongly taken away the territory from Finland, and the sight of Finnish tourists tearing up at the sight of the abandoned houses of their ancestors have further strengthened this. There was a curious "moral war" between the Finns and the Russians, which, unlike the Winter War, could not be won by the Russians. The returning Finnish "nostalgia tourists" and the locals have special relationships, thus changing the representations of space (Hanula M. 2006). The combination of Lutheran and Orthodox churches, old Finnish buildings, abandoned and functioning Soviet industrial facilities, military objects, and modern buildings distinguish the Karelian Isthmus from its neighbouring territories. Furthermore, the memory-oriented performativity of Finnish tourists, and the interaction with local Slavic communities, has contributed to a reinterpretation of the concepts of Karelian identity. This territorialized regional identity is independent from Karelian ethnicity, but has essential connections to the Karelian Isthmus as a region.

Rescaling Moldovan Identities

Tamás Illés; Zsolt Bottlik

Introduction

The Republic of Moldova is situated in the immediate vicinity of the European Union, in the area currently defined as "In-Between Europe" (*Zwischeneuropa*). Caught in the grip of post-Soviet imperial aspirations and pan-Romanian pressure, its territory has been a buffer zone for centuries, which has created characteristic cultural differences, as well as numerous existential and social fault lines. The weakness of local structures has provided a favorable climate not only for the formation of ethnic and national identities imported from different centers of power, but also for playing these identities against each other in accordance with changing geopolitical interests. As no great powers have been able to permanently integrate the area and fully impose their cultural politics upon it, there is an exceptionally broad spectrum of national identities in the region, which bear the marks of fluidity and fragmentation. The consequences of misunderstood identities, as well as the relevance of carrying out research on the topic, are underscored by Gagauz separatist aspirations, the "frozen" armed conflict in Transnistria, and other warzones of the post-Soviet realm that are stuck in a similar geopolitical vacuum (for example, Eastern Ukraine or South Ossetia).

This chapter deals with the imprints left by the identity politics and interventions of great powers on different territories of Moldova and various strata of Moldovan society. Intended as a means to integrate the area into their own sphere of interest, these interventions defined different eras in the region. This chapter will shed light on the background of ethnic tensions that culminated in the de facto statehood of Transnistria. The authors scrutinize the background of these ethnic tensions in *longue durée*, tracing the roots of these tensions over several centuries from a macro-level perspective. The peripherality, and at the same time also centuries-long colonial exposure of the region, provides a particularly suitable ground for applying postcolonial approaches, and warns us about the pitfalls of normative, totalizing discourses. The complexity of local identities, however, and the entangled nature of interethnic relations, requires an approach to research that that makes room not only for postcolonialism, but also for the consideration of geographical scales. The aim of this chapter is to provide a basis for interpreting the identity politics that bind the everyday lives of Moldovans, while simultaneously addressing these relationships in their own complexity.

Theoretical frameworks

The Western interpretative framework of the post-Soviet realm's local characteristics

The idea of "layers" of Moldovan identity is a result of the wider spectrum of changes, as the meta-geographies of the three worlds and the geopolitical discourses of the Cold War era obscured the uneven geographical conditions of the periphery, which also led to the oversimplification of the question of national identities in the post-Soviet realm. The simplifying notions attached to the eastern part of Europe were not only the products of the Cold War era, but were also saturated with metaphors of "in-between otherness" (neither fully civilized, nor completely barbaric) in the period of the Enlightenment (Wolff, L. 1994). The essentialization of identities was also reproduced by Soviet authorities who strongly supported the national institutionalization of favored (for example, non-Muslim) ethnic groups, under the control of state leadership. Though the break-up of the Soviet Union shed new light on the identities of the region, the approach of researchers has generally been limited by an adherence to narrow, oversimplifying theoretical frames. Impoverished by lingering misconceptions and often pointless debates, our understanding of these emergent identities thus remains incomplete.

A key question lies in how the European post-Soviet realm, and the Republic of Moldova more specifically, is represented in the production and mediation of scientific knowledge. Despite the epistemological shifts of previous decades, a well-entrenched tendency prevails in Western-dominated human geography, one which insists stubbornly on the insensitive application of universalist claims in the case of local social contexts (Robinson, J. 2003). According to Berg (2004), theories originating from outside the West are usually portrayed as having no explanatory power, whereas Western approaches are more likely to circulate without being tied to a specific place. Timár (2004) notes how Western scholars became experts of post-socialism overnight by applying their theories to Eastern European phenomena, so that local studies were conducted according to the uneven formula of "Western, (predominantly Anglo-American) theory coupled with Eastern empirics".

As this chapter argues, "post-socialism" serves best as the underlying theoretical framework for the understanding of

European post-Soviet social processes. However, Western perspectives often conflate these processes in a teleological way with the process of democratization and Europeanization (Stenning, A. and Hörschelmann, K. 2008). The majority of discourses on (hyper-)globalization also envisioned the "end of history" (see, for instance, Fukuyama, F. 1992), placing their emphasis on transitional conditions and the "Westernization" of Eastern countries (Illés T. 2018a). Unsurprisingly, for human geographers dealing with the region throughout the 1990s, the paradigm of transitology (primarily in an economic sense) became dominant, if not monopolistic (Dingsdale, A. 1999). However, it is impossible to describe, or analyze, the complexity of the transitional period of Eastern European countries based on the a priori concepts of the West. Nor is it possible to do so with reference to terms such as perestroika or glasnost when they are used without consideration of their actual contexts (Tőkés R. 1998). That is why it is necessary to clarify theoretically and conceptually the post-socialism of the post-Soviet realm from an Eastern European perspective.

As a result of the dominant teleological approach focusing on the future and the West, rather than the present and the East, the historical and local geographical characteristics of the post-Soviet realm have become obscured (Stenning, A. ; Hörschelmann, K. 2008). Under the spell of transitology, the Eastern Bloc was, at best, associated with critiques of the normative conception of democratization (Suchland, J. 2011), but the deconstruction of deterministic notions — for example in the case of identities — has not yet been done. The equating of post-socialism with transitology was also the work of intellectuals from the Second World (for example, Milan Kundera, Czesław Miłosz and Tzvetan Todorov) who, in contrast to the intellectual elites of the Third World, maintained a critical attitude towards the Soviet system and totalitarianism, while also expressing their unconditional sympathy towards the West as well (Suchland, J. 2011). Consequently, critical analyses of the relationship between the two worlds on both sides of the Iron Curtain did not emerge until the collapse of the Soviet Union. However, the Russian/Soviet model, as a peculiar variant of modernity, was also portrayed as a kind of modernity that was always compared to (and seen as imitating) the West (with the associated slogan: "to catch up and leave behind") (Tlostanova, M. 2012). As the Second World ceased to exist virtually overnight, "post-Soviet" was conceptualized in Western narratives in terms of temporality rather than spatiality, a factor that continues to contribute to the perpetuation of transitology, and to the lack of critical perspectives in postcolonial studies (Tlostanova, M. 2012).

Embracing postcolonial discourses

Situated within a broadly understood postmodern intellectual current, postcolonialism has greatly influenced the production of geographical knowledge over the past three decades (and therefore also the geographical imaginations of various regions) by investigating the relationship between ruling and subordinate social groups (Cullen, D. and Ryan, J. and Winders, J. 2013). By challenging Eurocentric bias, postcolonial studies have revealed the continuities of colonization in nationalisms, sovereignty, spatial inequalities of power, and the accumulation of capital, as well as in the limited opportunities of acquiring knowledge (Sharp, J. P. 2009). As one of their greatest contributions, postcolonial critiques are constantly questioning universal(ist), global-scale explanations and metanarratives built on modernization, development, and world-systems theories. However, these have been examined almost exclusively in the case of non-Western, developing countries, while the Second World has not received similar attention (Chari, S. and Verdery, K. 2009).

Like orientalism (Said, E. 1978), Eastern Europe's "second-hand orientalism" (see Park, M. 2010) is also traditional and modern at the same time, and was intertwined with empire-building aspirations as well. Yet, this region was not identified as an antipode to civilization, nor was it conceived as being equivalent to barbarism. Instead, "Eastern Europeanness" was seen as a transitional stage on a development scale, with Western modernity as the most important point of reference (Wolff, L. 1994). At the same time, specific forms of creolization, hybridity, multilingualism, and transculturation are also found in the region, which can be paralleled with their postcolonial counterparts (Tlostanova, M. 2012). As a conspicuous similarity, Soviet and post-Soviet national aspirations did not emerge as the aspirations of nations, but rather as a struggle between institutionalized national elites and their opposing counter-elites (Brubaker, R. 1994). The situation of Soviet-influenced Central and Eastern Europe can also be linked to postcolonialism in the way certain states sought to homogenize their populations in accordance with the idea of a nation-state (for example, the Baltic States in the 1990s, or Ukraine today). Thus, Eastern European nationalisms can be interpreted as analogous to postcolonial state-building (Verdery, K. 1996).

Despite calls by some scholars (Sidaway, J. D., Woon, C. T. and Jacobs, J. M. 2014), only a few attempts have been made to extend postcolonialism in an Eastern European (post-Soviet) direction. According to Moore (2006), there are two main reasons for this "silence." First, since the majority of postcolonial scholars are Marxists, they refuse to depict the Soviet Union as "vicious", saving their harsh critique for French or British imperial practices. As Račevskis has observed, "according to the Western critical canon, it is not possible to be both a victim of Marxism and colonialism" (Račevskis, K. 2002). Second, while Western intellectuals feel guilty for the conditions of the Third World, they do not consider the same kind of solidarity towards the Second World (Moore, D. C. 2006). In addition, postcolonial studies attach too much importance to the transoceanic dimension of imperialism, as they see the overseas aspirations of Western states as colonialization, whereas the Russian/Soviet project has been characterized as mere territorial expansion (Lazarus, N. 2012). The Second World's differences compared to the West do not seem to be significant enough to rise to the rank of Said's postcolonial "Other" (Koobak, R. and Marling, R. 2014).

The equating of the two "posts" in postcolonial and post-Soviet is also hampered by other factors. Moscow was different from Western colonizers because it did not seek to integrate its dependent territories through capital accumulation, but rather through the accumulation of "redistributive" power (Chari, S. and Verdery K. 2009). Additionally, according to Todorova (2010), we cannot speak of the Soviet colonization of (In-Between) Europe because these states retained significant control over their social processes in contrast to the African colonial system. Therefore, instead of the "postcolonial paradigm", she proposes an approach that starts from concrete historical legacies. Although Kovačević (2008) agrees that no European states have undergone the same sort of extensive colonial exploitation as many of their African or Asian counterparts, she argues that this way of thinking still binds the region to the stereotypes created by the West (i.e. to the dichotomies of despised, backward, or mythologized conservatism). Instead, she proposes the notion of a specific Eastern European Orientalism. Since there is no consensus on the definition and the territorial extent of colonization, post-socialism — as an empty label — should instead be interpreted as a de-territorialized concept (Tuvikene, T. 2016) in order to saturate it with the rich theoretical achievements of postcolonialism (Owczarzak, J. 2009). This epistemological shift is also in line with Todorova's standpoint which considers the rejection of postcolonial theoretical frameworks unacceptable only from the side of the subject, since self-colonization and its related practices examined from the subject's point of view raise further questions as well. In this regard, subjects of the periphery marginalize themselves, thereby perpetuating the center (Kiossev, A. 2011). According to Koobak and Marling (2014), it is exactly the "complex and continuing process of self-colonization" which makes the post-socialist region relevant for postcolonial studies.

The embracing of a critical postcolonial position provides an opportunity to dismantle rigid dichotomies, as well as deconstruct the hierarchies formed according to the needs of the external centers of power. Thus, the "postcolonial post-Soviet" approach is necessarily critical of the neoliberal promises of the market economy and democracy, of the socialist past and socialist futures, and of the possibilities of acquiring knowledge. Instead of relationships built on binary oppositions interwoven with politics and power, the postcolonial notion of hybridity (Bhabha, H. K. 1994) may be suitable for grasping and (re)interpreting post-regime change contradictions, ambivalences, and frightening contrasts. This "post-socialist hybridity" may offer a way out of the insurmountable conflicts between left-wing narratives that mourn the end of the socialist experiment, and the opposite side depicting the socialist era as demonic totalitarian oppression (Marciniak, K. 2009). Hybridity also reminds us that cultures are not necessarily homogeneous and coherent.

In the case of countries in the western part of the European post-socialist realm, the adaptation of postcolonial perspectives may be questionable, and even constrained, due to their specific historical legacy and western orientation. However, in the case of the eastern (post-Soviet) states, the weak local structures that determine social processes, the constant dependency, and the more intense impact of Moscow's colonializing aspirations, allow and justify the use of postcolonialism as an underlying theoretical framework. Nonetheless, it is necessary to avoid replacing the previous holistic epistemology with new ones. As Tlostanova (2012) points out, instead of "universalist applications of ready-made discourses and travelling theories", the goal should be to explore various local histories determined by colonial and imperialist differences, evading the role of both the heroic resister and the sacrificial lamb. It is also important to avoid overemphasizing the importance of post-socialism or postcolonialism, which can lead possibly to the trap of historicism (Stenning, A. and Hörschelmann, K. 2008). A solution to this problem may be to use post-socialism not merely as a kind of periodization, but also as a way of revealing the intersections between pre- and post-socialism. In doing so, post-socialism should not be considered a mere variant of postcolonialism. Rather, in a heuristic way, the insights of postcolonial studies should be applied in order to gain a more nuanced understanding of post-Soviet identities. The scrutiny of Moldovan identity and its spatiality provides a suitable starting point to meet this call.

The importance of geographical scales in the (trans)formation of Moldovan identity

In addition to the theoretical foundations laid out above, the complexity of the topic requires a framework that helps to overcome the historicizing narratives dominating ethnic, religious, and political geography studies in the eastern part of Europe. In this chapter, we rely on the concept of geographical scale. The distinct and intertwined factors influencing Moldovan identity on supranational, national, and regional levels point to the usability of scale. Although scale has been one of the key concepts in the field of human geography since the 1980s, it gradually lost its explanatory power in the so-called "scale debate" which began in the 1990s, and then lost its ontological status as well (Berki M. 2017). The paper by Marston, Jones, and Woodward (2005) may be considered the climax of the debate. It identified scale not only as an unfruitful concept for geography, but also as a downright harmful category. Currently, there is a cautious reconsideration in the literature that is aimed at least partially at reclaiming the methodological usefulness of scale, which is understood as a categorization tool for examining social processes (Häkli, J. 2018). With regard to the importance of flows, interconnectedness, and networks intensifying with globalization, it must be emphasized that this chapter does not intend to attribute either material or deterministic features to scale, but rather to look at it epistemologically (Jones, K. T. 1998). Accordingly, in this study, there is no presumption of a hierarchically defined continuity between the local and global scales influencing the layers of Moldovan identity. Instead, the chapter draws attention to the dynamically changing nature of the elements of identity.

Constant in-betweenness on the supranational scale

The foundations of today's modern Moldovan state were established in the early 19th century, and its boundaries (except for its northwestern part) were established in August 1940, when it became a member republic of the Soviet Union. However, this political frame is not a continuation of the Principality of Moldavia, which had its heyday in the 15th century. The political contours of the area have changed several times, mostly because of the aspirations of neighboring powers (Figure 3.2.1). When trying to grasp the in-betweenness of identities present in the current territory, we must first take into consideration the various impacts that the great powers have had on the local society, especially in light of the role they played in determining the area's geopolitical position. The most important of these impacts are the ones that have become a part of identity-forming collective memory, either by subsequent national movements, or by various political formations.

The area's character as a geopolitical buffer zone has been evident since the early medieval period (Hofbauer, H. and Roman, V. 1997). Recognizing the strategic importance stemming from its geographical location, the emerging states of the region,

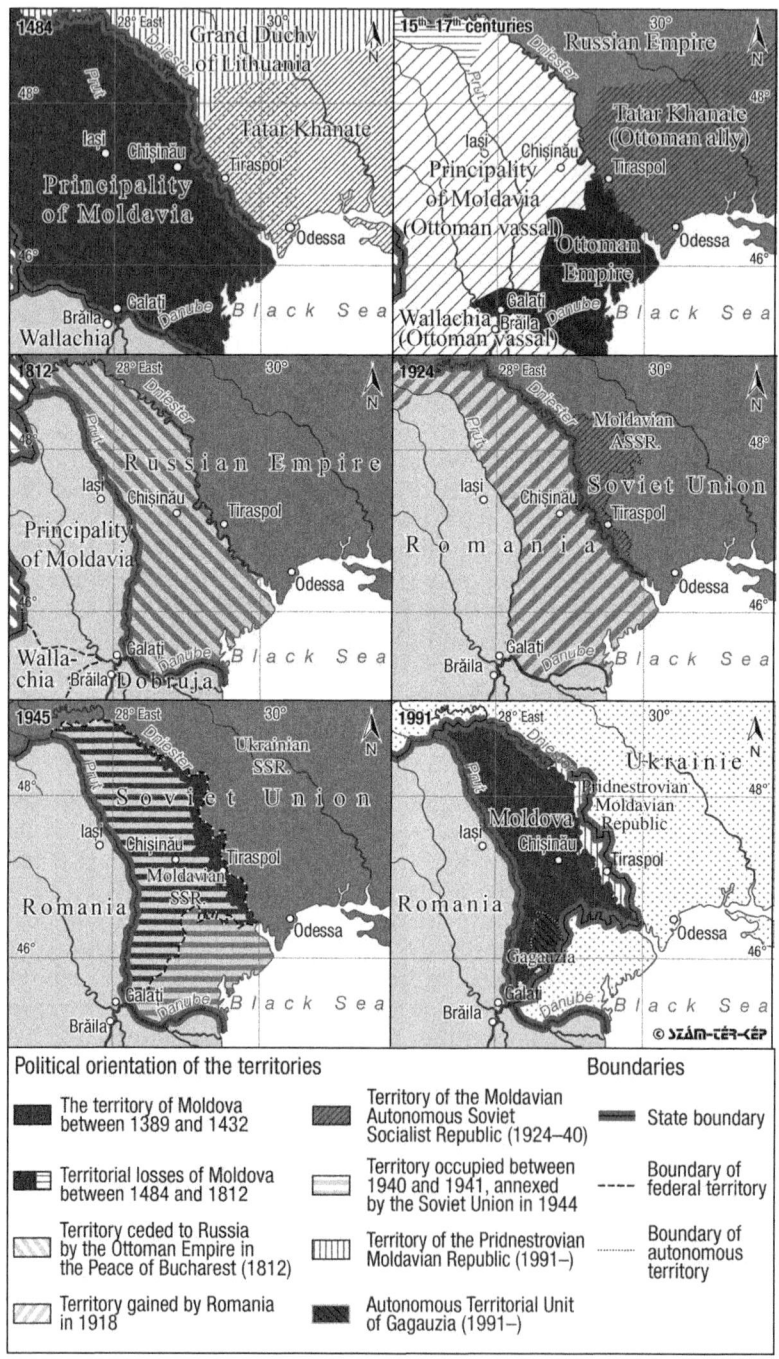

Figure 3.2.1 *The changing territory of Moldova from the 14th century to the present; (Source:* Sellier, A. ; Sellier, J. 1991*)*

which included Kievan Rus, the Kingdom of Hungary, and Poland, would have liked to have integrated the area into their state. Still, as an external power, it was the Ottoman Empire that first appeared in the region. However, Ottomans occupied only the Lower Danube tributary area that was strategically important for them, and were satisfied with the vassal status of the Principality.

It was not until 1812 that the territory known as Bessarabia, situated roughly between the Prut and the Dniester, became an integral part of a foreign power. As a result of Russian aspirations towards the Balkans, it was conquered by the Russian Empire. This had a number of consequences that were, and still are, affecting the ethnic identity of Eastern Neo-Latin-speaking communities living in the territory of the Republic of Moldova. From 1812, the history of the former Principality of Moldavia started to follow two distinct paths along which the group identity of the local population was steered in different directions, despite their shared foundations (Tontsch, G. H. 1996). The areas with fundamentally different trajectories were characterized by changed geopolitical orientations, and were also affected differently by the nation-building strategies of the 19th century (Zabarah, D. A. 2013). It should also be emphasized that in the area between the Prut and the Dniester, following the empire-building logic of tsarist Russia, the promotion of the language of its administration and culture was a high priority (King, C. 2000). It was in this light that the influence of Russian language and culture increased significantly, and that, from the 1860s onwards, the local Neo-Latin (Romanian) language was gradually restricted, both in education and in ecclesiastical liturgy.

From the first half of the 19th century, the ethnic spatial structure of the population also started to change significantly, which led to the loosening of the local Neo-Latin-speaking majority that had been more homogeneous in the Middle Ages. This meant the gradual emigration of Romanian-speaking people to the Principality of Moldavia situated west of Prut, and the immigration of Russian-speaking people from inner Russian territories, who mainly entered into the domains of public administration and the economy (Cazacu, M. and Trifon, N. 2017). In addition to changes in ethnic proportions, territorial polarization could also be observed, as Neo-Latin speakers were gradually pushed into rural areas. In towns, Slavic speakers and Jews formed an almost absolute majority (Bochmann, K. et al. 2012) (Figure 3.2.2).

The aim of the Romanian national movement, which was already forming in the first half of the 19th century, was to create the linguistic and cultural unity of the Principality of Wallachia and

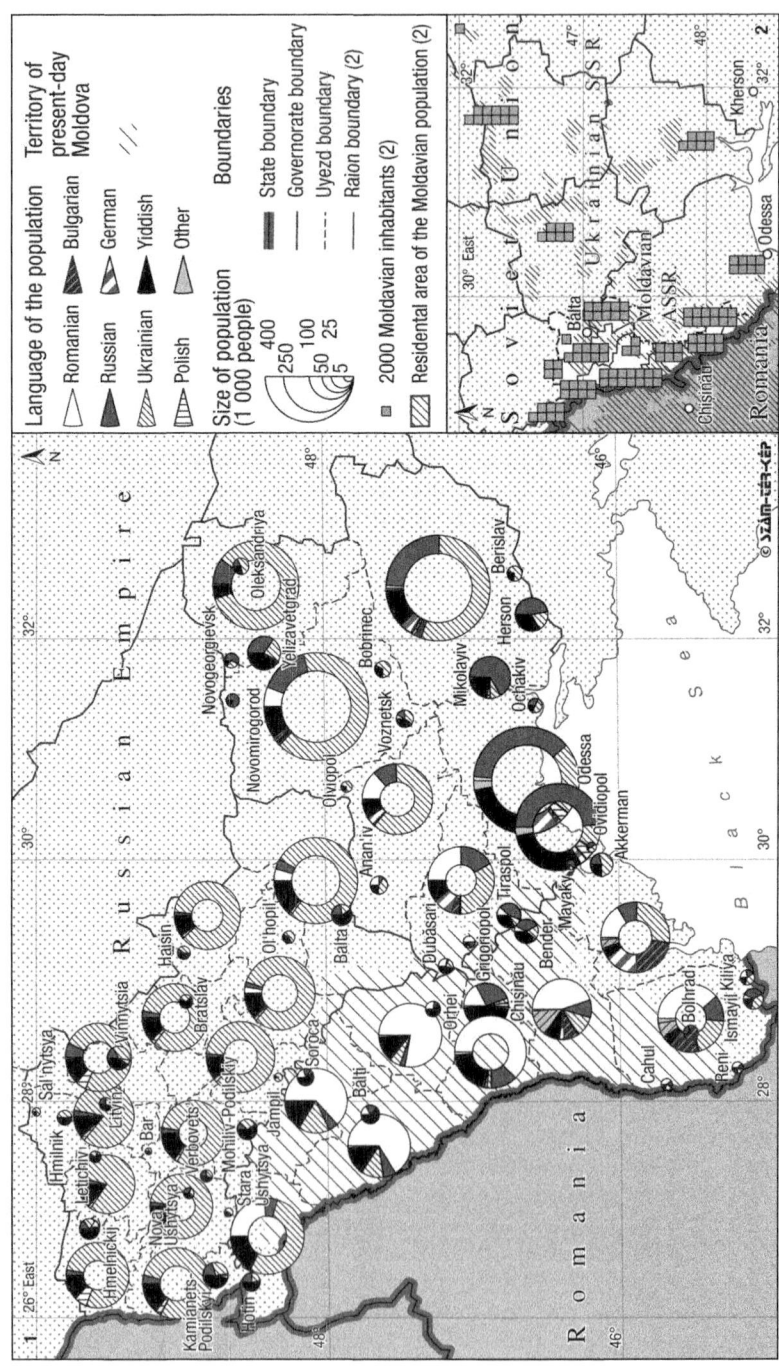

Figure 3.2.2 *The ethnic composition of the settlement area of Romanians living in the Russian Empire in 1897 (1) and the size and residential area of the Moldovan population in 1926 (2); (Sources:* [26]; [28]; [29])

the still-independent Principality of Moldavia (situated between the Prut and the Carpathians). It was an essential part of the birth of the Romanian nation, and provided the Romanians with opportunities to strengthen their political position. Becoming a modern nation, the group living beyond the Carpathians (in the territory of Wallachia and the Principality of Moldavia) had a much more intense cultural relationship with the Romanians of Transylvania and Bukovina, while the Bessarabian Neo-Latin-speaking population (living in the eastern part of the former Principality of Moldavia) had been practically left out of the experience of Romanian nation-building (Goina, C. 2005; Wagner, M. 2008). At the same time, the cultural threads of the intellectual elite of the latter group were still tied to the west, to Iaşi, importing the cultural products of Romanian nation-forming from there (Dumbrava, V. 2006). However, due to the small size of the intellectual stratum, the Romanian language — which had meanwhile been consolidated and modernized according to Western standards — could not find a breeding ground in Bessarabia among the population exposed to Russification, and who still used the Cyrillic alphabet (Solomon, F. 2002).

The opportunity to fulfil the political goal of the Romanian national movement (namely, to make all Romanians the citizens of the modern Romanian nation-state founded in 1859) emerged after World War I, with the creation of "Greater Romania". This was the time when Bessarabia, between the Prut and the Dniester, also came under Romanian rule. Nonetheless, despite the undoubted common cultural and linguistic roots, the above-mentioned economic and social differences dating from 1812 could not be reduced by the Romanian central authorities either. One of the reasons for this was that the Soviet Union did not recognize Romania's right to the territories beyond the Prut, which contributed to a constant unstable atmosphere in local everyday life. Thus, from the Romanian side, the primary goal was to integrate the area — which had only a 56% Romanian/Moldovan majority — as quickly, and in some cases as aggressively, as possible (Tontsch, G. H. 1996, van Meurs, W. 2003). However, the intensifying governmental centralization and the restrictive nationality politics aroused not only the antipathy of non-Romanian speakers, but also the dissatisfaction and marginalization of the Moldovan population. Because they led a more traditional lifestyle, and had become accustomed to a greater degree of subsidiarity, attempts at centralization reinforced their non-Romanian group consciousness (Petrescu, C. 2001).

Over the 20th century, and mainly due to two distinct historical trajectories, the dissimilarity between the eastern and the western part of the former Principality of Moldavia further deepened, especially after the area was re-annexed to the Soviet Union during World War II. As a consequence of the Sovietization of the Moldavian Soviet Socialist Republic, which had been organized within a different territorial framework (Figure 3.2.1), authorities placed an increasing emphasis on the cultural and historical differences of the region's ethnic groups, distinguishing Neo-Latin-speaking groups from the Romanian ones. This was reinforced by the reintroduction of the Cyrillic alphabet, the marginalization of the Romanian literary language, the deportation of Romanophile intellectuals, and the disruption of their physical and cultural ties with the above-mentioned Romanian ethnic core area (Dumbrava, V. 2002, Illés T. 2018b). In parallel with this, the authorities supported the resettlement of workers and other functionaries from inner Russian territories through a targeted cadre policy. As a result of this practice, a new social stratum emerged, one that strengthened the imperial (colonial) dimension by placing the hierarchies of local society on new foundations. These new foundations, however, intersected with existing ethnic fault lines.

In Romania itself, maintaining and even mentioning the historical and cultural relations that existed with the areas beyond the Prut was a taboo subject until the 1960s. On the Romanian side, the state border was not the only obstacle. There were also systematic attempts to build walls between the societies of the two countries that had shared cultural roots. Though the Romanian national idea was once again spatially extended beyond the state boundaries during the Ceaușescu era, the "Bessarabian question" could not be raised officially among the two friendly socialist states (Tontsch, G. H. 1996, van Meurs, W. 2003).

The national scale(s) of Moldovan identity(ies)

One of the fundamental conflicts in Moldova's identity struggles is that the political geographical concept of "Moldova" has changed several times historically. Various social groups have understood it differently, moreover, and it was also often uncertain whether it referred to a political or a historical region for them (Cazacu, M. 1996, Siupur, E. 1993) (Figure 3.2.1). The first modern state framework that was developed in accordance with a distinct Moldovan national identity was erected by the Moldavian Autonomous Soviet Socialist Republic, which was established by the USSR in 1924, and which was located entirely within the Ukrainian Soviet Socialist Republic. Even though the very concept of Moldovan identity raises a question about the existence of a non-Romanian Moldovan ethnic group, the establishment of an autonomous Moldovan territory was also linked to the Soviet need to secure the territories between the Prut and the Dniester, a strategic interest that they shared with their tsarist predecessors. Additionally, in keeping with Soviet foreign policy strategy at the time, the area could also have served as a foundation for subversive actions aimed at weakening Romania (Cazacu, M. 1996). Later on, this autonomous territory served as an explicit reference point for the establishment of the larger Moldavian Soviet Socialist Republic (MSSR), a member republic of the Soviet Union (Figure 3.2.1).

From the 1950s, the state formation of the newly-constituted MSSR provided not only the political support and comprehensive societal frames necessary for Moldovan identity formation, but also the basis upon which dissimilarities from the Romanians could be stressed. Slavic cultural expansion, coupled with the Sovietization of society, emerged as a general tendency which distanced the Neo-Latin-speaking majority from the Romanian nation. Its steps included the deportation of individuals stigmatized as anti-Soviet elements, the settlement of the supporters of the Soviet system into the territory, and the strengthening of the role of the Russian language as a means of social uplift. In addition to making it impossible to establish cultural contacts by banning individual travel, any kind of personal contact with Romania was prevented (even visiting relatives was possible only on rare occasions until 1989) (Berindei, D. 1996). This not only disrupted the common cultural and linguistic roots between Moldovans and Romanians, but also contributed to the desire to create an essentialized, independent Moldovan language. This linguistic construct bears the marks both of premodern Moldovanness (which was not easily discernible geographically) and Soviet culture. However, as a localized linguistic project, it was also deliberately aimed at blending together all the dialects spoken in the territory of the MSSR. In addition to state-governing bodies (the assembly of the member republic and the Communist Party of Moldavia), this politics of language was backed by a number of other key institutions as well (for example, the Academy of Sciences of Moldova or the Moldova State University in Chişinău).

Although the Soviet Union was more or less successful in repressing local political opposition groups in the early 1980s, in the second half of the decade Gorbachev's appointment as general secretary in the spirit of "political rejuvenation", as well as perestroika and glasnost, created a fundamentally different situation. In the case of Moldavia, the first tangible signs of this were the measures initiated in August 1989 by the People's Front (Frontul Popular). Led by the local elite who had been excluded from political and economic power but were willing to grab it, the People's Front advocated maintaining closer ties with Romanian culture. These measures included the official recognition of Romanian language and the introduction of the Latin alphabet (Solomon, F. 2002). As a result, language became a key element of the national project again. At the same time the MSSR, taking advantage of the greater room to maneuver politically, sought to forge closer ties with Romania, even though one of the articles of the agreement signed during the Iliescu–Gorbachev meeting in April 1991 affirmed the inviolability of borders. The rapprochement with Romania and the possible unification that was mentioned increasingly at the political level was evident in other ways, too. As a counter-reaction, a Russian-oriented political group also emerged who were interested in maintaining or reviving the old structures as widely as possible. They consisted predominantly of the communist elites of the capital city and the territories beyond the Dniester, as well as of the Gagauz and Bulgarian minorities who enjoyed a more privileged position in the Soviet system than the Moldovan majority (March, L. 2007). Under these circumstances, the independence of the MSSR was proclaimed under the name Republic of Moldova in August 1991. It was the first independent, internationally recognized state of the local Neo-Latin-speaking population, whose elite initially defined itself as Romanian and called for unification with Romania as soon as possible.

Almost simultaneously with this, the Gagauz people and the mostly Russian and Ukrainian speaking inhabitants of Transnistria also declared their independence. During the outbreak of the civil war, and with the dissolution of the Soviet Union in December 1991, the Republic of Moldova became de jure independent as well. In addition, separatists with strong Russian support established the internationally unrecognized Pridnestrovian Moldavian Republic (Transnistria), whereas an autonomous territorial unit called Gagauzia was also formed. This, in turn, sharpened the debates over Romanian orientation, not only in the context of the "Romanian–non-Romanian" relationship, but also within the Neo-Latin-speaking population. Among the latter, the previously clear opinion on the tight relationship with Romanians was questioned, and regional factors increasingly became the focal points of self-identification.

Premodern Moldovanness manifesting on the regional scale

Although modern nationalisms are based on the structures of modern states, in many cases in "In-between Europe" (*Zwischeneuropa*), these states are not necessarily the legal continuations of medieval antecedents of the same name. Yet, these early state formations play an important role in collective memory. Therefore, in order to examine the regional scale of Moldovan identity essentialized by Soviet politics, we must reach back to the already-mentioned medieval political formation, which had a Christian, Neo-Latin-speaking population.

In the period between the 5th and the 13th centuries, the wider territory of today's Republic of Moldova functioned as a military staging area for equestrian nomadic tribes. As a result, relatively solid state structures could only develop in the last third of the Middle Ages. In the former staging area of the Mongolian army, which had largely been under Hungarian rule, the first consolidated state — the independent Principality of Moldavia — was founded by Prince Bogdan in 1359. With the Prut as its central axis, the territory of the principality was bordered by the Dniester in the east, the Black Sea and the Lower Danube in the south, and the Carpathians (or more precisely, the eastern border of the Kingdom of Hungary) in the west. It only lacked a stable natural and political geographical boundary in the north, towards the Polish territories. Thus, its character as a buffer zone was also stronger in this direction (Hausleitner, M. 2008). The principality included the Moldavian territories that are now parts of Romania as well as the territory of the present-day Republic of Moldova, which is situated between the Prut and the Dniester (Figure 3.2.1). Consequently, and also unsurprisingly, collective historical memory on both sides of the Prut regards this state formation as the foundation of national identity.

The buffer-zone character of the territory did not change in later historical periods. Due to the weakness (or, rather, the power balance) of external forces, and following its heyday in the 15th century, the area became a vassal of the Ottoman Empire, which at that time was pursuing a particularly intensive foreign policy towards the Balkans and the Crimea. The Ottomans did not integrate this region into their state in the same way as their territories in the Balkans, however. A certain level of cultural independence was granted to the people in this buffer zone, especially in the northern territory that was strategically less important for the Sublime Porte and therefore had a less heterogeneous ethnic spatial structure (Kőszegi M. 2016a). As a result of these factors, the area is characterized by a deeply-rooted linguistic and cultural fabric and a certain degree of political cohesion, which has survived up to this day, and that continues to exhibit an important degree of social cohesion in spite of constantly changing power and external (counter)influences (Neukirch, C. 1996, 2003).

Discussion: Identity politics on different scales

The political background of identity constructions in the present-day Republic of Moldova

As demonstrated above, the statehood of the Republic of Moldova, and in many cases also the identity of its inhabitants, was largely determined by supranational forces over the *longue durée*. The will of the local elite, in turn, has only been expressed for a relatively short period of time. With the independent Republic of Moldova, however, it seemed that the conditions had been set for those living in the area to define themselves at the national level according to their own ideas. At the same time, all the factors discussed above — that is, the multi-scalar exposures to power, the internal social structures, and the characteristically Eastern European identity elements (especially the role of language, the peripheral position of religion in the Soviet period, the unprocessed traumas of the past, and the inability to find national consensus) — have rendered national self-consciousness and the identity of the country's inhabitants highly contradictory. Their postcolonial negotiations of identity mark the starting point of the acute social problems that have consumed the region since the regime change. As a further contradiction, the formation of this nation-state under such circumstances is not the prerequisite of Moldovan national history (as it is typical in the region), but rather its product (Bochmann, K. et al. 2012).

From an outsider's point of view, two foreign policy strategies (as well as economic strategies) seemed feasible to stabilize the new state: union with Romania or the existence of two Romanian states. While nation-building was aimed at integrating minorities and emphasizing Europeanness in the majority of post-socialist countries, the situation was markedly different in the case of states torn apart along the lines of their federal units (such as Yugoslavia or the Soviet Union), the parts of which suddenly became new (nation-)states. Among these newly created countries, Moldova is even more special in the sense that its existence was questioned right at the moment of its birth, and the century-long antecedent of a desired, future Moldovan identity did not result in a stable sense of self-consciousness either (van Meurs, W. 2003). Moreover, in Transnistria, in parallel with gaining independence, a new national movement also emerged.

In the now independent country, the crisis caused by the regime change led to a breakup among the Romanian-speaking population as well. As in all former socialist countries, with the dissipation of the euphoria that accompanied political change, new conflicts evolved and intensified. In Moldova, unification with

Romania was removed from the agenda mainly because the society turned towards its own internal problems and gave its vote of confidence in the mid-1990s to a political force promising the relative calmness of the Soviet era (Benkö, A., Malek, M. 2005).

This has resulted in a process in which the old-new holders of power reached back to the ideology of "Moldovenism", albeit not to its Soviet interpretation (Zabarah, D. 2013). This mostly meant the rethinking of their geopolitical positions on the supranational scale. Renouncing unity with Romania reassured minorities in particular, while the mobilization of the rural population was another aim of this political shift. Among others, the post-Soviet leadership argued for linguistic independence, highlighted the continuity of medieval Moldavian statehood, and emphasized the multinational character of the population. In contrast, for another group ("*Românists*", the supporters of Western orientation), the need to emphasize the commonalities with Romanian culture also remained important. The competition of these two groups, which were different in their ethnic identity, has had an impact on various aspects of domestic policy as well (Belina, B. and Arambaşa, M. 2007). The opposition between the group more tightly linked to the old system and the nationalist circles continues to influence the interpretation of history and memory politics (Bochmann, K. et al. 2012).

"Transnistrianism", however, presents a challenge for the two previous ideas on a regional scale, as the breakaway state was established in a well-defined area (consisting of a strip of territory along the left bank of the Dniester and two bridgeheads west of the river). Thus, in this area, Moldovan/Romanian identity management also has to reckon with an independent identity that is still being shaped (van Meurs, W. 2003; Neukirch, C. 1996, 2003). The identity of the inhabitants of this ethnically extremely heterogeneous territory (Figure 3.2.3) has already been characterized by in-betweenness in historical times as well, which made Romanian attempts at national unification uncertain in this area (Zabarah, D. 2013). After the regime change, the separatists' arguments were directed against Moldovan/Romanian dominance, as breaking the status quo would have jeopardized the economic advantages gained during the Soviet period. Given that Transnistria does not share a border with Russia, and that Russia is thus supporting the Transnistrian project from afar, the leaders of the breakaway state had no other choice than to solidify independent statehood and formulate a national strategy (Heller, M. and Arambaşa, M. N. 2009). Therefore, while the Moldovan line prefers a multi-ethnic direction vis-à-vis the Romanian orientation, Transnistrian identity management seeks to provide a cultural basis for their de facto statehood.

In addition, the Autonomous Territorial Unit of Gagauzia is situated in the southern part of the country, where the

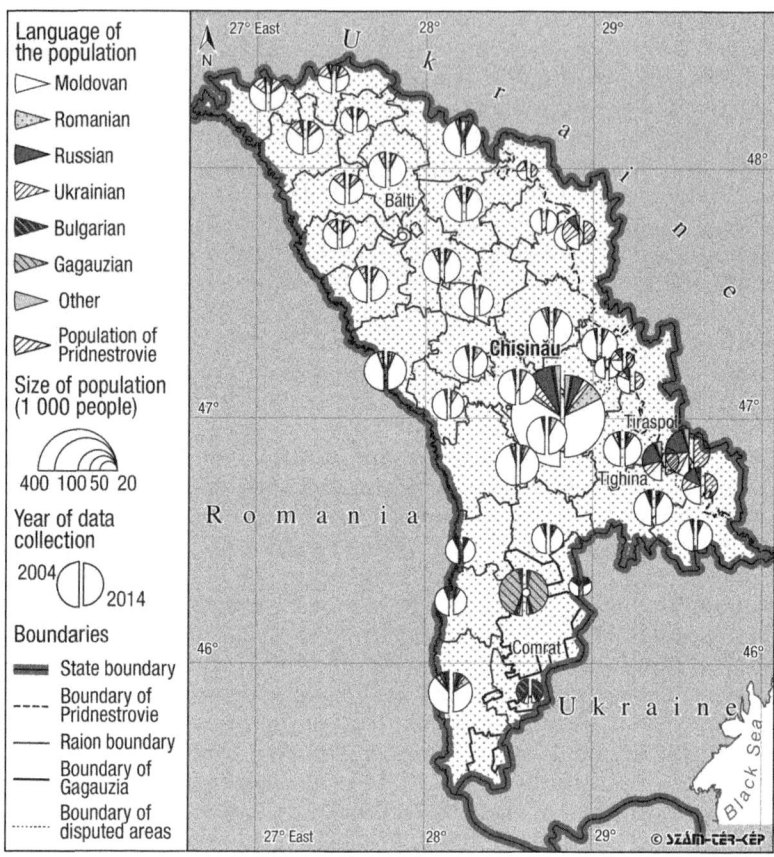

Figure 3.2.3 *The distribution of the population of Moldova by native language by raions between 2004 and 2014; (Sources:* [21]; [22])

Turkish-speaking Orthodox population is granted autonomous rights. The regionalism of both areas, imbued with an odd nostalgia, is based on the cultural politics of the Russian/Soviet era that protected them against Romanian/Moldovan national aspirations (Kőszegi M. 2016b). Thus, while Transnistrian independence can be primarily attributed to Russia's geopolitical interests, the autonomy of Gagauzia owes its existence to the Moldovan leadership, and has resulted from their compromise on separatism.

Since the beginning of the politico-economic transition, in certain countries of post-socialist (and even more typically post-Soviet) Europe, state power is not very strong, the will to reform is weak, and the social need to adopt Western patterns (for example, in the form of EU accession) is low. Taken together, these factors are also coupled with ethnic tensions. In several instances, even if indirectly, these states likely fall into the crossfire of external power games (van Meurs, W. 2013). This can be seen in the case of Moldova as well, which is simultaneously exposed to Russian energy and Western financial assistance, especially because ethnic differences have clear political determinations. Despite the escalation of the tensions into an armed conflict, these determinations were not really perceived by the international public in the early 1990s, a fact that also stems from the region's neglect by the West.

Summary: the layeredness of Moldovan identity

Postcolonialism is less associated with a well-defined historical event, a change in political status, or a geographical area; rather, it represents a critical commitment against the consequences of colonialism and its role in knowledge formation (Gregory, D. 2004, Radcliffe, S. A. 1997). This approach provides a suitable theoretical framework for rethinking the cultural patterns of the region; Moldovan identities, for instance, may gain new meanings not only through the prisms of the centers of power but also in the context of the continuity of colonialism.

In the Republic of Moldova, after having undergone several changes of power over the past centuries, nationalisms associated with the slow process of modernism usually developed in accordance with the needs of geographically distant centers. As a result of border changes, a premodern identity that emerged on a regional scale was harnessed first to pan-Slavic and then later to pan-Romanian political aspirations. As in other peripheral regions of the Soviet Union, the socialist system eventually produced its own identity constructs in Moldova as well which, by propagating "Moldovenism" to create a national scale, ultimately sought to solidify the uniqueness of Moldovan identity.

At the same time, globalization has posed yet another challenge to nation-building by adding a supranational scale to the already interconnected local, regional, and national scales. Given the emergence of transnational mobility within this globalized context, the national attachment of Moldovans has become the product of a more progressive and self-reflexive choice, rather than the automatic acceptance of a socially conserved structure. Owing to the dire economic situation, the Moldovan population is particularly exposed to this. In the 2005–2010 period alone, at least 20–25% of the country's working-age population had to work abroad permanently (Nita, S. 2016).

Also due to the rise of global processes and their associated networks, national identity can no longer be linked exclusively to the national scale, as globalization has overturned the primacy of identity politics organized on the national scale, and has increased the importance of both the sub- and the supranational scales (Brenner N. 1999). At the same time, however, it is also important to note that this scale-jumping was not accompanied by the diminishing relevance of the national idea (Antonsich, M. 2009). Instead, it is clear that national identity is embedded between various forms of supranational and regional identities, although these three scales do not complement or enable each other in a static way, but rather function within the context of complex interaction (Kaplan, D. H. 2018). Therefore, Moldovan identity cannot be linked only to the national scale, since people's collective memory is associated neither with a centuries-old state formation, nor with a standardized language. On the contrary, Moldovan identity can only be interpreted relationally, with mutually interconnected and interdependent multi-scalar layers. The local layer can be manifested on the national scale (for example, in the case of the Moldovan line which builds on the elements of authenticity and traditionalism stemming from the sense of place), just as the national scale may have an impact on concrete localities (for example, in the form of the occasional demonstrations rejecting the convergence of Romanian or Russian foreign policy).

Because of the layeredness of identity elements resulting from multiple influences, it is not surprising that in the conflict of current geopolitical discourses, centers of power cannot play off a given slice of collective identity that would be otherwise beneficial for them. Thus, beyond blaming postmodernity or cultural globalization for the fluidity of Moldovan identity, an unprocessed historical past burdened with geopolitical tensions can also be evoked as a peculiar kind of in-betweenness that has caused long centuries of political failures imposed from higher geographical scales.

The Post-Soviet Azerbaijani National Identity

Margit Kőszegi; Zsolt Bottlik

Introduction

Widely known for its diversity of peoples, the Caucasus is home to the so-called Transcaucasian states, which include Azerbaijan, Georgia, and Armenia. Formed as member republics of the Soviet Union in the early 20th century, these nation-states became independent after 1990. Though they in many ways owed their existence to Soviet policy, and of course also to Soviet power, the peoples of this region nevertheless regarded their countries as legitimate nations, and saw themselves as proud custodians of thousands of years of culture and statehood.

Like their neighbours, the Azerbaijanis have laid claim to a long history of civilization and development in the Caucasus. Beyond this, they also profess to live in the first democratic state of the Islamic world. This self-definition already carries in itself the peculiarities of their peripheral position, namely the hybridity of their collective identity (Bhabha, H. 2004). As part of Islam, but as a result of tsarist Russian expansionist efforts, they became involved in the process of forming "imagined communities" (Anderson, B. 1991) which resulted in the proclamation in 1918 of their short-lived independent nation-state. However, the formation of their national identity over the rest of the 20th century was determined by Soviet-type state power, which meant the abolition of the role of religion in defining identity. The effects of the Soviet period, in addition to the nature of political leadership, also illustrates continuity in everyday life, even after the break-up of the Soviet Union, and in parallel with the revival of Islam.

Among the lingering effects of the Soviet period, the territorial-based debate arising from the formation of borders has become especially important in the formation of national identity. The territorial dispute with neighbouring Armenia over Nagorno-Karabakh escalated tensions during the 1980s. These tensions resulted in an armed conflict between the two countries in the 1990s, as well as between the Azerbaijani majority and the Armenian minority within Azerbaijan itself. The presence of a common enemy, coupled with threats to their territorial integrity, were particularly strong factors in the development of national consciousness in Azerbaijan in the years following independence (Fig. 3.3.1).

Post-Soviet identity formation in Azerbaijan is complicated by the fact that the northern regions of Iran, which border present-day Azerbaijan to the south, have a significant Azerbaijani-speaking Shia Muslim population, known as the Azeris. These parts of Iran, which include the sub-territorial units of East and West Azerbaijan, count more than 18 million Azerbaijani-speaking Azeris, a number two-and-a-half times higher than the Azerbaijani inhabitants of Azerbaijan (Ulasiuk, I. 2013) (Fig. 3.3.1). A widespread conspiracy theory from the Soviet period has long suggested that the Azerbaijani people were deliberately cut in two by the dividing powers (the Russian and Persian Empires). Public opinion in Azerbaijan has fuelled a widespread sense of belonging with the Azeris living on the other side of the border, which has led to border conflicts and also illegal border crossings at the time of the regime change. This phenomenon has put the political elite of post-Soviet Azerbaijan at a sensitive crossroads.

Another important factor that informs identity politics in Azerbaijan is oil, which is the country's strategically important raw material and most important economic asset. With its origins in the forced industrialization of the Soviet period, oil as an energy source is tied directly to notions of the motherland, and is considered a national treasure. A key economic determinant in the 21st century, oil directly affects the daily life and livelihoods of the people, and forms an integral part of the "nationnes" of contemporary Azerbaijan.

Given its history in the short 20th century, Azerbaijan understandably retains specific post-Soviet characteristics. This chapter will focus specifically on the effects of power, hegemony and leadership that determined the formation of the Azerbaijani nation. In terms of the national consciousness of Azerbaijanis more generally, as in many other examples presented in this book, the direct and indirect influence on the periphery by centralized leadership, whether Soviet or now Russia, is paramount.

Forming the imagined Azerbaijani community

In examining Azerbaijani national identity, this chapter accepts the theory of the imagined community developed by Anderson (1991). According to this theoretical point of view, with the spread of print capitalism and the wider communication-enhancing effects of modernization since the 19th century, as well as the efficient organization of government-run administrative and educational institutions, there was a growing opportunity to form and shape national communities (Anderson, B. 1991). At the same time, drawing on Brubaker's institutionalist approach, we also interpret "nationnes" in the Soviet successor states as taking an institutionalized form, both

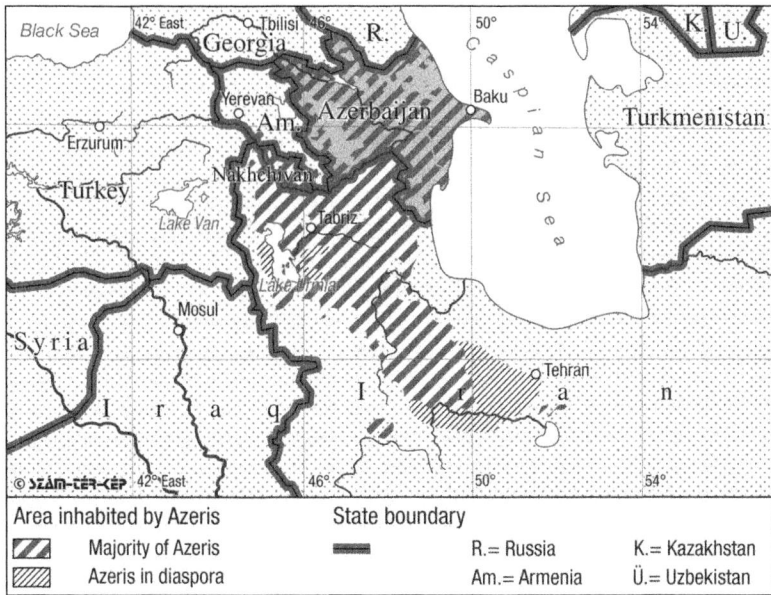

Figure 3.3.1 *Azeri Settlement Areas in 2011; (Sources:* [7]; [8]; [9]; [11]; [12]; [23]; [24]*)*

as a practical category and a possible event (Brubaker, R. 1996). The conclusions drawn in this chapter are also informed by theoretical insights into the ethnic character of nations and their relation to constructions of power (Eriksen, T. H. 2010 [1993]). By examining the post-Soviet characteristics of Azerbaijani "nationnes", this chapter builds on research that has promoted the scientific embeddedness of post-socialist and post-Soviet terms in recent decades. In this chapter, post-Soviet is not seen as a container that delimits time and space, or as a transitional period (Tuvikene, T. 2016). Instead, it emphasizes the framework of these spatial and temporal connections and the characteristics of specific processes and features. Seen in this light, the Azerbaijani national identity can be interpreted as post-Soviet.

Running parallel with these theoretical foundations, the chapter also outlines the process involved in the formation of Azerbaijani national identity through a discourse analysis carried out with the help of extant literature. Aided by this research, the chapter aims to shed light on the effects that modernization, which followed in the wake of Russian expansion, had on the formation of the Azerbaijani national community. Making a clear distinction between the specific character and goals of Russian and Soviet nation-building, the chapter draws attention to ethnic peculiarities that have been strengthened in Azerbaijani communities through Soviet-type national identity constructions (Cornell S. E. 1998, 1999). We also emphasize the role of the latter as critical background to understanding armed conflict in Nagorno-Karabakh. At the same time, the chapter will also highlight the peculiarities of Azerbaijani society, which changed as a result of Soviet-type modernization. By exploring the complex mechanisms of influence of the Soviet period and embedding Azerbaijan in geopolitical context at the turn of the millennium, this chapter points to the post-Soviet peculiarities of 21st-century Azerbaijani national consciousness.

Emergence and effects of tsarist Russian power in Azerbaijan

The Russian annexation of the entire territory of present-day Azerbaijan took place in the first half of the 19th century. The symbolic significance of this annexation is highlighted by the fact that it took place in the shadow of the great power game, and that it occurred within the context of the so-called "Eastern question". While the future of the Ottoman Empire was an important issue for Western powers in terms of continental European balance, Russian expansion at the expense of the Persian Empire was not significant at the time. In the second half of the 19th century, as part of the so-called "Great Game," the Persian Empire was still more or less invisible to the Western powers, largely because Persia's eastern neighbours had become their primary focus. Russian expansion in the region was itself linked to the events of the Decembrist uprising in 1825. Attempting to take advantage of the Russian nationalist revolt against tsarist power, the Persian leadership launched an attack on the Caucasian Russian army led by General Jermolov. The Persian army suffered a catastrophic defeat at the hands of the Russian military forces under the command of General Paskevich, and as a result the Shah was forced to make peace on February 13, 1828, in the city of Turkmenchai. The Persian defeat resulted in the loss of territory, and also bolstered Russia's growing influence in the Caucasus. The treaty not only confirmed the Russian territorial gains of the 1813 Russian-Persian peace Treaty of Gulistan, but also transferred significant territories to Russian rule. Moreover, the current border between Azerbaijan, Iran, and Armenia was also established (Horváth Cs. 2011). The plan to dismantle the Persian state was not realized at that time because Tsar Nicolas I did not agree to depriving the legitimate Persian ruler of his power.

Though Persia did not disappear as a state, their power in the Caucasus began to decline precipitously as a result of these peace agreements. Under the pressure of tsarist expansion, Persian losses accelerated. After defeating Muslim-majority Dagestan in the northeastern Caucasus, the entire territory of present-day Georgia and northern Azerbaijan came under tsarist rule. In 1828, the present northwestern border of Iran was drawn along the Aras River. Though centuries of Persian influence ceased in the region as a result of Russian gains, Shia Islam and the Persian language persisted, and have had a continued cultural presence within Azerbaijani communities to this day. While the language was almost entirely supplanted by Russian in the 20th century, Shi'ism is again a substantial factor in Azerbaijan's national identity.

At the same time, the gradual rise of Russian power and the change of geopolitical influence could be felt on the western side of the Caspian Sea as early as the 18th century. Nearly a hundred years earlier, at the end of Peter I's reign, a peace treaty had been signed between the Russians and the Persians, which transferred the coast and the city of Baku to the tsar, who had marshalled a large force to achieve his objectives, but had suffered significant losses as a result. Although the conquered territory was again handed over to the Persians for tactical reasons during the course of the Russian–Ottoman wars, the strengthening of Russian influence remained continuous until the end of the century. Under Catherine II, who carried out large-scale expansion during her reign, the annexation of the western coast of the Caspian Sea to the Russian Empire was raised again. This planned annexation was not realized at that time, however, because of the death of the Empress (Catherine II). Mikhail Heller, who has written on the history of the Russian Empire, has also emphasized that economic considerations, and in particular the need for direct trade relations with India, were at the centre of the conquests of Peter I and Catherine II, and that these conquests came at the expense of the Persians (Heller, M. 1996). It was in this light that the two central cities with significant port traffic, Derbent in Dagestan, and Baku (which later became the capital of Azerbaijan) came into Russian hands at the end of the 18th century.

The territorial expansion of the Russian Empire initiated significant migration from occupied territories to Persia. In the second half of the 19th century, after a few decades of military administration, two governorates were established in what is now Azerbaijan. The centres were significant cities in the region: Yelizavetpol (formerly Ganja), and the largest port on the Caspian Sea, Baku (O'Loughlin, J. and Kolossov, V. and Radvanyi, J. 2007). Bringing with it a new system and set of political tools, the establishment of Russian power in the region in the first half of the 19th century effected a transition between the former khanates and the tsarist imperial administration. Customary Islamic law was gradually pushed back to the level of families, while Christian subjects enjoyed a clear advantage over their Muslim counterparts. The latter had also become targets of Russian converts. Differences in treatment, and tensions stemming from religious discrimination, led to a sharpening of ethnic differences, especially in the cities. Tensions between Armenians and Azerbaijanis also deepened, and ran parallel both to the establishment of Russian power and to the emergence of modernization. The pro-Christian policy of the Tsarist administration resulted in an influx of Armenians, which undermined Muslim blocs in many places and increased Armenian settlements in the South Caucasus region, a move that is clearly seen as anti-Muslim in today's Azerbaijani context (Gasimov, Z. 2013).

In terms of the territorial effects of Russian power, Baku's change is most conspicuous. With the revival of trade in the port city, the expansion and reconstruction of the settlement, and with this also the change of its image, had already begun by the first half of the 19th century. Due to the growing importance of crude oil, more and more immigrants from different parts of the Russian Empire settled in the city. Economic and population growth intensified, especially after the 1870s, and was tied to the emergence of industries that were required for the exploration of oil deposits, as well as extraction and processing. It was there that the world's first oil well was drilled in 1846, followed shortly afterwards by the construction of an oil refinery in 1859, and a petroleum plant in 1863. The rise of the oil industry led to the development of transportation links, such as the Trans-Caucasus Railway and other services, and the rise of mass communication. Given the growing demand for labour, the development of the oil sector also attracted workers from all areas of the empire, as well as from neighbouring Iran. However, Baku's transformation into a multicultural city resulted in the further marginalization of Muslims, in large part because the circle of ownership was restricted mainly to Russian and Armenian investors.

The rapid economic upswing and unilateral development also made the new oil industry vulnerable, which was immediately felt during the economic crisis that unfolded in the early 20th century in the wake of the protracted Russo-Japanese War. As unemployment rose, ethnic tensions also surfaced, leading to clashes between Muslims and Armenians. The tsarist leadership saw the maintenance of ethnic differences as a manifestation of its power, and therefore repeatedly overlooked violence against Muslims and Armenians (Rauf A. G. 1996).

The Transcaucasian governorates that became more open to the world during this period as a result of rapid modernization also became sites of a changed worldview. The increase in direct contact with the Russian and Ottoman worlds brought with it the spread of radical social ideologies as well. At the beginning of the century, the young revolutionary Joseph Stalin, who promoted communist ideology and criticized the oppressive power of oil magnates, attracted attention by organizing workers' strikes in Baku. His party partner and friend, Grigoriy Ordzhonikidze, also of Georgian descent, was active here as well. The emergence of radical political movements ran alongside the intensification of Muslim nationalist movements in the region. Radical Azerbaijani intellectuals capitalized on the community-forming power of negative discrimination and drew on this discontent to advance the interests of the Muslim population in the region. Based on all this, it can be said that the essential elements of Azerbaijani national identity mentioned in the introduction had appeared already in the 19th century as a result of social changes generated by the Russian tsarist power.

Social changes were less prevalent in the everyday lives of rural communities, as well as in urban Muslim communities that were less affected by industrialization (e.g. Tbilisi, Ganja). Islamic religious ideology continued to define the daily lives of those who lived in these more traditional areas. The patriarchal social order preferred traditional female roles and dress habits, making it difficult to implement and adopt Tsarist Russian modernization efforts in education and public life (Najafizadeh, M. 2012). In contrast, urban Muslim communities, especially in Baku, were more open to European cultural influences, which resulted in increased secularization, and the rise of Western-type roles for women. Highlighted by the work of enlightened Muslim thinkers and philanthropists (e.g. Mirza Fathali Akhundov and Haji Taghiyev), the need to adapt to and work within the new framework emerged within the Muslim community.

Circumstances behind the establishment of independent Azerbaijan

The outbreak of the Russian Revolution and the end of tsarist power led to independence movements on the European periphery of the Russian Empire. These events fit organically into the great power contexts of the First World War. The disintegrating state structures in revolutionary Russia weakened the ties of peripheral territories to Russian power, and activated other interests. On the one hand, this led to a strengthening of Ottoman influence. On the other hand, in the period of allied intervention, the Caucasus was one of the main areas of the British expeditionary forces. However, since none of the great powers were able to concentrate significant military force in the region, the transitional situation opened up by the Bolshevik revolution provided an opportunity for independence in the Caucasus. This was realized by the mass movements initiated by the emerging radical intelligentsia. The so-called Transcaucasian Republic, for example, was established to counter the Ottoman threat, primarily on the initiative of Christian Georgia and Armenia. As a result of the different interests expressed by the large Muslim population, and also on account of the political differences with respect to the assessment of the situation, the regional organization also amplified ethnic divides that ultimately paved the way for the formation of independent nation-states. Nationalist movements thus found fertile ground for success, and on May 28, 1918, the Democratic Republic of Azerbaijan was proclaimed.

The new state of Azerbaijan was created in nearly the same area as it exists today, though its western boundaries were unclear. Its name was borrowed from the northwestern provinces of neighbouring Persia, where administrative units of Eastern and Western Azerbaijan already existed. Thus, by choosing a name, they also entered into a community with the Turkic-speaking Azerbaijani population under Persian rule, who formed a significant majority in the northwestern region of Persia. It also underscored the fact that a new nation-state had been formed in the Caucasus, one which was dominated by and under the leadership of its Muslim population. However, the mainly Armenian and Russian Christian leadership and inhabitants of Baku did not accept the sovereignty of the newly-proclaimed Azerbaijani state. Among the oil workers in Baku, the Bolsheviks had a significant base, which in turn prompted the British to occupy the city to avert the red threat. In the unfolding struggles, the city's Muslim population often became a target, but as a result of alternating power relations, clashes stemming from ethnic conflict claimed significant casualties on both sides. With Ottoman military assistance, Baku eventually became the capital of the new republic. The memory of this assistance has become an inalienable basis for fostering friendly relations with Turkey, the successor to the Ottoman Empire, in "re-independent" post-Soviet Azerbaijan.

In the functioning of parliamentary democracy, liberal, social democratic, and conservative views were included, which was an indication of the increasing modernization of society and the embeddedness of the state in the European framework. The Democratic Republic of Azerbaijan also took part in the negotiations that led to the signing of the Treaty of Versailles, so it was de facto recognized by the international community as an independent state. Most of the leaders of the newly formed country looked to Europe, as did their policies. The Bolshevik regime, however, which by 1920 had emerged victorious from the Russian Civil War, was a clear threat to the region, a concern that soon became realized in military attacks. "The Reds," in fact, engaged in a concerted effort to reoccupy the territories in the Caucasus that had belonged to the former Russian Empire. The war claimed many Azerbaijani lives.

The Azerbaijanis, however, had to deal with more than just the Bolshevik attack. Armed uprisings took place almost continuously in Nagorno-Karabakh, a fact that became more widely known to the world in the 1990s (Yamskov, A. N. 1991). The consolidation of Azerbaijan's western borders led to conflict and war with neighbouring Armenia, which had been established on the same day as the Democratic Republic of Azerbaijan. Armenian–Azerbaijani relations were further strained by the crackdown on Armenians in the former Ottoman Empire, which prompted a mass migration to the Caucasus. The newcomers changed the ethnic pattern of the region (Mutlu, S. 2003). The difficult conditions, coupled with the deprivations of war, only served to exacerbate tensions between Armenians and Azerbaijanis.

On April 28, 1920, the Red Army, with the participation of Sergei Kirov and Grigoriy Ordzhonikidze (who later would be responsible for the establishment of the Caucasian Communist administration), occupied the Democratic Republic of Azerbaijan, then Armenia, and finally Georgia. Communism had a mass local base, especially among Baku workers, so that after the bloody war between the Red Army and the Azerbaijani troops, the communist takeover took place in Azerbaijan without significant resistance. During the transitional period during the First World War, it became clear that Moscow would continue to determine the lives of the Azerbaijanis living north of the Aras River, and with it, the process of nation-building in Azerbaijan and its future opportunities.

After the First World War, the Bolsheviks were also very active on the other side of the border, in northwestern Iran. The ensuing "communist" movement, in line with the policy of *korenizatsiya*, emphasized the separation of the Azeri group. This was driven by the desire for the expansion of communist ideology, and the weakening of Iran's influence on Shia Muslims. The weakness of the Persian school network in Iranian Azerbaijan also meant a relatively weak connection of local societies to Tehran. This situation strengthened the Azerbaijani national consciousness in the Soviet period. However, after the change of regime, the post-Soviet Azerbaijani leadership interpreted it as a "national democratic liberation struggle", forgetting the otherwise internationalist, Bolshevik nature of these movements (Gasimov, Z. 2013).

Azerbaijani identity in the Soviet Socialist Republic of Azerbaijan

The ideological duality that determined the nationality policy of the Soviet period — namely, the enforcement of the right of peoples to self-determination, and the principle of the efficient operation of a centralized, multi-ethnic state bound together for the future victory of the world revolution — shifted increasingly towards centralization, with the consolidation of Bolshevik power and the rise of Stalin to power in the wake of Lenin's illness and death. The treaty signed with Azerbaijan on September 20, 1920 became the template for settling relations between the Russian Federation and the Soviet republics (Heller, M. and Nyekrics A. 1996). The agreement articulated an extremely close military, economic, and financial alliance, one that that in actuality merged the territories and institutional systems of the signees. The agreement effectively deprived the member state of its own domestic policy, which led to Moscow's continual interference in the internal affairs of the member republic. The application of Leninist principles made it possible in 1922 to secure the sovereignty of individual member republics with the slogan of federalization, and to reserve the right to possible secession. Still, with Lenin's death and the consolidation of Stalin's power, its practical significance rapidly declined. From the beginning, Stalin consistently applied his system of arguments based on communist ideology, in which he considered it feasible to reshape the peasant-dominated periphery by relying on the working class of the more industrialized central areas (Heller, M. and Nyekrics A. 1996). In the case of Azerbaijan, this Moscow-centred perspective entailed not only the exercise of external control, but also a different perception of the capital and the countryside. By abolishing Islamic-based community organization, and by fundamentally subverting the organization of traditional families by putting women to work, the drastic political changes had far-reaching effects, mainly in the life of rural society (Najafizadeh, M. 2012).

The policy of *korenizatsiya* that was put into force in the 1920s in the Soviet Socialist Republic of Azerbaijan also provided an opportunity for the rise of credible local party cadres who encouraged the inhabitants to accept Soviet and Marxist-Leninist ideologies. During this period, young radical intellectuals, with the support of Moscow, played a significant role in the creation of local culture. The principle that each member republic had to have its own independent language played an important dual role in the peripheral areas as well, including in the Caucasus. The ideology of communism was to be disseminated through print media to the local population in a local language, while a modernized, centralized education system was to make this language and the ideological messages it conveyed understandable to everyone. The consistent emphasis on the mother tongues of the member republics helped to eradicate the previously-used mediator languages, such as Persian, in the Caucasus. This also increased the cultural distance between the population of the member republics and the groups with similar languages and cultures living across the border. As a result, a particular bilingual, multi-language environment was formed (Pravikova, L. and Lazarev, V. 2005). The construction of national histories played a similar role in this process by justifying the separation of peoples of the periphery from the larger state formations that previously defined their lives. In the case of Azerbaijan, historical narratives were deployed to justify the nation's separation from the Persian Empire.

The policy of *korenizatsiya* in turn aimed at the complete abolition of Islamic religious identity. Beyond the introduction of the Soviet-type education and administrative system, the construction of a state language on ethnic foundations, as well as the modification of collective memory (for example, by the rewriting of national myths) served as tools of Soviet power (O'Lear, S. 2008). Enthusiastic local party cadres like Mustafa Kuliev, the People's Commissioner for Education), aided in this process, thus demonstrating the effectiveness of the *korenizatsiya* project. The demolition of mosques, or their transformation into shops and communal spaces, was a spectacular form of secularization, and signalled the rejection of Islamic traditions (Najafizadeh, M. 2012). In 1929, there were 1360 mosques in Azerbaijan, but by 1933, their number was only 17 (Najafizadeh, M. 2012). The elimination of the Koran, and other Arabic texts, also contributed to the decline of Islam. In addition to being unavailable, the mere possession of old religious artefacts was punished. Thus, most Azerbaijanis could not learn to read Arabic or Persian texts. The transmission of Islamic traditions was possible only within a small family circle, and was based on oral communication. As a result, religion was pushed to the social periphery, and the community became less and less connected to the Azerbaijanis living in Iran, and to the Muslim world in general.

The alphabetical rendering of the state language of Azerbaijan changed four times during the 20th century, which illustrates the changing cultural peculiarities mentioned above. At the beginning of the century, Arabic lettering was still used to write the Azerbaijani language, which was modified by the Soviet policy of the 1920s when the language was converted to Latin script. The strong centralization measures of the 1930s brought the use of Cyrillic lettering, which persisted until the break-up of the Soviet Union. In the 1990s, however, Azerbaijani as a written language returned once more to the Latin script, and move that was widely seen as a manifestation of the geopolitical orientation of the newly-independent state.

Although the apparent independence of the member Soviet republics prevailed within a narrower framework during the existence of the Soviet Union, the cultural independence remained characteristic in later decades as well, albeit with a constantly changing intensity. The practical implementation of ideological principles was reflected in the foreign immigrant workers of the member republics, mainly Russian workers, and in the cultural influences they represented, and in the presence of the Soviet school system, which can also be seen as a pledge to support the social uplifting of the people within the framework of the system. Knowledge of the Russian language, in addition to the acquisition of a modern way of life characteristic of Russian-speaking people, and the acceptance of the cultural influences associated with them, modified significantly the collective identity of the majority population, strengthening their attachment to Moscow and to the supposedly spontaneous Russification process. Arab and Persian influences that were spread through Islam and that served previously as the basis for collective identity were replaced by Russian cultural influences. The use of the Russian language became a common manifestation of this process during the Soviet period, especially among the urban population (O'Lear, S. 2008).

Nagorno-Karabakh and Azerbaijan's self-definition against the "Other"

When the Soviet Union ceased to exist in the early 1990s, the Azerbaijani political elite maintained its power without significant changes. Soviet and socialist flags were abandoned as early as the end of 1990, while state symbols were modified, and the 1918 flag was restored. Following the creation of the presidency, a 1991 referendum confirmed the independence of the Republic of Azerbaijan. Independent of the Soviet Union, Azerbaijan faced a severe political and military challenge, which overshadows the everyday life of the republic as an unresolved issue to this day, while very actively defining the national identity of the new state (Auch, E-M., 2008).

The Transcaucasian states of Georgia, Armenia, and Azerbaijan began their independent statehood in the 1990s within the territorial framework established for them by the central Soviet leadership in Moscow in the 1920s in the wake of the Soviet military occupation of the Caucasus which had displaced both English and Turkish military forces. The events of the first two decades of the 20th century not only brought emerging national identities in the Caucasus into sharp focus, but also reinforced the conviction that the establishment of independent states along the lines laid out by Leninist principles was a necessary step.

Drawing concrete boundaries in the midst of entangled interests, however, was hardly a clear or simple task, a fact that has haunted the region since the 1980s, as ethnic tensions on the Soviet periphery intensified, and escalated into bloody armed conflicts in the 1990s (Cornell, S. E. 2002). One such fatal decision by the Bolshevik central leadership was the annexation of the Armenian-majority Nagorno-Karabakh region to Azerbaijan. Though the creation of the Nagorno-Karabakh Autonomous Oblast in 1923 helped keep a lid on tensions during most of the Soviet period, the transfer of direct control of the region to Baku in 1990, coupled with the desire of Armenians living in Nagorno-Karabakh to gain independence from Azerbaijan, lay the groundwork for the outbreak of war in 1991, especially after Armenian separatists declared the independent Republic of Nagorno-Karabakh (Arcah). The civil war intersected with a territorial dispute between neighbouring Armenia and Azerbaijan. The armed clashes ended in 1994 with a ceasefire between Nagorno-Karabakh and Azerbaijan (Auch, E-M. 2008).

The war had an elemental impact on the national identity of the majority of people in independent Azerbaijan. With the animosity between Armenians and Azerbaijanis deepening in the wake of clashes and the significant casualties on both sides, perceptions of difference intensified (Croissant, M. P. 1998). For the Azerbaijanis, the Islamic traditions that had regained importance among the people played an important role in the process of self-definition against the "other". In turn, the fate of the Azerbaijani people of Nagorno-Karabakh (many survivors of the war had been forced to flee or were expelled) contributed to the sense of existential danger that many Azerbaijanis felt, and thus reinforced the ethnic foundations of their national identity (Gasimov, Z. 2011a). The image of Armenians endangering a common Azerbaijani homeland, moreover, brought the territorial aspects of national identity into sharp focus, and pointed to the need for a sacred and inviolable state territory (Gasimov, Z. 2011a).

Post-Soviet Azerbaijani national identity

In October 2003, Ilham Aliev assumed office as the fourth president of Azerbaijan. Succeeding his father, Heydar Aliev, who had been the most influential Azerbaijani politician of the post-World War II era, and who served as president from 1993 to 2003, Ilham Aliev's election assured his family's place within Azerbaijan's system of power. However, whereas his father first rose to an influential position within a system based on the principle of proletarian internationalism, both father and son assumed the presidency in an independent Azerbaijan whose ideological base and source of legitimacy was grounded in ethnic nationalism. Not unlike many other states in the post-Soviet sphere, ethno-nationalist narratives have gained a prominent place in Azerbaijani politics and culture. When voicing national slogans, the power elite, who came from the former Soviet leadership, looked back to the pre-Soviet era, to the period of the first democratic Islamic state. National policy, therefore, gained a certain hybridity in this light. On the one hand, the word "democracy" was a legacy of the Soviets, who defined their own dictatorial system as democratic in contrast to the "imperialist and tyrannical" system of the tsarist regime. On the other hand, the emphasis placed on a previous period of national independence is of singular importance among the successor states, because it serves to legitimate their independence from the Soviet Union.

Azerbaijan's current nation builders also make use of important aspects of the collective memory that was cultivated in the Soviet period, and that was formed on even earlier elements of nationalist consciousness. This collective memory has long distinguished the Azerbaijani people not only from their expansive Russian imperialist neighbour, but also from the former, centuries-old Persian Empire (Gasimov, Z. 2011b). In this context, the awareness of the Turkic origins of the Azerbaijani language, coupled with a sense of belonging to the Altai language family and a positive view of pan-Turkic relations, are essential, and have generated widespread support for closer foreign relations with Turkey as well as the former Soviet republics of Central Asia (Sidikov, B. 2008). The symbolic import of language itself cannot be understated in this context. The replacement of the Azerbaijani Cyrillic script with Latin script has become an important symbol of independence from Russia, and from Russian influence.

Beyond language, Azerbaijani authorities have granted Islam a central role in the generation of Azerbaijani national consciousness. The importance of Islam in this respect was reflected in concrete terms by the mosque-building fever of the 1990s, which increased the number of mosques to over 1,300 by the end of the decade. This nationalist project continued into the 2000s, with the number of mosques in Azerbaijan exceeding 1,700 (Najafizadeh, M. 2012). The Bibi-Heybat Mosque, which is of particular symbolic significance, stands out among them. The cult site, which has existed since the 13th century, was demolished in 1934. It was rebuilt by the independent state in 1997 in a conscious and very public attempt to break with the Soviet past, and then expanded in 2008. The change in the built environment can be interpreted as a symbol of independence and national consciousness in opposition to the legacy and memory of Soviet power.

As suggested above, the central element of Azerbaijani national consciousness is the Islamic faith, even though the number of people who actively practise their religion is negligible (Najafizadeh, M. 2012). A secular country, Azerbaijan nevertheless defines itself as an Islamic state, though Islamic traditions are returning relatively slowly in everyday life (unlike in the built environment). In cities, the wearing of a veil, which is considered a Muslim symbol, is almost non-existent, and in rural communities, the headscarf is worn primarily for practical reasons. Azerbaijan's special relationship with religion is, therefore, a legacy of the Soviet period. Despite Azerbaijan's longstanding secularization, over 90% of the people (Najafizadeh M. 2012) define themselves as Muslims. The centrality of Islam to Azerbaijani identity is reinforced by the nation's leadership, which has declared Azerbaijan a part of the Islamic political community. In addition to the construction of mosques, "national Islam" has also necessitated the translation of the Qur'an into Azerbaijani. It is important to note that, similarly to the Soviet period, religion is a public rather than primarily private affair. Perhaps in keeping with Azerbaijan's Soviet past, the state controls religion closely, and all religious literature is subject to strict state control (Najafizadeh, M. 2012).

The national self-definition of Christian Armenians, especially as this has played out in relation to the struggle over Nagorno-Karabakh, has only amplified the significance that Islam has gained with respect to Azerbaijani nation-building since the 1990s. As an unresolved challenge to Azerbaijani power, the Nagorno-Karabakh question, and tensions with Armenia more generally, have fuelled one of the essential elements of constructed national consciousness: protecting territorial integrity and securing Azerbaijan's sovereignty against "Armenian aggression" (Brown, C. S. 2004). This ever-present issue has remained a key focus of the Azerbaijani media, and is also embedded in the thinking of Azerbaijan's inhabitants (Brown, C. S. 2004, O'Lear, S. 2008). A resolution to the current stalemate with Armenia is, therefore, likely to take a long time.

Related to the Armenian question, the myth of a divided people lives in the public consciousness as a central element of Azerbaijani nationalism (Fig. 3.3.2). At the heart of the collective memory formed during the Soviet period was the belief that the two great powers, Russia and Persia, deliberately divided the Azerbaijani people along the Aras River in the early 19th century so that they could not build a stable state. The issue of unification presents a paradoxical situation for advocates of Azerbaijani nationalism, however, as they emphasize territorial integrity in the case of Nagorno-Karabakh, while calling for an ethnically-justified territorial expansion towards Iran based on the principle of self-determination. For the time being, the political elite has avoided this contradiction by renouncing the latter position (Brown, C. S. 2004). However, their official speeches are addressed to all Azerbaijanis in the world.

An essential element of current Azerbaijani self-determination revolves around the sense of loss. Inspired by the idea of "Greater Armenia," and by assertions of a "Greater Persia" based on the rather broad territorial base of Persian culture (Gasimov, Z. 2013), the notion of a "Greater Azerbaijan" projects an

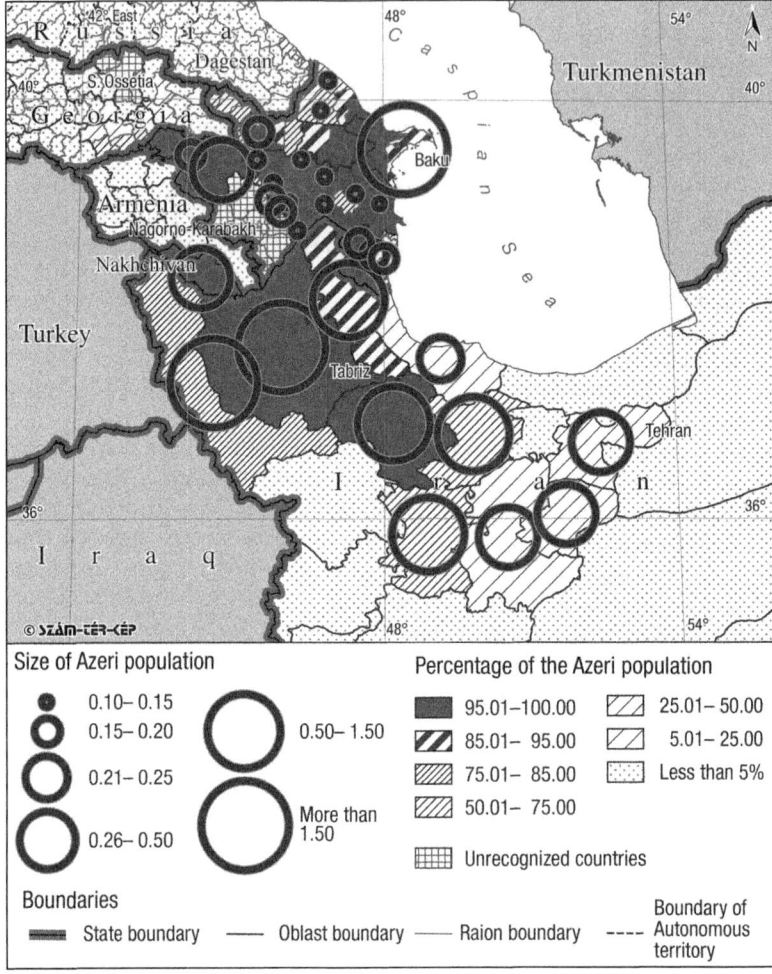

Figure 3.3.2 *The number and proportion of Azeris in 2011; (Sources: [9]; [13]; [25])*

image of past territorial expanse and unity. In this light, the smaller state territory today is explained as a regrettable result of great power intrigue (on the part primarily of tsarist Russia, Persia, and the Soviet Union), and more recently of the actions and foreign policy of Iran, Putin's Russia, and Armenia. The primary losses in this context are Nagorno-Karabakh (which represents 15% of the country's territory) and Northern Iran (the Azerbaijani inhabitants call this problem "Tabriz"). These discourses of loss are reinforced also by the Talysh and Lezgin problem. The ethnic territories of both groups are cut in half by the current Azerbaijani border, with significant numbers of both groups living in blocs in Dagestan and Iran. Situated directly along the border, the Talysh and Lezgin questions constitute a situation that is perceived as dangerous to territorial integrity.

Finally, oil also figures as a key aspect in the formation of Azerbaijani national identity, especially as this is promoted by those in power. Regarded as the "treasure of the motherland", crude oil is represented as an element intimately connected to the homeland. It is of course important in this context to note that Azerbaijan's political elite is also the largest owner of the energy industry, which defines all other economic sectors in the country. Opening up extraction and refining to international oil companies is thus presented as a symbolic opening to the rest of the world. Referred to as the oil industry's hometown, Baku has become even more separated from the rest of the country since the turn of the millennium. The influx of capital and expressions of political power has led to striking differences in the built environment as well, and has resulted in the extreme separation of the capital from the countryside.

In regards to international relations, Azerbaijan's political and economic elite have also stressed Azerbaijani control of the oil industry in their defence of state sovereignty. In particular, control of the nation's energy sector was mobilized as a key argument for independence from the former Soviet Union. However, at the same time, the importance of relations with Russia and the Soviet heritage has also been underlined. As a member of the Commonwealth of Independent States, Azerbaijan maintains close and friendly relations with neighbouring Russia.

Summary

In the eastern part of Europe, the formation of national identities, and the emergence of nationalism, was influenced significantly by both Russian and Soviet power. The western foothills of the Caspian Sea became a zone of influence in the former Russian Empire in the 18th century, and the central leadership of the rapidly growing state pursued a policy of powerful military interventions as a means of achieving its geopolitical aims (Herzig, E. 1999). The negative connotations associated with the Caucasus developed in the framework of expansive Russian power policies. In addition to failures of Russian troops in the region, the Caucasus reflects the ambivalent relationship of the people living here with the conquerors, a reflection of the peculiarities of peripheral existence.

Borders were established in this ethnically heterogeneous region in the 20th century, during the Soviet period. This situation continues to determine the framework of nation-state existence in the 21st century. Within these borders, the formation of a unified, homogeneous identity has been a continuous process, even during the period of party-state dictatorships. Since the change of regime, identity formation has taken on an openly national character, which is also reflected in the ethnic spatial structure of the wider region. This process is special in several respects in the Soviet successor state of Azerbaijan.

National consciousness in Azerbaijan was formed within a framework regulated first by Russian, and then by Soviet power. Although Azerbaijani speakers live in large numbers beyond the borders of Azerbaijan, Azerbaijani national identity is explicitly tied to the framework of the modern nation-state. As a legacy of the Soviet period, although Azerbaijani society was secularized, its national identity is still significantly determined by Islam. As a result, it has a special system of foreign policy relations with its three neighbours — Russia, Iran, and Turkey — countires which are also dominant in world politics. Its unresolved border dispute with the neighbouring Transcaucasian state of Armenia, which has generated military conflict, affects its national identity through hate myths, and a collective image of the enemy. From an economic point of view, its strategic raw materials base continues to ensure the geopolitical significance of its state territory in the 21st century.

Tajik Identities: Ageless Alternatives to an Unborn Nation

Csaba Baroch

Since the 19th century, Central Asia has been subject to various interpretations in international (and particularly Western) discourse. Most of these territorial narratives and imaginations have been led by western-type imperialist perceptions of the region, which developed following the Russian-Soviet conquests. As a result of its colonial heritage, and the second-wave structures that were created, we can identify post-Soviet Central Asia, which is comprised of historical layers and elements from the pre-colonial and colonial period, through the end of the Second World War, to the period of political (glasnost) and economical (perestroika) change, up until the post-Soviet era.

In Western interpretations, Central Asia's socio-economic context has aligned with the territorial administration and spatial divisions of the former Soviet Union. However, before Russian expansion, this region was marked by a cultural duality, with roots that can be traced back to antiquity. Two groups, the settled Indo-Aryan peoples and the nomadic Turkish peoples, had coexisted as a matter of necessity, despite the often sharp hostility between them. This so called "Iran–Turan" historical duality of the region manifested itself in the division of Central Asian peoples in terms of production, lifestyle, and culture. The Iranian peoples had Indo-Aryan language and descent, and consisted of mostly-settled groups in the Central Asian oasis belt, where they filled the role of East-West culture-transfer carriers. The nomadic, more standoffish Turks, on the other hand, lived in the northern steppe and desert regions of Central Asia. As a result of British and Russian imperial expansion, this complementary coexistence was eliminated, thereby artificially separating the Iranians and the Turks, and reinforcing their cultural differences into direct opposition. Over time, as political boundaries solidified, the Iranian–Tajik groups became a wedge between the region's growing Turkish (Uzbek) leadership, the extended Russian geostrategic activity, and their Iranian roots. The long-term consequence of great-power interventions in Central Asia was the creation of a colonial dichotomy from what was historically a dialectic duality.

With the evolution of the capitalist world system, Central Asia came to embody the liminality, economic asymmetry, and poorly-connected social ties that characterize internal and external peripheries (Wallerstein, I. 2004). The ever-reigning hegemonies

(Gramsci, A. 1959) or their sediments of power (Laclau, E. 1990) and political economic superstructure (Marx, K. 1909 [1867]) not only dominated their specific ages, but have also manifested themselves in the everyday realities of present-day societies. Because of this political time-space compression (Harvey, D. 1992 [1989]), we cannot examine the post-Soviet present without collectively examining the Soviet period, the era of tsarist colonialization, and the ages of Islamic expansion. By analyzing the interrelations between these periods, through locally-engaged literature, we can explore the complex identities or social conditions that exist in Central Asia, including the specific situation of Tajik (un)consciousness and imagined community (Anderson, B. 2016 [1983]). Because of the Tajik people's experience of both multiple oppressions and cultural vulnerability, this study necessarily applies a postcolonial and subaltern analysis (Prakash, G. 1994). To this end, the supporting literature has been limited to these approaches, and is strongly rooted in critical social theory and Marxist and autonomist critique.

Postcolonial post-Soviet

Social analysis within the postcolonialist theoretical framework examines the relationships between dominant and subaltern groups, and the politics and ideologies that originate from these relationships. But above all, it emphasizes the subaltern's oppression and disregarded point of view. These theories analyze how imperial hegemony is established, how it operates in the culture, politics, and economies of colonized areas, and the impact it has on colonized societies (Gramsci, A. 1959). The origin of postcolonialism can be traced to the disintegration of colonial empires in the 19th and 20th centuries, and the criticisms brought to light by Edward Said's theory of orientalism. Postcolonial theory imagines nominal and political liberation for colonized people, and analyzes the continuation of economic oppression through global capitalism and present-day Western imperialism (neocolonialism). It questions the prevailing eurocentrism in all spheres of social science, and criticizes the determinist–Orientalist view of Western academic and political discourse. This view imagines the global South and East as "developing" or "underdeveloped" as compared to the "developed", and therefore superior West (Said, E. W. 1978, Bhabha, H. K. 2004 [1994]). Postcolonial thinking has roots in critical theory, and thus is not only capable of revealing the injustices of a given historical or spatial context, but also uncovers global exploitation as a whole. Its temporal and spatial analysis reveals much more than the classical colonial positions: the postcolonial point of view deals with the internal (e.g. urban or domestic) (Gutiérrez, R. A. 2004) and necessarily remaining (neo)colonization (Lenin, V. I. 1963 [1917]; Nkrumah, K. 1965). These can include post-socialist or post-Soviet spaces, because these former state-capitalist or state-socialist countries also adapted to the capitalist world system (Wallernstein, I. 2004, Éber M. Á. et al. 2014, Gille Zs. 2019). The postcolonial view with regard to temporal extension reveals that imperialism dates back to before the period of "classical colonialism" and still operates intensely today. An examination like this should show the entire social hierarchy on a scale-free basis, thus revealing the colonizing forces inherent in factors such as racism, male chauvinism, or even gentrification. In the extended spatial case, this means considering those parts of the world system that colonized in a specific way under the illusion of an anti-imperialist (Stalinist) ideology (Illés T. and Bottlik, Zs. 2018).

If we want to study the Tajik people's postcolonial identity, both temporal and spatial extensions are needed. Oppression by colonial powers was not only determinative at the state level, but also at the micropolitical level, by fueling regionalism, localism, micro resistances, and entrenched gender roles, and by animating unique cultural patterns, such as languages, religions, and everyday practices (Foucault, M. 1978 [1976]; Roy, O. 1993). In the so called post-Soviet space, colonialism has been accompanied by forced modernization, which has resulted in time-space compression and an increase in social tensions (Bhabha, H. 1994, Kandiyoti, D. 2002a). One of the most impactful Soviet projects was the creation of an ethnic and national identity for the Tajik people, which aimed at masking the fragmented and contradictory goals of Tajik actors and groups, and blunting their real class struggle. This project was only successful with respect to certain aspects of identity, but in the post-Soviet era, its effects were evident in the hostilities that came to the surface, such as differences among regions or clan and ethnic origin, as well as between social classes. As a result of the post-Soviet colonial project, Tajikistan is now considered to be the weakest nation state in present-day Central Asia (Kandiyoti, D. 2002a, 2002b; Nourzhanov, K. and Bleuer, C. 2013).

The Tajik language as a common unconscious

The Tajik people are distinct from other groups in Central Asia because of their Iranian language, some particular cultural and anthropological characteristics, and their current state framework. From a European perspective, the state of Tajikistan, with its exact political borders, is a product of the 20th century, and is seen as having been separated from the Russian imperial protectorate, which it once shared with the Turkish people. Between 1924 and 1926, the Bolshevik leadership listed the territory as the Tajik Autonomous Soviet Socialist Republic. In this region, most of the population spoke the Iranian language, but political hegemony was in Uzbek hands. In 1929, the Tajik Soviet Socialist Republic was created as part of Stalin's National Territorial Delimitation policy (Nourzhanov, K. and Bleuer, C. 2013). The boundaries drawn by the Soviet leadership in 1929 represent the current borders of the state of Tajikistan, which has been independent since 1991. Thus, the current state framework in Tajikistan is the result of external, imperial interests.

When "Tajik identity" is considered outside the post-Westphalian paradigm of the nation-state, it becomes an exogenous, umbrella term. The Tajik population is organized in small ethnographic groups that share a Persian/Iranian background, and see themselves as part of a specific region or local territory, rather than as part of a politically delimited state (Olimov, M. A. and Olimova, S. 2002, Nourzhanov, K. and Bleuer, C. 2013). The reason for this formal disintegration is the presence of various cultural and social characteristics such as religion, clans, political considerations, habitation, lifestyle, ethnicity, and the extent of ethnic mixing (Akiner, S. 2001, Kilavuz, I. T. 2007). Perhaps the only cohesive force within this diverse population is the Tajik language, which spread across the region during the Soviet modernization project, along with the transformation of the public education system and political bureaucracy. However, Tajik diversity is well illustrated by the cultural presence of Uzbek, Kyrgyz, and Russian peoples. In fact, the linguistic standard for Tajik became generalized in 1988, while in the very isolated, mountainous Gorno-Badakhshan region (which amounts to 45% of Tajikistan's territory), the Pamirian dialects are still popular (Akbarzadeh, S. 1996, Nourzhanov, K. and Bleuer, C. 2013) (Figure 3.4.1).

Tajik is a southwest-Iranian language and belongs to the Indo-Iranian group of Indo-European languages. Because of the many linguistic similarities, Tajik's closest linguistic relatives are the New Persian languages of Farsi, which is mostly spoken in Iran, and Dari, which is spoken in Afghanistan. New Persian (Farsi) is the dominant language of this macroregion, but the next-most dominant Iranian language is Tajik, because of its state-standardized version, and the large number of speakers. The roots of standard Tajik are located in Bukhara, which is now part of Uzbekistan, and this is a fact that obviously raises a potential problem around national affiliation. However, the northeast Iranian Tajik people have traditionally been a settled society, living in the Central Asian oasis belt in the merchant cities of Samarkand, Bukhara, and Ferghana.

The Tajik people trace their history back to the Paniranian Samanid Empire, and to the Empire's expansion of Islam and

Figure 3.4.1 *The distribution of modern Persian/Farsi and its dialects in 2010; (Sources:* [7]; [11]; [12]; [23])

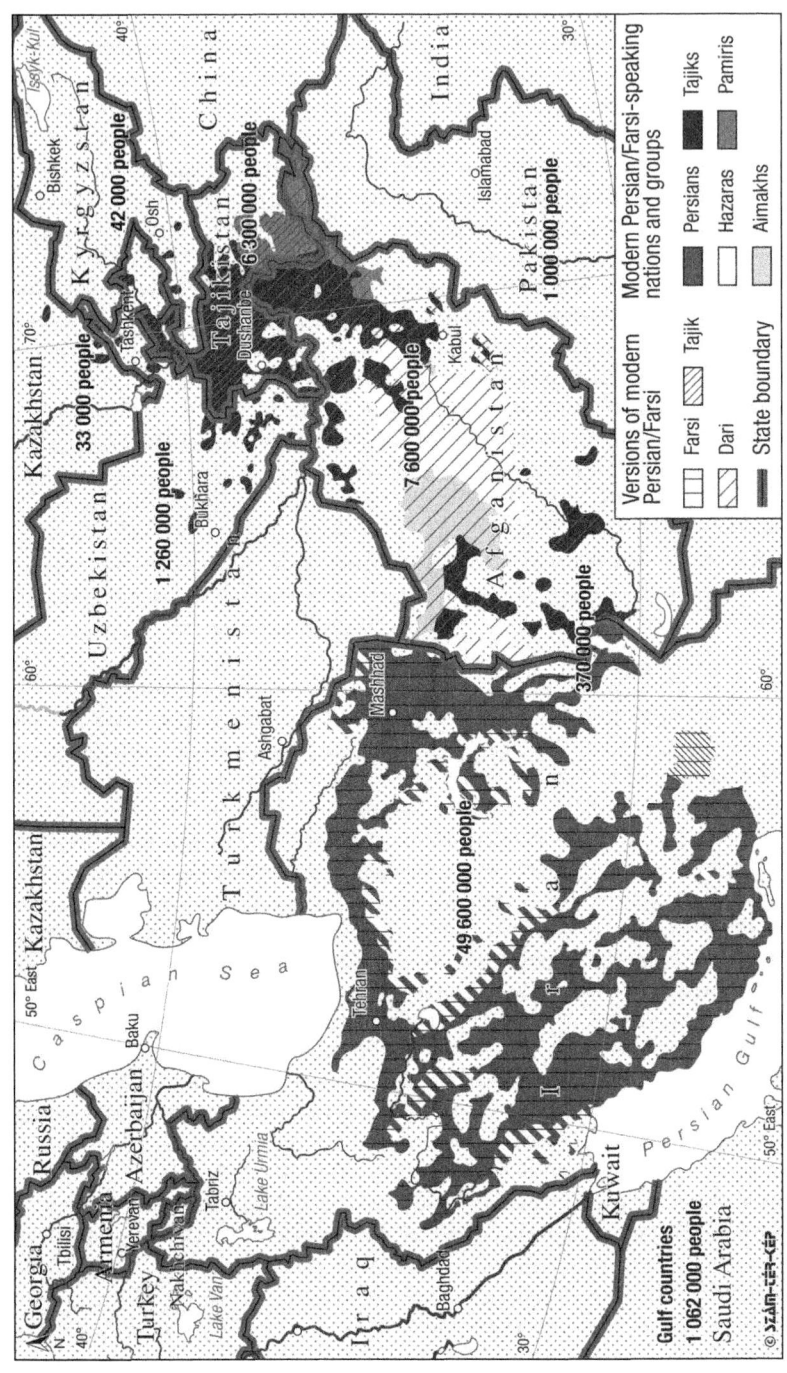

the Arabic language throughout the Central Asian region. Islam brought with it an Arabic language heritage. The word "Tai", which is the root of "Tajik", derived from an Arabic tribe's name. In this light, the "Tajik" denomination initially referred to the locally mixed, coherent Arabic and Persian community. Another aspect of Tajik ancestry was Sogdia, an independent, Samarkand-centered, indigenous Iranian culture (today we can recognize it in the name of the Sughd Region of Tajikistan). The Tajiks (as people of Persian descent) typically legitimized their subsequent presence (over the Turks) with reference to their Sogdian origin (Nourzhanov, K. and Bleuer, C. 2013). Thus, the Tajik language functioned as a social and national binder par excellence. Existing at first on the level of linguistic dialect, the language was enhanced with the later arrival of Turkish and, even more significantly, Russian loanwords and the Cyrillic alphabet. Such influences, if fact, account for the significant difference between Tajik and other Iranian-Persian languages. The formerly-dominant Tajik Communist Party, and its current political leadership, have begun to unite and standardize the various Tajik dialects. However, the original "Tai" cultural core and point of reference, which is connected to the dominant dialects in Samarkand and Bukhara, has long been outside the competence of Tajik central political power. Samarkand, Bukhara, and Ferghana were the fortresses of ancient and medieval Persian culture, and they are still primordial symbols of the Tajik language and its ethnogenesis.

Turkish immigration in the 10th century led to a domination of Turkish people in the culture and economy of rural spaces in the region. Later, Turks began moving into the merchant cities. With an established cultural identity in the countryside, they ultimately usurped the Persian hegemony of these settlements. When tsarist Russia initiated its imperialist expansion in Central Asia, Uzbek–Turkish culture had already become dominant in the cities, and was evident in the ethnicity and daily lives of the Ferghanian and Khujandian Tajik people (Nourzhanov, K. and Bleuer, C. 2013). Running even deeper than the generalized level of the Tajik literary language, therefore, the most significant divide for the Tajik people runs along the fault line between the north (eg. Sughd, Khujand) and the south (eg. Goro-Badakhshan, Khatlon) (Kilavuz, I. T. 2007).

Within this broad north-south divide, it is important to note that the northern valley Tajiks have always been the inhabitants of the economically prosperous rural areas. In these basins, the Uzbek–Tajik ethnic mix is more typical and the people are therefore anthropologically distinguishable from the more isolated southern or southeastern mountain Tajiks. These two cultural and economic entities had little contact with each other, even during the Soviet period, and this is still reflected in languages spoken in the region. People from the north have been much more receptive to Uzbek and Russian influences, while the Southern populations have been more aligned with Pashto, Dari, and Pamir languages. Of course, Russification, which manifested itself in various forms, from public education to the use of the Cyrillic alphabet, as well as the Islamic/Arabic affection, had a broad impact on the entirety of Tajik society (Akiner, S. 2001, Nourzhanov, K. and Bleuer, C. 2013).

The role of a "mother-tongue" language in identity formation is not just the result of a top-down cultural policy of a nation-state. Minorities and subcultures can also turn to the important power of an independent language. The Iranian people of Goro-Badakhshan, who use the Pamir dialects, have done this to preserve their own local attachment and autonomy. Languages spoken in the villages of Goro-Badakhshan, such as Wakhi and Sughni, belong to the Pamir branch of Southeastern Iranian languages, which make them distinct from the Tajik language. Owing to widespread illiteracy, none of them have become a literary language. However, these languages nevertheless have a high level of everyday usage which aids in the preservation of a local identity. There are many forms of cultural attachment among the Tajik people, but the Pamirians are more distinct with regards to their internal, and especially domestic, relations. Although the Tajik central leadership has endeavored to emphasize that the Pamir languages are Tajik dialects, analyses made on the basis of modern linguistics tend to stress the obvious differences from Tajik (Nourzhanov, K. and Bleuer, C. 2013, Novák, L. 2014). Cultural minorities that self-identify on the basis of their distinct language and origins are not alone in their claim to specific identities. Tajik citizens who do not speak Tajik at all also retain a specific identity. Much like the former socialist elite, members of this elite are advocates of formal internationalism, and thus consider the ethnic or linguistic component of identity formation unnecessary. These groups are largely either settled Russians or urban Tajik officials, intellectuals, and bureaucrats who have abandoned the language of their ancestors. In 1989, the Tajik central government initiated a process to dissolve communities whose identity was distinct from the newly-imagined, and artificial, national identity. Launched before the nation had gained independence from the Soviet Union, this was the first case of a post-Soviet Central Asian state introducing their own language mediated by the "national" elite (Akbarzadeh, S. 1996).

Fragmented imagined communities

Since 1991, the Tajik language has become the dominant form of internal discourse and articulation in Tajikistan, and has been the language sanctioned by its political leadership. However, various subnational differences and socio-cultural dimensions continue to divide Tajik society in many ways, and have thus prevented the creation of a European-style, universal national identity (Figure 3.4.2). Because of this fragmentation, the state has concentrated its political power on central, regional, and local levels. Regardless of these centralized efforts, a variety of non-state-sanctioned narratives persist in everyday life. These local narratives, however, do not have the political autonomy they need to realize the social goals of Tajikistan's many imagined sub-communities (Akbarzadeh, S. 1996). Though small social groups have emerged within Tajikistan's post-Soviet system, they are largely powerless as a result of the totalitarian features of the regime, one whose roots can be traced to the oppressive nature of the former centralized local Soviet leadership (Akbarzadeh, S. 1996, Nourzhanov, K. and Bleuer, C. 2013). With these facts in mind, the identities of the Tajik people need to be examined on different geographic-spatial scales that express their unique political desires, and not according to a spatial hierarchy.

On the basis of personal perceptions and communal manifestations, the idea of a unified Tajik identity, or the concept of the state framework, is an artificial social formation created by an external point of view (Akiner, S. 2001, Olimov, M. A. and Olimova, S. 2002, Nourzhanov, K. and Bleuer, C. 2013). The sub-state regional scale has produced multiple meanings. According to one interpretation, Tsarist colonization created a parallel, privileged, Russian-speaking society. This was both counteracted, and augmented, by the sudden and drastic modernization of the Soviet states, which replaced the urban-rural dichotomy with a separation between industrialized and developing regions. By changing feudal dependence into a support-base system, the Soviet leadership created a narrative of the northern, cotton-producing elite, who were located in highly urbanized, industrialized spaces such as Dushanbe and Nurek, while at the same time stigmatizing the underdevelopment of the local mountainous areas (Kandiyoti, D. 2002b). In addition to an identity that can be gleaned from the economic support and productivity of an area, regionalism also has a specific territorial attachment. The sense of historical origin in this region is not necessarily ethnic or clan-based, but rather has a spatial traceability. The attachment to these regions have been formed over three generations, especially on the paternal side.

In the forced mobilities of the modernist era, a multi-generational identity could be carried by one individual and embedded in a new environment. For example, in housing estates in the suburbs of Dushanbe, settlers and immigrants have formed groups and communities according to their region of origin. This is manifested not only with respect to public housing relations, but also in the use of public spaces (Kilavuz, I. T. 2007). The historical

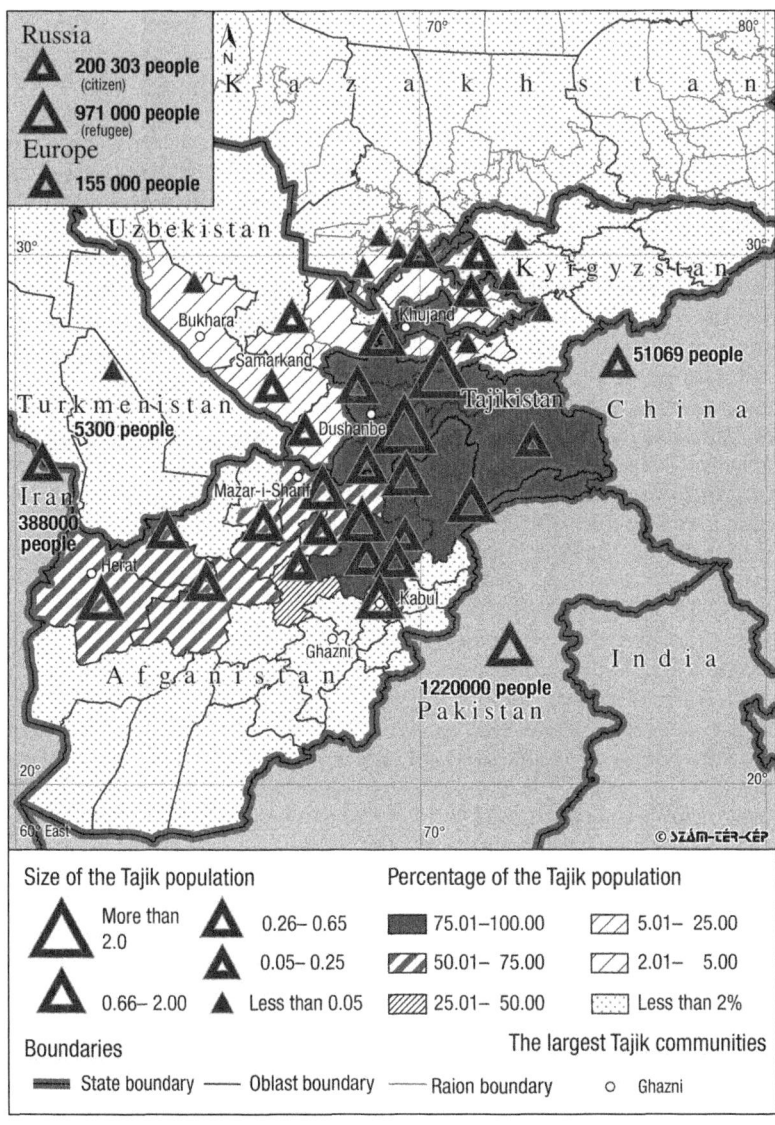

Figure 3.4.2 *The number and proportion of Tajiks in 2011; (Sources:* [1]; [16]; [19]; [34]; [35]; [36])

narratives of the three "great powers" — Islam, Tsardom, and the Soviet Union — also play an important role in the formation and production of urban spaces. In traditional Muslim society, the visiting of public spaces is segregated and strictly regulated. The ability to move through public spaces, like the performativity of the individual, was determined by patriarchal and conservative norms. The era of Soviet modernization pushed the rhythms of public life in two directions. On the one hand, trends of social mobility and family sociology were transformed by an increase in the urban population and the building of massive housing estates. However, the scarcity of housing estates made it impossible for large families to live in the same flat, thus facilitating the nuclearization of the traditional family model. On the other hand, with the survival of the extended social network and the multi-step urban migration within the generations, even entire staircases and blocks could be semi-privatized by a family. This social phenomenon disrupted the European interpretation of the urban dichotomy of public and private spaces (Sgibnev, W. 2015). After the change of the regime in 1991, capitalization further extended the privatization of public spaces. In the end, what Soviet modernization achieved in the field of gender emancipation, was undermined by the synchronicity of privatization and traditional, re-emerging Islamist social organization (Jung, C. G. 1972, Sgibnev, W. 2015).

In the southern and eastern mountain regions of Tajikistan, which have been considered to be less developed, localism is even more marked than regionalism (Roy, O. 1993). Expression of this localism is seen in the small, separated settlements in areas with a high rurality index. Here we find ethnically homogeneous and highly segregated spaces, separated by dialects of fragmented subcultures, or by relationships that extend beyond the endogenic families. In the eastern, more sparsely populated part of the country, it would have been impossible to develop an identity resulting from modern production conditions. Even before the advent of Communist ideology (and then the realized state-socialist system), the form of agricultural capitalism, practiced by the Valley Tajiks, had been unknown in the mountainous region, and the socialist system initiated a process of social emancipation and homogenization more than it changed the methods of economic production.

Another form of local territorial attachment is a widespread dual system in Tajikistan, which is the result of the Muslim traditional family model and Soviet social organization (Nourzhanov; K. Bleuer, C. 2013). Thanks to the survival of tribal communities and Islamic family centrism, the basic social cornerstone, the *avlod*, is still important today. The patriarchal-functional community of blood lineage relatives relies heavily on communal property and central economic planning. Thus, principles of "war communist" collectivism arrived in a somewhat familiar environment, and thus repressive, traditionalist practices survived (Kandiyoti, D. 2002b). The collective leadership of the economy, and the organization of production, was taken over by the *kolkhozes* and brigades, but the *avlod* has remained as a dominant category of origin (Abdullaev, K. 2004, Nekbakhtshoev, N. R. 2006). This is also due to the fact that, contrary to general European trends, the nuclearization of the rural family was not a dominant trend even in the 1990s (Nourzhanov, K. and Bleuer, C. 2013).

Another traditional system of councils connecting families with symbolic power is the *mahalla*. This system of organization is a kind of transition between the community forum and the elder's council. The *mahalla* is a forum for public expression, and also plays a role in imposing punishment and tax collection. However, in contemporary Tajik society, *mahallas* are more often a platform for Islamic law and celebratory rituals (Freizer, S. 2005, Nekbakhtshoev, N. R. 2006).

While economic decisions were invariably brought under the control of the *kolkhozes*, the organization of *mahallas* and *avlods* have played a significant role in determining not only an individual's life path, but also categories of performativity and identity, even after the change of regime. The residual effect of these traditional social systems has suppressed female actors in the community. But they can also organize the locals in order to mount fast and flexible resistance to centralized power (Nourzhanov, K. and Bleuer, C. 2013).

In traditional Tajik society, gender roles were rigidly defined, but during Soviet times, these gender roles were significantly dissolved, particularly in the religious realm. However, because of the isolation of rural populations, and the dominance of Soviet development interests, gender emancipation showed very large regional differences to the detriment of the rural female population (Kandiyoti, D. 2002b). The traditional (pre-Soviet) system of honor (*nomus*), and of shame (*ayb*), was predominantly enforced by senior men, but, on some issues, older women also had some representational power. Social standards are defined by the *mahalla* council, which are then transmitted to all male householders. As a result, the direct pressure is placed on men, leaving the individual male responsible for exerting pressure on the rest of the family to comply to assigned norms. Thus, Tajik women suffered and continue to suffer multiple oppressions that ensure their identity becomes part of a specific *nomus-ayb* conforming constraint-system. This system, which was at work regionally during the period of Soviet modernization, resulted in competition among women living in rural communities, which inhibited the organization of solidarity and resistance, and slowed the progress of emancipation, which more or less happened in the urban areas. It has also encouraged the development of a network of informers set up to monitor the proper functioning of gender roles as an extension of the power of the *mahalla*.

Another key to the survival of conservative social structures, especially in the countryside, is the education of children by women. In the *avlods*, young women are under the most severe repression and social dogmas are transmitted to their children in an unquestionable form (Harris, C. 2004). The liberation of women's identities from the control of the central government could have been achieved through education, but grassroots organizations would have needed to push back against the constraints of Islamic law and traditionalism, and the rigidity of the Soviet educational infrastructure.

The dissolution of the Soviet Union, combined with intensifying local, regional, ethnic, and religious conflicts, resulted in a civil war that raged between 1992 and 1997. Ethnic and national identities, constructed by the former Soviet power, were never successful in unifying the region. The consolidation of language and tradition, the ethnic privileges of social mobility, and the suppression of local identities, have not led to construction of a nation-state, but rather to the fragmentation of distinct groups in society which have been forced to turn inward, and then against one another (Nourzhanov, K. and Bleuer, C. 2013).

Two distinct sides emerged in the chaos of the civil war. On one side was The People's Front, which promoted the interests of the former communist elite with the support of Uzbekistan and Russia. On the other side was the Islamic Renaissance Party, which integrated elements of the United Tajik Resistance, such as the Islamists (with the support of Afghanistan), the Gorno-Badakhshan Autonomous Movement, and the nominally democratic opposition (Akbarzadeh, S. 1996). Occasionally, the regional identities within the two opposing sides were more politicized. In this conflict, the main difference between the parties was rooted in their ethno-regional basis, with a focus on a common area of origin. This was exacerbated by clan conflicts, feudal patron-client relationships, and attitudes toward Islam (Foster, D. W. 2015).

While the northern areas were controlled by the People's Front, where local leaders and warlords competed for power and economic position, the divisions in the eastern region of the country were based on identity differences that were caused either by localism, or by the opposition between the majority Sunni and the Shia of Gorno-Badakhshan (Roy, O. 1993, Akbarzadeh, S. 1996). The spatial relations of the civil war reflected the divisional opposition between the northwestern and southeastern regions of the country. Northwestern Tajikistan's industrialized, urban, "developed" regions represented the alliance of political and clan elites, with the help of Uzbeks and Russians. On the other side, the people of the marginalized spaces of the southeast found cohesion in religious movements, including Islamic radicalism. This identity divide in Tajik society was also evident in the fact that the civil war ended with different momentum in different regions (Foster, D. W. 2015). In many cases, the ideological background of the struggle was not determined by the two political narratives, but by local ruptures and conflicts (Kalyvas, S. N. 2006, Foster, D. W. 2015). Subnational cleavages have continued to determine the country's self-image, which has been dominated by Emomali Rahmon's People's Party since independence from the Soviet Union. In the eastern and southern territories, an individual remains loyal to local powers with respect to political and economic actions, and considers the national government irrelevant. In the isolated mountains, however, imagined communities are nonexistent with respect to the regional press or the economic division of labor (Anderson, B. 2016 [1983]; Akbarzadeh, S. 1996).

Antihegemony: opportunities and options instead of the state

Tajik identity can be understood on three geographical scales, where the attachment can be endowed with different meaning according to different situations and discourses. In addition, identities of the scales are not organized in a nested hierarchy like in the nation-state model. As a result, all-encompassing power and control does not emanate from a single center, but rather ruled individuals in the context of competition between the different scales (national, regional, local) (Foucault, M. 1995 [1975]; Van Assche, K. and Hornidge, A-K. 2014). The fragmentation and internal competition for power is manifested in gaps that allow for informality, new forms of social mobility, previously illegal forms of self-organization and creativity, and the opening up of new social boundaries, which ultimately result in a nomadization over state power (Eriksen, T. H. 2010 [1993]; Deleuze, G. and Guattari, F. 2005 [1987]; Van Assche; K. Hornidge, A-K. 2014). The fragmentation of identities can often lead to more debt or rootlessness, which can serve the controlling power on the state-scale, but reinforces community to the risk-taking of loyalty and solidarity at the local level (Engvall, J. 2006).

The control of state territory cannot be considered continuous when compared to the European nation-state framework. From 1992 to 1997, the emergent Tajik Civil War intensified divisions among clan leaders and warlords. In addition to the creation of local para-states, different rules were created rather than a uniform system. Thus, domestic mobility and population registration are not as strict as in the surrounding states. This situation allows various survival tactics, thus diversifying the individual's relationship with a social group or an imagined community (Anderson, B. 2016 [1983]; Van Assche, K. and Hornidge, A-K. 2014). Besides facilitating a variety of alternative economic activities and mobility, this political-institutional vacuum is not only the manifestation of people representing themselves, but has also provided NGOs with an opportunity to reveal their interests and to entice the elites by strengthening their individual positions with regards to economic power. Without the organization and power of the state, no social organization could be considered a real part of the Tajik nation. Relying on the worldwide hegemony of neoliberal capitalism, elites continued to reinforce the short-term economic thinking of the former socialist system, while nationalist intellectuals and people from the rural parts of the country took comfort in old, conservative ideas. However, each para-state structure has assisted clan-organizations and the reemergence of Islam (Kandiyoti, D. 2002b; Freizer, S. 2005, Van Assche, K. and Hornidge, A-K. 2014).

With the fall of the Soviet Union, the tactics and propaganda of the political and economic elite remained similar, which has rendered people skeptical of the official national narrative. With the disappearance of socialist-era public development, the state reduced long-term goals, and as a result the strength of community cohesion was also reduced. On the one hand, the disintegrated state has been a breeding ground for micro-politics and micro-resistances borne of particular or localized social desires and interactions. On the other hand, the fragmentation of the state has produced informal spaces that can be harmful for the society as a whole (Foucault, M. 1978 [1976]; Deleuze, G. and Guattari, F. 2005 [1987]; Van Assche, K. and Hornidge, A-K. 2014).

The unstable internal integration of Tajikistan, coupled with a weak identity policy and fragmented sense of identity, is largely due to the presence of long-standing Russian-Soviet power. Although we associate classical colonization with the period of Russian tsardom, the Stalinist era also created new oppressive structures. The resulting crisis allowed old pressures to deepen and new ones to emerge. The Soviet leadership interpreted the region's revolutionary left-wing politics in a vanguardist way, but Stalin supplemented it with a highly nationalist Russification, and distorted the revolutionary intent of Soviet-Bolshevik political ideas (Kiss V. 2018). Their Marxist roots and dedication to anti-imperialism should have been a decisive element of their ideology, but in Central Asia, it was only another manifestation of propaganda (Sidaway, J. D. 2002).

After the death of Lenin and Trotsky, Soviet-minded internationalism functioned as a new expansive hegemony, rather than as an anti-capitalist, anti-imperialist counter-hegemony. This system only sought to push Russia out of its subaltern imperial claustrophobia (Gramsci, A. 1959, Morozov, V. 2015). Central Asia remained a part and also victim of this superpower ambition. Even today, Tajikistan remains an important geopolitical frontier for Russian interests, a reality that has an impact on the country's domestic politics (Nourzhanov, K. and Bleuer, C. 2013).

It is clear that the post-Soviet situation is a result of both general structures and various identity crisis phenomena. But among the factors that have held back the development of imagined communities, we can find numerous components that are left behind by traditional perception (especially in rural spaces), forced modernization (mostly in urban areas) and, lately (since so-called independence), a new type of arbitrariness ushered in by the neoliberal world system (Anderson, B. 2016 [1983]; Sidaway, J. D. 2002). In Tajikistan, the hybrid identities of the four great narratives of traditional Islam, tsarist Russia, Soviet-Stalinism, and post-Sovietism, can be observed with significant territorial variation (Bhabha, H. K. 2004 [1994]). The only common frame of reference continues to be the Tajik language. Although it has proven to be a successful political project, and has had a significant role in communication and cultural transfer, it has not been able to build a united community of destiny, or ultimately, a nation.

The main element of these presumptive hybrid identities has been either the evolving regionalism or local spatial ties, which may include specific mobility and networking. Local and regional power replace the state and reproduce the fragmentation of central politics, but offer the potential for a new nomadization in Central Asia, which may be the utopia of a horizontal, decentralized society based on networks of autonomous regional or local municipalities. Taking this approach, we think about fluid social alliances (which are not as monolithic as social class) rather than hierarchies of power (Bhabha, H. K. 2004 [1994]; Deleuze, G. and Guattari, F. 2005 [1987]). However, present-day Tajikistan still mirrors the Soviet system, including the ambivalent relations of the old and the new elites (Bhabha, H. K. 1990). This narrow political-economic elite can be seen as the keepers of the development narrative, which represents the limited and interest-driven "catching-up" of postcolonial societies. The developments that have taken place in the controlled Western framework include acquired and produced knowledge and real political power that has had an external origin, while eternal developmentalism and backwardness have been inscribed in the local and regional landscape (Illés, T. and Bottlik, Zs. 2018). In contrast, informal power and economic activities are meeting points of central power and bottom-up organizations (Engvall, J. 2006). We can conclude that postcolonial independence does not necessarily lead to organized nationalism, nor is it necessarily expressed in a consistent nation-state with the "expected" European traditions (Akbarzadeh, S. 1996, Spivak, G. C. et al. 2006). In this case, the prevailing Tajik central power has become, and will continue to act, as a colonizer in the guise of a postcolonial actor.

Bibliography

Sources

Afghanistan

[1] Таджики в Афганистане https://ru.wikipedia.org/wiki/Таджики в Афганистане

Baltic countries

[2] Latvijas 2011. gada tautas skaitīšanas rezultāti – Centrālā statistikas pārvalde Rīga, 2015. 234 p.

[3] Pieejamo tabulu saraksts tēmā: 2000. gada tautas skaitīšanas rezultāti Latvijas iedzīvotāji republikas pilsētās un rajonos pēc vecuma, dzimuma un tautības – Latvijas Statistika (http://data.csb.gov.lv/pxweb/en/iedz/iedz__tautassk__taut__tsk2011/?tablelist=true)

[4] Statistika andmebaasi uuendus Rahva ja eluruumide loendus – Rahva ja eluruumide loendus 2011 – Elamistingimused Statistikaamet, Endla 15, 15174 Tallinn 2013

Belarus

[5] Статистические бюллетени «Национальный состав населения» – Перепись населения – 2009 Национальный статистический комитет Республики Беларусь (https://www.belstat.gov.by/informatsiya-dlya-respondenta/perepis-naseleniya/perepis-naseleniya-2009-goda/)

[6] Wakar, W. 1917: Rozwój terytorialny narodowości polskiej Part 3. Statystyka narodowościowa Królestwa Polskiego

Caucasus countries

[7] Izady M. 2000: Infographs, Maps and Statistics Collection (https://gulf2000.columbia.edu/maps.shtml)

[8] Major Muslim ethnic groups in Armenia, Iran, and the Islamic Commonwealth states. (https://upload.wikimedia.org/wikipedia/commons/3/3a/Major_Muslim_ethnic_groups_in_Armenia%2C_Iran%2C_and_the_Islamic_Commonwealth_states._LOC_92683743.jpg)

[9] Ethno-Caucasus – http://www.ethno-kavkaz.narod.ru/russkiy.html

Crimean peninsula

[10] Перепись населения в Республике Крым 2014. Итоги. Территориальный орган Федеральной службы государственной статистики в Республике Крым (Крымстат). 4.1. Национальный состав населения.Проверено 10 апреля 2016. (http://crimea.gks.ru/wps/wcm/connect/rosstat_ts/crimea/ru/census_and_research-ing/census/crimea_census_2014/score_2010/)

Iran

[11] Izady M. 2006-2009: Languages of Middle East (https://www.reddit.com/r/MapPorn/comments/2er1g7/detailed_map_of_languages_within_the_middle_east/)

References

[12] Izady M. 2006: Linguistic Composition of Iran (http://www.farsinet.com/farsi/linguistic_composition_of_iran.html)

[13] Азербайджанцы в Иране – (https://ru.wikipedia.org/wiki/Азербайджанцы_в_Иране)

Kazakhstan

[14] Итоги Национальной переписи населения 2009 года „Население Республики Казахстан" Департамент социальной и демографической статистики

[15] (http://www.stat.kz/p_perepis/novosty/Pages/itogi_po_regionam.aspx)

[16] 1999: Agentsvo Respubliki Kazakhstan po Statistike

[17] 2014: Ministry of National Economy of the Republic of Kazakhstan Committee on Statistics

[18] Mayor Ethnic Groups in Central Asia II. (https://upload.wikimedia.org/wikipedia/commons/d/d5/Central_Asia_Ethnic_en.svg)

Kyrgyzstan

[19] 2009, 2013 Bureau of Statistics of Kyrgyzstan (2009, 2013 Bureau of Statistics of Kyrgyzstan

Republic of Moldova

[20] Recensămîntul populației 2004, Culegere statistică. Vol. 1. Caracteristici demografice, naționale, lingvistice, culturale – Biroul Național de Statistică, 492 p.

[21] Recensămăntul populației și al locuințelor din 2014, Biroul Național de Statistică (http://recensamant.statistica.md)

[22] Atlas dmr 2004: Atlas of the Dniester Moldavien Republik. „Sheriff" Publishing and Printing Center Tiraspol 60. p.

Russia

[23] Брук С. И.– Апенченко В. С. (отв. ред.) 1964: Атлас народов мира. – Издательство: М. Академии наук, Москва. 184 p.

[24] Брук С. И – Пучков П. И. 2010: Карта Народов (Масштаб 1:25 000 000) (http://iamruss.ru/map-of-the-ethnic-composition-of-russia/)

[25] Всероссийская перепись населения 2002, 2010 года Национальный состав населения по регионам России

[26] Всесоюзная перепись населения 1926, 1939, 1959, 1970, 1979, 1989 года Национальный состав населения по регионам республик СССР

[27] Demoskop, Weekly – (http://www.demoscope.ru/weekly/ssp/census.php?cy=0)

[28] Population statistics of Eastern Europe & former USSR – (http://pop-stat.mashke.org/)

[29] Первая Всеобщая перепись населения Российской Империи 1897 г. Под ред. Н.А. Тройницкого. т. II. Общий свод по Империи результатов разработки данных Первой Всеобщей переписи населения, произведенной 28 января 1897 года. С.-Петербург, 1905. Таблица XIII. Распределение населения по родному языку.

[30] Росстат. (б.г.): Официальная статистика (http://www.gks.ru/wps/wcm/connect/rosstat_main/rosstat/ru/statistics/accounts/ (25. 02. 2019.)

[31] Chudinovskikh, O; Denisenko, M. 2017: Russia: A Migration System with Soviet Roots. Migration Information Source – The ONLINE Journal of the Migration Policy Institut (https://www.migrationpolicy.org/article/russia-migration-system-soviet-roots)

[32] Официальный сайт ФМС России (https://web.archive.org/web/20150316032709/http://www.fms.gov.ru/about/statistics/data/)

[33] Список российских военных объектов за рубежом https://ru.wikipedia.org/wiki/Список_российских_военных_объектов_за_рубежом; https://de.wikipedia.org/wiki/Streitkr%C3%A4fte_Russlands#Milit%C3%A4ranlagen_im_Ausland

Tajikistan

[34] 2000, 2010 Agency on Statistics under the President of the Republic of Tajikistan

Turkmenistan

[35] Türkmenistanyň Statistika baradaky döwlet komiteti statistika, 2010

Uzbekistan

[36] O'zbekiston Respublikasi Davlat Statistika Qo'mitasi (The State Comitee of the Republic of Uzbekistan on Statistics) 2013

[37] Цыряпкина, Ю., Н. 2015: Русские в Узбекистане: Языковые практики и самоидентификация (На примере полевых исследований в фергане) Томский журнал ЛИНГ и АНТР. Tomsk Journal LING & ANTHRO 3(9); pp. 18-28.

Ukraine

[38] Всеукраїнського перепису населення 2001, Національний склад населення України та його мовні ознаки – Державний комітет статистики України ТAzbir

[39] Про кількість та склад населення України за підсумками Всеукраїнського перепису населення 2001 року – Державний комітет статистики України (http://2001.ukrcensus.gov.ua/results/general/nationality/)

Unrecognized areas (Donetsk PR. and Luhansk PR.)

[40] http://glavstat.govdnr.ru/pdf/naselenie/chisl_naselenie_0118.pdf

[41] https://www.gkslnr.su/files/chisl_260418.pdf

References

A. Gergely A. 1997: Kisebbség, etnikum, nacionalizmus. MTA PTI, Budapest. 176 p.

Abdullaev, K. 2004: Current Local Government Policy Situation in Tajikistan. In: De Martino, L. (Ed.): Tajikistan at Crossroads: The Politics of Decentrlization. Cimera, Genova, pp. 8–16.

Abushenko, V. (Абушенко, В.) 2004: Креольство как ино-модерность Восточной Европы (Возможные стратегии исследования) ["Creolity" as the Other Modernity of Eastern Europe (Possible Research Strategies)]. Перекрестки, 4(1–2) pp. 124–160.

Ackermann, F. 2006: Ein sowjetisches Mitteleuropa. Annus Albaruthenicus 2006 – Год Беларускі сёмы том 2006. Рэдактар Сакрат Яновіч. Krynki: Villa Sokrates, pp. 7–31.

Ackermann, F. 2011: Die eigentliche Minderheit? Die staatliche Inszenierung weißrussischer Ethnizität in der Republik Belarus. In: Bohn, T. M. and Shadurski, V. (Hrsg.): Ein weißer Fleck in Europa …: Die Imagination der Belarus als Kontaktzone zwischen Ost und West, transcript Verlag, Bielefeld pp. 233–241.

Ackermann, F. and Urbansky, S. 2016: Einleitung - Introduction: Reframing Postwar Sovietization: Power, Conflict, and Accommodation. Jahrbücher für Geschichte Osteuropas, Neue Folge, 64(3), pp. 353-362

Akbarzadeh, S. 1996: Why Did Nationalism Fail in Tajikistan? Europe-Asia Studies, London, 48(7), pp. 1105–1129.

Akiner, S. 2001: Tajikistan: Disintegration or Reconciliation? Royal Institute of International Affairs, London, 95 p.

Alasuutari, P. and Alasuutari, N. 2009: Narration and Ritual Formation of Diasporic Identity: The Case of Second Generation Karelian Evacuees. Identities: Global Studies in Culture and Power, 16(3), pp. 321–341.

Alexandrova, O. and Timmermann, H. 1997: Integration und Desintegration in den Beziehungen Russlands. Belarus´ GUS. Osteuropa 47(10–11) pp. 1022–1037.

Allen, D. 2015: Russian Karelia looks to the past and future. South China Morning Post 28. Februar 2015.

Allworth, E. 1989: Preface to Central Asia. In: Central Asia. 120 Years of Russian Rule. Duke University Press, Durkham and London. pp. xv-xiii.

Anderson, B. 2016 [1983]: Imagined Communities: Reflections on the Origin and Spread of Nationalism. Verso, London & New York, 256 p.

Anderson, B. A. and Silver, B. D. 1983: Estimating Russification of Ethnic Identity Among Non-Russians in the USSR. Demography, 20(4), pp. 461–489.

References

Antonsich, M. 2005: Cardinal Markers of Finland's Identity Politics and National Identity, Eurasian Geography and Economics 46(4), pp. 290–305

Antonsich, M. 2009: National identities in the age of globalisation: The case of Western Europe. National Identities, 11(3), 281–299.

Arel, D. 2002: Demography and Politics in the First Post-Soviet Censuses: Mistrusted State, Contested Identities. Population, 57(6) pp. 801–827.

Aspaturian, V. V. 1968: The Non-Russian Nationalities. In: Kassof, Allen (ed.): Prospects for Soviet Society. New York: Praeger. pp. 143–198.

Atatürk, S. 2012: Regimes of Ethnicity and Nationhood in Germany, Russia and Turkey. Cambridge University Press, Cambridge. 321 p.

Auch, E-M. 2008: Berg Karabach – Krieg um die "Schwarzen Berge". In: von Guppenberg, M-C. and Steinbach, U. (Hrsg.): Der Kaukasus: Geschichte – Kultur – Politik. Verlag C. H. Beck, München pp. 111–122.

Augé, M. 1995: Non-places. Verso 98 p.

Austin, P. M. 1992: Soviet Karelian: The Language that Failed. Slavic Review, 51(1) pp. 16-35.

Aydıngün, I. and Aydıngün, A. 2007: Crimean Tatars Return Home: Identity and Cultural Revival. Journal of Ethnic and Migration Studies. 33(1), pp. 113–128.

Bacon, E. 1947: Soviet Policy in Turkestan. Middle East Journal. 1(4), pp. 386–400.

Baron, N. 2002: Production and Terror: The Operation of the Karelian Gulag, 1933-1939. Cahiers du Monde russe, 43(1). pp. 139-179.

Baron, N. 2007: Nature, nationalism and revolutionary regionalism: constructing Soviet Karelia, 1920-1923. Journal of Historical Geography 33(3), pp. 565-595.

Barta G; Illés T; Bottlik Zs. 2018: Orosz és szovjet népszámlálások etnikai-nemzeti kontextusban. In: Etnikai földrajzi kutatások a posztszovjet térségben. Szerk.: Kőszegi, M. and Barta, G. and Illés, T. and Berki, M. ELTE, Budapest, pp. 81-99.

Bartha A. 1996: Genocídiumok és nemzeti feltámadás. Történelmi Szemle 38(4), pp. 383-400.

Belina, B. and Arambaşa, M. 2007: Alltägliche Identitätskonstruktionen in der Republik Moldau zwischen Rumänismus und Moldovenismus. Europa Regional, 15(4), pp. 189–198.

Benkö, A., Malek, M. 2005: Akteure des Konflikts um Transnistrien (Moldau). Südosteuropa, 53(1), pp. 56–79.

Berg, L. D. 2004: Scaling knowledge: towards a critical geography of critical geographies. Geoforum, 35(5), 553–558.

Berindei, D. 1996: Die Kulturbeziehungen zwischen der Republik Moldova und Rumänien. Der Donauraum, 30(3–4) (Republik Moldova: Sonderheft), 103–106.

REFERENCES

Berki M. 2017: A földrajzi lépték változó értelmezése és a cselekvőhálózat-elmélet. Földrajzi Közlemények, 141(3), 203–215.

Besters-Dilger, J. 2000: Die aktuelle Sprachensituation in der Ukraine. Österreichisches Osthefte, 42(3–4) pp. 497–523.

Besters-Dilger, J. 2013: Prüfstein der europäischen Sprachenpolitik: Die Ukraine. Europa Ethnica, 69(1–2) pp. 23–31.

Bhabha, H. K. 1990: Nation and Narration. Routledge, London, 333 p.

Bhabha, H. K. 2004 [1994]: Location of Culture. Routledge, 2nd Edition, London & New York, 440 p.

Bieder, H. 2000: Konfession, Ethnie und Sprache in Weißrußland im 20. Jahrhundert. Zeitschrift für Slawistik J 45(3) pp. 200–214.

Bieder, H. 2001: Der Kampf um die Sprachen im 20. Jahrhundert. In: Beyrau, D. and Lindner, R. (Hrsg.): Handbuch der Geschichte Weißrußlands. Vandenhoeck & Ruprecht Verlag, Göttingen pp. 451–471.

Bieder, H. 2003: Die Normentwicklung der ostslawischen Standardsprachen in der postsowjetischen Periode. Wiener Slawistischer Almanach 52 pp. 19–35.

Bilinsky, Y. 1981: Expanding the Use of Russian or Russification? Some Critical Thoughts on Russian As a Lingua Franca and the "Language of Friendship and Cooperation of the Peoples of the USSR". The Russian Review. 40. 3. pp. 317–332.

Birtalan Á. and Rákos A. 2002: Kalmükök: egy európai mongol nép. Terebess Kiadó, Budapest. 260 p.

Bitis, A. 2005: The 1828–1829 Russo-Turkish War and the Resettlement of Balkan Peoples into Novorossiia. Jahrbücher für Geschichte Osteuropas, Neue Folge. 53(4), pp. 506–525.

Bochmann, K. 1996: „Moldauisch" oder „Rumänisch" Linguistische, kulturelle und politische Aspekte der Amtssprache. Der Donauraum, 30(3–4) (Republik Moldova: Sonderheft), pp. 95–102.

Bochmann, K., Dumbrava, V., Müller, D., Reinhardt, V. (Hrsg.) 2012: Die Republik Moldau (Republica Moldova) – Ein Handbuch. Universitätsverlag, Leipzig, 748 p.

Bohdanowitz, L. 1942: The Muslims in Poland: Their Origin, History, and Cultural Life. The Journal of the Royal Asiatic Society of Great Britain and Ireland. 109(3), pp. 163–180.

Bormanshinov, A. 1998: Kalmyk Pilgrims to Tibet and Mongolia. Central Asiatic Journal 42(1), pp. 1–23.

Bottlik Zs. 2008: Geographische Hintergründe zur nationalen Identität der Montenegriner. Geographische Rundschau, 59(10), pp. 54–61.

Bottlik Zs. 2013: A lengyel etnikai törzsterület földrajzi vizsgálata. Földrajzi Közlemények, 137(2), pp. 133–152.

Bottlik Zs. 2016: A belarusz lakosság nyelvhasználatának etnikai földrajzi vizsgálata. Földrajzi Közlemények, 140(2), pp 312–327.

Bottoni, S. 2014: A várva várt nyugat. MTA Bölcsészettudományi Kutatóközpont Történettudományi Intézet, Budapest. 362 p.

Brade-Schulze 1997: Rußland – aktuell. Beiträge zur regionalen Geographie, Band 4. Leibniz Institut für Länderkunde, Leipzig 120 p.

Braunmüller, K. and Ferraresi, G. 2003: Aspects of Multilingualism in European Language History. Hamburg Studies on Multiliungalism, John Benjamins Publishing Com. Amsterdam. 291 p.

Brenner, N. 1999: Beyond state-centrism? Space, territoriality, and geographical scale in globalization studies. Theory and Society, 1., pp 39–78.

Bressey, C. 2011: Race/Ethnicity. In: Agnew, J.A., Livingstone D.N. (ed.): The SAGE Handbook of Geographical Knowledge. SAGE, London. pp. 418–429.

Brom, L. 1988: Dialectical Identity and Destiny: A General Introduction to Alexander Zinoviev's Theory of the Soviet Man. Rocky Mountain Review of Language and Literature. 42(1–2), pp. 15–27

Brown, C. S. 2004: Wanting to Have Their Cake and Their Neighbor's Too: Azerbaijani Attitudes towards Karabakh and Iranian Azerbaijan. Middle East Journal, 58(4), (Autumn), pp. 576–596.

Brubaker, R. and Cooper, F. 2000: Beyond "Identity". Theory and Society. 29(1) pp. 1–47.

Brubaker, R. 1994: Nationhood and the national question in the Soviet Union and post-Soviet Eurasia: An institutionalist account. Theory and Societ 23(1) 47–78.

Brubaker, R. 1996: Nationalism Reframed: Nationhood and the National Question in the New Europe Cambridge, Cambridge University Press 202 p.

Brunnbauer, U. (Hg.) 2002: Umstrittene Identitäten. Ethnizität und Nationalität in Südosteuropa. Peter Lang, Frankfurt am Main. 234 p.

Brüggemann, M. 2014: Zwischen Anlehnung an Russland und Eigenständigkeit: Zur Sprachpolitik in Belarus. Europa Ethnica 71(3–4), pp. 88–94.

Burlyka, I. 2004: Do Belarusians Speak Belarusian in the Street? Annus Albaruthenicus 2004 – Год Беларускі пяты том 2004. Рэдактар Сакрат Яновіч. Krynki: Villa Sokrates, pp. 103–109.

Cadiot, J. 2005: Searching for Nationality: Statistics and National Categories at the End of the Russian Empire (1897–1917). The Russian Review, 64(3), pp. 440–455.

Calhoun, C. 1993: Nationalism and Ethnicity. Annual Review of Sociology. 19., pp. 211–239.

Carney, C. and Moran, J. P. 2000: Imagining Communities in Central Asia: Nationalism and Interstate Affect in the Post-Soviet Era. Asian Affairs. 26(4), pp. 179–198.

References

Cashaback, D. 2012: Assessing Asymmetrical Federal Design in the Russian Federation: A Case Study of Language Policy in Tatarstan. Europe-Asia Studies. 60(2), pp. 249–275.

Cazacu, M. 1996: Moldau – Bessarabien – Transnistrien. Der Donauraum, 30(3–4) (Republik Moldova: Sonderheft), pp. 14–21.

Cazacu, M., Trifon, N. 2017: Republica Moldova. Un stat în căutarea națiunii. Cartier, Chișinău 416 p.

Chari, S., Verdery, K. 2009: Thinking between the posts: Postcolonialism, postsocialism, and ethnography after the Cold War. Comparative Studies in Society and History, 51(1), pp. 6–34.

Cheshire, H. 1934: The Expansion of Imperial Russia to the Indian Border. The Slavonic and East European Review. 13(37), pp. 85–97.

Ciscel, M. 2007: The Language of the Moldovans: Romania, Russia, and Identity in an Ex-Soviet Republic. Lexington Books, Lanham 186 p.

Collins, K. 2003: The Political Role of Clans in Central Asia. Comparative Politics. 35(2) pp. 171–190.

Cornell, S. E. 1998: Religion as a Factor in Caucasian Conflicts. Civil Wars, 1(3), pp. 46–64.

Cornell, S. E. 1999: The Nagorno-Karabakh Conflict. Report no. 46. Department of East European Studies, Uppsala University. 162 p.

Cornell, S. E. 2002: Autonomy and Conflict. Ethnoterritoriality and Separatism in the South Caucasus – Cases in Georgia. Department of Peace and Conflict Research, Uppsala Report No. 61. 258 p.

Cosgrove, D. 1989: Geography is everywhere: culture and symbolism in human landscapes. In: Gregory D & R Walford (eds: Horizons in human geography. Macmillan, London pp. 118–135.

Cox, K. R. 2002: Political Geography. Territory, State, and Society. Blackwell, Oxford. 382 p.

Croissant, M. P. 1998: Armenia-Azerbaijan Conflict: Causes and Implications. Westport, CT: Praeger, 172 p.

Crowther, W. 1991: The Politics of Ethno-National Mobilization: Nationalism and Reform in Soviet Moldavia. The Russian Review. 50(2), pp. 183–202.

Cullen, D. and Ryan, J. and Winders, J. 2013: Postcolonialism. In: Johnson, N. C. and Schein, R. H. and Winders, J. (eds.: The Wiley-Blackwell companion to cultural geography. Wiley-Blackwell, Chichester, pp. 508–523.

Cusco, A. 2017: A contested borderland. Competing Russian and Romanian visions of Bessarabia in the late nineteenth and early twentieth century. Central European University Press, Budapest, New York 345 p.

Danylenko, A. 2006: On the Language of Early Lithuanian Tatars or, Have Lithuanian Tatars Ever Written in Ukrainian? The Slavonic and East European Review. 84.(2), pp. 201-236.

Darrow, D. W. 2002: Census as a Technology of Empire. Ab Imperio, 4. pp. 145-176.

Deleuze, G. and Guattari, F. 2005 [1987]: A Thousand Plateaus: Capitalism and Schizophrenia. University of Minnesota Press, Minneapolis, 610 p.

Dembinska, M., Campana, A. 2017: Frozen Conflicts and Internal Dynamics of De Facto States: Perspectives and Directions for Research. International Studies Review, 19(2), pp. 254-278.

Demeter G. 2010: Montenegró két arca: gazdasági sikerek és belpolitikai válságok (2005-2008). In: Demeter G., Radics Zs. (szerk.): Kompországok, ahol a part szakad. Szemelvények Köztes-Európa integrációs törekvéseiből (1990-2008). Didakt Kiadó, Debrecen, pp. 315-339.

Demeter G. 2018: A történelem nyomai a mai térszerkezetben – belső törésvonalak az európai posztszovjet térségben. (The impact of history – persistent fault lines in the post-Soviet region). Tér és társadalom 32(4), pp. 7-30.

Deutsch, K. W. 1961: Social Mobilization and Political Development. American Political Science Review. 55(3), pp. 634-647.

Deutsch, K. W. 1966: Nationalism and Social Communication: An Inquiry into the Foundations of Nationality. Cambridge, MIT Press. 345 p.

Devlet, N. 1991: Islamic Revival in the Volga-Ural Region. Cahiers du Monde russe et soviétique. 32. 1. En asie centrale soviétique: Ethnies, nations, états. pp. 107-116.

Dingley, J. 2001: Sprachen in Weißrussland bis zum Ende des 19. Jhs. In: Beyrau, D. and Lindner, R: Handbuch der Geschichte Weißrußlands Vandenhoeck & Ruprecht Verlag, Göttingen pp. 437-450.

Dingsdale, A. 1999: New geographies of post-socialist Europe. The Geographical Journal, 165(2), pp. 145-153.

Dumbrava, V. 2002: Die „Last der Geschichte" in der Republik Moldau. Südosteuropa, pp. 51(7-9), 431-448.

Dumbrava, V. 2006: Sprachpolitik in der Republik Moldova. Europa Ethnica, 63(1-2) pp. 33-38.

Éber M. Á. et al. 2014: 1989: Szempontok a rendszerváltás globális politikai gazdaságtanához. Fordulat, Budapest, 21, pp. 10-63.

Eberhardt, P. 2000: Polacy na Kresach Wschodnich – rodowód, dzieje. Przegląd Geograficzny T. 62(1-2) pp. 5-14.

Eberhardt, P. 2001: Ethnic Groups and Population Changes in Twentieth-Century Central-Eastern Europe. M.E. Sharpe Amonk, New York 559 p.

References

Eberhardt, P. 2002: Ethnic Problems in Poland and in Her Eastern Neighbours. Geografickỳ Časopis, 54(3) pp. 191–201.

Engvall, J. 2006: The State Under Seige: The Drug Trade and Organised Crime in Tajikistan. Europe–Asia Studies, London. 58(6) pp. 827–854.

Eriksen, T. H. 2010 [1993]: Ethnicity and Nationalism: Anthropological Perspectives. Pluto Press, 3rd Edition, London, 256 p.

Fanon, F. 2008 [1952; 1967]: Black Skin, White Masks. Grove Press, New York. 206 p.

Fanon, F. 1963 [1963]: The Wretched of the Earth. Grove Press, New York. 320 p.

Fingerroos, O. 2006: The Karelia of Memories – Utopias of a Place. Folklore vol. 33 (Estonian Folklore), pp. 95-108.

Foster, D. W. 2015: Militarism in Tajikistan: Realities of Post-Soviet Nation Building. University of Oregon, Eugene, 291 p.

Foucault, M. 1978 [1976]: The History of Sexuality. Volume I: An Introduction. Pantheon Books, New York, 168 p.

Foucault, M. 1995 [1975]: Discipline & Punish: The Birth of the Prison. Vintage Books, New York, 333 p.

Frank, A. J. 2000: Varieties of Islamization in Inner Asia: The Case of the Baraba Tatars, 1740-1917. Cahiers du Monde russe (En islam sibérien) 41(2–3), pp. 245–262.

Freizer, S. 2005: Neo-liberal and Communal Civil Society in Tajikistan: Merging or Dividing in the Post War Period? Civil Society in Central Asia and the Caucasus, Milton Park, 24(3), pp. 225–243.

Froese, P. 2004: Forced Secularization in Soviet Russia: Why an Atheistic Monopoly Failed. Journal for the Scientific Study of Religion 43(1), pp. 35–50.

Fukuyama, F. 1992: The end of history and the last man. Free Press, New York

Gammer, M. 2000: Post-Soviet Central Asia and Post-Colonial Francophone Africa: Some Associations. Middle Eastern Studies. 36. 2. pp. 124–149.

Gasimov, Z. 2010: Mova und Jazyk Die Sprachenfrage in der Ukraine In: Osteuropa 60(2-4), pp. 403-411.

Gasimov, Z. 2011a: The Caucasus, in: European History Online (EGO), published by the Institute of European History (IEG), Mainz 23 p. URL: http://www.ieg-ego.eu/gasimovz-2011-en URN: urn:nbn:de:0159-2011081894

Gasimov, Z. 2011b: Zwischen Europa, Turan und Orient: Raumkonzepte in der modernen aserbaidschanischen Geschichtsschreibung und Geschichtspolitik Jahrbücher für Geschichte Osteuropas; Neue Folge, 59(4), pp. 534–558

Gasimov, Z. 2013: Aserbaidschan: Befreiung und Konflikt – der Umgang mit Verlusten in einer postkolonialen Gesellschaft In.: Hilger A. and von Wrochem, O. (Hrsg): Die geteilte Nation: nationale Verluste und Identitäten im 20. Jahrhundert Oldenburg Verlag; München pp. 135-151.

Gelb, M. 1993:'Karelian Fever': The Finnish Immigrant Community during Stalin's Purges. Europe-Asia Studies, 45(6), pp. 1091-1116.

Gellner, E. 2008 [1983]: Nations and nationalism. Cornell, Ithaka. 152 p.

Gille Zs. 2019: Létezik-e szocialocén? Fordulat, Budapest, 25, pp. 79–103.

Giuliano, E. 2000: Who Determines the Self in the Politics of Self-Determination? Identity and PreferenceFormation in Tatarstan's Nationalist Mobilization. Comparative Politics. 32. 3. pp. 295–316.

Goina, C. 2005: How the state shaped the nation: an essay on the making of the Romanian nation. Regio. Minorities, Politics, Society, 1.,154–169.

Golz, S. 2011: Quo Vadis, Weißrussisch; Entwicklungslinien einer (Standard)Sprache. In: Bohn, T. and Shadurski, V. (Hrsg.): Ein weißer Fleck in Europa …: Die Imagination der Belarus als Kontaktzone zwischen Ost und West. Trancript Verlag, Bielefeld pp. 39–47.

Govorukhin, S. and Ganina, M. and Lavrov, K. and Dudintsev, V. 1989: Homo Sovieticus. World Affairs (The Soviet Union on the Brink: Part Two) 152(2), pp. 104–108.

Gramsci, A. 1959: The Modern Prince and Other Writings. International Publishers, New York, 192 p.

Graney, K. E. 1999: Education Reform in Tatarstan and Bashkortostan: Sovereignty Projects in Post-Soviet Russia. Europe-Asia Studies. 51(4), pp. 611–632.

Gregory, D. 2004: The colonial present. Blackwell, Malden, Oxford, Carlton 367 p.

Grin, F. 2000: Kalmykia: From Oblivion to Reassertion? ECMI Working Paper # 10. European Centre for Minority Issues (ECMI). 38 p.

Grousset, R. 1970: The Empire of the Steppes: A History of Central Asia. Rutgers University Press, New Brunswick. 718 p.

Guchinova, E. B. 2005: У каждого своя Сибирь. Два рассказа о депортации калмыков. Антропологический форум 3. pp. 400–442.

Gutiérrez, R. A. 2004: Internal Colonialism: An American Theory of Race. Du Bois Review, Cambridge, 1(2), pp. 281–295.

Gyuris F. 2018: Szovjet és posztszovjet: Rendszerszintű társadalmi és gazdasági keretek a szovjet szocialist rendszerben és utána. In: Etnikai földrajzi kutatások a posztszovjet térségben. Szerk.: Kőszegi, M. and Barta, G. and Illés, T. and Berki, M. ELTE, Budapest, 31–50.

Hagendoorn, L. and Poppe, E. and Minescu, A. 2008: Support for Separatism in Ethnic Republics of the Russian Federation. Europe-Asia Studies, 60(3), pp. 353-373.

Häkli, J. 2018: Afterword. Transcending scale. In: Herb, G. H., Kaplan, D. H. (eds.): Scaling identities. Nationalism and territoriality. Rowman & Littlefield, Lanham, pp. 271–282.

Halperin, C. J. 1982: "Know Thy Enemy": Medieval Russian Familiarity with the Mongols of the Golden Horde. Jahrbücher für Geschichte Osteuropas, Neue Folge. 30(2) pp. 161–175.

Hann, C. and Pelkmans, M. 2009: Realigning Religion and Power in Central Asia: Islam, Nation-State and (Post)Socialism. Europe-Asia Studies. 61(9), pp. 1517–1541.

Hannula M. 2006: The transformation of the identity of the Karelian Isthmus of Russia. Alue ja Ympäristö, 35(2), pp. 32–41.

Harris, C. 2004: Control and Subversion: Gender Relations in Tajikistan. Pluto Press, London, 212 p.

Harvey, D. 1992 [1989]: The Condition of Postmodernity. Blackwell, Cambridge & Oxford, 379 p.

Hasse, A. and Hudseljak, I. 2000: Perspektiven und Probleme der neuen polnisch-ukrainischen Nachbarschaft. Europa Regional, 8(2), pp. 2–19.

Hausleitner, M. 2008: Bessarabien als historische Region In: Khal, T., Metzeltin, M., Ungureanu, M. R. (Hrsg.): Rumänien. Raum und Bevölkerung, Geschichte und Geschichtsbilder, Kultur, Gesellschaft und Politik heute, Wirtschaft, Recht und Verfassung, historische Regionen. LIT Verlag, Berlin, Münster, Wien, Zürich, London, pp. 825–839.

Häyrynen, M. 2004: A periphery lost: the representation of Karelia in Finnish national landscape imagery. Fennia 182(1), pp. 23–32.

Heller, M. 1996: Az Orosz Birodalom története (Orosz történelem I. kötet). Osiris-2000, Budapest. 668p.

Heller, M. and Nyekerics, A. 1996: A Szovjetunió története (Orosz történelem II. kötet). Osiris-2000, Budapest 610 p.

Heller, W., Arambaşa, M. N. (Hrsg.) 2009: Am östlichen Rand der Euriopäischen Union – Geopolitische, ethnische und nationale sowie ökonomische und soziale Probleme und ihre Folgen für die Grenzraumbevölkeerung. Universitätsverlag Potsdam, Potsdam (Potsdamer Geographische Forschungen; 28.)

Hellie, R. 2005: The Structure of Russian Imperial History. History and Theory. 44(1), pp. 88–112.

Hentschel, G. and Kittel, B. 2011. Zur weißrussisch-russischen Zweisprachigkeit in Weißrussland – nicht zuletzt aus Sicht der Weißrussen [On Belarusian-Russian Bilingualism – Not Least from the Belarusian View]. In: Bohn, T. M. – Shadurski, V. (Hrsg.): Ein weißer Fleck in Europa…: Die Imagination der Belarus als Kontaktzone zwischen Ost und West, transcript Verlag, Bielefeld. pp. 49–67.

Herb, G. H. 2018: Power, Territory and National Identity. In: Herb, G. H. and Kaplan, D. H.: Scaling identities: nationalism and territoriality. Rowman & Littlefield. pp. 7–29.

Herrschel, T. 2007: Global geographies of post–socialist transition: geographies, societies, policies. Routledge studies in human geography 14. Routledge, London, 288 p.

Herzig, E.1999: The new Caucasus: Armenia, Azerbaijan and Georgia. Royal Institute of International Affairs, London. 165 p.

Hirsch, F. 2005: Empire of Nations: Ethnographic Knowledge and the Making of the Soviet Union. Cornell University Press, Ithaca – London. 392 p.

Hirschhausen, B. von 2017a: The lessons of phantom borders: The vestiges of the past come (also) from the future. L'Espace geographique, 45(2), 106–125.

Hirschhausen, B. von 2017b: The heuristic interest of the concept of "phantom borders" in the understanding of cultural regionalization. L'Espace geographique, 45(2), 126–142.

Hirschhausen, B. von. and Grandits, H. and Kraft, C. and Müller, D. and Serrier, T. 2015: Phantomgrenzen: Räume und Akteure in der Zeit neu denken. Wallstein Verlag, Göttingen. (Phantomgrenzen in Östlichen Europa Bd. 1.), 224 p.

Hobsbawm, Eric J. 1962: The Age of Revolution. Europe 1789–1848. Wiedenfeld and Nicolson, London. 366 p.

Hofbauer, H. and Roman, V. 1997: Bukowina, Bessarabien, Moldawien: Vergessenes Land zwischen Westeuropa, Rußland und der Türkei. Promedia Verlag, Wien

Holland, E. C. 2015: Competing Interpretations of Buddhism's Revival in the Russian Republic of Kalmykia. Europe-Asia Studies 67. 6. pp. 948–969.

Honkasalo, M-L. 2009: Grips and Ties: Agency, Uncertainty, and the Problem of Suffering in North Karelia. Medical Anthropology Quarterly, New Series (Nordic Medical Anthropology), 23(1), pp. 51-69.

Hopkirk, P. 2006: The Great Game: On Secret Service in High Asia. John Murray, London 566 p.

Horváth, Cs. 2010: Ethnographic Metamorphosis of East Karelia during the 20th Century. Délkelet-Európa – South-East Europe International Relations Quarterly, 1(2), 27 p.

Horváth, Cs. 2011: Ethno Demographic Changes in the Caucasus 1860-1960. Délkelet-Európa – South-East Europe International Relations Quarterly. 2(6), pp. 1–20. https://www.southeast-europe.org/pdf/06/DKE_06_A_K_HORVATH_CSABA.pdf

Höfinghoff, M. 2006: Zur Frage russisch-ukrainischer Zweisprachigkeit in der Ukraine. Europa Ethnica, 63(1–2) pp. 25–32.

References

Hrycak, J. 2000: Die Formierung der modernen ukrainischen Nation. Österreichisches Osthefte, 42(3-4) pp. 189-210.

Illés T. and Bottlik, Zs. 2018: A moldáv identitás rétegei. Tér és Társadalom, Budapest, 32(4) pp. 84-105.

Illés T. 2018a: A kulturális globalizáció földrajzi vonásai. Tér és Társadalom, 32(2), pp. 3-20.

Illés T. 2018b: Kelet és Nyugat között - a román csoportok etnikai földrajzi vizsgálata a kezdetektől napjainkig. Földrajzi Közlemények, 142(2), 137-153.

Ioffe, G. 2003a: Understanding Belarus: Question of Language. Europe-Asia Studies, 55(7), pp. 1009-1047.

Ioffe, G. 2003b: Understanding Belarus: Belarusian Identity. Europe-Asia Studies, 55(8), pp. 1241-1272.

Ioffe, G. 2006: The Phenomenon of Belarus: A Book Review Essay. Eurasian Geography and Economics, 47(5), pp. 622-634.

Iwanow, N. 1994: Die Polen in Weißrusslands. Osteuropa, 44(5), pp. 473-482.

Jańczak, J. 2015: Phantom borders and electoral behavior in Poland. Historical legacies, political culture and their influence on contemporary politics. Erdkunde, 69(2), 125-137.

Jones, K. T. 1998: Scale as epistemology. Political Geography, 17(1), pp. 25-28.

Jung, C. G. 1972: Synchronicity: An Acausal Connecting Principle. In: Jung, C.: Collected Works of C. G. Jung, Volume 8 (2nd Edition). Princeton University Press, Princeton, pp. 417-420.

K. Horváth Zs. 1999: Az eltűnt emlékezet nyomában. Pierre Nora és a történeti emlékezetkutatás francia látképe. Aetas Történettudományi Folyóirat 14(3), pp. 132-141.

Kalyvas, S. N. 2006: The Logic of Violence in Civil War. Cambridge University Press, Cambridge, 485 p.

Kandiyoti, D. 2002a: How Far Do Analyses of Postsocialism Travel? The Case of Central Asia. In: Hann, C. (Ed.): Postsocialism: Ideals, Ideologies and Practices in Eurasia. Routledge, London-New York, pp. 238-257.

Kandiyoti, D. 2002b: Post-Colonialism Compared: Potentials and Limitations in the Middle East and Central Asia. International Journal of Middle East Studies, Cambridge, 34(2) pp. 279-297.

Kaplan, D. H. 2018: National identity and scalar processes. In: Herb, G. H., Kaplan, D. H. (eds.): Scaling identities. Nationalism and territoriality. Rowman & Littlefield, Lanham, pp. 31-47.

Karácsonyi D. 2006: A területi tagoltság és a régiók eredete, arculata Ukrajnában. Földrajzi Értesítő, 55(3-4), pp. 375-391.

Karácsonyi D. 2008: A kelet-európai sztyep és a Magyar Alföld, Mint frontier területek. Földrajzi Értesítő, 57(1-2), pp. 185-211.

Karácsonyi D. 2009: Ein Versuch der Typologie der ländlichen Räume in der Ukraine. Europa Regional, 17(1), pp. 34–50.

Karácsonyi D. 2014b: A csernobili baleset térbeli hatása a Poleszje demográfiai és urbanizációs folyamataira. Tér és társadalom, 28(1), 130–154.

Karácsonyi D. and Bottlik Zs. 2018: Ukrajna kétarcúságának etnikai földrajzi háttere. In: Bottlik Zs. (szerk.): Etnikai földrajzi kutatások Köztes-Európában. ELTE, Budapest, pp. 43–61.

Karácsonyi D. and Kocsis K. and Bottlik Zs. 2017: Belarus in maps. HAS Research Center for Astronomy and Earth Sciences, Budapest, 194. p.

Karácsonyi D. and Kocsis K. and Kovály K. and Molnár J. and Póti L. 2014a: East–West dichotomy and political conflict in Ukraine – Was Huntington right? Hungarian Geographical Bulletin, 63(2), pp. 99–134.

Karim, M. 2005: Globalization and Post-Soviet Revival of Islam in Central Asia and the Caucasus. Journal of Muslim Minority Affairs. 25(3), pp. 439–448.

Karimova, L. 2013: Muslim Revival in Tatarstan: Tatar Women's Narratives as Indicators of Competing Islamic Traditions. Nova Religio: The Journal of Alternative and Emergent Religions. 17(1), pp. 38–58.

Katchanovski, I. 2005: Small Nations but Great Differences: Political Orientations and Cultures of the Crimean Tatars and the Gagauz. Europe-Asia Studies. 57(6), pp. 877–894.

Kendirbai, G. 2018: The Politics of the Inner Asian Frontier and the 1771 Exodus of the Kalmyks. Inner Asia 20. pp. 263–292.

Kennedy, J. 2016: John Porter Lecture: Liberal Nationalisms Revisited. In: Canadian Review of Sociology. 53(1), pp. 7–25.

Keough, L. J. 2006: Globalizing 'Postsocialism': Mobile Mothers and Neoliberalism on the Margins of Europe. Anthropological Quarterly. 79(3), pp. 431–461.

Khodarkovsky, M. 2004: Russia's Steppe Frontier: The Making of a Colonial Empire, 1500-1800. Indiana University Press, Bloomington, 304 p.

Kilavuz, I. 2007: Understanding Violent Conflict: A Comparative Study of Tajikistan and Uzbekistan. Indiana University, Bloomington, 222 p.

King, C. 1993: Moldova and the New Bessarabian Questions. The World Today. 49(7), pp. 135–139.

King, C. 2000: The Moldovans: Romania, Russia, and the Politics of culture. Hoover Institution Press, Stanford, 303 p.

Kiossev, A. 2011: The self-colonizing metaphor. Atlas of transformation. http://monumenttotransformation.org/atlas-of-transformation/html/s/self-colonization/the-self-colonizing-metaphor-alexander-kiossev.html (Retrieved: 3 October 2018)

Kirimli, H. 1993: The "Young Tatar" Movement in the Crimea, 1905-1909. Cahiers du Monde russe et soviétique. 34(4), pp. 529–560.

References

Kirimli, H. 2003: The Famine of 1921-22 in the Crimea and the Volga Basin and the Relief from Turkey. Middle Eastern Studies. 39(1), pp. 37-88.

Kirkinen, H. and Nevalainen, P. and Sihvo, H. 1994: Karjalan kansan historia. Helsinki: WSOY, 605 p.

Kitinov, B. U. 2016: Buddhism and Polity in Caspian Region. Himalayan and Central Asian Studies 20(1), pp. 26-40.

Kittel, B. and Lindner, D. 2011: Der soziale Hintergrund von Sprachwahlen in Bearus. Kölner Zeitschrift für Soziologie und Sozialpsychologie, 63(4) pp. 623-647.

Knappe, E. and Wust, A. and Ratchina M. 2012: Weißrussland – Aktuelle Probleme und Entwicklungen. Daten-Fakten-Literatur 11. zur Geographie Europas Leibnitz Institut für Länderkunde, Leipzig 124 p.

Kocsis K. 2002: Etnikai földrajz. In: Tóth József (szerk.): Általános társadalomföldrajz. Dialóg – Campus, Budapest – Pécs, pp. 313-335.

Kocsis K., Rudenko, L., Schweitzer F. 2008: Ukraine in Maps. HAS, Geographical Research Institute, Budapest, 147 p.

Kolstø, P. 2016: Introduction: Russian Nationalism is Back – but Precisely What Does that Mean? In: Kolstø, P. and Blakkisrud, H. (Eds.): The New Russian Nationalism: Imperialism, Ethnicity and Authoritarianism 2000-15. Edinburgh University Press, Edinburgh, pp. 1-17.

Koobak, R. and Marling, R. 2014: The decolonial challenge: Framing post-socialist Central and Eastern Europe within transnational feminist studies. European Journal of Women's Studies, 21(4), pp. 330-343.

Kostiainen, A. 1996: Genocide in Soviet Karelia: Stalin's Terror and the Finns of Soviet Karelia. Scandinavian Journal of History, 21(4), pp. 332-341.

Kovačević, N. 2008: Narrating post/communism. Colonial discourse and Europe's borderline civilization. Routledge, Abingdon, 236 p.

Kőszegi M. 2016a: Nacionalizmusok Európa keleti felében. In: Bottlik Zs. (szerk.): Etnikai földrajzi kutatások Köztes-Európában. ELTE, Budapest, pp. 35-43.

Kőszegi M. 2016b: Kis népek nacionalizmusa az európai posztszovjet térségben: a krími tatárok és a gagauzok. Földrajzi Közlemények, 140(4), pp. 285-296.

Kőszegi M. 2018: Az orosz nacionalizmus arcai. In: Kőszegi, M. and Barta, G. and Illés, T. and Berki, M. (szerk.): Etnikai földrajzi kutatások a posztszovjet térségben. ELTE, Budapest, pp. 57-71.

Kőszegi M. 2019: Tatárok a posztszovjet térben. In: Kőszegi M. and Barta G. and Illés T. and Berki M. (Eds.): Etnikai földrajzi kutatások a posztszovjet térségben. ELTE TTK, Budapest pp. 115-124.

Kőszegi M., Pete M. 2018: Köztes-Európa és az orosz nemzeti identitás In: Bottlik Zs. (szerk): Etnikai földrajzi kutatások Köztes Európában. ELTE TTK, Budapest, pp. 135-144.

Krajkó Gy. 1987: A Szovjetunió gazdaságföldrajza. Tankönyvkiadó, Budapest 239 p.

Kratochvil, A. and Mokienko, W. 2004: Sprachliche Prozesse in der Ukraine seit Anfang der neunziger Jahre. In: Makarska, R. and Kerski, B. (Hrsg.): Die Ukraine, Polen und Europa: Eurpäische Identität an der neuen EU-Ostgrenzen (Veröffentlichungen der Deutsch-Polnischen Gesellschaft, 3.) Fibre Verlag, Osnabrück pp. 135–150.

Kulyk, V. 2010: Gespaltene Zungen: Sprache und Sprachpolitik in der Ukraine. Osteuropa, 60(2–4), pp. 391–402.

Kupari, H. 2016: Studying Displaced Karelian Orthodox Women. In: Kupari, H.: Lifelong Religious as Habitus: Religious Practice among Displaced Karelian Orthodox Women in Finland, Brill, pp. 34-58.

Kvilinkova, E. 2013: The Gagauz Language Through the Prism of Gagauz Ethnic Identity. Anthropology & Archeology of Eurasia, 52(1), pp. 74–94.

Laclau, E. 1990: New Reflections on the Revolution of Our Time. Verso, London & New York, 284 p.

Lagzi G. 2001: A szovjet rendszer öröksége: Nemzet- és államépítési nehézségek Belaruszban az 1990-es években [The Legacy of the Soviet System: Difficulties of Nation- and State-Building in Belarus in the 1990s]. Pro Minoritate, 10(2) pp. 187–206.

Laitila, T. 2001: Struggle over the Karelian language(s) and Identity. Етнічна історія народів Європи, Вип. 9. pp. 107-110.

Lankina, T. 2002: Local Administration and Ethno-social Consensus in Russia. Europa-Asia Studies, 54(7), pp. 1037-1053.

Lapidus, G. W. 1984: Ethnonationalism and Political Stability: The Soviet Case. World Politics. 36(4), pp 555–580.

Lazarus, N. 2012: Spectres haunting: Postcommunism and postcolonialism. Journal of Postcolonial Writing, 2., 117–129.

Lazzerini, E.J. 1981: Tatarovedenie and the "New Historiography" in the Soviet Union: Revising the Interpretation of the Tatar-Russian Relationship. Slavic Review. 40(4), pp. 625–635.

Lee, J-Y. 2016: "Were the Historical Oirats "Western Mongols"?: An Examination of their Uniqueness in Relation to the Mongols." Études mongoles et sibériennes, centrasiatiques et tibétaines 47. pp. 1–24.

Lenin, V. I. 1963 [1917]: Imperialism, the Highest Stage of Capitalism. In: Lenin's Selected Works. Progress Publishers, Moscow, 1. pp. 667–766.

Levene, M. 2008: Empires, Native Peoples, and Genocide. In: Moses, A. D. (ed.): Empires, Colony, Genocide: Conquest, Occupation, and Subaltern Resistance in World History. Berghahn Books, New York – Oxford. pp. 183–205.

Lieven, D. 1998: Russian, Imperial and Soviet Identities. Transactions of the Royal Historical Society, 8. pp. 253–269.

REFERENCES

Löwis, S. von 2015a: Phantom Borders in the Political Geography of East Central Europe: an Introduction. Erdkunde, 69(2), pp. 99–106.

Löwis, S. von 2015b: Ambivalente Identifikationsräume in der Westukraine: das Phantom der alten Grenze an Zbruč. Europa Regional, 23(3–4), 148–162.

Löwis, S. von 2017: Phantom Borders and Ambivalent Spaces of Identification in Ukraine. L'Espace geographique, 45(2), 143–157.

Lunacharsky, A. V. 1918: To All Who Teach. In.: A. V. Lunacharsky: The Class Struggle Vol. II, No. III, May-June 1918. Lunacharsky Internet Archive (https://www.marxists.org/archive/lunachar/works/teachers.htm)

Luostarien, H. 1989: Finnish Russophobia: The Story of an Enemy Image. Journal of Peace Research, 26(2), pp. 123-137.

Mackenzie, D. 1967: Kaufman of Turkestan: An Assessment of His Administration 1867–1881. Slavic Review. 26(2), pp. 265–285.

Mackenzie, D. 1974: Turkestan's Significance to Russia (1850–1917). The Russian Review. 33(2), pp. 167–188.

Magomedov, A. 2001: Oil and Caspian Pipeline Consortium, as Instruments of Astrakhan and Kalmyk Leaders. Central Asia and the Caucasus 2(8), pp. 87–95.

Maksimov, K. N. 2008: Kalmykia in Russia's Past and Present: National Policies and Administrative System. Central European University Press, Budapest – New York, 454 + 8 p.

Mandel, W. M. 1942: Soviet Central Asia. Pacific Affairs. 15(4) pp. 389–409.

Manninen, O. 1980: Suur-Suomen ääriviivat: Kysymys tulevaisuudesta ja turvallisuudesta Suomen Saksan-politiikassa 1941. Helsinki: Kirjayhtymä, 328 p.

March, L. 2007: From Moldovanism to Europeanization? Moldova's communists and nation building. Nationalities Papers, 35(4), pp. 601–626.

Marciniak, K. 2009: Post-socialist hybrids. European Journal of Cultural Studies (Media globalization and post-socialist identities), 12(2), pp. 173–190.

Mark, R. A. 2011: Eine verspätete Nation; Anfänge weißrussischer Identitätsfindung im ausgehenden Zarenreich. In: Bohn, T. M. and Shadurski, V. (Hrsg.): Ein weißer Fleck in Europa …: Die Imagination der Belarus als Kontaktzone zwischen Ost und West, transcript Verlag, Bielefeld, pp. 139–150.

Marples, D. R. 1999: Belarus: A Denationalized Nation. Harwood Academic Publishers, Amsterdam 139 p.

Marston, S. A., Jones, J. P., Woodward, K. 2005: Human geography without scale. Transactions of the Institute of British Geographers, 30(4), pp 416–432.

Martin, J. 2005: Identity. Atkinson, D., Jackson, P., Sibley, D., Washbourne, N. (ed.): Cultural Geography. I.B. Tauris, London. pp. 97–102.

Martin, T. 2001: The Affirmative Action Empire: Nations and Nationalism in the Soviet Union, 1923–1939. Cornell University Press, Ithaca – London. 528 p.

Marx, K. 1909 [1867]: Capital: A Critique of Political Economy. Volume I: The Process of Capitalist Production. Charles H. Kerr & Company, Chicago, 618 p.

Matley, I. M. 1989: The Population and the Land. In: Allworth, E. (Ed.): Central Asia: 120 Years of Russian Rule. Duke University Press, Durkham–London. pp. 92–130.

Mead, W. R. 1952: Finnish Karelia: An International Borderland. The Royal Geographical Society, The Geographical Journal, 118(1), pp. 40-54.

Minescu, A. and Poppe, E. 2011: Poppe Source Intergroup Conflict in Russia: Testing the Group Position Model. Social Psychology Quarterly, 74(2), pp. 166-191

Mironov, B. N., Eklof, B. 2000: The Social History of Imperial Russia, 1700–1917. Westview Press, Boulder, 600 p.

Moon, D. 1996: Estimating the Peasant Population of Late Imperial Russia from the 1897 Census: A Research Note. Europe-Asia Studies, 48(1) pp. 141–153.

Moore, D. C. 2006: Is the post- in postcolonial the post- in post-Soviet? Towards a global postcolonial critique. In: Kelertas, V. (ed.): Baltic postcolonialism. Rodopi, Amsterdam, New York, 11–43.

Morozov, V. 2015: Russia's Postcolonial Identity: A Subaltern Empire in a Eurocentric World. Palgrave Macmillan, Basingstoke, 218 p.

Morrison, A. 2006: Russian Rule in Turkestan and the Example of British India, c. 1860–1917. The Slavonic and East European Review. 84(4), pp. 666–707.

Moser, M. 2000: Die Entwicklung der ukrainischen Schriftsprache. Österreichisches Osthefte, 42(3–4) pp. 482–495.

Murphy, A. B. 2002: National claims to territory in the modern state system: geographical considerations. Geopolitics, 7(2), pp. 193–214.

Mutlu, S. 2003: Late Ottoman Population and Its Ethnic Distribution. Turkish Journal of Population Studies, 25(1), pp. 3–38.

Najafizadeh, M. 2012: Gender and Ideology: Social Change and Islam In Post-Soviet Azerbaijan. Journal of Third World Studies. 29(1), pp 81–101.

Nekbakhtshoev, N. 2006: Clan Politics: Explaining the Persistence of Subethnic Divisions in Tajikistan: Comparative Approach. Duquesne University, Pittsburgh, 107 p.

Nekrich, A. M. 1978: The punished peoples: The deportation and tragic fate of the Soviet minorities at the end of the Second World War. W.W. Norton & Company, New York. 256 p.

Neukirch, C. 1996: Die Republik Moldau: Nations- und Staatsbildung in Osteuropa. LIT Verlag, Münster (Osteuropa: Geschichte, Wirtschaft, Politik; 9.)

Neukirch, C. 2003: Moldau und Europa: Mehr als eine Nachbarschaft? Südosteuropa Mitteilungen, 43(4-5), pp. 15-29.

Nita, S. 2016: Circular migration within the EU-Moldova mobility partnership. In: Solé, C., Parella, S., Martí, T. S., Nita, S. (eds.): Impact of circular migration on human, political and civil rights. A global perspective. Springer, New York, pp. 23-44.

Nkrumah, K. 1965: Neo-Colonialism, the Last Stage of Imperialism. Thomas Nelson & Sons, London, 280 p.

Nora, P. 1996: From Lieux de Mémorie to Realms of Memory. In: Nora, Pierre: Realms of Memory: The Construction of the French Past (Volume 1). English Language Edition edited & with foreword by Lawrence D. Kritzman. Columbia University Press pp. XV - XXIV.

Nordenskiöld, E. 1919: Finnland: The Land and the Pople. Geographical Review - American Geographical Society, 7(6), pp. 361-376.

Nourzhanov, K. and Bleuer, C. 2013: Tajikistan: A Political and Social History. ANU Press, Canberra, 404 p.

Novák, L. 2014: Question of (Re)classification of Eastern Iranian Languages. Linguistica Brunesia, Brno, 62(1) pp. 77-87.

Nuksunova, A. M. 2009: The Cultural Identity of Today's Kalmyk Young People. Russian Social Science Review 50. 5. pp. 63-70.

O'Lear, S. 2008: Azerbaijan In: G. H. Herb; D. H. Kaplan: Nations and nationalism: A Global Historical Overview (volume 4.), ABC-CLIO. pp. 1714-1721.

O'Loughlin, J. and Kolossov, V. and Radvanyi, J. 2007: The Caucasus in a Time of Conflict, Demographic Transition, and Economic Change. Eurasian Geography and Economics 49(2), pp. 135-156.

Olimov, M. and Olimova, S. 2002: Ethnic Factors and Local Self-Government in Tajikistan. In: Tishkov, V. - Filippova, E. (Eds.): Local Governance and Minority Empowerment in the CIS. Open Society Institute, Budapest, pp. 235-262.

Osterhammel, J. 1997: Colonialism: A Theoretical Overview. Markus Wiener. 164 p.

Owczarzak, J. 2009: Introduction: Postcolonial studies and postsocialism in Eastern Europe. Focaal-European Journal of Anthropology, (53), pp. 3-19.

Özkirimli, U. 2010: Theories of Nationalism. Palgrave Macmillan, NY. 244 p.

Paasi, A. 1996: Territories, Boundaries and Consciousness: The Changing Geographies of the Finnish-Russian Border. J. Wiley & Sons, New York, 353 p.

Pain, E. 2016: The imperial syndrome and its influence on Russian nationalism. In: Kolstø, P. and Blakkisrud, H (eds.): The New Russian Nationalism. Imperialism, Ethnicity and Authoritarianism 2000–2015. pp. 46–74.

Pándi L. 1997: Köztes-Európa 1763-1993. Térképgyűjtemény. Osiris, Budapest. 798 p.

Park, M. 2010: South reads Western and Eastern East: Second-hand orientalism in Kiltro, a Chilean martial arts film. In: López-Calvo, I. (ed.): One world periphery reads the other: Knowing the "oriental" in the Americas and the Iberian peninsula. Cambridge Scholars Publishing, Newcastle upon Tyne, pp. 393–405.

Pavlenko, A. 2011: Linguistic russification in the Russian Empire: peasants into Russians? Russian Linguistics. 35(3), pp. 331–350.

Perdue, P. C. 2005: China Marches West: The Qing Conquest of Central Eurasia. Harvard University Press, Cambridge–London. 752 p.

Petrescu, C. 2001: Contrasting/conflicting identities. Bessarabians, Romanians, Moldovans. In: Trencsényi, B., Petrescu, D., Petrescu, C., Iordachi, C., Kántor, Z. (eds.): Nation-building and contested identities: Romanian and Hungarian case studies. Regio Books, Editura Polirom, Budapest, Iași, pp. 153–179.

Pockney, B. 1991: Soviet Statistics since 1950. Aldershot, Dartmouth, 333 p.

Pohl, J. O. 2000: Stalin's genocide against the "Repressed Peoples". Journal of Genocide Research 2(2), pp. 267–293.

Posch, E. 2011: Limba Noastra – Sprache in der Republik Moldau: Bestandsaufnahmeeiner schwierigen Situation. In: Oppenheimer, Ch. (Hrsg.): Blicke auf die Republik Moldau: Eine Annäherung an ein unbekanntes Land. Edition Chrop, Wehrheim pp. 70–79.

Prakash, G. 1994: Subaltern Studies as Postcolonial Criticism. The American Historical Review, 99(5), pp. 1475–1490.

Pravikova, L. and Lazarev, V. 2005: The North Caucasus Bilingualism and Language Identity. In: James Cohen, Kara T. McAlister, Kellie Rolstad, and Jeff MacSwan (Ed): Proceedings of the 4th International Symposium on Bilingualism. Cascadilla Press Somerville, MA. pp. 1309–1327.

Prina, F. 2016: National Minorities in Putin's Russia. Diversity and Assimilation. Routledge, 266 p.

Pütz, R. 1998: Polen im Transformationprozes. Geographische Rundschau, 49(1), 4–11.

Račevskis, K. 2002: Toward a postcolonial perspective on the Baltic states. Journal of Baltic Studies, 33(1), pp 37–56.

Radcliffe, S. A. 1997: Different heroes: Genealogies of postcolonial geographies. Environment and Planning A: Society and Space, 29(8), pp. 1331–1333.

Radzik R. 2002: Between Russia and Poland: national and cultural evolution of the Belarusian society in the last two centuries. Annus Albaruthenicus. Villa Socrates, Krynki, pp. 7–13.

Rauf A. G. 1996: Ethnic Situation int he Caucasus. Center for Strategic Research – Republic of Turkey Ministry of Foreign Affairs 9 p.: https://sam.gov.tr/ethnic-situation-in-the-caucasus/

Richardson, C. 2002: Stalinist terror and the Kalmyks' national revival: A cultural and historical perspective. Journal of Genocide Research 4(3), pp. 441–451.

Richly G. 2010: A finn nemzeti himnusz. Kortárs 54(2), pp. 82–86.

Robinson, J. 2003: Postcolonializing geography: Tactics and pitfalls. Singapore Journal of Tropical Geography, 24(3), pp. 273–289.

Romsics I. 1998: Nemzet, nemzetiség és állam Kelet-Közép- és Délkelet-Európában a 19. és a 20. században. Napvilág Kiadó, Bp. 420 p.

Rónai A. 1945: Atlas of Central Europe. Institute of Political Sciences, Budapest – Balatonfüred. 367 p.

Rowland, R. H. 2003: Nationality Population Trends in Belarus during the Recent Intercensal Period 1989–1999. Eurasian Geography and Economics, 44(7) pp. 535–556.

Roy, O. 1993: The Civil War in Tajikistan: Causes and Implications. United States Institute of Peace, Washington DC, 34 p.

Said, E. W. 1978: Orientalism. Pantheon Books, New York, 368 p.

Saphiro, M. J. 2003: Nation-states. In: Agnew, J., Mitchell K., Toal, G.: A Companion to Political Geography. Blackwell, Oxford. pp. 271–288.

Sapper, M. and Wagner, R. P. and Wagner, C. 2003: Rußlands kulturelle Ausstrahlung auf die Staaten der GUS. In: Alexandrova, O. and Götz, R. and Halbach, U. (Hrsg.): Rußland und der postsowjetische Raum, Nomos Verlagsgesellschaft, Baden Baden pp. 175–196.

Sarhimaa, A. 2016: Karelian in Finland ELDIA Case-Spesific Report. Studies in European Language Diversity 27, European Language Diversity for All, 291 p.

Saunders, D. 1995: Russia's Ukrainian Policy (1847–1905): A Demographic Approach. European History Quarterly, 25(2) pp. 181–208.

Savitzkaya, N. 2011: Weißrussisch: Eine Verkehrssprache oder eine Sprache von Verkehrsschildern? In: Bohn, T. M. and Shadurski, V. (Hrsg.): Ein weißer Fleck in Europa …: Die Imagination der Belarus als Kontaktzone zwischen Ost und West. transcript Verlag, Bielefeld pp. 27–38.

Schöpflin Gy. 2003: A modern nemzet. Attraktor, Máriabesnyő-Gödöllő. 180 p.

Sellier, A. and Sellier, J. 1991: Atlas des peuples d'Europe centrale. La Découverte, Paris, 200 p.

Seton-Watson, H. 1977: Nations and States. An Enquiry into the Origins of Nations and the Politics of Nationalism. Westview Press. Methuen, London. 563 p.

Sgibnev, W. 2015: Rhythms of Being Together: Public Space in Urban Tajikistan Through the Lens of Rhythmanalysis. International Journal of Sociology and Social Policy, Bingley, 35(7-8) pp. 533-549.

Sharp, J. P. 2009: Geographies of postcolonialism. Spaces of power and representation. Sage, Los Angeles, London, 176 p.

Shiller, R. J. and Boycko, M. and Korobov, V. Sidney; G. Winter; Thomas Schelling 1992: Hunting for Homo Sovieticus: Situational versus Attitudinal Factors in Economic Behavior. Brookings Papers on Economic Activity. 1992(1), pp. 127-194.

Šibeka, Z. 2002. Historia Białorusi, 1895-2000 [History of Belarus, 1895-2000]. IESW, Lublin. 571 p.

Šibeka, Z. 2011: Von der urbanen zur nationalen Identität. die belarussische Variante. In: Bohn, T. M. and Shadurski, V. (Hrsg.): Ein weißer Fleck in Europa ...: Die Imagination der Belarus als Kontaktzone zwischen Ost und West, transcript Verlag, Bielefeld, pp. 99-106.

Sidaway, J. 2002: Postcolonial Geographies: Survey-Explore-Review. In: Blunt, A. and McEwan, C. (Eds.): Postcolonial Geographies. Continuum, London-New York, pp. 11-28.

Sidaway, J. D., Woon, C. Y., Jacobs, J. M. 2014: Planetary postcolonialism. Singapore Journal of Tropical Geography, 35(1), pp. 4-21.

Sidikov, B. 2008: Aserbaidschan - Machtpoker um die Petrodollars In: von Guppenberg, M-C; Steinbach, U. (Hrsg.): Der Kaukasus: Geschichte - Kultur - Politik. Verlag C. H. Beck, München, pp. 49-63.

Sieg, H. M. 2011: Der Transnistrien-Konflikt: Voraussetzungen für eine Konfliktlösung. Südosteuropa Mitteilungen, 51(3), pp. 63-77.

Siikala, J. 2006: The Ethnography of Finland. Annual Review of Anthropology, 35, pp. 153-170.

Silver, B. D. 1986: The Ethnic and Language Dimensions in Russian and Soviet Censuses. In: Clem, R. S. (Ed.): Research Guide to the Russian and Soviet Censuses. Cornell University Press, Ithaca-London pp. 70-97.

Silver, B. 1974a: The Impact of Urbanization and Geographical Dispersion on the Linguistic Russification of Soviet Nationalities. Demography. 11(1), pp. 89-103.

Silver, B. 1974b: Social Mobilization and the Russification of Soviet Nationalities. The American Political Science Review. 68(1), pp. 45-66.

Sinclair, T. 2008: Tibetan Reform and the Kalmyk Revival of Buddhism. Inner Asia 10(2), pp. 241-259.

References

Siupur, E. 1993: Von Bessarabien zur Republik Moldau – die historischen Wurzeln eines Konflikts. Südosteuropa, 42(3–4), 153–162.

Smalianchuk, A. 2007: Belarusian National Idea in the Early Twentieth Century. Annus Albaruthenicus 2007 – Год Беларускі восьмы том 2007. Рэдактар Сакрат Яновіч. Krynki: Villa Sokrates, pp. 55–69.

Smith, A. D. 1986: The Ethnic Origins of Nationalism. Blackwell, Oxford. 312 p.

Solomon, F. 2002: Auf der Suche nach Identität: Ethno-kulturelle Auseinandersetzungen in der Republik Moldau. Südosteuropa, 51(7–9) pp. 449–464.

Spivak, G. and Condee, N. and Ram, H. and Chernetsky, V. 2006: Are We Postcolonial? Post-Soviet Space. PMLA, 121(3) pp. 828–836.

Statiev, A. 2005: The Nature of Anti-Soviet Armed Resistance, 1942-44: The North Caucasus, the Kalmyk Autonomous Republic, and Crimea Kritika: Explorations in Russian and Eurasian History 6(2) pp. 285–318.

Stenning, A., Hörschelmann, K. 2008: History, geography and difference in the post-socialist world: Or, do we still need post-socialism? Antipode, 40(2), pp. 312–335.

Suchland, J. 2011: Is postsocialism transnational? Signs: Journal of Women in Culture and Society, 37(4), pp. 837–862.

Suny, R. G. 1993: The Revenge of the Past: Nationalism, Revolution, and the Collapse of the Soviet Union. Stanford University Press, Stanford. 200 p.

Sz. Bíró Z. 2018: Miért és miként bomlott fel a Szovjetunió. Világtörténet 8(4), pp. 589-611.

Taagepera, R. 2011: The Finno-Ugric Republics and the Russian State. Routledge, 340 p.

Tepora, T. and Roselius, A. 2014: The Finnish Civil War 1918. Brill 451 p.

Thaden, E.C. 1981: Russification in the Baltic Provinces and Finland, 1855–1914. Princeton University Press, New Jersey. 514 p.

Timár J. 2004: More than "Anglo-American', it is "Western': Hegemony in geography from a Hungarian perspective. Geoforum, 35(5), 533–538.

Tishkov, V. 1997: Ethnicity, Nationalism and Conflict in and after the Soviet Union: The Mind Aflame. SAGE Publications, London – Thousand Oaks – New Delhi. 352 p.

Tlostanova, M. 2012: Postsocialist ≠ postcolonial? On post-Soviet imaginary and global coloniality. Journal of Postcolonial Writing, 48(2), pp. 130–142.

Tobler, W. R. 1970: A Computer Model Simulating Urban Growth in the Detroit Region. Economic Geography, 46(1sup), pp. 234–240.

Todorova, M. 2010: Balkanism and postcolonialism, or on the beauty of the airplane view. In: Bradatan, C., Oushakine, S. A. (eds.): In Marx's shadow. Knowledge, power, and intellectuals in Eastern Europe and Russia. Lexington Books, Lanham. pp. 175–195.

Toft, M. D. 2003: The Geography of Ethnic Violence: Identity, Interests and the Indivisibility of Territory. Princeton, NJ: Princeton University Press, 226 p.

Tolz, V. 2005: Orientalism, Nationalism, and Ethnic Diversity in Late Imperial Russia. The Historical Journal, 48(1) pp. 127–150.

Tomilov, N.A. and Frank, A.J. 2000: Ethnic Processes within the Turkic Population of the West Siberian Plain (Sixteenth-Twentieth Centuries). Cahiers du Monde (Russe En Islam Sibérien), 41(2–3), pp. 221–232.

Tontsch, G. H. 1996: Der verlorene Sohn: Moldova und Rumänien. Südosteuropa Mitteilungen, 4., 336–343.

Tőkés R. 1998: Iránytű vagy zsákutca? – A legújabb tranzitológiai irodalommal vitázva. Beszélő, 3(2), pp. 31–38.

Törnquist-Plewa, B. 2005: Language and Belarusian Nation-Building in the Light of Modern Theories on Nationalism. Annus Albaruthenicus 2005 – Год Беларускі шосты том 2005. Рэдактар Сакрат Яновіч. Krynki: Villa Sokrates, pp. 109–118.

Trepte, H-C. 2004: Das Problem der „Hiesigen"(Tutejsi) im polnisch-weißrussischen Grenzraum – Regionale Identitäten. Annus Albaruthenicus 2004 – Год Беларускі пяты том 2004. Рэдактар Сакрат Яновіч. Krynki: Villa Sokrates, pp. 67–84.

Tudoroiu, T. 2012: The European Union, Russia, and the Future of the Transnistrian Frozen Conflict. East European Politics and Societies: and Cultures, 26(1), 135–161.

Tudoroiu, T. 2016: Unfreezing Failed Frozen Conflicts: A Post-Soviet Case Study, Journal of Contemporary European Studies, 24(3), 375–396.

Tuvikene, T. 2016: Strategies for comparative urbanism: Post-socialism as a de-territorialized concept. International Journal of Urban and Regional Research, 40(1), pp. 132–146.

Uehling, G. 2000: Squatting, Self-Immolation, and the Repatriation of Crimean Tatars. Nationalities Papers. 28(2), pp. 317–341.

Uehling, G. 2001: The Crimean Tatars in Uzbekistan: speaking with the dead and living homeland. Central Asian Survey. 20(3), pp.391–404.

Ulasiuk, I. 2013: National Minorities and Migration in Armenia, Azerbaijan, Belarus, Georgia, Moldova, Russia and Ukraine. In: CARIM-East Research Report No. 33.

Vakar, N. 1935: The Annexation of Chinese Turkestan. The Slavonic and East European Review. 14(40), pp. 118–123.

Vámbéry Á. 1865/1873: "Reise in Mittelasien". Leipzig. [Travel in Middle Asia], 384 p.

Van Assche, K. and Hornidge, A.-K. 2014: Hidden Mobilities in Post-Soviet Spaces: Boundaries, Scales, Identities and Informal Routes to Livelihood (Crossroads Asia Working Paper Series 20). University of Bonn, Bonn, 51 p.

van Meurs, W. 2003: Moldova – nationale Identität als politisches Programm. Südosteuropa Mitteilungen, 43(4–5), pp. 31–43.

Varfolomeeva, A. 2014: Past and Present of Indigenous Rights in Karelia. In: Kati Lepojarvi (ed): The Arctic and Barents Regions – Cooperation, Human Rights and Security Challenges. Nordic Forum 2014 Organizers pp. 29-32.

Vaškevič, J. 2009. Sowjetische Kultur in Belarus [Soviet Culture in Belarus]. In: Albaruthenicus 2009 – Год Беларускі 2009. Дзесяты том; Рэдактар Сакрат Яновіч. Krynki: Villa Sokrates, pp. 7–25.

Verdery, K. 1996: Nationalism, postsocialism, and space in Eastern Europe. Social Research, 63(1), pp. 77–95.

Vitukhnovskaya, M. 2001: Cultural and Political Reaction in Russian Karelia in 1906-1907. State Power, the Orthodox Church and the "Black Hundreds" against Karelian Nationalism. Jahrbücher für Geschichte Osteuropas, Neue Folge, 49(1), pp. 24-44.

Voitura, E. 2014: Ideology, history, and politics in service of repatriation Pontic Greeks and Crimean Tatars. Focaal – Journal of Global and Historical Anthropology, (70), pp. 37–48.

Wagner, M. 2008: Ethnische Schichtung der Ost-Balkan-Länder – Ursachen und Konsequenzen. Der Donauraum 48(4), pp. 373–387.

Wallerstein, I. 2004: World-systems Analysis: An Introduction. Duke University Press, 1st Edition, Durham & London, 109 p.

Weeks, T. R. 2004: Russification: Word and Practice 1863-1914. Proceedings of the American Philosophical Society. 148(4), pp. 471–489.

Weiner, A. 1999: Nature, Nurture, and Memory in a Socialist Utopia: Delineating the Soviet Socio-Ethnic Body in the Age of Socialism. The American Historical Review 104(4), pp. 1114–1155.

Whitman, J. 1956: Turkestan Cotton in Imperial Russia. The American Slavic and East European Review. 15(2), pp. 190–205.

Wiebe, R. 2000: Imagined Communities: Nationalist Experiences. Journal of the Historical Society. 1(1), pp. 33–63.

Williams, B. G. 2002: Hidden ethnocide in the Soviet Muslim borderlands: the ethnic cleansing of the Crimean Tatars. Journal of Genocide Research. 4(3), pp. 357–373.

Williams, C. H. 2003: Nationalism in a democratic context. In: Agnew, J., Mitchell K., Toal, G.: A Companion to Political Geography. Blackwell, Oxford. pp. 356–377.

Wilson, A. 2013: The Crimean Tatars: A Quarter of a Century after Their Return. Security and Human Rights. 24(3-4), pp. 418–431.

References

Wilson, W. A. 2006: Sibelius, the *Kalevala*, and Karelianism. In: Jill Terry Rudy, Diane Call (ed.): The Marrow of Human Experience. University Press of Colorado, Utah State University Press pp. 124-141.

Wirtshafter, E. K. 2009: Social Categories in Russian Imperial History. Cahiers du Monde russe, 50(1) pp. 231-250.

Wolff, L. 1994: Inventing Eastern Europe. The map of civilization on the mind of the Enlightenment. Stanford University Press, Stanford 436 p.

Yamskov, A. N. 1991: Ethnic Conflict in the Transcaucasus: The Case of Nagorno-Karabakh. Theory and Society. 20(5), pp. 631-660.

Yaroshevski, D. B. 1987: Russian Regionalism in Turkestan. The Slavonic and East European Review. 65(1), pp. 77-100.

Zabarah, D. 2013: Die Republik Moldau: Staatswerdung im Spannungsfeld zwischen historischen Ansprüchen und dem Zerfall alter Ordnungen. In: Hilger, A. and von Wrochem, O. (Hrsg.): Die geteilte Nation: Nationale Verluste und Identitäten im 20. Jahrhundert. Oldenburg Verlag, München pp. 117-134.

Zamfira, A. 2015: Methodological limitations in studying the effect of interethnicity on voting behaviour, with examples from Bulgaria, Romania and Slovakia. Erdkunde, 69(2), pp. 161-173.

Zarycki, T. 2015: The electoral geography of Poland: between stable spatial structures and their changing interpretations. Erdkunde, 69(2), pp. 107-124.

Zeraschkowitsch, P. 2001: Ethnischer Wandel und Nationalitätenpolitik in den weißrussischen Provinzen (1795-1914). In: Beyrau, D. and Lindner, R. (Hrsg.): Handbuch der Geschichte Weißrußlands. Vandenhoeck & Ruprecht Verlag, Göttingen pp. 359-376.

Zhurzhenko, T. 2001: Sprache und Nationsbildung: Dilemmata der Sprachenpolitik in der Ukraine. Transit – Europäische Revue, 21 pp. 144-169.

List of figures

Figure 0.0.1 The geopolitical situation in the post-Soviet realm; (Sources: [2]; [3]; [4]; [5]; [9]; [10]; [15]; [19]; [21]; [22]; [30]; [31]; [32]; [33]; [34]; [35]; [36]; [38]; [40]; [41]).......................................viii

Figure 1.1.1. Regional differences in the Russian Empire based on the variables of the 1897 census I (Source: [29]).........................13

Figure 1.1.2 Regional differences in the Russian Empire based on the variables of the 1897 census II. (Source: [29]).......................15

Figure 1.1.3 Regional patterns of literacy rate — literacy in towns and difference between towns and rural areas (1897) (Source: [29]) 18

Figure 1.1.4 Regional pattern of the Orthodox population in towns and the rural hinterland (1897); (Source: [29]) 20

Figure 1.1.5 Regional pattern of the aggregated development level of towns in 1897 and the differences of development between urban centres and their rural hinterland; (Source: [29]) 21

Figure 1.1.6 Rural cluster types based on the character of differences between towns and their hinterland and urban clusters based on the difference in urban features; (Source: [29]) 23

Figure 1.1.7 Aggregated development level and the cluster types of raions in the post-Soviet realm; (Sources: [30]; [39])............37

Figure 1.2.1 The proportion of Christian Orthodox inhabitants in Russia in 1897; (Source: [29])..49

Figure 1.2.2 The proportion and number of native Russian speakers in Russia in 1897; (Source: [29]) 51

Figure 1.3.1 The change of the linguistic situation among Eastern Slavic speakers..63

Figure 1.3.2 The change of linguistic and political orientation in the territory of Moldova 67

Figure 1.3.3 The proportion and number of Russian native speakers in Ukraine in 2001; (Sources: [26]; [27]; [28]; [38]) 71

Figure 1.3.4 The situation of the Russian language in the European post-Soviet realm; (Sources: [2]; [3]; [4]; [5]; [10]; [21]; [28]; [38]). 74

List of figures

Figure 1.3.5 Ethnic composition in the Belarusian-inhabited territories of the Russian Empire in 1897; (Source: [29]) 78

Figure 1.3.6 The ethnic composition of the population in Belarus between 1897 and 2009; (Sources: [5]; [28]; [29]; Eberhardt, P. 2000) 84

Figure 1.3.7 The ethnic composition of the population and the proportion of non-Belarusians in Belarus by raions in 2009; (Source: [5]) 86

Figure 1.3.8 The distribution of the population by native language and actually-used language in Belarus by raions; (Source: [5]) 88

Figure 1.4.1 The ethnic composition of the central and western territories of the Russian Empire and the governorates with a Russian majority in 1897; (Source: [29]) 94

Figure 1.4.2 The distribution of the ethnic minorities in Russia between 1926 and 2010; (Sources: [25]; [26]) 100

Figure 1.4.3 The ethnic composition of the Russian population in 2010 (see page 300) (Sources: [23]; [24]; [25]; [28]) 102

Figure 2.1.1 The ethnic composition of the Turkestan population and the proportion of Russians in 1897; (Source: [29]) 122

Figure 2.1.2 Changes in the ethnic composition of former Soviet Central Asia (1926-2010); (Sources: [14]; [16]; [17]; [19]; [26]; [34]; [35]; [36]; [37]) 126

Figure 2.1.3 The ethnic composition of former Soviet Central Asia in 2010; (Source: [18]) 130

Figure 2.2.1 The territorial presence of Tatars in Russia in 2010; Source: [25]) 137

Figure 2.2.2 Changes in the ethnic composition of Tatarstan (1897–2010); (Sources: [25]; [26]; [27]; [29]) 145

Figure 2.3.1 Changes in the ethnic composition of Crimea (1850–2014)(Sources: [10]; [26]; [29]; [38]) 155

Figure 2.3.2 The ethnic composition of the Crimean population by municipalities in 2014; (Source: [10]) 159

Figure 2.3.3 The proportion of Gagauz inhabitants and their larger communities in Budjak and Moldova 2001/2014; (Sources: [21]; [22]; [38]).. 165

Figure 2.3.4 The proportion of Bulgarians inhabitants and their larger communities in Budjak and Moldova 2001/2014 165

Figure 2.3.5 Linguistic composition of the population of Budjak 2001/2004; (Sources: [20]; [38])... 166

Figure 2.4.1 The change in the number of Kalmyks between 1897 and 2010; (Sources: [25]; [26]) 175

Figure 2.4.2 The change in the ethnic composition and population of Kalmykia between 1926 and 2010; (Sources: [25]; [26]) 177

Figure 2.4.3 The settlement area of Kalmyks in 2010; (Source: [25]).. 178

Figure 3.1.1 Regions of Karelia and significant territorial changes of the region (Source: Kirkinen, H., Nevalainen, P. and Sihvo, H. 1994).. 185

Figure 3.1.2 The settlement area of the Karelians and population changes between 1926 and 2010; (Sources: [25]; [26]) 187

Figure 3.1.3 The concept of "Finland as an island" as the modest version of Greater Finland notions (Source: Manninen, O. 1980) 190

Figure 3.1.4 Changes in the population of ethnic groups in Karelia between 1897 and 2010; (Sources: [25]; [26]; [29]) 197

Figure 3.2.1 The changing territory of Moldova from the 14th century to the present; (Source: Sellier, A. ; Sellier, J. 1991)......... 215

Figure 3.2.2 The ethnic composition of the settlement area of Romanians living in the Russian Empire in 1897 (1) and the size and residential area of the Moldovan population in 1926 (2); (Sources: [26]; [28]; [29]) 217

Figure 3.2.3 The distribution of the population of Moldova by native language by raions between 2004 and 2014; (Sources: [21]; [22]) 224

Figure 3.3.1 Azeri Settlement Areas in 2011; (Sources: [7]; [8]; [9]; [11]; [12]; [23]; [24])... 229

Figure 3.3.2 The number and proportion of Azeris in 2011;

(Sources: [9]; [13]; [25]) 242

Figure 3.4.1 The distribution of modern Persian/Farsi and its dialects in 2010; (Sources: [7]; [11]; [12]; [23]) 248

Figure 3.4.2 The number and proportion of Tajiks in 2011; (Sources: [1]; [16]; [19]; [34]; [35]; [36]) 253

Authors of the book:

Baroch, Csaba (chapter 3.4)

Master's student of Geography (Department of Social and Economic Geography, Eötvös Loránd University, Budapest)
Csaba earned a bachelor's degree in 2017 with a specialization in settlement and regional development. The topic of his undergraduate dissertation was "Symbolic Spaces of Budapest and Ways of Occupying Space through Public Space Names," which he defended at the Department of Social and Economic Geography at Eötvös Loránd University. His research interests include urban geography, radical and critical geography, and related social theories.

Barta, Géza (chapter 1.4 and 3.1)

PhD student (Department of Social and Economic Geography, Eötvös Loránd University, Budapest)
Before graduating as a cultural anthropologist, Géza obtained his master's degree in geography from Eötvös Loránd University, Budapest. After gaining teaching experience at the secondary-school level, he commenced his PhD studies in 2017 at the Doctoral School of Earth Sciences at Eötvös Loránd University. His cross-disciplinary research interests encompass the frontiers of cultural anthropology and human geography. His main research fields include ethnic, regional, hybrid and place identities, along with social theories.

Berki, Márton (ed.)

PhD, Senior Lecturer (Department of Social and Economic Geography, Eötvös Loránd University, Budapest), Research Fellow (Institute for Regional Studies, Centre for Economic and Regional Studies, Eötvös Loránd Research Network, Budapest)
After graduating as a geographer, Márton began his PhD studies in the Doctoral School of Earth Sciences at Eötvös Loránd University in 2009. Between 2012 and 2016 he was a Junior Research Fellow in the Institute for Sociology of the Hungarian Academy of Sciences. He defended his PhD dissertation in 2014, and returned to the Department of Social and Economic Geography at Eötvös Loránd University, where he is currently working as a Senior Lecturer. He also works in the Institute for Regional Studies of the Centre for Economic and Regional Studies of Eötvös Loránd Research Network as a Research Fellow. His main fields of research include cultural geography, urban geography, socialist and post-socialist urbanism, and critical social and spatial theory.

Bottlik, Zsolt (ed.) (chapter 1.3, 1.4, 2.1, 3.2 and 3.3)

PhD, Associate Professor (Department of Social and Economic Geography, Eötvös Loránd University, Budapest)
Zsolt took up a position in the Geographical Institute of the Hungarian Academy of Sciences after several years of secondary school teaching. His main fields of research include ethnic geography and the regional geographies of In-Between Europe (*Zwischeneuropa*). He is currently Associate Professor in the Department of Social and Economic Geography of Eötvös Loránd University, and is the founder and leader of the university's Research Group on Ethnicity and Religion.

Demeter, Gábor (chapter 1.1)

PhD, senior researcher (Hungarian Academy of Sciences, Research Center for the Humanities, Institute of History).
Gábor is a historian and geographer, and an English special translator in geography. He was a Junior prima prize winner in 2009, and Assistant Professor in the Department of Physical Geography and GIS at the University of Debrecen until 2010. His research field includes the application of GIS and statistics (cliometrics) in history. He also focuses on the diplomatic and socio-economic history of the Balkans and Austria-Hungary, the socio-economic history and historical geography of Hungary in the 19th century (with a specific focus on migration, urbanization, land use changes, and regional inequalities). He was a Hungarian Academy of Science award winner in 2018 and 2019, and a Bolyai plaque winner in 2019.

Illés, Tamás (chapter 1.4, 2.4 and 3.2)

PhD candidate, (Department of Social and Economic Geography, Eötvös Loránd University, Budapest; research fellow at the Institute for Public Policies in Szeklerland, Sepsiszentgyörgy/Sf. Gheorghe)
Tamás obtained his bachelor's and then master's degree in geography at Eötvös Loránd University's Faculty of Science. He also spent a semester as a visiting student at the University of Heidelberg. He started his PhD studies in 2016 at the Doctoral School of Earth Sciences at Eötvös Loránd University. His primary focus is in political geography, population geography and the geography of religions, while his main research topic covers the historical fertility transition in a multidenominational region.

Jobbitt, Steven (ed.)

PhD, Associate Professor (Department of History, Lakehead University, Thunder Bay, Ontario, Canada)
Steven earned his PhD in history from the University of Toronto in 2008. Between 2008 and 2013 he was Assistant Professor of Eu-

ropean history at California State University, Fullerton. In 2013, he returned home with his family to Thunder Bay, where he teaches Russian and East European history, as well as world history. His research focuses primarily on identity and the history of geography in twentieth-century Hungary.

Kőszegi, Margit (chapter 1.2, 2.1, 2.2, 2.3 and 3.3)
PhD, research Fellow (Eötvös Loránd University, Budapest, Hungary)
Margit graduated as a geography and history teacher and is currently a research fellow at Eötvös Loránd University. Her research interests include political geography and cultural geography, and she investigates the various nationalisms of Eastern Europe. Her current research topics include the theories of nationalism and the characteristics of ethnonationalism in the post-Soviet realm.

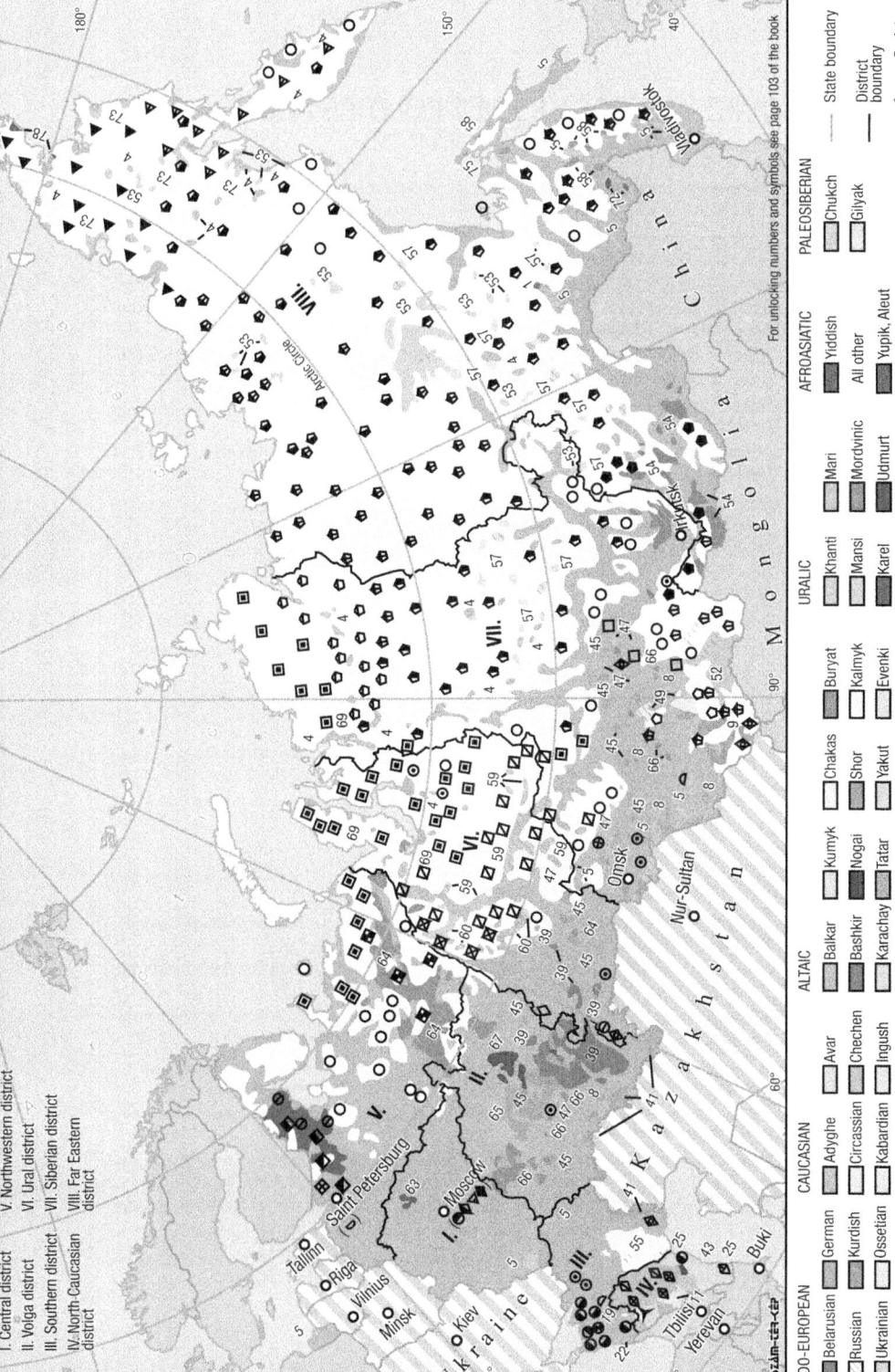

SOVIET AND POST-SOVIET POLITICS AND SOCIETY
Edited by Dr. Andreas Umland | ISSN 1614-3515

1. *Андреас Умланд (ред.)* | Воплощение Европейской конвенции по правам человека в России. Философские, юридические и эмпирические исследования | ISBN 3-89821-387-0

2. *Christian Wipperfürth* | Russland – ein vertrauenswürdiger Partner? Grundlagen, Hintergründe und Praxis gegenwärtiger russischer Außenpolitik | Mit einem Vorwort von Heinz Timmermann | ISBN 3-89821-401-X

3. *Manja Hussner* | Die Übernahme internationalen Rechts in die russische und deutsche Rechtsordnung. Eine vergleichende Analyse zur Völkerrechtsfreundlichkeit der Verfassungen der Russländischen Föderation und der Bundesrepublik Deutschland | Mit einem Vorwort von Rainer Arnold | ISBN 3-89821-438-9

4. *Matthew Tejada* | Bulgaria's Democratic Consolidation and the Kozloduy Nuclear Power Plant (KNPP). The Unattainability of Closure | With a foreword by Richard J. Crampton | ISBN 3-89821-439-7

5. *Марк Григорьевич Меерович* | Квадратные метры, определяющие сознание. Государственная жилищная политика в СССР. 1921 – 1941 гг | ISBN 3-89821-474-5

6. *Andrei P. Tsygankov, Pavel A. Tsygankov (Eds.)* | New Directions in Russian International Studies | ISBN 3-89821-422-2

7. *Марк Григорьевич Меерович* | Как власть народ к труду приучала. Жилище в СССР – средство управления людьми. 1917 – 1941 гг. | С предисловием Елены Осокиной | ISBN 3-89821-495-8

8. *David J. Galbreath* | Nation-Building and Minority Politics in Post-Socialist States. Interests, Influence and Identities in Estonia and Latvia | With a foreword by David J. Smith | ISBN 3-89821-467-2

9. *Алексей Юрьевич Безугольный* | Народы Кавказа в Вооруженных силах СССР в годы Великой Отечественной войны 1941-1945 гг. | С предисловием Николая Бугая | ISBN 3-89821-475-3

10. *Вячеслав Лихачев и Владимир Прибыловский (ред.)* | Русское Национальное Единство, 1990-2000. В 2-х томах | ISBN 3-89821-523-7

11. *Николай Бугай (ред.)* | Народы стран Балтии в условиях сталинизма (1940-е – 1950-е годы). Документированная история | ISBN 3-89821-525-3

12. *Ingmar Bredies (Hrsg.)* | Zur Anatomie der Orange Revolution in der Ukraine. Wechsel des Elitenregimes oder Triumph des Parlamentarismus? | ISBN 3-89821-524-5

13. *Anastasia V. Mitrofanova* | The Politicization of Russian Orthodoxy. Actors and Ideas | With a foreword by William C. Gay | ISBN 3-89821-481-8

14. *Nathan D. Larson* | Alexander Solzhenitsyn and the Russo-Jewish Question | ISBN 3-89821-483-4

15. *Guido Houben* | Kulturpolitik und Ethnizität. Staatliche Kunstförderung im Russland der neunziger Jahre | Mit einem Vorwort von Gert Weisskirchen | ISBN 3-89821-542-3

16. *Leonid Luks* | Der russische „Sonderweg"? Aufsätze zur neuesten Geschichte Russlands im europäischen Kontext | ISBN 3-89821-496-6

17. *Евгений Мороз* | История «Мёртвой воды» – от страшной сказки к большой политике. Политическое неоязычество в постсоветской России | ISBN 3-89821-551-2

18. *Александр Верховский и Галина Кожевникова (ред.)* | Этническая и религиозная интолерантность в российских СМИ. Результаты мониторинга 2001-2004 гг. | ISBN 3-89821-569-5

19. *Christian Ganzer* | Sowjetisches Erbe und ukrainische Nation. Das Museum der Geschichte des Zaporoger Kosakentums auf der Insel Chortycja | Mit einem Vorwort von Frank Golczewski | ISBN 3-89821-504-0

20. *Эльза-Баир Гучинова* | Помнить нельзя забыть. Антропология депортационной травмы калмыков | С предисловием Кэролайн Хамфри | ISBN 3-89821-506-7

21. *Юлия Лидерман* | Мотивы «проверки» и «испытания» в постсоветской культуре. Советское прошлое в российском кинематографе 1990-х годов | С предисловием Евгения Марголита | ISBN 3-89821-511-3

22. *Tanya Lokshina, Ray Thomas, Mary Mayer (Eds.)* | The Imposition of a Fake Political Settlement in the Northern Caucasus. The 2003 Chechen Presidential Election | ISBN 3-89821-436-2

23. *Timothy McCajor Hall, Rosie Read (Eds.)* | Changes in the Heart of Europe. Recent Ethnographies of Czechs, Slovaks, Roma, and Sorbs | With an afterword by Zdeněk Salzmann | ISBN 3-89821-606-5

24 *Christian Autengruber* | Die politischen Parteien in Bulgarien und Rumänien. Eine vergleichende Analyse seit Beginn der 90er Jahre | Mit einem Vorwort von Dorothée de Nève | ISBN 3-89821-476-1

25 *Annette Freyberg-Inan with Radu Cristescu* | The Ghosts in Our Classrooms, or: John Dewey Meets Ceauşescu. The Promise and the Failures of Civic Education in Romania | ISBN 3-89821-416-8

26 *John B. Dunlop* | The 2002 Dubrovka and 2004 Beslan Hostage Crises. A Critique of Russian Counter-Terrorism | With a foreword by Donald N. Jensen | ISBN 3-89821-608-X

27 *Peter Koller* | Das touristische Potenzial von Kam"janec'–Podil's'kyj. Eine fremdenverkehrsgeographische Untersuchung der Zukunftsperspektiven und Maßnahmenplanung zur Destinationsentwicklung des „ukrainischen Rothenburg" | Mit einem Vorwort von Kristiane Klemm | ISBN 3-89821-640-3

28 *Françoise Daucé, Elisabeth Sieca-Kozlowski (Eds.)* | Dedovshchina in the Post-Soviet Military. Hazing of Russian Army Conscripts in a Comparative Perspective | With a foreword by Dale Herspring | ISBN 3-89821-616-0

29 *Florian Strasser* | Zivilgesellschaftliche Einflüsse auf die Orange Revolution. Die gewaltlose Massenbewegung und die ukrainische Wahlkrise 2004 | Mit einem Vorwort von Egbert Jahn | ISBN 3-89821-648-9

30 *Rebecca S. Katz* | The Georgian Regime Crisis of 2003-2004. A Case Study in Post-Soviet Media Representation of Politics, Crime and Corruption | ISBN 3-89821-413-3

31 *Vladimir Kantor* | Willkür oder Freiheit. Beiträge zur russischen Geschichtsphilosophie | Ediert von Dagmar Herrmann sowie mit einem Vorwort versehen von Leonid Luks | ISBN 3-89821-589-X

32 *Laura A. Victoir* | The Russian Land Estate Today. A Case Study of Cultural Politics in Post-Soviet Russia | With a foreword by Priscilla Roosevelt | ISBN 3-89821-426-5

33 *Ivan Katchanovski* | Cleft Countries. Regional Political Divisions and Cultures in Post-Soviet Ukraine and Moldova | With a foreword by Francis Fukuyama | ISBN 3-89821-558-X

34 *Florian Mühlfried* | Postsowjetische Feiern. Das Georgische Bankett im Wandel | Mit einem Vorwort von Kevin Tuite | ISBN 3-89821-601-2

35 *Roger Griffin, Werner Loh, Andreas Umland (Eds.)* | Fascism Past and Present, West and East. An International Debate on Concepts and Cases in the Comparative Study of the Extreme Right | With an afterword by Walter Laqueur | ISBN 3-89821-674-8

36 *Sebastian Schlegel* | Der „Weiße Archipel". Sowjetische Atomstädte 1945-1991 | Mit einem Geleitwort von Thomas Bohn | ISBN 3-89821-679-9

37 *Vyacheslav Likhachev* | Political Anti-Semitism in Post-Soviet Russia. Actors and Ideas in 1991-2003 | Edited and translated from Russian by Eugene Veklerov | ISBN 3-89821-529-6

38 *Josette Baer (Ed.)* | Preparing Liberty in Central Europe. Political Texts from the Spring of Nations 1848 to the Spring of Prague 1968 | With a foreword by Zdeněk V. David | ISBN 3-89821-546-6

39 *Михаил Лукьянов* | Российский консерватизм и реформа, 1907-1914 | С предисловием Марка Д. Стейнберга | ISBN 3-89821-503-2

40 *Nicola Melloni* | Market Without Economy. The 1998 Russian Financial Crisis | With a foreword by Eiji Furukawa | ISBN 3-89821-407-9

41 *Dmitrij Chmelnizki* | Die Architektur Stalins | Bd. 1: Studien zu Ideologie und Stil | Bd. 2: Bilddokumentation | Mit einem Vorwort von Bruno Flierl | ISBN 3-89821-515-6

42 *Katja Yafimava* | Post-Soviet Russian-Belarussian Relationships. The Role of Gas Transit Pipelines | With a foreword by Jonathan P. Stern | ISBN 3-89821-655-1

43 *Boris Chavkin* | Verflechtungen der deutschen und russischen Zeitgeschichte. Aufsätze und Archivfunde zu den Beziehungen Deutschlands und der Sowjetunion von 1917 bis 1991 | Ediert von Markus Edlinger sowie mit einem Vorwort versehen von Leonid Luks | ISBN 3-89821-756-0

44 *Anastasija Grynenko in Zusammenarbeit mit Claudia Dathe* | Die Terminologie des Gerichtswesens der Ukraine und Deutschlands im Vergleich. Eine übersetzungswissenschaftliche Analyse juristischer Fachbegriffe im Deutschen, Ukrainischen und Russischen | Mit einem Vorwort von Ulrich Hartmann | ISBN 3-89821-691-8

45 *Anton Burkov* | The Impact of the European Convention on Human Rights on Russian Law. Legislation and Application in 1996-2006 | With a foreword by Françoise Hampson | ISBN 978-3-89821-639-5

46 *Stina Torjesen, Indra Overland (Eds.)* | International Election Observers in Post-Soviet Azerbaijan. Geopolitical Pawns or Agents of Change? | ISBN 978-3-89821-743-9

47 *Taras Kuzio* | Ukraine – Crimea – Russia. Triangle of Conflict | ISBN 978-3-89821-761-3

48 *Claudia Šabić* | „Ich erinnere mich nicht, aber L'viv!" Zur Funktion kultureller Faktoren für die Institutionalisierung und Entwicklung einer ukrainischen Region | Mit einem Vorwort von Melanie Tatur | ISBN 978-3-89821-752-1

49 *Marlies Bilz* | Tatarstan in der Transformation. Nationaler Diskurs und Politische Praxis 1988-1994 | Mit einem Vorwort von Frank Golczewski | ISBN 978-3-89821-722-4

50 *Марлен Ларюэль (ред.)* | Современные интерпретации русского национализма | ISBN 978-3-89821-795-8

51 *Sonja Schüler* | Die ethnische Dimension der Armut. Roma im postsozialistischen Rumänien | Mit einem Vorwort von Anton Sterbling | ISBN 978-3-89821-776-7

52 *Галина Кожевникова* | Радикальный национализм в России и противодействие ему. Сборник докладов Центра «Сова» за 2004-2007 гг. | С предисловием Александра Верховского | ISBN 978-3-89821-721-7

53 *Галина Кожевникова и Владимир Прибыловский* | Российская власть в биографиях I. Высшие должностные лица РФ в 2004 г. | ISBN 978-3-89821-796-5

54 *Галина Кожевникова и Владимир Прибыловский* | Российская власть в биографиях II. Члены Правительства РФ в 2004 г. | ISBN 978-3-89821-797-2

55 *Галина Кожевникова и Владимир Прибыловский* | Российская власть в биографиях III. Руководители федеральных служб и агентств РФ в 2004 г.| ISBN 978-3-89821-798-9

56 *Ileana Petroniu* | Privatisierung in Transformationsökonomien. Determinanten der Restrukturierungs-Bereitschaft am Beispiel Polens, Rumäniens und der Ukraine | Mit einem Vorwort von Rainer W. Schäfer | ISBN 978-3-89821-790-3

57 *Christian Wipperfürth* | Russland und seine GUS-Nachbarn. Hintergründe, aktuelle Entwicklungen und Konflikte in einer ressourcenreichen Region| ISBN 978-3-89821-801-6

58 *Togzhan Kassenova* | From Antagonism to Partnership. The Uneasy Path of the U.S.-Russian Cooperative Threat Reduction | With a foreword by Christoph Bluth | ISBN 978-3-89821-707-1

59 *Alexander Höllwerth* | Das sakrale eurasische Imperium des Aleksandr Dugin. Eine Diskursanalyse zum postsowjetischen russischen Rechtsextremismus | Mit einem Vorwort von Dirk Uffelmann | ISBN 978-3-89821-813-9

60 *Олег Рябов* | «Россия-Матушка». Национализм, гендер и война в России XX века | С предисловием Елены Гощило | ISBN 978-3-89821-487-2

61 *Ivan Maistrenko* | Borot'bism. A Chapter in the History of the Ukrainian Revolution | With a new Introduction by Chris Ford | Translated by George S. N. Luckyj with the assistance of Ivan L. Rudnytsky | Second, Revised and Expanded Edition ISBN 978-3-8382-1107-7

62 *Maryna Romanets* | Anamorphosic Texts and Reconfigured Visions. Improvised Traditions in Contemporary Ukrainian and Irish Literature | ISBN 978-3-89821-576-3

63 *Paul D'Anieri and Taras Kuzio (Eds.)* | Aspects of the Orange Revolution I. Democratization and Elections in Post-Communist Ukraine | ISBN 978-3-89821-698-2

64 *Bohdan Harasymiw in collaboration with Oleh S. Ilnytzkyj (Eds.)* | Aspects of the Orange Revolution II. Information and Manipulation Strategies in the 2004 Ukrainian Presidential Elections | ISBN 978-3-89821-699-9

65 *Ingmar Bredies, Andreas Umland and Valentin Yakushik (Eds.)* | Aspects of the Orange Revolution III. The Context and Dynamics of the 2004 Ukrainian Presidential Elections | ISBN 978-3-89821-803-0

66 *Ingmar Bredies, Andreas Umland and Valentin Yakushik (Eds.)* | Aspects of the Orange Revolution IV. Foreign Assistance and Civic Action in the 2004 Ukrainian Presidential Elections | ISBN 978-3-89821-808-5

67 *Ingmar Bredies, Andreas Umland and Valentin Yakushik (Eds.)* | Aspects of the Orange Revolution V. Institutional Observation Reports on the 2004 Ukrainian Presidential Elections | ISBN 978-3-89821-809-2

68 *Taras Kuzio (Ed.)* | Aspects of the Orange Revolution VI. Post-Communist Democratic Revolutions in Comparative Perspective | ISBN 978-3-89821-820-7

69 *Tim Bohse* | Autoritarismus statt Selbstverwaltung. Die Transformation der kommunalen Politik in der Stadt Kaliningrad 1990-2005 | Mit einem Geleitwort von Stefan Troebst | ISBN 978-3-89821-782-8

70 *David Rupp* | Die Rußländische Föderation und die russischsprachige Minderheit in Lettland. Eine Fallstudie zur Anwaltspolitik Moskaus gegenüber den russophonen Minderheiten im „Nahen Ausland" von 1991 bis 2002 | Mit einem Vorwort von Helmut Wagner | ISBN 978-3-89821-778-1

71 *Taras Kuzio* | Theoretical and Comparative Perspectives on Nationalism. New Directions in Cross-Cultural and Post-Communist Studies | With a foreword by Paul Robert Magocsi | ISBN 978-3-89821-815-3

72 *Christine Teichmann* | Die Hochschultransformation im heutigen Osteuropa. Kontinuität und Wandel bei der Entwicklung des postkommunistischen Universitätswesens | Mit einem Vorwort von Oskar Anweiler | ISBN 978-3-89821-842-3

73 *Julia Kusznir* | Der politische Einfluss von Wirtschaftseliten in russischen Regionen. Eine Analyse am Beispiel der Erdöl- und Erdgasindustrie, 1992-2005 | Mit einem Vorwort von Wolfgang Eichwede | ISBN 978-3-89821-821-4

74 Alena Vysotskaya | Russland, Belarus und die EU-Osterweiterung. Zur Minderheitenfrage und zum Problem der Freizügigkeit des Personenverkehrs | Mit einem Vorwort von Katlijn Malfliet | ISBN 978-3-89821-822-1

75 Heiko Pleines (Hrsg.) | Corporate Governance in post-sozialistischen Volkswirtschaften | ISBN 978-3-89821-766-8

76 Stefan Ihrig | Wer sind die Moldawier? Rumänismus versus Moldowanismus in Historiographie und Schulbüchern der Republik Moldova, 1991-2006 | Mit einem Vorwort von Holm Sundhaussen | ISBN 978-3-89821-466-7

77 Galina Kozhevnikova in collaboration with Alexander Verkhovsky and Eugene Veklerov | Ultra-Nationalism and Hate Crimes in Contemporary Russia. The 2004-2006 Annual Reports of Moscow's SOVA Center | With a foreword by Stephen D. Shenfield | ISBN 978-3-89821-868-9

78 Florian Küchler | The Role of the European Union in Moldova's Transnistria Conflict | With a foreword by Christopher Hill | ISBN 978-3-89821-850-4

79 Bernd Rechel | The Long Way Back to Europe. Minority Protection in Bulgaria | With a foreword by Richard Crampton | ISBN 978-3-89821-863-4

80 Peter W. Rodgers | Nation, Region and History in Post-Communist Transitions. Identity Politics in Ukraine, 1991-2006 | With a foreword by Vera Tolz | ISBN 978-3-89821-903-7

81 Stephanie Solywoda | The Life and Work of Semen L. Frank. A Study of Russian Religious Philosophy | With a foreword by Philip Walters | ISBN 978-3-89821-457-5

82 Vera Sokolova | Cultural Politics of Ethnicity. Discourses on Roma in Communist Czechoslovakia | ISBN 978-3-89821-864-1

83 Natalya Shevchik Ketenci | Kazakhstani Enterprises in Transition. The Role of Historical Regional Development in Kazakhstan's Post-Soviet Economic Transformation | ISBN 978-3-89821-831-3

84 Martin Malek, Anna Schor-Tschudnowskaja (Hgg.) | Europa im Tschetschenienkrieg. Zwischen politischer Ohnmacht und Gleichgültigkeit | Mit einem Vorwort von Lipchan Basajewa | ISBN 978-3-89821-676-0

85 Stefan Meister | Das postsowjetische Universitätswesen zwischen nationalem und internationalem Wandel. Die Entwicklung der regionalen Hochschule in Russland als Gradmesser der Systemtransformation | Mit einem Vorwort von Joan DeBardeleben | ISBN 978-3-89821-891-7

86 Konstantin Sheiko in collaboration with Stephen Brown | Nationalist Imaginings of the Russian Past. Anatolii Fomenko and the Rise of Alternative History in Post-Communist Russia | With a foreword by Donald Ostrowski | ISBN 978-3-89821-915-0

87 Sabine Jenni | Wie stark ist das „Einige Russland"? Zur Parteibindung der Eliten und zum Wahlerfolg der Machtpartei im Dezember 2007 | Mit einem Vorwort von Klaus Armingeon | ISBN 978-3-89821-961-7

88 Thomas Borén | Meeting-Places of Transformation. Urban Identity, Spatial Representations and Local Politics in Post-Soviet St Petersburg | ISBN 978-3-89821-739-2

89 Aygul Ashirova | Stalinismus und Stalin-Kult in Zentralasien. Turkmenistan 1924-1953 | Mit einem Vorwort von Leonid Luks | ISBN 978-3-89821-987-7

90 Leonid Luks | Freiheit oder imperiale Größe? Essays zu einem russischen Dilemma | ISBN 978-3-8382-0011-8

91 Christopher Gilley | The 'Change of Signposts' in the Ukrainian Emigration. A Contribution to the History of Sovietophilism in the 1920s | With a foreword by Frank Golczewski | ISBN 978-3-89821-965-5

92 Philipp Casula, Jeronim Perovic (Eds.) | Identities and Politics During the Putin Presidency. The Discursive Foundations of Russia's Stability | With a foreword by Heiko Haumann | ISBN 978-3-8382-0015-6

93 Marcel Viëtor | Europa und die Frage nach seinen Grenzen im Osten. Zur Konstruktion ‚europäischer Identität' in Geschichte und Gegenwart | Mit einem Vorwort von Albrecht Lehmann | ISBN 978-3-8382-0045-3

94 Ben Hellman, Andrei Rogachevskii | Filming the Unfilmable. Casper Wrede's 'One Day in the Life of Ivan Denisovich' | Second, Revised and Expanded Edition | ISBN 978-3-8382-0044-6

95 Eva Fuchslocher | Vaterland, Sprache, Glaube. Orthodoxie und Nationenbildung am Beispiel Georgiens | Mit einem Vorwort von Christina von Braun | ISBN 978-3-89821-884-9

96 Vladimir Kantor | Das Westlertum und der Weg Russlands. Zur Entwicklung der russischen Literatur und Philosophie | Ediert von Dagmar Herrmann | Mit einem Beitrag von Nikolaus Lobkowicz | ISBN 978-3-8382-0102-3

97 Kamran Musayev | Die postsowjetische Transformation im Baltikum und Südkaukasus. Eine vergleichende Untersuchung der politischen Entwicklung Lettlands und Aserbaidschans 1985-2009 | Mit einem Vorwort von Leonid Luks | Ediert von Sandro Henschel | ISBN 978-3-8382-0103-0

98 Tatiana Zhurzhenko | Borderlands into Bordered Lands. Geopolitics of Identity in Post-Soviet Ukraine | With a foreword by Dieter Segert | ISBN 978-3-8382-0042-2

99 *Кирилл Галушко, Лидия Смола (ред.)* | Пределы падения – варианты украинского будущего. Аналитико-прогностические исследования | ISBN 978-3-8382-0148-1

100 *Michael Minkenberg (Ed.)* | Historical Legacies and the Radical Right in Post-Cold War Central and Eastern Europe | With an afterword by Sabrina P. Ramet | ISBN 978-3-8382-0124-5

101 *David-Emil Wickström* | Rocking St. Petersburg. Transcultural Flows and Identity Politics in the St. Petersburg Popular Music Scene | With a foreword by Yngvar B. Steinholt | Second, Revised and Expanded Edition | ISBN 978-3-8382-0100-9

102 *Eva Zabka* | Eine neue „Zeit der Wirren"? Der spät- und postsowjetische Systemwandel 1985-2000 im Spiegel russischer gesellschaftspolitischer Diskurse | Mit einem Vorwort von Margareta Mommsen | ISBN 978-3-8382-0161-0

103 *Ulrike Ziemer* | Ethnic Belonging, Gender and Cultural Practices. Youth Identitites in Contemporary Russia | With a foreword by Anoop Nayak | ISBN 978-3-8382-0152-8

104 *Ksenia Chepikova* | ‚Einiges Russland' - eine zweite KPdSU? Aspekte der Identitätskonstruktion einer postsowjetischen „Partei der Macht" | Mit einem Vorwort von Torsten Oppelland | ISBN 978-3-8382-0311-9

105 *Леонид Люкс* | Западничество или евразийство? Демократия или идеократия? Сборник статей об исторических дилеммах России | С предисловием Владимира Кантора | ISBN 978-3-8382-0211-2

106 *Anna Dost* | Das russische Verfassungsrecht auf dem Weg zum Föderalismus und zurück. Zum Konflikt von Rechtsnormen und -wirklichkeit in der Russländischen Föderation von 1991 bis 2009 | Mit einem Vorwort von Alexander Blankenagel | ISBN 978-3-8382-0292-1

107 *Philipp Herzog* | Sozialistische Völkerfreundschaft, nationaler Widerstand oder harmloser Zeitvertreib? Zur politischen Funktion der Volkskunst im sowjetischen Estland | Mit einem Vorwort von Andreas Kappeler | ISBN 978-3-8382-0216-7

108 *Marlène Laruelle (Ed.)* | Russian Nationalism, Foreign Policy, and Identity Debates in Putin's Russia. New Ideological Patterns after the Orange Revolution | ISBN 978-3-8382-0325-6

109 *Michail Logvinov* | Russlands Kampf gegen den internationalen Terrorismus. Eine kritische Bestandsaufnahme des Bekämpfungsansatzes | Mit einem Geleitwort von Hans-Henning Schröder und einem Vorwort von Eckhard Jesse | ISBN 978-3-8382-0329-4

110 *John B. Dunlop* | The Moscow Bombings of September 1999. Examinations of Russian Terrorist Attacks at the Onset of Vladimir Putin's Rule | Second, Revised and Expanded Edition | ISBN 978-3-8382-0388-1

111 *Андрей А. Ковалёв* | Свидетельство из-за кулис российской политики I. Можно ли делать добро из зла? (Воспоминания и размышления о последних советских и первых послесоветских годах) | With a foreword by Peter Reddaway | ISBN 978-3-8382-0302-7

112 *Андрей А. Ковалёв* | Свидетельство из-за кулис российской политики II. Угроза для себя и окружающих (Наблюдения и предостережения относительно происходящего после 2000 г.) | ISBN 978-3-8382-0303-4

113 *Bernd Kappenberg* | Zeichen setzen für Europa. Der Gebrauch europäischer lateinischer Sonderzeichen in der deutschen Öffentlichkeit | Mit einem Vorwort von Peter Schlobinski | ISBN 978-3-89821-749-1

114 *Ivo Mijnssen* | The Quest for an Ideal Youth in Putin's Russia I. Back to Our Future! History, Modernity, and Patriotism according to Nashi, 2005-2013 | With a foreword by Jeronim Perović | Second, Revised and Expanded Edition | ISBN 978-3-8382-0368-3

115 *Jussi Lassila* | The Quest for an Ideal Youth in Putin's Russia II. The Search for Distinctive Conformism in the Political Communication of Nashi, 2005-2009 | With a foreword by Kirill Postoutenko | Second, Revised and Expanded Edition | ISBN 978-3-8382-0415-4

116 *Valerio Trabandt* | Neue Nachbarn, gute Nachbarschaft? Die EU als internationaler Akteur am Beispiel ihrer Demokratieförderung in Belarus und der Ukraine 2004-2009 | Mit einem Vorwort von Jutta Joachim | ISBN 978-3-8382-0437-6

117 *Fabian Pfeiffer* | Estlands Außen- und Sicherheitspolitik I. Der estnische Atlantizismus nach der wiedererlangten Unabhängigkeit 1991-2004 | Mit einem Vorwort von Helmut Hubel | ISBN 978-3-8382-0127-6

118 *Jana Podßuweit* | Estlands Außen- und Sicherheitspolitik II. Handlungsoptionen eines Kleinstaates im Rahmen seiner EU-Mitgliedschaft (2004-2008) | Mit einem Vorwort von Helmut Hubel | ISBN 978-3-8382-0440-6

119 *Karin Pointner* | Estlands Außen- und Sicherheitspolitik III. Eine gedächtnispolitische Analyse estnischer Entwicklungskooperation 2006-2010 | Mit einem Vorwort von Karin Liebhart | ISBN 978-3-8382-0435-2

120 *Ruslana Vovk* | Die Offenheit der ukrainischen Verfassung für das Völkerrecht und die europäische Integration | Mit einem Vorwort von Alexander Blankenagel | ISBN 978-3-8382-0481-9

121　*Mykhaylo Banakh* | Die Relevanz der Zivilgesellschaft bei den postkommunistischen Transformationsprozessen in mittel- und osteuropäischen Ländern. Das Beispiel der spät- und postsowjetischen Ukraine 1986-2009 | Mit einem Vorwort von Gerhard Simon | ISBN 978-3-8382-0499-4

122　*Michael Moser* | Language Policy and the Discourse on Languages in Ukraine under President Viktor Yanukovych (25 February 2010–28 October 2012) | ISBN 978-3-8382-0497-0 (Paperback edition) | ISBN 978-3-8382-0507-6 (Hardcover edition)

123　*Nicole Krome* | Russischer Netzwerkkapitalismus Restrukturierungsprozesse in der Russischen Föderation am Beispiel des Luftfahrtunternehmens „Aviastar" | Mit einem Vorwort von Petra Stykow | ISBN 978-3-8382-0534-2

124　*David R. Marples* | 'Our Glorious Past'. Lukashenka's Belarus and the Great Patriotic War | ISBN 978-3-8382-0574-8 (Paperback edition) | ISBN 978-3-8382-0675-2 (Hardcover edition)

125　*Ulf Walther* | Russlands „neuer Adel". Die Macht des Geheimdienstes von Gorbatschow bis Putin | Mit einem Vorwort von Hans-Georg Wieck | ISBN 978-3-8382-0584-7

126　*Simon Geissbühler (Hrsg.)* | Kiew – Revolution 3.0. Der Euromaidan 2013/14 und die Zukunftsperspektiven der Ukraine | ISBN 978-3-8382-0581-6 (Paperback edition) | ISBN 978-3-8382-0681-3 (Hardcover edition)

127　*Andrey Makarychev* | Russia and the EU in a Multipolar World. Discourses, Identities, Norms | With a foreword by Klaus Segbers | ISBN 978-3-8382-0629-5

128　*Roland Scharff* | Kasachstan als postsowjetischer Wohlfahrtsstaat. Die Transformation des sozialen Schutzsystems | Mit einem Vorwort von Joachim Ahrens | ISBN 978-3-8382-0622-6

129　*Katja Grupp* | Bild Lücke Deutschland. Kaliningrader Studierende sprechen über Deutschland | Mit einem Vorwort von Martin Schulz | ISBN 978-3-8382-0552-6

130　*Konstantin Sheiko, Stephen Brown* | History as Therapy. Alternative History and Nationalist Imaginings in Russia, 1991-2014 | ISBN 978-3-8382-0665-3

131　*Elisa Kriza* | Alexander Solzhenitsyn: Cold War Icon, Gulag Author, Russian Nationalist? A Study of the Western Reception of his Literary Writings, Historical Interpretations, and Political Ideas | With a foreword by Andrei Rogatchevski | ISBN 978-3-8382-0589-2 (Paperback edition) | ISBN 978-3-8382-0690-5 (Hardcover edition)

132　*Serghei Golunov* | The Elephant in the Room. Corruption and Cheating in Russian Universities | ISBN 978-3-8382-0570-0

133　*Manja Hussner, Rainer Arnold (Hgg.)* | Verfassungsgerichtsbarkeit in Zentralasien I. Sammlung von Verfassungstexten | ISBN 978-3-8382-0595-3

134　*Nikolay Mitrokhin* | Die „Russische Partei". Die Bewegung der russischen Nationalisten in der UdSSR 1953-1985 | Aus dem Russischen übertragen von einem Übersetzerteam unter der Leitung von Larisa Schippel | ISBN 978-3-8382-0024-8

135　*Manja Hussner, Rainer Arnold (Hgg.)* | Verfassungsgerichtsbarkeit in Zentralasien II. Sammlung von Verfassungstexten | ISBN 978-3-8382-0597-7

136　*Manfred Zeller* | Das sowjetische Fieber. Fußballfans im poststalinistischen Vielvölkerreich | Mit einem Vorwort von Nikolaus Katzer | ISBN 978-3-8382-0757-5

137　*Kristin Schreiter* | Stellung und Entwicklungspotential zivilgesellschaftlicher Gruppen in Russland. Menschenrechtsorganisationen im Vergleich | ISBN 978-3-8382-0673-8

138　*David R. Marples, Frederick V. Mills (Eds.)* | Ukraine's Euromaidan. Analyses of a Civil Revolution | ISBN 978-3-8382-0660-8

139　*Bernd Kappenberg* | Setting Signs for Europe. Why Diacritics Matter for European Integration | With a foreword by Peter Schlobinski | ISBN 978-3-8382-0663-9

140　*René Lenz* | Internationalisierung, Kooperation und Transfer. Externe bildungspolitische Akteure in der Russischen Föderation | Mit einem Vorwort von Frank Ettrich | ISBN 978-3-8382-0751-3

141　*Juri Plusnin, Yana Zausaeva, Natalia Zhidkevich, Artemy Pozanenko* | Wandering Workers. Mores, Behavior, Way of Life, and Political Status of Domestic Russian Labor Migrants | Translated by Julia Kazantseva | ISBN 978-3-8382-0653-0

142　*David J. Smith (Eds.)* | Latvia – A Work in Progress? 100 Years of State- and Nation-Building | ISBN 978-3-8382-0648-6

143　*Инна Чувычкина (ред.)* | Экспортные нефте- и газопроводы на постсоветском пространстве. Анализ трубопроводной политики в свете теории международных отношений | ISBN 978-3-8382-0822-0

144 *Johann Zajaczkowski* | Russland – eine pragmatische Großmacht? Eine rollentheoretische Untersuchung russischer Außenpolitik am Beispiel der Zusammenarbeit mit den USA nach 9/11 und des Georgienkrieges von 2008 | Mit einem Vorwort von Siegfried Schieder | ISBN 978-3-8382-0837-4

145 *Boris Popivanov* | Changing Images of the Left in Bulgaria. The Challenge of Post-Communism in the Early 21st Century | ISBN 978-3-8382-0667-7

146 *Lenka Krátká* | A History of the Czechoslovak Ocean Shipping Company 1948-1989. How a Small, Landlocked Country Ran Maritime Business During the Cold War | ISBN 978-3-8382-0666-0

147 *Alexander Sergunin* | Explaining Russian Foreign Policy Behavior. Theory and Practice | ISBN 978-3-8382-0752-0

148 *Darya Malyutina* | Migrant Friendships in a Super-Diverse City. Russian-Speakers and their Social Relationships in London in the 21st Century | With a foreword by Claire Dwyer | ISBN 978-3-8382-0652-3

149 *Alexander Sergunin, Valery Konyshev* | Russia in the Arctic. Hard or Soft Power? | ISBN 978-3-8382-0753-7

150 *John J. Maresca* | Helsinki Revisited. A Key U.S. Negotiator's Memoirs on the Development of the CSCE into the OSCE | With a foreword by Hafiz Pashayev | ISBN 978-3-8382-0852-7

151 *Jardar Østbø* | The New Third Rome. Readings of a Russian Nationalist Myth | With a foreword by Pål Kolstø | ISBN 978-3-8382-0870-1

152 *Simon Kordonsky* | Socio-Economic Foundations of the Russian Post-Soviet Regime. The Resource-Based Economy and Estate-Based Social Structure of Contemporary Russia | With a foreword by Svetlana Barsukova | ISBN 978-3-8382-0775-9

153 *Duncan Leitch* | Assisting Reform in Post-Communist Ukraine 2000–2012. The Illusions of Donors and the Disillusion of Beneficiaries | With a foreword by Kataryna Wolczuk | ISBN 978-3-8382-0844-2

154 *Abel Polese* | Limits of a Post-Soviet State. How Informality Replaces, Renegotiates, and Reshapes Governance in Contemporary Ukraine | With a foreword by Colin Williams | ISBN 978-3-8382-0845-9

155 *Mikhail Suslov (Ed.)* | Digital Orthodoxy in the Post-Soviet World. The Russian Orthodox Church and Web 2.0 | With a foreword by Father Cyril Hovorun | ISBN 978-3-8382-0871-8

156 *Leonid Luks* | Zwei „Sonderwege"? Russisch-deutsche Parallelen und Kontraste (1917-2014). Vergleichende Essays | ISBN 978-3-8382-0823-7

157 *Vladimir V. Karacharovskiy, Ovsey I. Shkaratan, Gordey A. Yastrebov* | Towards a New Russian Work Culture. Can Western Companies and Expatriates Change Russian Society? | With a foreword by Elena N. Danilova | Translated by Julia Kazantseva | ISBN 978-3-8382-0902-9

158 *Edmund Griffiths* | Aleksandr Prokhanov and Post-Soviet Esotericism | ISBN 978-3-8382-0903-6

159 *Timm Beichelt, Susann Worschech (Eds.)* | Transnational Ukraine? Networks and Ties that Influence(d) Contemporary Ukraine | ISBN 978-3-8382-0944-9

160 *Mieste Hotopp-Riecke* | Die Tataren der Krim zwischen Assimilation und Selbstbehauptung. Der Aufbau des krimtatarischen Bildungswesens nach Deportation und Heimkehr (1990-2005) | Mit einem Vorwort von Swetlana Czerwonnaja | ISBN 978-3-89821-940-2

161 *Olga Bertelsen (Ed.)* | Revolution and War in Contemporary Ukraine. The Challenge of Change | ISBN 978-3-8382-1016-2

162 *Natalya Ryabinska* | Ukraine's Post-Communist Mass Media. Between Capture and Commercialization | With a foreword by Marta Dyczok | ISBN 978-3-8382-1011-7

163 *Alexandra Cotofana, James M. Nyce (Eds.)* | Religion and Magic in Socialist and Post-Socialist Contexts. Historic and Ethnographic Case Studies of Orthodoxy, Heterodoxy, and Alternative Spirituality | With a foreword by Patrick L. Michelson | ISBN 978-3-8382-0989-0

164 *Nozima Akhrarkhodjaeva* | The Instrumentalisation of Mass Media in Electoral Authoritarian Regimes. Evidence from Russia's Presidential Election Campaigns of 2000 and 2008 | ISBN 978-3-8382-1013-1

165 *Yulia Krasheninnikova* | Informal Healthcare in Contemporary Russia. Sociographic Essays on the Post-Soviet Infrastructure for Alternative Healing Practices | ISBN 978-3-8382-0970-8

166 *Peter Kaiser* | Das Schachbrett der Macht. Die Handlungsspielräume eines sowjetischen Funktionärs unter Stalin am Beispiel des Generalsekretärs des Komsomol Aleksandr Kosarev (1929-1938) | Mit einem Vorwort von Dietmar Neutatz | ISBN 978-3-8382-1052-0

167 *Oksana Kim* | The Effects and Implications of Kazakhstan's Adoption of International Financial Reporting Standards. A Resource Dependence Perspective | With a foreword by Svetlana Vlady | ISBN 978-3-8382-0987-6

168 *Anna Sanina* | Patriotic Education in Contemporary Russia. Sociological Studies in the Making of the Post-Soviet Citizen | With a foreword by Anna Oldfield | ISBN 978-3-8382-0993-7

169 *Rudolf Wolters* | Spezialist in Sibirien Faksimile der 1933 erschienenen ersten Ausgabe | Mit einem Vorwort von Dmitrij Chmelnizki | ISBN 978-3-8382-0515-1

170 *Michal Vit, Magdalena M. Baran (Eds.)* | Transregional versus National Perspectives on Contemporary Central European History. Studies on the Building of Nation-States and Their Cooperation in the 20th and 21st Century | With a foreword by Petr Vágner | ISBN 978-3-8382-1015-5

171 *Philip Gamaghelyan* | Conflict Resolution Beyond the International Relations Paradigm. Evolving Designs as a Transformative Practice in Nagorno-Karabakh and Syria | With a foreword by Susan Allen | ISBN 978-3-8382-1057-5

172 *Maria Shagina* | Joining a Prestigious Club. Cooperation with Europarties and Its Impact on Party Development in Georgia, Moldova, and Ukraine 2004–2015 | With a foreword by Kataryna Wolczuk | ISBN 978-3-8382-1084-1

173 *Alexandra Cotofana, James M. Nyce (Eds.)* | Religion and Magic in Socialist and Post-Socialist Contexts II. Baltic, Eastern European, and Post-USSR Case Studies | With a foreword by Anita Stasulane | ISBN 978-3-8382-0990-6

174 *Barbara Kunz* | Kind Words, Cruise Missiles, and Everything in Between. The Use of Power Resources in U.S. Policies towards Poland, Ukraine, and Belarus 1989–2008 | With a foreword by William Hill | ISBN 978-3-8382-1065-0

175 *Eduard Klein* | Bildungskorruption in Russland und der Ukraine. Eine komparative Analyse der Performanz staatlicher Antikorruptionsmaßnahmen im Hochschulsektor am Beispiel universitärer Aufnahmeprüfungen | Mit einem Vorwort von Heiko Pleines | ISBN 978-3-8382-0995-1

176 *Markus Soldner* | Politischer Kapitalismus im postsowjetischen Russland. Die politische, wirtschaftliche und mediale Transformation in den 1990er Jahren | Mit einem Vorwort von Wolfgang Ismayr | ISBN 978-3-8382-1222-7

177 *Anton Oleinik* | Building Ukraine from Within. A Sociological, Institutional, and Economic Analysis of a Nation-State in the Making | ISBN 978-3-8382-1150-3

178 *Peter Rollberg, Marlene Laruelle (Eds.)* | Mass Media in the Post-Soviet World. Market Forces, State Actors, and Political Manipulation in the Informational Environment after Communism | ISBN 978-3-8382-1116-9

179 *Mikhail Minakov* | Development and Dystopia. Studies in Post-Soviet Ukraine and Eastern Europe | With a foreword by Alexander Etkind | ISBN 978-3-8382-1112-1

180 *Aijan Sharshenova* | The European Union's Democracy Promotion in Central Asia. A Study of Political Interests, Influence, and Development in Kazakhstan and Kyrgyzstan in 2007–2013 | With a foreword by Gordon Crawford | ISBN 978-3-8382-1151-0

181 *Andrey Makarychev, Alexandra Yatsyk (Eds.)* | Boris Nemtsov and Russian Politics. Power and Resistance | With a foreword by Zhanna Nemtsova | ISBN 978-3-8382-1122-0

182 *Sophie Falsini* | The Euromaidan's Effect on Civil Society. Why and How Ukrainian Social Capital Increased after the Revolution of Dignity | With a foreword by Susann Worschech | ISBN 978-3-8382-1131-2

183 *Valentyna Romanova, Andreas Umland (Eds.)* | Ukraine's Decentralization. Challenges and Implications of the Local Governance Reform after the Euromaidan Revolution | ISBN 978-3-8382-1162-6

184 *Leonid Luks* | A Fateful Triangle. Essays on Contemporary Russian, German and Polish History | ISBN 978-3-8382-1143-5

185 *John B. Dunlop* | The February 2015 Assassination of Boris Nemtsov and the Flawed Trial of his Alleged Killers. An Exploration of Russia's "Crime of the 21st Century" | ISBN 978-3-8382-1188-6

186 *Vasile Rotaru* | Russia, the EU, and the Eastern Partnership. Building Bridges or Digging Trenches? | ISBN 978-3-8382-1134-3

187 *Marina Lebedeva* | Russian Studies of International Relations. From the Soviet Past to the Post-Cold-War Present | With a foreword by Andrei P. Tsygankov | ISBN 978-3-8382-0851-0

188 *Tomasz Stępniewski, George Soroka (Eds.)* | Ukraine after Maidan. Revisiting Domestic and Regional Security | ISBN 978-3-8382-1075-9

189 *Petar Cholakov* | Ethnic Entrepreneurs Unmasked. Political Institutions and Ethnic Conflicts in Contemporary Bulgaria | ISBN 978-3-8382-1189-3

190 *A. Salem, G. Hazeldine, D. Morgan (Eds.)* | Higher Education in Post-Communist States. Comparative and Sociological Perspectives | ISBN 978-3-8382-1183-1

191 *Igor Torbakov* | After Empire. Nationalist Imagination and Symbolic Politics in Russia and Eurasia in the Twentieth and Twenty-First Century | With a foreword by Serhii Plokhy | ISBN 978-3-8382-1217-3

192 *Aleksandr Burakovskiy* | Jewish-Ukrainian Relations in Late and Post-Soviet Ukraine. Articles, Lectures and Essays from 1986 to 2016 | ISBN 978-3-8382-1210-4

193 *Natalia Shapovalova, Olga Burlyuk (Eds.)* | Civil Society in Post-Euromaidan Ukraine. From Revolution to Consolidation | With a foreword by Richard Youngs | ISBN 978-3-8382-1216-6

194 *Franz Preissler* | Positionsverteidigung, Imperialismus oder Irredentismus? Russland und die „Russischsprachigen", 1991–2015 | ISBN 978-3-8382-1262-3

195 *Marian Madeła* | Der Reformprozess in der Ukraine 2014-2017. Eine Fallstudie zur Reform der öffentlichen Verwaltung | Mit einem Vorwort von Martin Malek | ISBN 978-3-8382-1266-1

196 *Anke Giesen* | „Wie kann denn der Sieger ein Verbrecher sein?" Eine diskursanalytische Untersuchung der russlandweiten Debatte über Konzept und Verstaatlichungsprozess der Lagergedenkstätte „Perm'-36" im Ural | ISBN 978-3-8382-1284-5

197 *Alla Leukavets* | The Integration Policies of Belarus and Ukraine vis-à-vis the EU and Russia. A Comparative Case Study Through the Prism of a Two-Level Game Approach | ISBN 978-3-8382-1247-0

198 *Oksana Kim* | The Development and Challenges of Russian Corporate Governance I. The Roles and Functions of Boards of Directors | With a foreword by Sheila M. Puffer | ISBN 978-3-8382-1287-6

199 *Thomas D. Grant* | International Law and the Post-Soviet Space I. Essays on Chechnya and the Baltic States | With a foreword by Stephen M. Schwebel | ISBN 978-3-8382-1279-1

200 *Thomas D. Grant* | International Law and the Post-Soviet Space II. Essays on Ukraine, Intervention, and Non-Proliferation | ISBN 978-3-8382-1280-7

201 *Slavomír Michálek, Michal Štefansky* | The Age of Fear. The Cold War and Its Influence on Czechoslovakia 1945–1968 | ISBN 978-3-8382-1285-2

202 *Iulia-Sabina Joja* | Romania's Strategic Culture 1990–2014. Continuity and Change in a Post-Communist Country's Evolution of National Interests and Security Policies | With a foreword by Heiko Biehl | ISBN 978-3-8382-1286-9

203 *Andrei Rogatchevski, Yngvar B. Steinholt, Arve Hansen, David-Emil Wickström* | War of Songs. Popular Music and Recent Russia-Ukraine Relations | With a foreword by Artemy Troitsky | ISBN 978-3-8382-1173-2

204 *Maria Lipman (Ed.)* | Russian Voices on Post-Crimea Russia. An Almanac of Counterpoint Essays from 2015–2018 | ISBN 978-3-8382-1251-7

205 *Ksenia Maksimovtsova* | Language Conflicts in Contemporary Estonia, Latvia, and Ukraine. A Comparative Exploration of Discourses in Post-Soviet Russian-Language Digital Media | With a foreword by Ammon Cheskin | ISBN 978-3-8382-1282-1

206 *Michal Vít* | The EU's Impact on Identity Formation in East-Central Europe between 2004 and 2013. Perceptions of the Nation and Europe in Political Parties of the Czech Republic, Poland, and Slovakia | With a foreword by Andrea Pető | ISBN 978-3-8382-1275-3

207 *Per A. Rudling* | Tarnished Heroes. The Organization of Ukrainian Nationalists in the Memory Politics of Post-Soviet Ukraine | ISBN 978-3-8382-0999-9

208 *Kaja Gadowska, Peter Solomon (Eds.)* | Legal Change in Post-Communist States. Progress, Reversions, Explanations | ISBN 978-3-8382-1312-5

209 *Paweł Kowal, Georges Mink, Iwona Reichardt (Eds.)* | Three Revolutions: Mobilization and Change in Contemporary Ukraine I. Theoretical Aspects and Analyses on Religion, Memory, and Identity | ISBN 978-3-8382-1321-7

210 *Paweł Kowal, Georges Mink, Adam Reichardt, Iwona Reichardt (Eds.)* | Three Revolutions: Mobilization and Change in Contemporary Ukraine II. An Oral History of the Revolution on Granite, Orange Revolution, and Revolution of Dignity | ISBN 978-3-8382-1323-1

211 *Li Bennich-Björkman, Sergiy Kurbatov (Eds.)* | When the Future Came. The Collapse of the USSR and the Emergence of National Memory in Post-Soviet History Textbooks | ISBN 978-3-8382-1335-4

212 *Olga R. Gulina* | Migration as a (Geo-)Political Challenge in the Post-Soviet Space. Border Regimes, Policy Choices, Visa Agendas | With a foreword by Nils Muižnieks | ISBN 978-3-8382-1338-5

213 *Sanna Turoma, Kaarina Aitamurto, Slobodanka Vladiv-Glover (Eds.)* | Religion, Expression, and Patriotism in Russia. Essays on Post-Soviet Society and the State. ISBN 978-3-8382-1346-0

214 *Vasif Huseynov* | Geopolitical Rivalries in the "Common Neighborhood". Russia's Conflict with the West, Soft Power, and Neoclassical Realism | With a foreword by Nicholas Ross Smith | ISBN 978-3-8382-1277-7

215 *Mikhail Suslov* | Geopolitical Imagination. Ideology and Utopia in Post-Soviet Russia | With a foreword by Mark Bassin | ISBN 978-3-8382-1361-3

216 *Alexander Etkind, Mikhail Minakov (Eds.)* | Ideology after Union. Political Doctrines, Discourses, and Debates in Post-Soviet Societies | ISBN 978-3-8382-1388-0

217 *Jakob Mischke, Oleksandr Zabirko (Hgg.)* | Protestbewegungen im langen Schatten des Kreml. Aufbruch und Resignation in Russland und der Ukraine | ISBN 978-3-8382-0926-5

218 *Oksana Huss* | How Corruption and Anti-Corruption Policies Sustain Hybrid Regimes. Strategies of Political Domination under Ukraine's Presidents in 1994-2014 | With a foreword by Tobias Debiel and Andrea Gawrich | ISBN 978-3-8382-1430-6

219 *Dmitry Travin, Vladimir Gel'man, Otar Marganiya* | The Russian Path. Ideas, Interests, Institutions, Illusions | With a foreword by Vladimir Ryzhkov | ISBN 978-3-8382-1421-4

220 *Gergana Dimova* | Political Uncertainty. A Comparative Exploration | With a foreword by Todor Yalamov and Rumena Filipova | ISBN 978-3-8382-1385-9

221 *Torben Waschke* | Russland in Transition. Geopolitik zwischen Raum, Identität und Machtinteressen | Mit einem Vorwort von Andreas Dittmann | ISBN 978-3-8382-1480-1

222 *Steven Jobbitt, Zsolt Bottlik, Marton Berki (Eds.)* | Power and Identity in the Post-Soviet Realm. Geographies of Ethnicity and Nationality after 1991 | ISBN 978-3-8382-1399-6

223 *Daria Buteiko* | Erinnerungsort. Ort des Gedenkens, der Erholung oder der Einkehr? Kommunismus-Erinnerung am Beispiel der Gedenkstätte Berliner Mauer sowie des Soloveckij-Klosters und -Museumsparks | ISBN 978-3-8382-1367-5

224 *Olga Bertelsen (Ed.)* | Russian Active Measures. Yesterday, Today, Tomorrow | With a foreword by Jan Goldman | ISBN 978-3-8382-1529-7

225 *David Mandel* | "Optimizing" Higher Education in Russia. University Teachers and their Union "Universitetskaya solidarnost'" | ISBN 978-3-8382-1519-8

226 *Mikhail Minakov, Gwendolyn Sasse, Daria Isachenko (Eds.)* | Post-Soviet Secessionism. Nation-Building and State-Failure after Communism | ISBN 978-3-8382-1538-9

227 *Jakob Hauter (Ed.)* | Civil War? Interstate War? Hybrid War? Dimensions and Interpretations of the Donbas Conflict in 2014–2020 | With a foreword by Andrew Wilson | ISBN 978-3-8382-1383-5

228 *Tima T. Moldogaziev, Gene A. Brewer, J. Edward Kellough (Eds.)* | Public Policy and Politics in Georgia. Lessons from Post-Soviet Transition | With a foreword by Dan Durning | ISBN 978-3-8382-1535-8

229 *Oxana Schmies (Ed.)* | NATO's Enlargement and Russia. A Strategic Challenge in the Past and Future | With a foreword by Vladimir Kara-Murza | ISBN 978-3-8382-1478-8

230 *Christopher Ford* | Ukapisme – Une Gauche perdue. Le marxisme anti-colonial dans la révolution ukrainienne 1917-1925 | Avec une préface de Vincent Présumey | ISBN 978-3-8382-0899-2

231 *Anna Kutkina* | Between Lenin and Bandera. Decommunization and Multivocality in Post-Euromaidan Ukraine | With a foreword by Juri Mykkänen | ISBN 978-3-8382-1506-8

232 *Lincoln E. Flake* | Defending the Faith. The Russian Orthodox Church and the Demise of Religious Pluralism | With a foreword by Peter Martland | ISBN 978-3-8382-1378-1

233 *Nikoloz Samkharadze* | Russia's Recognition of the Independence of Abkhazia and South Ossetia. Analysis of a Deviant Case in Moscow's Foreign Policy | With a foreword by Neil MacFarlane | ISBN 978-3-8382-1414-6

ibidem.eu